p... oda...

D0317700

MANCHESTER
1824

Manchester University Press

Politics Today

Series editor: Bill Jones

US politics today

Second edition

Edward Ashbee

U.W.E.L.
LEARNING RESOURCES
ACC. No.
2397819
CONTROL
0719068193
DATE.
26. SEP. 2006
SITE
WV
CLASS
116

Manchester University Press
Manchester and New York

distributed exclusively in the USA by Palgrave

Copyright © Edward Ashbee and Nigel Ashford 1999, 2004

New material in second edition copyright © Edward Ashbee 2004

The right of Edward Ashbee and Nigel Ashford to be identified as the authors of this work has been asserted by them in accordance with the Copyright, Designs and Patents Act 1988.

First edition published by Manchester University Press 1999
Reprinted 2001, 2002, 2003

This edition published by Manchester University Press
Oxford Road, Manchester M13 9NR, UK
and Room 400, 175 Fifth Avenue, New York, NY 10010, USA
www.manchesteruniversitypress.co.uk

Distributed exclusively in the USA by
Palgrave, 175 Fifth Avenue, New York,
NY 10010, USA

Distributed exclusively in Canada by
UBC Press, University of British Columbia, 2029 West Mall,
Vancouver, BC, Canada V6T 1Z2

British Library Cataloguing-in-Publication Data
A catalogue record for this book is available from the British Library

Library of Congress Cataloging-in-Publication Data applied for

ISBN 0 7190 6819 3 *paperback*

This edition first published 2004

13 12 11 10 09 08 07 06   10 9 8 7 6 5 4 3 2

Typeset in Photina
by Servis Filmsetting Ltd, Manchester
Printed in Great Britain
by Biddles Ltd, King's Lynn

Contents

List of tables

List of boxes

Preface and acknowledgements

Although the 2003 Iraq war illustrated the limitations as well as the scale of American power, the political, economic and cultural importance of the United States is beyond question. Both its critics and friends now employ the term 'hyperpower'.

Events and developments within the US since the first edition of *US politics today* was published have reaffirmed the importance of understanding the American political process and subjecting it to sustained scrutiny. The contested aftermath of the 2000 presidential election highlighted the continuing relevance of a constitution written over two centuries ago and the pivotal role of the Supreme Court. The nation's response to al Qaeda's attacks on 11 September 2001 and the launching of the 'war on terrorism' drew attention to both the powers of the president and the constraints imposed upon him.

US politics today considers and assesses US political institutions and the broader context within which they function. In particular, the book:

- offers an introduction to the structures of government, most notably the presidency, Congress, and the federal courts;
- examines the role of parties and interest groups; and
- evaluates the variables shaping the outcome of presidential and Congressional elections.

The book has been updated so as to incorporate events since 1998 and offer a more developed picture of the arguments and debates that are taking place among observers of the political process. It also includes a new chapter that examines the core political issues facing the US today and, at the same time, provides opportunities for follow-up work by readers.

I am immensely grateful to those who have helped the book come to fruition. My students – past and present – have assisted me in countless ways. Nigel Ashford and Martin Durham have always been ready with invaluable advice and thoughtful reflection. David Phelps's careful and scrupulous work improved many of the chapters. I would, however, particularly like to thank all my new colleagues at the Copenhagen Business School – most notably Niels Bjerre-Poulsen – for providing a friendly, constructive, and purposeful environ-ment within which the final stages of work on the book were completed.

I should, however, stress that the responsibility for errors, ambiguities and omissions remains mine alone.

Edward Ashbee
Copenhagen Business School,
Frederiksberg, Denmark.

1

Differences and divisions

At the time of its founding two centuries ago, the US was – despite some significant regional differences – a relatively homogeneous society dominated by White Anglo-Saxon Protestants or WASPs. They were the descendants of settlers from the British Isles who had established colonies along the eastern seaboard of the American continent from the early seventeenth century onwards.

The contemporary US is very different. On 1 April 2000, the Census Bureau recorded a population of 281,421,906. The nation not only occupies a far greater land mass – stretching across the continent – but is also much more diverse. There are significant fissures based upon race, ethnicity, and region. Some observers assert that the divisions are such that they will lead to *Balkanisation* and the eventual break-up of the US. Arthur Schlesinger Jr., a distinguished historian and former adviser to President Kennedy, has for example warned of 'the fragmentation of the national community into a quarrelsome spatter of enclaves, ghettos, tribes' (1992: 137–8). This chapter assesses the character of American society and considers the basis for these claims.

Race

About 12.1 per cent of the US population is black or *African-American*. Over half still live in the southern states, where their ancestors worked as slaves until the end of the Civil War in 1865. Others are the grandchildren and great-grandchildren of those who migrated – from the First World War onwards – to the northern cities. They were drawn by the promise of industrial employment and the chance to escape the rural poverty and the 'Jim Crow' segregation laws of the south. Blacks now constitute 39 per cent and 75 per cent of those living in Chicago and Detroit respectively.

Since the ending of segregation and the extension of the franchise in the 1960s, African-Americans have made sustained economic progress. A substantial black middle class has emerged. There are also growing numbers

Box 1.1   Race: the American dilemma

Many immigrants thought in terms of religious, economic and political freedom. About one-and-a-half million Africans were, however, brought across the Atlantic in leg and neck irons. They were mostly destined for the southern states such as South Carolina, Virginia and Mississippi. Although slavery came to an end in 1865, when the south was defeated in the Civil War, southern blacks faced continuing discrimination. Until the reforms of the 1960s, public facilities were *segregated* and many blacks were unable to vote. There was a gulf between the democratic ideals that constituted the American creed and political institutions structured around racial oppression. Gunnar Myrdal, a Swedish sociologist, termed this *the American dilemma*.

Amidst all this, black Americans are sometimes portrayed as passive victims. However, despite endemic racism, slaves and their descendants made an enduring mark on American life and society. For a brief period – in the after-math of the Civil War – blacks in the southern states gained *political* rights. They were elected to state legislatures and the US Congress, although they lost these positions as whites regained their dominance in the region. There were also a number of black *economic* success stories. Madam C. J. Walker made her fortune from beauty salons. John Merrick founded the North Carolina Mutual Insurance Company. Blacks also 'voted with their feet'. In the early years of the twentieth century, large numbers migrated from the south to northern cities. The growing black electorate in cities such as Detroit and Chicago created the conditions in which blacks could organise and again win political representa-tion. In 1928, Oscar DePriest, a Republican, was elected to the House of Representatives. Others supported Marcus Garvey's radical 'Back to Africa' movement. Black *culture* also began to gain recognition as the Harlem Renaissance took shape. Novelists, poets and jazz musicians carved out a dis-tinctive black culture in uptown New York City that influenced black and white Americans alike.

In the 1950s and 1960s the civil rights movement, led by figures such as Martin Luther King and coordinated by organisations such as the Southern Christian Leadership Conference, began to gain substantive victories. Against a background of Cold War pressures, the Montgomery bus boycott of 1955–56, the 'freedom rides', sit-ins and marches compelled federal legislators to act. The

of black public officials, including Congressmen. Nonetheless, there are still entrenched inequalities. In 2001, 22.7 per cent of the black population lived below the poverty level. Just 7.8 per cent of (non-Hispanic) whites faced similar difficulties (US Census Bureau 2002a). The infant mortality rate for blacks is twice that for whites. In 2002, 27.3 per cent of African-Americans aged 15 or over had failed to graduate or complete their studies at high school successfully. The figure for (non-Hispanic) whites was 16.4 per cent (US Census Bureau 2002b). Blacks are disproportionately likely to be victims of crime. Significant numbers are also offenders. According to a 1991 study, black males born in

1964 Civil Rights Act and the 1965 Voting Rights Act finally brought segregation to an end and allowed African-Americans to vote freely.

Despite legal – or *de jure* – equality, there are still significant differences between the races. African-Americans lag behind in terms of both educational achievement and income levels. Indeed, the gap widened during the boom years of the late 1990s and at the beginning of the new century. This was because living standards rose for whites at a faster rate than for blacks, the boom faltered from 2000 onwards, and in 1996 a report by the Children's Defense Fund suggested that the number of black children and young people in extreme poverty rose sharply between 2000 and 2003 (*New York Times*, 30 April 2003).

Median household income, 2001 (dollars)

Households	Income
All households	42,228
White (non-Hispanic)	46,305
Black	29,470
Hispanic	33,565

Source: adapted from US Census Bureau (2003), *Income 2001*, www.census.gov/hhes/income01/inctab1.html.

What should be done? Liberals emphasise the continuing hold of *institutionalised* discrimination. The disparities between whites and blacks – in terms of poverty, educational attainment, and jailings – suggest to them that federal government action is required. They call for large-scale public investment in the inner-city neighbourhoods and the maintenance of affirmative action programmes so as to ensure that minorities are proportionately represented on educational courses and in senior management positions. For their part, conservatives – and black nationalist organisations such as the Nation of Islam – adopt a different approach. They argue that although government regulations prevent individuals building up their own business enterprises, many of the former obstacles to black progress have now been eliminated. The black communities, they argue, need to rediscover the entrepreneurial spirit, and to address the problems of illegitimacy, criminality and drug abuse within their own communities.

that year would have had a greater than one in four chance of incarceration in federal prisons, state jails, or juvenile institutions during their lifetimes. In contrast, white males would have had a 1 in 23 chance of serving time (Joint Center for Political and Economic Studies 2003).

Race is also important because it informs social and political attitudes. The races have different priorities. Significantly more blacks than whites, for example, regard issues such as crime, violence, drugs, poverty and homelessness as the most important problems facing the US (Bositis 1999: 12). Furthermore, whereas a clear majority of African-Americans believe that the federal government should set basic national standards in the provision of welfare and other forms of social assistance, less than a third of the population as a whole share this opinion. Similarly, whereas 78.3 per cent of whites favour the use of the death penalty, it is backed by only 49.9 per cent of African-Americans (General Social Survey 1998). Although there was a 'rally round the flag' effect in the aftermath of the 11 September attacks – as both blacks and whites pulled together behind the president and the nation – the differences between blacks and whites re-emerged as the war against Iraq drew close. According to polls conducted by the Gallup Organization, only 29 per cent of blacks backed the war effort, compared with 78 per cent of whites (Gallup Organization 2003). These attitudinal differences are reflected in voting patterns. African-Americans are the Democrats' most loyal constituency. In the 2000 election, 90 per cent of black voters supported Al Gore, the Democratic Party candidate for the presidency. Just 8 per cent of blacks backed George W. Bush, the Republican candidate.

White attitudes should also be considered. While there is evidence to suggest that racism may have either diminished or taken a less overt form over the past half century, it is still evident. A 1991 survey suggested that racial stereotypes were widely accepted. Almost half of whites agreed that 'blacks tend to be lazy'. A clear majority endorsed claims that blacks 'prefer welfare'. Almost half said that they were 'unintelligent' (Smith 1995: 39). Sentiments such as these have at times been translated into votes, particularly during periods of economic uncertainty. David Duke, a former Ku Klux Klan leader, who still maintained many of his earlier opinions, stood as a candidate in the 1992 Republican presidential primaries. He gained 11 and 7 per cent of the votes among Republican primary voters in Mississippi and South Carolina respectively.

Ethnicity

Although hostility towards the black population bound whites together during America's formative years, the whites should not be seen as a homogeneous bloc. The white 'race' is constructed from different ethnic – or cultural – groupings. This is because the US is – in President John F. Kennedy's words – a 'nation of immigrants'.

In the 2000 Census, 10.3 per cent of the population claimed English ancestry. A further 4.6 per cent have roots in Wales, Scotland and from among the 'Scotch-Irish' of northern Ireland (US Census Bureau 2003a).

The British were the first permanent 'immigrants' on the mainland of north America. In May 1607, a settlement was established at Jamestown, Virginia. Despite many hardships, it survived by exporting tobacco. In 1620, the Pilgrim Fathers landed at Plymouth Bay in what was to become Massachusetts. In contrast with the Jamestown settlers, who were commercial adventurers, the Puritans sought to build a self-governing Christian commonwealth. Later in the seventeenth century, Quaker communities were founded in the Delaware valley. During the eighteenth century, others came from the borderlands between England and Scotland and the northern counties of Ireland (Fischer 1989).

These beginnings evolved into stable and ordered communities stretching along much of the eastern seaboard. Although the settlers were British colonists and subject to the rule of Governors appointed by the authorities in London, a separate and distinct American identity began to emerge. While there were significant differences between the northern 'Yankees' and the southerners, this identity formed a basis for rebellion against British rule. The Declaration of Independence was published in 1776. The War of Independence followed, culminating in the defeat of the British forces at Yorktown in 1781.

Although WASPs formed the backbone of the new nation, others followed. During the nineteenth and early twentieth centuries, millions of migrants made the journey from Europe. Before the Civil War (1861–65), they were largely drawn from northern European countries such as Ireland, Germany and Sweden. After the war, it was the turn of those from eastern and southern Europe. Between 1845 and 1854, three million crossed the Atlantic. In 1907 alone, 1.3 million people arrived in the US.

Why did they make the journey? The answer is that both 'push' and 'pull' factors were at work. 'Push' factors are the pressures that encourage migrants to abandon their country of origin. For example, in Poland, peasants were forced from the land because of competition from more advanced forms of agriculture in Western Europe and the US. Their difficulties were compounded by both a high birth-rate and the occupation and partition of the country by neighbouring powers. However, 'pull' factors also played their part. The Poles were drawn to the US by the promise of employment in industrial cities such as Chicago, Buffalo and Pittsburgh. At the same time, the transatlantic journey became less arduous and costly. The advent of the steamship cut the crossing time to weeks rather than months, and intense competition between shipping companies reduced the fares. There were broadly similar pressures in other European countries. The failure of the potato crop led to mass famine in Ireland. From 1847 until 1855, over 100,000 Irish emigrated annually. In 1851, the outflow reached a peak of 221,000. In the US, the men found employment in construction projects, such as canals and railroads along the east coast. Women worked in the textile industries.

The US offered more, however, than a regular wage. Although – as Martin Scorsese depicted in his 2002 film, *Gangs of New York* – immigrants often encountered *nativist* resentment from those who had been in the country for many generations, America represented freedom. It promised economic freedom to those who had been adversely affected by the process of economic change. In Europe, the displaced craftsman – or *artisan* – faced only unemployment or absorption into the ranks of the industrial working class. In the US, he might rebuild a business of his own. The commercial history of the US is adorned by individual success stories. German-American artisans established

Box 1.2   Latinos

There was a Hispanic or *Latino* presence in the south-west long before the region was incorporated into the US. Numbers grew significantly from the 1880s onwards, when Mexican labourers came to border states such as Texas and California in search of work. There has been renewed growth in recent years following the liberalisation of immigration laws in 1965. Between 1990 and 2000, the number of Latinos rose by 57.9 per cent (US Census Bureau 2003b). Many settled in the metropolitan regions in and around cities such as Chicago and New York as well as the south-western states. In July 2002, the Census Bureau announced that Latinos had overtaken African-Americans and were now the largest minority grouping in the country. The rise in numbers can be attributed to immigration and a relatively high birth-rate.

To an extent, Latinos share the problems facing the black communities. Disproportionate numbers are unemployed and in poverty. Median income is significantly lower than for whites, although this can partly be explained by the relative youth of the Latino population. It would, however, be wrong to make too many generalisations. As the US Census Bureau emphasises, the term 'Hispanic' embraces those of Mexican, Puerto Rican, Cuban, and Central or South American origin. It is, furthermore, an ethnic category, and there are both white and black Hispanics. These cleavages form the basis for significant economic and cultural differences within the Latino population.

The Latino population 2002 (%)

	Total US	Mexican	Puerto Rican	Cuban	All Central and South American
Failure to graduate from high school	15.9	49.4	33.2	29.2	35.3
Below poverty level	11.7	22.8	26.1	16.5	15.2
In managerial and / or professional employment	31.4	11.9	19.5	23.0	14.7

Source: adapted from US Census Bureau (2003), The Hispanic Population in the United States: March 2002 – Detailed Tables (PPL-165), www.census.gov/population/socdemo/hispanic/ppl-165.html.

companies such as Steinway and Sons, the piano makers, and Levi Strauss, the clothing manufacturers. For other migrants, there were hopes of religious liberty. Sects such as the Amish and the Mennonites sought the freedom to live independently of others. They survive to this day as autonomous communities in states such as Pennsylvania and Ohio. The US also offered political freedom and civic rights. In Europe, Jews faced discrimination. In the years before the First World War, there were violent anti-Semitic massacres in Poland and

There are also variations in the economic, cultural and political relationship between the Latino communities and the wider population. In California, there have been tensions that were reflected in the passage of Proposition 187. Passed in November 1994, the measure sought to deny non-emergency state benefits to illegal immigrants. It was supported by 63 per cent of 'Anglos' and opposed by 69 per cent of Hispanics. In Texas, however, polarisation is less marked. Cities such as Houston seem to have been restructured around a 'Tex–Mex' identity. Although well over two-thirds of Latinos across the US vote Democratic, there are some signs that minority politics in Texas are being 'normalised', and there is serious competition between the parties for the Latino vote.

Latinos and the overall US population compared

	Total US population	Latinos
Population (000s)	282,082	37,438
Median household income	$38,275	$25,083
Median age (years)	35.6	26.3

Source: adapted from US Census Bureau (2003), *Selected Summary Measures of Age and Income by Hispanic Origin and Race*, www.census.gov/population/socdemo/hispanic/ppl-165/sumtab01.xls.

References and further reading

US Census Bureau (2003g), *Difference in Population by Race and Hispanic or Latino Origin, for the United States: 1990 to 2000*, www.census.gov/population/cen2000/phc-t1/tab04.txt.

Russia. After the war, prejudice against the Jewish communities was sustained as the newly formed Slav nations began to establish themselves.

However, from 1921 onwards, admissions to the US were severely restricted, and skewed towards northern Europe. This policy lasted until the 1965 amendments to the Immigration and Nationality Act abandoned the system of quotas for particular nations and established 'family reunification' as the defining criterion for entry. As a consequence of reform, the number of immigrants has risen dramatically, and they have again become a significant element within American society. In 2002, the foreign-born constituted an estimated 11.5 per cent of the American population (US Census Bureau 2003b). Between 1991 and 2000, 9,095,417 immigrants were admitted (Bureau of Citizenship and Immigration Services 2003). The majority of the new immigrants are Hispanic, or *Latino*, and are drawn from Central and South America. However, there are also growing numbers from the countries of Asia.

A significant proportion of the immigrant population are in the country illegally. Studies by the Immigration and Naturalization Service suggest that, in 2000, there were about 7 million illegal immigrants, a number growing by more than 300,000 annually (CNN.com 2003). During the early and middle 1990s, illegal immigration became a defining political issue in California. In November 1994, the state's voters passed Proposition 187, which sought to end the provision of non-emergency state benefits, such as health care and education, to 'undocumented aliens'. However, political circumstances changed during the latter half of the decade. There was increasing economic prosperity, and some in the Republican Party became increasingly conscious of the need to court the Latino vote. Against this background, despite increased numbers, both legal and illegal immigration became less pressing concerns, and legislators were more reluctant to see them placed on the political agenda.

Table 1.1 *Immigration to the US, 1951–2000*

Year	Number
1951–60	2,515,479
1961–70	3,321,677
1971–80	4,493,314
1981–90	7,338,062
1991–2000	9,095,417

Source: adapted from Bureau of Citizenship and Immigration Services (2003), *Immigration to the United States: Fiscal Years 1820–2001*, www.immigration.gov/graphics/aboutus/statistics/IMM01yrbk/ExcIMM01/Table1.xls.

Immigration has been on such a scale that – despite continuing WASP predominance – it has reshaped the cultural and political character of the US. This is evident in five ways:

1 Immigration fractured the geography of many American cities. To this day, New York City has a Chinatown, a Little Italy and an El Barrio. More recent immigrants have also made their mark. The Atlantic Avenue district in Brooklyn, a borough of New York City, is predominantly Arabic. The Brighton Beach neighbourhood is now known as 'Little Odessa' following an influx of Russians.
2 Recent immigration has contributed to a increasingly visible cultural and political divide between immigrant 'gateway' cities such as New York, Chicago, and Los Angeles – which are around the 'rim' of the US – and the overwhelmingly white 'heartland' states.
3 Mass immigration has led to religious diversity. Although they belonged to different denominations, the early settlers were united by a shared commitment to the Protestant faith. Some brought Anglican traditions with them. Others – particularly in New England – were committed to Puritanism. There were also sects such as the Shakers and the Amish, who isolated themselves from outsiders.

Since the mid-nineteenth century, however, the US has progressively become a less Protestant and a more pluralistic nation. Immigrants from eastern and southern Europe, and recent immigrants from central and south America, brought both Roman Catholicism and Judaism with them. By 2001, about 24 per cent of the American population was Catholic, and there are almost three million Jews. Other faiths – most notably Islam – are also growing, although estimates of the Muslim population vary. Islam draws adherents from both Asian immigrants and the native-born black population.

Table 1.2 *Selected religious faiths and denominations, 2001*

	Number of adult adherents	% of adult US population
Catholic	50,873,000	24.5
Baptist	33,830,000	16.3
Methodist / Wesleyan	14,150,000	6.8
Lutheran	9,580,000	4.6
Presbyterian	5,596,000	2.7
Judaism	2,831,000	1.3
Islam	Estimates vary between 2.8 and 4.1 million	

Source: adapted from Adherents.com (2003), *Largest Religious Groups in the United States of America*, www.adherents.com/rel_USA.html#Pew_branches.

4 Although there has been a steady process of assimilation into the American mainstream, and many of the ethnic neighbourhoods have lost their formerly distinctive character, ethnicity still offers a basis for self-identification. Indeed, in recent decades, there has been a renewal of commitment to ethnic celebrations, festivals and organisations. Denver holds an annual *Oktoberfest*. In Savannah, the schools are closed on St Patrick's Day (Dinnerstein, Nichols and Reimers 1996: 266). The annual St Patrick's Day parade in New York City attracts about 150,000 participants.

5 Ethnicity also has political significance. In many states, an ethnically balanced ticket is still essential for electoral success. In Minnesota, every state governor between 1925 and 1976 had a Scandinavian background. Since the mid-nineteenth century, the Irish vote has had to be courted in cities such as New York and Boston. There was, from 1916 until 1969, a 'Jewish seat' on the US Supreme Court bench. It is likely that a Hispanic seat will be established and institutionalised within the coming years.

Projections by the US Census Bureau suggest that the ethnic composition of the country will change dramatically over the coming half-century. Their forecasts indicate that by 2060 non-Hispanic whites will be a minority. The proportion of African-Americans will only rise marginally, to about 13.3 per cent. However, there will have been a dramatic increase in the number of Latinos. By

2060, they will constitute a quarter of the country's population. At about the same time, the proportion of the population who are Asian-American will rise to almost 10 per cent.

Table 1.3 *US population projections by race and Hispanic origin (% of the total US population)*

	White	Black	Hispanic	Asian	American Indian
2000	69.1	12.1	12.5	3.6	0.7
2025	62.0	12.9	18.2	6.2	0.8
2050	52.8	13.2	24.3	8.9	0.8
2060	49.6	13.3	26.6	9.8	0.8

Note: 'Hispanic' is an ethnic description, and can be applied to those of any race. The figures for whites, blacks, Asians and American Indians *exclude* those who are also Hispanic.
Source: adapted from US Census Bureau (2003h), *Projections of the resident population by race, Hispanic origin, and nativity,* www.census.gov/population/projections/nation/summary/pp-t5-f.txt.

Although opinion is divided among conservatives, some – most notably Peter Brimelow, author of *Alien Nation* – believe that these demographic shifts will have dramatic consequences for the US. He asserts that many Latino immigrants have maintained their ties with their former countries and have little loyalty towards the US. Indeed, he argues, some within the Latino population may eventually seek the break-up of the country. He warns that 'throughout the lifetime of my little son, American patriots will be fighting to salvage as much as possible from the shipwreck of their great republic' (1996: 268).

Other commentators are more sanguine. They argue that just as earlier generations of immigrants were progressively absorbed into the American mainstream, Hispanics will also be assimilated. They insist that the US is – in contrast

---

Box 1.3   The immigrant experience: *Gangs of New York* (2002)

Director: Martin Scorsese
Starring: Leonardo DiCaprio, Cameron Diaz, Daniel Day-Lewis, Liam Neeson, Jim Broadbent, Pete Postlethwaite

Martin Scorsese's epic film is set in New York City between the 1840s and 1863. It is structured around the relationship between a young man who seeks vengeance against Bill 'The Butcher', the man who killed his father. All this takes place against a background of violent struggles in the Five Points neighbourhood between newly arrived immigrants from Europe and native-born Americans. The film depicts the role played by the corrupt 'machine politics' of patronage based around Tammany Hall and events in New York during the Civil War.

Website: www.gangsofnewyork.com.

with the countries of Europe and Asia – open to all those who accept its founding principles of liberty and democracy. Attempts to limit admissions are a denial of those principles and therefore 'unAmerican'.

Underclass and overclass

A significant proportion of Americans place themselves in the middle class. However, US society is marked by significant socioeconomic divisions. There are those who are separated from the remainder of society by being permanently 'locked' into poverty. Inner-city neighbourhoods or 'ghettos', such as Harlem or the Bronx in New York, the Chicago South Side, and the Watts neighbourhood of Los Angeles, became synonymous with the most severe forms of urban deprivation. Members of the *underclass* have few job-based skills, and are either unemployed or under-employed. African-Americans, Latinos and other minorities are disproportionately represented in its ranks.

The 'underclass' is, however, a contested concept. The economic boom of the late 1990s led to a significance rise in living standards for the poor as well as the wealthier groupings. Furthermore, many who use the term 'underclass' have drawn on the work of Charles Murray, a conservative commentator, who has tied it to cultural as well as economic dimensions. It has become associated in the popular mind with criminality, drug abuse, a high teenage pregnancy rate, the collapse of family structures, and welfare dependency. This, it has been argued, is a cruel stereotype that hides the realities of life in urban neighbourhoods. Few however dispute that although economic opportunities opened up during the latter half of the 1990s, there is still a pervasive sense of isolation and helplessness in many of the inner-cities. As Cornel West, a noted black social commentator, puts it: 'we have created rootless, dangling people with little link to the supportive networks – family, friends, school – that sustain some sense of purpose in life' (1993: 9).

Urban poverty is explained in different ways. Liberals stress economic factors and emphasise the decline of manufacturing industry. Some also point to the

Table 1.4 *Percentage of the population in different income categories, 1998*

Income categories	%
$0–$19,999	26.7
$20,000–$29,999	17.0
$30,000–$49,999	25.6
$50,000–$89,999	21.0
Over $90,000	9.7
Total	100

Source: adapted from the General Social Survey (2003), *Income98 (Recoded) / Year(1998)*, www.icpsr.umich.edu/.

way in which inner-city neighbourhoods lost their vitality as more affluent white and black families moved out to the suburbs. All too often, they assert, financial institutions fail to offer start-up capital for minority businesses. From this perspective, the solution to the urban crisis lies in federal government intervention and increased funding for inner-city regeneration.

For their part, conservatives accept that economic factors play a role. They suggest, however, that greater competition and the adoption of *laissez-faire* economic policies – through *deregulation* – would create the conditions for urban renewal. They also emphasise the importance of cultural change in the inner-city neighbourhoods. They suggest that the initiatives adopted during the 1990s – including welfare reform and strict 'zero-tolerance' law and order policies – have encouraged responsible behaviour, a commitment to the work ethic, self-reliance, and small-scale entrepreneurship. Conservative commentators point, in particular, to the 1996 Personal Responsibility and Work Opportunity Reconciliation Act, which ended the principle of welfare as an entitlement, established work requirements as a condition for the receipt of assistance, and imposed a five-year lifetime limit on the provision of benefits.

The 'underclass' entered the popular vocabulary some years ago. However – during the 1990s – a number of observers began to talk of an elite or *overclass*. The term refers to an economically and socially privileged grouping – between about 5 and 10 per cent of the American people – that consists of those with advanced degrees and their families. Members of the 'overclass' have views and interests that mark them out from other sections of the population. Although they back tax reductions and other policies associated with economic conservatism, they also endorse some proposals that are tied to social liberalism. For example, their need for domestic staff, particularly nannies, has led them to support open immigration (Lind 1996: 139–80).

Regional identities

The American regions have traditionally been associated with particular cultural identities. The Yankee north-east was shaped by its Puritan roots. Although the character of states such as New Hampshire and Maine is still defined by their forests, lakes, and mountains, the region was also the locus of the American industrial revolution. Cities such as Lowell in Massachusetts owed their origins to the textile mills. By 1846, they were producing almost a million yards of cloth a week. As time progressed, the tools and techniques used in the textile mills were applied to other industries. Machine shops and factories were established. In 1851, when the first World's Fair was held at the Crystal Palace in London, Americans won more prizes for their industrial products, compared to the number of entries, than any other nation. On the basis of such achievements, the north-east increasingly became economically, socially and politically predominant.

Box 1.4 Native Americans

By the 1840s, the US was committed to conquering much of the continent. The 'manifest destiny' of the nation was to occupy all the lands from the Atlantic to the Pacific. For the native Americans or 'Indians', the westward shift led to the final destruction of tribal societies and their nomadic way of life. Despite occasional victories – most notably the rout of General Custer and his soldiers at the Little Big Horn in 1874 – Indian resistance was crushed. The tribes were not only outgunned. Mass slaughter led to the near-extinction of the buffalo herds on which they depended. The capture of Geronimo in 1886 symbolised their final defeat.

Today, the remnants of native American society are to be found on the reservations. The largest – the Navajo nation – stretches across parts of Arizona, New Mexico, and Utah. Some of those living on the reservations have made a living by offering goods and services such as fireworks and gambling that are prohibited elsewhere under state law. There are also earnings from tourism. Some – most notably the Navajo – have sold coal and uranium mining rights.

Despite these initiatives, significant numbers of native Americans – particularly reservation dwellers – face severe problems, including economic hardship and unemployment.

Relative situations of Native Americans and the overall US population compared

	Total US population	Total Native American population
Population	248,709,873	1,937,391
College/university graduates	7.6%	2.1%
Median household income	30,056	19,900
Persons in poverty	13.1%	31.2%

Source: adapted from US Census Bureau (1995), *Selected Social and Economic Characteristics for the 25 Largest American Indian Tribes: 1990*, www.census.gov/population/socdemo/race/indian/ ailang2.txt.

The identity of the midwest is more difficult to define. It is popularly associated with agriculture, the small town and *isolationist* attitudes. For many, the character of the region has been captured by the Minnesota writer, Garrison Keillor, in his stories about the fictional Lake Wobegon. However, the midwest is not homogeneous. Agriculture is divided between corn, wheat and dairy production. The culture of the region was shaped by German, Scandinavian and British settlers. The midwest also includes the industrial belt around the Great Lakes, cities such as Detroit, and the metropolis of Chicago.

The west includes states such as Arizona and New Mexico. They were among the last to be brought into the US, and still retain a sense of the 'frontier' about them. Much of the terrain is arid and dramatic. There are large-scale, albeit impoverished, Indian reservations. The character of Utah has been shaped by Mormon settlers. Las Vegas – in Nevada – is the gambling capital of the US. On the west coast, California has – from the 'gold rush' of 1849 onwards – been seen as a land of opportunity.

Among the different regions, the south traditionally had the most distinct cultural character. In the years before the Civil War, it was structured around 'King Cotton', the plantation (although the small farm was, in practice, more representative), and slavery. Tensions between the south and the north grew as the century progressed. Abolitionists in the north called for an end to slavery. Northern manufacturers insisted upon protective tariffs, although these threatened the interests of the cotton trade. For southerners, the election of the Republican candidate, Abraham Lincoln, as president in November 1860 seemed to symbolise the determination of the north to impose its will upon the entire nation. His victory led eleven southern states to *secede* from the US and establish the Confederate States of America as an independent nation. Although Lincoln was, despite his opponents' fears, prepared to accept the maintenance of slavery, he could not countenance the dissolution of the US, and 620,000 were killed in the civil war that followed.

The northern victory in April 1865 led to the abolition of slavery and the long-term hegemony of the north. However, despite military defeat, the white south progressively reasserted itself. Its political representatives dominated Congressional committees for the greater part of the twentieth century. From the 1890s, segregation was imposed across the south, confining blacks to certain occupations and restricting their access to public facilities. Bogus 'tests' and rigged state constitutions were used to remove their right to vote. These forms of institutionalised racism – known as 'Jim Crow' laws – were only brought to an end in the 1960s.

Some observers talk today about the 'homogenisation' of the nation. The building of the interstate highways, the emergence of a national economic market, and the advent of television brought about a national culture. Nonetheless, some still talk of southern 'exceptionalism'. Carl Degler notes that the south is still marked by greater 'rurality'. Living standards are lower than the national average. Conservative thinking and traditionalist attitudes have a more entrenched hold (1997: 14–22).

However, although these regional differences remain, other cleavages have come to the fore in recent decades.

1 There has been a long-term process of deindustrialisation as capital-intensive industries in parts of the north-east and midwest have contracted and shed labour. The states that were once defined by manufacturing have been dubbed the *rustbelt*.

   In contrast, there have been high levels of growth in the *sunbelt* states of the south and the west. The network of interstate highways built during the

Eisenhower years transformed hitherto isolated rural communities. The federal government funded other infrastructural projects. Many defence installations were established in the sunbelt states. The space programme was based in Houston in Texas and at Cape Canaveral in Florida. These projects, the low cost of land, and the relative weak character of trade unionism encouraged the development of new industries. During the 1980s, employment in the south and west grew by 26.3 per cent and 29.8 per cent respectively.

The economic disparities between the regions inevitably led to population shifts. Although the US population grew significantly during the 1990s, growth in the rustbelt states was limited in character. During the same period, however, the population in the southern and western states increased substantially. For example, the population of Arizona rose by 40 per cent.

Table 1.5 *Percentage change in population, 1990–2000*

State	% change
Arizona	40.0
California	13.8
Colorado	30.6
Nevada	66.3
New York	5.5
Pennsylvania	3.4
Texas	22.8

Source: adapted from US Census Bureau (2001), *Census 2000, PHC-T-2, Ranking Tables for States: 1990 and 2000*, www.census.gov/population/cen2000/phc-t2/tab01.pdf.

2 There has been a second, parallel shift. Large numbers of immigrants have settled in metropolitan 'gateways' such as New York, Chicago, Los Angeles and Houston. These cities and the suburban regions which are tied to them – or metros – have also attracted significant numbers of young, single people, many of whom have professional qualifications and work in the high-tech 'post-industrial' sector.

However, at the same time, there has been a process of outward migration. A significant proportion of those with the financial means – who are predominantly white – have left the 'metros' and moved to the 'heartland' states, particularly in the west. This created an increasingly visible cultural and political cleavage between the 'gateway' regions – around the 'rim' of the US – and the remaining states. The divide is reflected in voting patterns. The former supported the Democratic candidate, Al Gore, in the 2000 presidential election, while the 'heartland' decisively backed George W. Bush, the Republican nominee.

Gender

Alongside talk of a 'Balkanisation' process based around racial, ethnic and regional cleavages, many political observers also speak of a 'gender gap'. Their comments are based upon differences in terms of both voting behaviour and attitudes. Women are more likely to vote for the Democrats. They also tend to see the role of government in more positive terms than men.

Table 1.6 *Attitudes towards the role of government, 1997–98 (%)*

	Men	Women
Too powerful	40	27
Right amount of power	32	31
Should use more power	27	40

Source: Pew Research Center for the People and the Press (1998), *How Americans View Government – Selected Tables,* people-press.org/reports/display.php3?PageID=597.

Although the extent and scale of the gender gap should not be exaggerated, it is rooted in three factors. Firstly, a high proportion of women are domestic carers, and many therefore look to government as a source of support. Secondly, as William Scheider has argued, the Republicans have used forms of language that are oriented, in particular, towards men. Thirdly, some suggest that the traditional role of men has been undermined by economic and cultural shifts. The decline of manufacturing industry and the growth of the service sector have led to a shrinkage in the number of traditionally 'male' forms of employment. As employment became more insecure and traditional certainties have been eroded, men have been drawn by their loss of status towards conservatism. They are seeking a restoration of an earlier age in which they were the 'breadwinners'.

Culture wars

The differences between the gateway regions and the 'heartland' lay the basis for what have been dubbed the 'culture wars'. The term refers to the battles between those with 'progressive' attitudes and moral traditionalists. Although largely a function of region, the warring cultures are also tied to the gender gap, levels of both geographic and social mobility, exposure to modernity, the specific experiences of different generations, and religious affiliations.

While the differences should not be exaggerated – partly because some immigrant communities are traditionalist in outlook – disproportionate numbers of those living in the metropolitan regions lean towards socially liberal or 'progressive' attitudes. Indeed, there are visible gay neighbourhoods in cities such as New York, Los Angeles and San Francisco. Although a majority in the 'metros' still leans towards traditionalism, moral *relativism* – the belief that different 'lifestyle choices' have equal validity – has gained increasing acceptance. Studies of attitudes towards abortion and homosexuality, for example, suggest significant differences between the cities and the rural areas.

Table 1.7 *Should abortion be allowed 'for any reason'? (%)*

	Large and medium-sized cities	Suburbs	Small cities, towns and rural areas
Yes	47	42.6	29.5
No	53	57.4	70.5

Question text: 'Please tell me whether or not *you* think it should be possible for a pregnant woman to obtain a *legal* abortion if . . . the woman wants it for any reason?'
Source: adapted from General Social Survey (2003), *ABANY / XNORCSIZ(Recoded)*, www.icpsr. umich.edu:8080/GSS/homepage.htm.

Table 1.8 *Are homosexual relationships wrong? (%)*

	Large and medium-sized cities	Suburbs	Small cities, towns and rural areas
Always / Almost always wrong	57.4	70.3	80
Wrong only sometimes / Not wrong at all	42.6	29.7	20

Question text: 'And what about sexual relations between two adults of the same sex, is it. . . .'
Source: adapted from General Social Survey (2003), *HOMOSEX1 / XNORCSIZ (Recoded)*, www.icpsr.umich.edu:8080/GSS/homepage.htm.

Changing attitudes are tied to shifting lifestyles. There are now fewer traditional households. According to the 2000 Census, there were 5.5 million unmarried couple households in the US compared with just 3.2 million in 1990. Census returns also pointed to 594 thousand same-sex households. These are mostly to be found within the metropolitan regions (US Census Bureau 2003c).

Outside the 'metros', a significant proportion of Americans still regard themselves as moral traditionalists. They stress the importance of the conventional family and – in some cases – fundamentalist forms of religion based upon a literal reading of Biblical texts.

Table 1.9 *Attitudes towards the Bible 1998 (%)*

Large and medium-sized cities	Suburbs	Small cities, towns, and rural areas
22.8	29.7	41.7

Question text: 'The Bible is the actual word of God and it is to be taken literally, word for word.'
Source: adapted from General Social Survey (2003), *BIBLE1 / XNORCSIZ(Recoded)*, www.icpsr. umich.edu:8080/GSS/homepage.htm.

The institutions of marriage and family are, they assert, not only rooted in biblical teaching, but also represent an important building-block for a stable and ordered society. Although they disagree about the extent to which government can or should 'legislate morality', there is agreement that homosexuality, attempts to devalue the marriage vow, and illegitimacy are immoral.

Conclusion

The contemporary US is a diverse and heterogeneous society. Some radicals and liberals see the country's ethnic, racial and gender differences in positive terms and as a basis for *identity politics*. They call for the maintenance and extension of policies such as *affirmative action*. In its most rigorous form, this attempts to ensure 'equality of outcome' by setting numerical goals – or 'quotas' – so that women and minorities are more fully represented in senior management positions or on educational courses. Many liberals also stress the importance of multiculturalism and diversity in education. School students, they assert, should be taught to understand and appreciate the different cultures from which the US is constructed.

For their part, conservatives and some more traditional liberals argue that such policies are socially divisive, and will lead to the fragmentation of the US as a nation. In place of policies such as multiculturalism and affirmative action, they instead stress the beliefs, principles and traditions that bring Americans together. These are considered and assessed in Chapter 2.

References and further reading

Bositis, D. A. (1999), *1999 National Opinion Poll*, Washington DC, Joint Center Political and Economic Studies.

Brimelow, P. (1996), *Alien Nation*, New York, HarperPerennial.

Bureau of Citizenship and Immigration Services (2003), *Immigration to the United States: Fiscal Years 1820–2001*, www.immigration.gov/graphics/aboutus/statistics/ IMM01yrbk/ExcIMM01/Table1.xls.

CNN.com (2003), *INS: 7 million illegal immigrants in United States*, 1 February www.cnn.com/2003/US/01/31/illegal.immigration/.

Degler, C. N. (1997), *Place Over Time: The Continuity of Southern Distinctiveness*, Athens, GA, University of Georgia Press.

Dinnerstein, L., R. L. Nichols and D. M. Reimers (1996), *Natives and Strangers: A Multicultural History of America*, New York, Oxford University Press.

Fischer, D. H. (1989), *Albion's Seed: Four British Folkways in America*, New York, Oxford University Press.

Gallup Organization (2003), *Poll Analyses – Blacks Show Biggest Decline in Support for War Compared with 1991: Other Traditional Democratic Groups Also Much Less Supportive of Current Iraq War*, April 4, www.gallup.com/poll/releases/pr030404.asp.

General Social Survey (1998), *CAPPUN*, www.icpsr.umich.edu:8080/GSS/home-page.htm.

Joint Center for Political and Economic Studies (2003), *African Americans and the Correctional System*, www.jointcenter.org/DB/factsheet/correctionalsys.htm.

Lind, M. (1996) *The Next American Nation: The New Nationalism and the Fourth American Revolution*, New York, The Free Press.

Schlesinger, Jr A. M. (1992), *The Disuniting of America: Reflections on a Multicultural Society*, New York, W. W. Norton.

Smith, R. C. (1995), *Racism in the Post-Civil Rights Era*, Albany, NY, State University of New York Press.

US Census Bureau (2002a) *Poverty Status of People by Family Relationship, Race, and Hispanic Origin: 1959 to 2001*, www.census.gov/hhes/poverty/histpov/hstpov2.html.

US Census Bureau (2002b) *Percent of High School and College Graduates of the Population 15 Years and Over, 1 by Age, Sex, Race, and Hispanic Origin: March 2002*, www.census.gov/population/socdemo/education/ppl-169/tab01a.txt.

US Census Bureau (2003a), *QT-02. Profile of Selected Social Characteristics: 2000*, factfinder.census.gov/home/en/c2ss.html.

US Census Bureau (2003b), *Foreign-Born Population Surpasses 32 Million, Census Bureau Estimates*, www.census.gov/Press-Release/www/2003/cb03–42.html.

US Census Bureau (2003c), *Married-Couple and Unmarried-Partner Households: 2000*, www.census.gov/prod/2003pubs/censr-5.pdf.

West, C. (1993), *Race Matters*, Boston, Beacon Press.

Websites

The website hosted by the American Studies Resources Centre (www.americansc.org.uk) offers an excellent starting-point for those studying US politics and government. Based at John Moores University in Liverpool, the site provides information about learning resources, student conferences, study days and degree courses in the UK. It incorporates *American Studies Today*, an on-line journal with a wide range of articles, news and book reviews.

2

A shared culture

Chapter 1 considered the claims of those who assert that the US is a divided and fractured nation. However, their arguments represent only part of the overall picture. Despite the cleavages and fissures, there are also unifying ideas that draw Americans together into a common nationality. These include a belief that the US offers the promise of upward mobility and principles such as self-reliance, democracy and freedom. For some commentators, notions such as these define what it means to be 'American'. Indeed they were dubbed the 'American creed' by Samuel P. Huntington in his book, *American Politics: The Promise of Disharmony* (Huntington 1982: 14). This chapter surveys and assesses these beliefs.

Mobility and the American dream

The 'American dream' is a familiar phrase. It is, however, defined in different ways. It has sometimes been used to describe the aspirations of those seeking to break away from the constraints of conventional life and escape to the American west. It has also been used – much more narrowly – to refer to the prospect of individual home ownership. However, it is most commonly employed to describe the belief that individuals can – with sufficient commit-ment, application, and initiative – achieve almost unlimited goals, bringing forth material reward. This is underpinned by the belief that the US offers boundless opportunities and possibilities. A contrast is often drawn with other nations, where, it is said, an individual's standing depended upon his or her inherited class position. The belief that the US is an open society offering upward mobility is widely accepted. In her study, *Facing Up to the American Dream*, Jennifer Hochschild concludes that Americans – including those on low incomes – are 'close to unanimous in endorsing the idea of the American dream' (1995: 55). James Truslow Adams (1878–1949), a historian, referred to 'that dream of a land in which life should be better and richer and fuller for every man, with opportunity for each according to his ability or achievement' (Fossum and Roth 1981: 6). In 1993, President Bill Clinton talked in similar terms: 'The American dream that we were all raised on is a simple but powerful one – if you work hard and play by the rules you should be given a chance to go as far as your God-given ability will take you' (Hochschild 1995: 18).

Table 2.1 *'America has an open society. What one achieves in life no longer depends on one's family background, but on the abilities one has and the education one acquires' (1983–87) (% of the population)*

Strongly agree	40.2
Somewhat agree	44.8
Somewhat disagree	13.4
Strongly disagree	1.7

Source: adapted from General Social Survey (2003a), *USCLASS3*, www.icpsr.umich.edu:8080/ GSS/homepage.htm.

The dream also takes a political form. It expresses itself in the belief that individuals can, like President Abraham Lincoln (1861–65), rise from 'log cabin to White House'. President James A. Garfield, who was assassinated shortly after taking office in 1881, is another celebrated example. He was born in a pioneer home in Ohio, distinguished himself in the Civil War, rose to be Speaker of the House of Representatives, and later gained the Republican nomination for the presidency. Other presidents have been hailed in similar terms. Following the presidential election of 1992, President Bill Clinton talked of his own progression from Hope in rural Arkansas to the White House.

The dream has a hold because it is, at least to some extent, rooted in the realities of life. Some individuals and families *have* begun with little and accumulated vast sums. Andrew Carnegie (1835–1919) was born in Scotland. He was sent to the US at the age of thirteen, and initially laboured in the mills for a salary of $1.20 a week. He eventually became a wealthy steel magnate. Today, figures such as Bill Gates of Microsoft, and Ross Perot, who built up a Texas computer company and contested the presidency in 1992 and 1996, seem to show that the dream is still a reality.

However, although the dream is widely accepted, and despite the successes of individual entrepreneurs who appear to represent its fulfilment, there are those who have questioned its legitimacy as a description of American society. Some have argued that – in practice – levels of upward mobility are similar in Europe and the US. Others assert that process of moving upwards is a much more brutal process than the depictions of the American dream generally suggest. For example, at the end of the nineteenth century, the novelist Jack London saw the US as a savagely competitive society in which only the fittest survived. In more recent decades, the late Christopher Lasch, a communitarian theorist, argued that the adoption of a dream based upon the acquisition of riches represented the abandonment of earlier hopes. In the original republican vision, there were to be large numbers of property holders and, although there would be economic inequalities, rigid class distinctions would be absent. Such a society would enable its citizens to move beyond the world of work and develop their intellectual and aesthetic abilities. The original ideal, Lasch asserted: 'was nothing less than a classless society, understood to mean not only the absence of hereditary privilege and legally recognized distinctions of rank but a refusal to tolerate the separation of learning and labor' (Lasch 1995: 64).

Self-reliance, individualism and *laissez-faire*

In its contemporary form, the American dream promises opportunity and reward to those who work hard. There is however a corollary to this. If individuals fail to advance, and are, for example, unemployed or in poverty, it is regarded, to a very large extent, as their own responsibility. There is a widely shared commitment to the principles of individualism and self-reliance. Individuals should not look towards the government. Instead, they are expected to provide for themselves, and there is a degree of impatience with those who fail to do this.

The emphasis upon self-reliance is tied to *laissez-faire* or free-market economics. There is a belief that companies and individuals should be left to make their own economic decisions, and that the government should play only a minimal role. A cross-national survey of public opinion conducted in 1985–86 showed some significant differences. Whereas 81 per cent of British people believed that the government should spend more on old-age pensions, only 47 per cent of Americans held the same opinion; and while 85 per cent of British people agreed that it was the responsibility of government to provide health care, only 40 per cent of Americans concurred.

American faith in self-reliance and *laissez-faire* has played a part in stifling attempts to establish a labour or social-democratic party committed to extending government ownership, control and provision. These efforts reached a peak in 1912, when Eugene V. Debs, a socialist and trade unionist, made the third of his four bids for the presidency. However, he gained only 6 per cent of the vote. In contrast, the socialist parties that emerged in the European countries during the closing decades of the nineteenth century had, by the end of the First World War, become parties of government.

There were other reasons why American socialism foundered. The pervasiveness of the American dream, and its at least partial basis in economic reality, provides part of the answer. The US appeared to offer greater opportunities for personal advancement than could be found in other nations and, in comparison with Europe, class barriers seemed much less rigid. Some have argued that the 'frontier' also had a role. The process of continuous expansion westwards, and the availability of free or cheap land through the Homestead Act of 1862, provided an escape route for those who were discontented. It constituted a 'safety valve' that released social tensions. Furthermore, many socialists were first-generation immigrants who lacked roots in American society. The cultural divisions between different ethnic groupings formed a barrier to working-class unity. Socialist calls for the regulation of business were co-opted by others – such as urban reformers – and absorbed into Progressivism, a much broader reforming movement.

Populism

Some of these ideas and principles – particularly the belief in the pivotal role of individual effort and the 'American dream' – are, however, tempered by another ideological strain or tradition. American attitudes have also been shaped by *populism*. This is a faith in the people and a belief that they are ill served by elite groupings. Although it is less pronounced than in the early 1990s, there is a profound suspicion and hostility towards government, particularly at federal level. This is evident in the University of Michigan's National Election Studies. The numbers prepared to trust the federal government 'most of the time' fell from 57 per cent in 1958 to 30 per cent in 1996. As a corollary, the proportion of the American population believing that 'quite a few' government officials are 'crooked' rose from 24 per cent in 1958 to a peak of 52 per cent in 1994.

Table 2.2 *'Are government officials crooked?' (1958–2000) (% of the population)*

	1958	1974	1994	2000
Quite a few	24	45	52	36
Not many	44	42	39	49
Hardly any	26	10	8	13
Don't know	6	3	1	2

Source: adapted from National Election Studies (2003), *The NES Guide to Public Opinion and Electoral Behavior – Are Government Officials Crooked?*, www.umich.edu/~nes/nesguide/toptable/tab5a_4.htm.

However, suspicions also extend beyond government towards big business. While there is the belief that individuals can – with sufficient effort and application – move up the economic and social ladder there is – alongside this – a significant degree of hostility towards the larger corporations. There is often a sense of identification with lone individuals who are pitted against anonymous companies. Stephen Soderbergh's film, *Erin Brockovich* (2000), told, for example, of a woman's struggle against corporate pollution. Furthermore, although socialist ideologies failed to take root in the US, notions of class – and class conflict – are accepted by a significant proportion of the population.

Table 2.3 *'In all countries, there are differences or conflicts between different social groups. In your opinion, in America, how much conflict is there between management and workers?' (1983–87) (% of the population)*

Very strong conflict	12.2
Strong conflict	44.1
Not strong conflict	40.4
No conflict	3.3

Source: adapted from General Social Survey (2003b), *CONUNION*, www.icpsr.umich.edu:8080/GSS/homepage.htm.

Democracy and freedom

Other beliefs are widely shared. The words 'democracy' and 'freedom' are widely used. Indeed, during the Cold War years, the US portrayed itself – and was widely seen – as a beacon of both by many of those opposing Soviet rule in the countries of eastern Europe and Asia. In the aftermath of the 11 September attacks, the terms were again often heard. At its simplest, the concept of democracy implies rule by the people, or, at least, by a majority of the people. However, this can be interpreted in different ways. The US is a *representative* democracy. This means that those who serve in government, whether at federal, state, or local level, should be subject to periodic election. This extends further than in many other representative democracies. Many positions that are taken by appointees in the United Kingdom and other European countries – including judges and sheriffs – are occupied by elected officials in the US. However, the US is not a 'pure' representative democracy. At local and state level, there are elements of *direct* democracy through constitutional provisions for initiatives, referendums and recall.

- *Initiatives* allow proposals for changes in state law to be placed on the ballot so that the people decide upon them.
- *Referendums* permit a law passed by the state legislature to be voted upon by the electorate before it is enacted.
- *Recall systems* allow voters to gather signatures and – if a specified number are collected – require that an elected representative face a special election to decide whether or not she or he should continue in office. In early 2003, a campaign – alleging financial mismanagement – was initiated to recall the California Governor, Gray Davis. To succeed, the campaign organisers had to gather 897,158 signatures from registered voters – 12 per cent of the votes cast when the Governor was elected. The growth of the internet has facilitated the process of publicising recall campaigns and collecting signatures (*Washington Post* 2003).

In a US context, the term 'freedom' also has a particular meaning. Although the Supreme Court and some forms of public policy rest upon the belief that some clauses in the Constitution confer positive freedoms requiring government intervention so as to promote a particular social goal, the conception of freedom that is most widely drawn upon in the US is essentially *negative*. It rests upon the belief that constraints should not be imposed upon individuals and groups by government. Such rights are not however absolute, in so far as the freedom of others must also be considered. In the words of the nineteenth-century political philosopher, John Stuart Mill, freedom means '. . . pursuing our own good in our own way, so long as we do not attempt to deprive others of theirs, or impede their efforts to obtain it'.

This conception of freedom can be contrasted with the *positive* conceptions of freedom that are associated with contemporary liberalism. These lead, for example, to calls for 'freedom from want' and 'freedom from ignorance'. They generally involve government action to redress the inequalities generated by free-market economies. Notions such as these gave rise to the welfare state and were widely accepted in Europe during the three decades that followed the Second World War. They also influenced the making of public policy in the US – particularly attempts to address racism and the legacy of institutionalised discrimination against African-Americans and other long-disadvantaged groupings. However, so conservative critics charge, positive freedoms are, in reality, an assertion that the government should provide particular services or goods, and that these should be funded from taxation. According to conservatives, such 'freedoms' constrain personal choices, and therefore limit rather than extend the freedom of the individual.

Rights and obligations

Commitment to freedom leads to a stress on the rights of the individual. Some of the most important rights are enumerated in the Bill of Rights – the first ten amendments to the US Constitution – and have particular importance. They include freedom of speech and religion, the right to 'bear arms', and freedom from the imposition of 'cruel and unusual punishments'.

For many, individual rights are originally granted by God. The Declaration of Independence spoke of people 'being endowed by their Creator with certain unalienable rights' (see Chapter 3). Furthermore, the early political philosophers, such as John Locke, who influenced the thinking of the founding fathers, talked of 'natural rights'. These existed in the *state of nature* that, they believed or supposed, preceded the emergence of governments. Only some had been surrendered when governments were formed. Others were retained by the people. Populist suspicions of government have added to notions such as these. From this perspective, rights represent an important line of defence against further encroachments on the freedom of the individual by Washington DC.

The emphasis that American citizens place on rights marks the US out from the countries of Europe. Many Americans believe that there is a private sphere which is sovereign, and into which the government cannot intrude. For example, in a 1990 cross-national survey of attitudes towards the compulsory wearing of seat belts, 82 per cent of West Germans accepted that they should be required by law. Only 49 per cent of Americans concurred.

The stress on rights is sometimes depicted as excessive or as constituting 'hyperindividualism'. 'Rights talk' ensures that controversies often become clashes between competing absolutes. American citizens assert their own individual interests and disregard those of others. There is a reluctance to compromise. This is, in turn, reflected in the 'legalisation' of everyday life, as individuals increasingly resort to lawyers and the law.

Furthermore, some observers suggest that the assertion of self-interest associated with a stress on rights has been compounded by the erosion of earlier notions of communal and civic obligation. The idea that citizens had responsibilities to others was undermined as the US became a predominantly industrial nation and traditional communities – based around small, intimate groupings of families and neighbours – were broken up.

However, the argument has been countered. Thomas Bender accepts that many traditional rural communities were lost, but he draws attention to the survival – albeit in a different form – of small communities represented by families, friends, work groups and other networks (1993: 135–6). Although Robert Putnam has charted the decline of civic participation, there is still a sense of obligation to fellow citizens.[1] This is, for example, evident in *volunteerism*. Even today, many towns have a part-time volunteer fire department. Peter Drucker notes that almost every other adult is working for at least three hours a week as a volunteer with a social-sector organisation.

Equality

When the American colonists declared their independence from the British crown in 1776, Thomas Jefferson proclaimed that, 'all men are created equal'. Commitment to equality represents another element within the American creed. However, in contrast with the ideologies of the left which stress equality of income, reward or outcome, America offers a different form of egalitarianism. The American conception of equality is structured around three principal characteristics:

1   There is an equality of regard for each individual. This stems from an absence of deference. Visitors to the US are often struck by the informal character of American culture, and the relatively unrestrained way in which strangers address each other. In the eighteenth century, a foreign observer noted that the American 'dictionary' was 'short in words of dignity, and names of honor'. Similarly, when Mrs Frances Trollope, an Englishwoman, visited in 1830, she noted the reluctance of Americans to seek employment

as domestic servants, and complained about the 'coarse familiarity, untempered by any shadow of respect, which is assumed by the grossest and lowest in their intercourse with the highest and most refined'.

2 The ideology of Americanism also rests on *equality of rights*. There is, at least today, a generally accepted insistence that basic rights – particularly those enshrined in the Bill of Rights (the first ten amendments to the Constitution, which were added in 1791) – apply to *all* citizens, regardless of income or status.

3 The American creed also proclaims *equality before the law*. All, whatever their rank or station, are subject to the rule of law. There would be no scope for the arbitrary judgements that characterised the regimes of Europe at the time when the Constitution and the Bill of Rights were written. Even the president is bound by court rulings. In 1974 – during the final days of the Watergate drama – the US Supreme Court compelled President Richard Nixon to release tape recordings he had made of his personal conversations. In 1998, President Bill Clinton – faced by allegations arising from the Monica Lewinsky affair – had to answer questions before a Grand Jury.

However, although a commitment to these forms of equality is at the heart of American thinking, realities have been very different for significant numbers of Americans. At the time of the Declaration of Independence, about half a million blacks, constituting 20 per cent of the population, were held as slaves. Although slavery was abolished at the end of the Civil War, segregation and institutionalised oppression did not come to an end until the mid-1960s. Other groups have also endured discrimination. In the nineteenth century, Native Americans faced what some call genocide as they lost their land, economy and culture. During the Second World War (1941–45), many Americans of Japanese descent were regarded as potentially disloyal and held in detention camps.

Patriotism

National symbols and the rituals of citizenship constitute a further component of the American creed. Visitors to the country often comment on the flying of the flag outside American homes. Statistical surveys invariably reveal a high level of loyalty and patriotism. A 1990 Gallup study reported that only 11 per cent of Americans would like to emigrate if the opportunity became open to them. In contrast, 38 per cent of British citizens, 20 per cent of the Japanese, and 30 per cent of Germans said that they would rather live abroad (Samuelson 1997: 259). In 1996, a study conducted by the General Social Survey asked respondents to quantify the personal importance of American nationality to them on a scale between 0 and 10: 69.8 per cent placed themselves at 8 or above.

Table 2.4 *'How important is being an American to you, where 0 is not at all important and 10 is the most important thing in your life?' (1996) (% of the population)*

0 – not important at all	1.6
1	0.7
2	1
3	1.2
4	1.9
5	9.7
6	4.5
7	9.7
8	14.2
9	9.9
10 – most important	45.7

Source: adapted from General Social Survey (2003), *AMIMP*, www.icpsr.umich.edu:8080/GSS/homepage.htm.

American patriotism is intensified in periods of crisis, conflict and national uncertainty. Nine months after the terrorist attacks on 11 September 2001, a CNN/USA Today/Gallup poll suggested that 83 per cent of Americans would display a flag during the Independence Day holiday weekend, and 90 per cent of Americans answered 'extremely' or 'very' when asked 'How proud are you to be an American?' Nearly two out of three (65 per cent) answered 'extremely', compared with 55 per cent when the same question was asked in a January 2001 poll (Gallup Organization 2002).

Religion and moralism

The US is, in the amended words of the Pledge of Allegiance, 'one nation, under God'. Gallup polling suggests, for example, that 96 per cent of the American public believe in God or a 'universal spirit', compared with just over 60 per cent of the British people. The differences between the US and Europe are even more striking if patterns of church attendance are considered. According to polls, 47 per cent of Americans claimed to have attended a church or synagogue service in the preceding seven days. In contrast, a 1998 study of the English churches suggested that just 11.1 per cent of population attended church at least once a month.

Many of the earliest settlers who established colonies in New England were Puritans. They were committed to a strict and austere form of worship. Their religious vision left a powerful ideological legacy. Alexis de Tocqueville, the French nobleman and writer who visited America in 1831–32, and is still celebrated as a groundbreaking commentator on American political culture, concluded: 'I think I can see the whole destiny of America contained in the first Puritan who landed on those shores.' This is evident in four principal ways.

1 As Max Weber was later to emphasise in his classic 1904–5 study, *The Protestant Ethic and the Spirit of Capitalism*, Puritanism was structured around values that corresponded with the development of American commerce, private enterprise and capitalism. It stressed the virtues of self-reliance, thrift, deferred gratification, hard work, humility and ambition.

2 Puritanism bequeathed a sense of purpose or mission that, some suggest, shaped the way in which America thought of itself and the character of US foreign policy. It led to periods of isolation as the country sought to cut itself off from the corruption of the 'Old World' and of interventionism as it attempted to 'export' its founding principles.

3 The structure of the early Churches also left a legacy. They had a relatively democratic character, in so far as they were structured around the congregation. The preacher was the servant of the Church membership rather than its master. The Puritan tradition infused American culture with the democratic egalitarianism that became one of its defining hallmarks.

4 Puritanism also tinged the US with what Seymour Martin Lipset terms 'utopian absolutism'. As he puts it, Americans 'tend to view social and political dramas as morality plays, as battles between God and the Devil, so that compromise is virtually unthinkable' (1997: 63).

Although Puritanism had a firm hold on the early New England communities, other denominations – and, at a later stage, faiths and sects – also found a place on the American continent. However, while there have always been theological differences between the different Churches, nearly all share a faith in the 'American creed'. The white evangelical Churches, in particular, have a profound commitment to the nation, share a negative conception of freedoms and rights, and embrace the principles associated with self-reliance and *laissez-faire*.

Shared values?

Chapter 1 emphasised the fissures and tensions that characterise contemporary American society. This chapter has suggested that these should be placed in context. Many beliefs and principles, they argue, are shared across different and divergent social groupings. Although, for example, race is a significant cleavage within contemporary American society, survey evidence suggests that both whites and blacks are committed to many of the same basic values. The black poor are socially and economically isolated, and might be expected to reject the American creed. However, as Jennifer Hochschild argues, while there are significant pressures and tensions, they subscribe to mainstream American values to a greater extent than many in the black middle-class (1995: 72).

Nor should ethnic differences be over-emphasised. Traditionally, the process of assimilation led to the absorption of the different ethnicities. Indeed, the process of integration, absorption and assimilation took such an all-encompassing form that American society came to be known as a *melting-pot*. The phrase was coined by a playwright, Israel Zangwill. In 1908, he described America as 'God's Crucible, the great Melting Pot where all the races of Europe are melting and reforming . . . German and Frenchman, Irishman and Englishman, Jews and Russians – into the Crucible with you all! God is making the American.' As Zangwill saw it, the US brought together the immigrant groupings from across the globe and fused them together so as to construct a new nationality. The mechanisms of assimilation traditionally included the public (or state) schools, the occupational ladder, and intermarriage. A hundred years ago, the schools had a largely Protestant ethos, taught in English and insisted upon 'American' forms of behaviour. Traditionally, the English language was essential for many of those seeking employment. The children of immigrants grew up as Americans, and, in many instances, married someone from a different ethnic background.

The two world wars also contributed to the assimilative process. Some groups rallied to the flag because the nation was threatened. Others sought to abandon their identity because they had family ties with the enemy country. For example, US participation in the First World War (1917–18) led many German-Americans to close down their clubs and newspapers and anglicise their names. They sought social 'invisibility'. Following the Second World War, the Cold War and fear of communism bound Americans together. In particular, it drew in the 'white ethnics' whose homelands had come under Soviet domination.

From this perspective, the mechanisms of assimilation are still at work. While schools teach some courses in minority languages, this is generally undertaken on a short-term basis while the student acquires proficiency in English. Although there are minority television channels, the language of the youth entertainment market is English. The breaking down of barriers through intermarriage and the formation of mixed households continues today. In the 2000 Census, almost seven million people reported that they belonged to more than one race. These trends are set to continue. The Census also revealed that about 4.0 per cent of American children were multiracial, compared with 1.9 per cent of adults (Singer 2002).

Some other cleavages should also be placed in context. Many past regional differences have been eroded as geographical mobility has increased and the communications industry has assumed initially a national and latterly an increasingly global character. In particular, the southern states have lost much of their former distinctiveness. Furthermore, the gender gap should not be over-stated. Although there are some differences, most men and women subscribe to broadly comparable values. Many women, for example, join with men in opposing affirmative action programmes. A 1995 survey suggested that 40 per cent of women and 51 per cent of men disapprove of such policies (Golay and Rollyson 1996: 60). Furthermore, although they have received scant attention, many other 'gaps' – such as the 'gap' between rural and urban voters – are considerably larger (Ashford 1996: 66). Attempts to depict the 'baby boom' generation, the sexual revolution of the 1960s and 1970s, and the rise of counter-cultures as a break with Americanism are also difficult to sustain. Although some aspects of these countercultures represented an affront to established values, the post-war generation accepted the fundamental tenets of the American creed, particularly its commitment to self-reliance and upward mobility. Furthermore, feminism, black politics, and gay activism have lost much of their former radicalism and have, at least partially, been integrated into mainstream politics through the Democratic Party.

However, there is a danger of overemphasising the scale and extent of the American *consensus*. There are still some important contemporary divisions and cleavages that should not be neglected.

1 Although there were traditional assimilative mechanisms – which drew immigrants from countries such as Italy, Ireland and Poland into the American mainstream – the process was confined to whites. African-Americans always remained outsiders, facing *de jure* and *de facto* discrimination. Indeed, it might be argued that assimilation was strengthened as the different white groupings – such as the Irish – collectively distanced themselves from blacks by subscribing to the racist practices that were commonplace during the nineteenth and early twentieth centuries. There is still a significant cultural divide between blacks and whites, and intermarriage rates remain low.

2 Although the different forms of measurement show a decline between 1980 and 2000, there is still substantial residential 'segregation', particularly between blacks and whites. Many people continue to live in largely separate neighbourhoods (US Census Bureau 2002).

3 Many of today's immigrants maintain ties with their former countries. Indeed, a 2002 study by the Pew Research Center suggested that 54 per cent of Latinos described themselves firstly or exclusively in terms of their, or their parents', country of origin. Only 24 per cent defined themselves as 'American'. Among foreign-born Latinos, the latter figure was just 6 per cent (Pew Hispanic Center / The Henry J. Kaiser Family Foundation 2002: 28).

Conclusion

Although the US is characterised by diversity, there are also *shared values*. Alexis de Tocqueville noted that Americans 'are unanimous upon the general principles that ought to rule human society'. For some observers, many of these 'general principles' are still evident today. However, others offer a more sanguine judgement, and suggest that contemporary social cleavages have a more profound character than those of the past.

Note

1   For a discussion of the Putnam thesis, see Ashbee 2002: 72–85.

References and further reading

Ashbee, E. (2002), *American Society Today*, Manchester, Manchester University Press.

Ashford, N. (1996), 'Angry white males', *Talking Politics*, Autumn, 64–8.

Bender, T. (1993), *Community and Social Change in America*, Baltimore, MD, The Johns Hopkins University Press.

Fossum, R. H. and J. K. Roth (1981) *The American Dream*, Durham, British Association for American Studies.

Golay, M. and C. Rollyson (1996), *Where America Stands 1996*, New York, John Wiley

Hochschild, J. L. (1995), *Facing Up to the American Dream: Race, Class, and the Soul of the Nation*, Princeton, NJ, Princeton University Press.

Huntington, S. P. (1982), *American Politics: The Promise of Disharmony*, Cambridge, MA, The Belknap Press of Harvard University Press.

Lasch, C. (1995), *The Revolt of the Elites and the Betrayal of Democracy*, New York, W. W. Norton.

Lipset, S. M. (1997), *American Exceptionalism: A Double-Edged Sword*, New York and London, W. W. Norton.

Pew Hispanic Center / The Henry J. Kaiser Family Foundation (2002), *2002 National Survey of Latinos – Summary of Findings*, Washington DC, Pew Hispanic Center / Kaiser Family Foundation.

Samuelson, R. J. (1997), *The Good Life and its Discontents*, New York, Vintage Books.

Singer, A. (2002), *America's Diversity at the Beginning of the Twenty First Century: Reflections from Census 2000*, Washington DC, The Brookings Institution, www.brookings.edu/dybdocroot/views/papers/singer/20020402.pdf.

US Census Bureau (2002), *Racial and Ethnic Segregation in the United States 1980–2000*, www.census.gov/prod/2002pubs/censr-3.pdf.

3

The US Constitution

Chapter 2 suggested that – despite cleavages and fissures – there is also a substantial degree of consensus. This is structured around a shared faith in the country and principles such as democracy and freedom. The consensus has, however, a further characteristic. Although there has long been considerable cynicism towards the politicians who serve in Washington DC, there is also a deeply rooted belief in the essential worth of the fundamental structures underpinning the American political system. There is, in particular, an ingrained faith in the US Constitution, the document upon which the US was founded. While the Constitution is often at the centre of political controversy, that debate is generally about the interpretation of the principles upon which it rests rather than the fundamental worth of those principles. Proposals for reform are nearly always put forward as a means by which the spirit of the Constitution can be more fully implemented. This chapter outlines the principal features of the US Constitution, considers the institutions that were created on the basis of it, and surveys the debates about the meaning of the Constitution today.

Origins of the US Constitution

By the eighteenth century, the original settlements that had been established on the eastern seaboard had evolved into thirteen colonies. As such, although some were corporate ventures, they were British possessions. However, despite the appointment of governors by the London authorities, the colonists had a tradition of limited self-government through colonial assemblies. There was wider property ownership than in Britain, allowing relatively large numbers to participate in civic affairs.

Against this background – and amidst growing talk of 'unalienable rights' and constraints upon the power of government – restrictions on the westward expansion of the colonies, the imposition of taxes, and other limits on trade by

the British laid a basis for protests and eventual rebellion. The 1773 Tea Act –
which sparked the protests that were dubbed the 'Boston Tea Party' – and the
1774 Quebec Act – which extended its boundaries so as to threaten the western
expansion of the American colonies – were particularly resented. American
leaders responded by establishing the Continental Congress, bringing together
delegates from the different colonies. The British refused to compromise and
demanded that the colonists recognise the authority of Parliament. The
Patriots – as supporters of American interests came to be known – began to
organise themselves. Attempts by British troops to disarm them and suppress
their activities triggered war. In a celebrated speech to the Virginia legislature,
which symbolised the shift from protest to rebellion, Patrick Henry said 'Give
me liberty, or give me death.'

After eighteen months of fighting – on 4 July 1776 – Congress approved the
Declaration of Independence. Written principally by Thomas Jefferson, the
Declaration offered a justification for the revolutionary repudiation of British
rule:

> We hold these truths to be self-evident, that all men are created equal, that they
> are endowed by their Creator with certain unalienable rights, that amongst these
> are life, liberty and the pursuit of happiness. That to secure these rights, govern-
> ments are instituted amongst men, deriving their just powers from the consent of
> the governed. That whenever any form of government becomes destructive of
> these ends, it is the right of the people to alter or abolish it, and to institute a new
> government. (Foley 1991: 31)

The arguments pursued in the Declaration drew on notions of liberty, rights
and limited government that had been established a century earlier:

1 All people – not only Americans – have certain natural rights, most notably
   'life, liberty and the pursuit of happiness'. These rights were granted by God
   and could not be taken away or 'alienated'. They were 'unalienable'.
2 The purpose of government – the reason why it is created – is to protect these
   rights. There is a social contract between the people and government in
   which the people accept a duty to obey the government. In return, those in
   government have an obligation to protect the people's rights.
3 The people have the right to withdraw that consent, and have the right of
   rebellion if the government fails to protect their rights.
4 King George III and the British Parliament had, through acts of oppression,
   broken their side of the social contract. The people had been denied their
   'unalienable' rights. The American colonists could therefore justifiably
   break their side of the contract and deny British authority on American
   soil.

The Declaration also put forward a list of twenty-seven specific grievances
against the British Crown to demonstrate the ways in which the rights of the

colonists were being denied. King George III was described in bitter terms: 'He has plundered our seas, ravaged our coasts, burned our towns, and destroyed the lives of our people . . . A prince, whose character is thus marked by every act which may define a tyrant, is unfit to be the ruler of a free people' (quoted in Henretta, Brownlee, Brody and Ware 1993: 168).

The Declaration has been portrayed in different ways. For some, it was an assertion of a distinct American nationhood. Others suggest that it represented an attempt to reclaim the tradational rights and liberties of the 'freeborn Englishman'. There are also less idealistic depictions. The rebels, it is said, were seeking to pursue commercial interests that had been placed in jeopardy by the British authorities. Furthermore, although the Declaration of Independence spoke in the name of the people, women, blacks, native Americans and propertyless whites were largely excluded from the political process. The war of independence can justly be described as 'a conservative revolution'.

The British were finally defeated by the Americans – fighting in alliance with the French – in October 1781 at Yorktown in Virginia. The Treaty of Paris, signed in September 1783, recognised American independence.

Articles of Confederation

A year after the writing of the Declaration of Independence, the Continental Congress adopted a constitution, the Articles of Confederation. These were not, however, ratified by all thirteen of the former colonies – now states – until 1781.

The Articles rested upon a loose and decentralised system based upon a very weak national government. Each state maintained 'its sovereignty, freedom, and independence', but the Congress – in which each state had one vote – had only limited powers. Important decisions and changes to national law required the backing of nine of the thirteen states. There was, furthermore, no separate executive branch. Decision-making was inevitably a slow, cumbersome and uncertain process.

The powers of the national government were limited for two reasons. Firstly, there was a reaction against the strongly centralised character of British rule. Secondly, many of the states jealously guarded their own prerogatives and were unwilling to surrender even a limited degree of power. However, although the Articles were eventually ratified, the Confederation faced difficulties from the beginning.

1 The weakness of Congress was highlighted by its inability to raise tax revenue. The states – upon which Congress depended for funds – failed to pay the sums that were required.
2 Trade was the responsibility of the states. They imposed tariffs against each other so as to protect their own immediate commercial interests. There were

also difficulties enforcing contracts between the citizens of different states. Such restrictions held back the economic development of the nation.

3 There were periods of turmoil when the country seemed to be falling apart. There were incipient tensions between the northern and southern states. In 1783, there was serious discontent and talk of a military coup – the Newburgh conspiracy – within the army. Furthermore, the Congress established under the Articles of Confederation, and the different state governments, could not enforce their decisions or impose their own authority. During a period of economic depression, the state of Massachusetts imposed property tax increases so as to pay off debts incurred during the war. When the taxes were not paid, farms and homes were seized. In 1786, many farmers took part in Shays's rebellion as a protest. The rebellion later collapsed; but it appeared to portend growing social discontent.

4 There were fears that foreign powers would seek a foothold for themselves within the new Republic. Britain, France and Spain all had possessions on the North American continent, and there were concerns that some of the states might be tempted into alliances with these powers that might break up the Confederation.

Because of these criticisms, a constitutional convention of delegates from the states was called in 1787 to modify or amend the Articles. Although the delegates who met in Philadelphia were not directly elected by the people, and one state (Rhode Island) was not represented at all, a new constitution emerged from their deliberations.

Philadelphia Convention (1787)

The debate at the convention continued throughout the summer of 1787. The fifty-five delegates – who became known as the 'Framers', founders or 'Founding Fathers' – considered two alternative models of government.

- The larger states supported James Madison's Virginia Plan. It rested on the 'supremacy of national authority', so that the states would lose much of the autonomy that they had been afforded under the Confederation. The national government would draw its authority from the American people rather than the states. There would be a bicameral legislature that would, in part, be directly elected. The legislature would choose those who would head the executive branch.
- The New Jersey Plan was backed by the smaller states, who were fearful of being engulfed. Although it also envisaged a greater degree of political centralisation than under the Confederation, it respected the authority of the states by proposing a unicameral legislature based upon the states, which would be allocated equal representation regardless of size. The states would also be able to remove members of the executive branch.

The different political forces at the convention agreed upon 'the Great Compromise'. The larger states favoured a system of government that assigned representation on the basis of population. However, the smaller states feared that they would have little influence over such a government. Therefore, numbers in the lower chamber, the House of Representatives, would be based on a state's population. This favoured the larger states. However, the Senate, the upper chamber, was based on equal representation. Each state was to have two Senators – who until the early twentieth century were appointed by the state legislatures rather than elected – regardless of its size or population. The Philadelphia Convention also pursued other forms of political accommodation.

1 There were differences at the convention between those who talked in terms of the 'people', although this often referred only to male property-holders, and those who were sceptical of unrestrained democracy. It was agreed that some form of democracy was required to act as a check on the abuse of power by the executive, but it was feared that unchecked majority rule might neglect the basic rights of the individual citizen. These concerns grew because of events in Pennsylvania. It had a directly elected, unicameral, and strong legislature. As a consequence, it was said, the liberties of minorities had not been protected, Quakers had lost the vote, and opponents of the war had faced sanctions. The convention therefore sought to place constraints on the will of the majority. They agreed that only the House of Representatives would be directly elected by the people. The president was to be indirectly elected through an electoral college. Senators would be chosen by the state legislatures. The judiciary would be appointed.

2 There were tensions between free states and the slave states. Many in the northern states wished to abolish slavery, but the five southern states would have refused to join the US if slavery had not been permitted. As a consequence, slavery was not addressed in the Constitution, although there was a provision that, for the purposes of representation, slaves would be counted as three-fifths of citizens. This was at the insistence of the free states, who wanted to limit the political influence of the slave states.

3 There was also a debate between advocates and opponents of a strong, centralised executive branch of government. Some of the founders, most notably Alexander Hamilton, argued that there had to be 'energy in the executive' so as to unify the nation. They called for a single executive that would have far-reaching powers. Others feared, however, that the placing of so much power in the hands of a single figure would lead to tyranny. They therefore agreed upon a single executive – the President – but restricted the powers of the office. These were concentrated in foreign policy-making, where swift and decisive action might be required. In the domestic sphere, the powers of the executive branch were to be more limited.

4 The Constitution also sought to establish a compromise between those who feared that the states would lose their independence and authority and

'nationalists' who believed that a stronger national government was required if the country was to survive. However, the character and extent of the 'states' rights' afforded by the US Constitution have been the subject of extensive controversy. Some, including President Ronald Reagan, have portrayed the US as a compact between the states. This implies that the states have far-reaching rights that cannot be abrogated. Others argue that the American people as a whole have *sovereignty*. From this perspective, the rights of the states are much more limited and the constraints placed upon the states in the Constitution are of particular importance.

Adopting the Constitution

The Constitution was eventually accepted – or *ratified* – by the states between 1787 and 1790. However, there was a fierce debate between supporters of the new Constitution, known as the Federalists, and opponents, the Antifederalists.

The Federalists argued that the Constitution offered a basis for a system of government that had strength and cohesion but would not threaten the fundamental rights and liberties of either the states or the American people. They wrote a series of newspaper articles – *The Federalist* – in its defence. The principal authors were James Madison, Alexander Hamilton and John Jay, who collectively wrote under the pseudonym of 'Publius'.

The Antifederalists feared that the Constitution would lead to an over-centralisation of power in the hands of the federal government, and that this would inevitably threaten the independence of the states and the rights of the citizen. Although the Antifederalists lost the debate, the concerns that they expressed still resonate in American politics today. So as to secure majorities in some of the states, the Federalists promised to amend the Constitution so as that individual rights and liberties would entrenched. As a consequence, ten amendments were added in 1791. These amendments – the Bill of Rights – placed constraints upon the powers of the national government. In later years, the US Supreme Court progressively extended these limits so that they also applied to the state governments as well.

Principles of the Constitution

The Constitution has five defining principles.

- It offered a form of government based – in part – upon the representation of the people. Indeed, the Constitution rests upon the belief that a government's right to rule – its *legitimacy* – depends upon the consent of the governed. This marked out the US from the autocratic regimes that dominated Europe at the time when the US Constitution was written.

- However, the representation of the people takes a constrained form. The Constitution promised a 'republic' that would be responsive but also responsible. The Founders' search for a compromise between democratic participation and constraints that would prevent a majority infringing or denying the rights of individuals led them towards constitutional mechanisms that would allow government to act only when there was a widely-shared consensus on a clearly and widely accepted public good. The Constitution not only sought to prevent impulsive decision-making, but was informed by a *counter-majoritarian* spirit.

- The Constitution was structured, thirdly, around a *separation of powers* or, in some accounts, separated institutions sharing powers. Political systems involve legislative, executive, and judicial responsibilities. These terms refer to the making, implementation and interpretation of the law. The Constitution established that these three responsibilities would be exercised by three separate institutions: Congress, the presidency and the federal courts. Yet although these are often described as the legislative, executive and judicial branches of government, each of the three branches plays a part in the legislative, executive and judicial processes. As Richard Neustadt, author of *Presidential Power and the Modern President* notes, the president is, for example, involved in the making of law. The Constitution allows him to veto bills or to mould the character of legislation by threatening the imposition of a veto: 'The Constitutional Convention of 1787 is supposed to have created a government of "separated powers." It did nothing of the sort. Rather, it created a government of separated institutions sharing powers. "I am part of the legislative process," Eisenhower often said in 1959 as a reminder of his veto' (Neustadt 1991: 29). The three branches of government are assigned different powers, methods of election or appointment, and terms of office.

- Fourthly, the Constitution also rested on *checks and balances*. The Founding Fathers built a degree of conflict between the branches of government into the fabric of the constitution. They sought to ensure that no single branch could become over-powerful or oppressive. The Constitution therefore required that many decisions must have the endorsement of more than one branch. For example, presidential appointments for the most important positions in the executive branch and to the federal judiciary have to be made with 'the advice and consent' of the Senate.

- The Constitution was based, fifthly, on federalism. The powers of government are divided between national and the individual state governments, although their relationship is not defined with clarity. The national or federal government is granted certain specified – or *enumerated* – powers. Its responsibilities include foreign policy, defence, foreign trade and commerce between the states. However, the states were offered some assurances. Their assent is required if the Constitution is to be amended. Their territorial boundaries have to be respected. Most significantly of all, as the Tenth Amendment emphasised, the powers and responsibilities not granted by the Constitution to the national government lie with the states or the people.

Box 3.1   Checks and balances

By the legislative branch on the executive

1 The Senate confirms or rejects major presidential appointments.
2 Congress has the 'power of the purse' through the budget process.
3 Congress can pass, reject, or amend all legislative proposals put forward by the president.
4 Congress can impeach and – on conviction – remove the president for 'high crimes and misdemeanours'.
5 Foreign treaties signed by the president must be ratified by the Senate with a two-thirds majority.
6 Congress can override a presidential veto if there is a two-thirds majority in both chambers.

By the legislative branch on the judiciary

1 The Senate has to confirm all appointments to the federal courts.
2 Congress can reorganise the federal court structure.
3 Congress can change the number of judges serving on federal courts.
4 Congress can impeach and remove judges.

By the executive branch on the legislature

1 The president can propose legislation.
2 The president can veto bills passed by Congress.
3 The president can call special sessions of Congress.

By the executive branch on the judiciary

The president appoints all federal judges.

By the judicial branch on the legislature

1 The Supreme Court can rule a law unconstitutional.
2 The Supreme Court interprets laws passed by Congress.

By the judicial branch on the executive

The Supreme Court can rule an action undertaken by the president – such as the issuing of an executive order – unconstitutional.

Structure of the Constitution

The Constitution consists of one single document of only seven thousand words. It is divided up into sections or *Articles*. These mostly consider the powers, responsibilities and characters of the three different branches of government.

Preamble

The introduction to the Constitution has two key features. Firstly, it begins with the phrase 'We the People' thereby establishing that it is the people who have the power to create, and so by implication also to end, the new constitution. Secondly, the Preamble identifies the broad purpose of the new federal government. It is to 'establish justice, insure domestic tranquillity, provide for the common defence, promote the general welfare, and secure the Blessings of Liberty'.

Article I: Congress

Congress, the national legislature, was to be the principal source of law and policy. *The Federalist* stated that 'in republican government, the legislature necessarily predominates'. Congress is also assigned specific powers. It has the right to declare war. It also has the 'power of the purse'; it decides upon the levying of taxes and the allocation of government spending. In a phrase that progressively acquired greater significance as the US became a modern industrial economy, Congress has the power to regulate 'interstate commerce'. Some observers suggest that the Framers thought in terms of Congressional hegemony. From this perspective, the role of the president was in large part to be a check on a potentially overpowerful Congress. His leadership responsibilities were largely confined to the making of foreign and defence policy. Early presidents, with the exceptions of Thomas Jefferson, Andrew Jackson and Abraham Lincoln, accepted the restrictions on their role. It was not until the twentieth century that the president came to assume the prominence he has today.

Congress was given a *bicameral* structure. It was, in other words, divided into two chambers. The Senate and the House of Representatives were to be elected in different ways and with different and sometimes overlapping powers. The House of Representatives was designed as the popular, directly elected chamber. Its members are elected every two years, and in single-member constituencies – or *districts* – so as to ensure its responsiveness and answerability to the electorate. It can be regarded as the equivalent of the House of Commons in the UK. Every state was guaranteed at least one Representative or 'Congressman', but otherwise representation was based on the population of a particular state. To take account of population shifts, there was to be a process of *reapportionment* and – within each state – *redistricting*, every ten years following the census.

Table 3.1 *Reapportionment: changes in Congressional representation, 1990–2000*

Gainers		Losers	
Arizona	2	New York	−2
Florida	2	Pennsylvania	−2
Georgia	2	Connecticut	−1
Texas	2	Illinois	−1
California	1	Indiana	−1
Colorado	1	Michigan	−1
Nevada	1	Mississippi	−1
North Carolina	1	Ohio	−1
		Oklahoma	−1
		Wisconsin	−1

Source: adapted from N. J. Ornstein, T. E. Mann, and M. J. Malbin (2002), *Vital Statistics on Congress 2001–2002*, Washington DC, The AEI Press, pp. 32–3.

The Senate is the upper chamber. It was intended to represent the individual states and have a more thoughtful and deliberative character. Through its six-year terms of office, it would be – according to James Madison – the stable 'anchor' of Congress, thereby acting as a check on the more populist House and, at the same time, offering accumulated experience, or what Garry Wills has termed, an 'institutional memory' (Wills 1999: 74). A rolling system of election was adopted, so that one-third of the Senate is subject to re-election every two years. This was established so as to ensure that the Senate would not surrender to the 'passions and panics of the moment' to which the House would be prone.

Every state, regardless of numerical size, is entitled to two Senators, from large states such as California to the least populous states such as South Dakota or Wyoming. Senators were originally elected by the state legislatures, but since 1913 have been directly elected by the voters of the state. If a Senator resigns from office or dies, the state governor can select a nominee to serve on a short-term basis. The governor will almost certainly pick an individual from his or her own party. This can, at times, have significant consequences for the overall balance between the parties in the Senate.

The Senate was assigned some specific constitutional responsibilities. It alone confirms appointments and ratifies treaties. This, Wills suggests, was because its stable and deliberative character would command the respect of foreign powers.

Article II: the president

The president is elected for a four-year term by an electoral college. The college was originally composed of elder statesmen chosen by the different state legis-latures. It now plays a nominal role, in so far as the 'Electors' almost always confirm the choice made by the voters in each state. However, the college can distort the popular vote and – in exceptional circumstances – this can lead to the election of a president who has lost the popular vote. This happened in 2000 (see Chapter 10). From 1951 onwards, the president has been restricted to two terms of office.

The founders believed that the executive branch of government should be headed by a single person so as to ensure that the federal government had direction and that foreign policy had the necessary degree of purpose and coherence. However, he has relatively few specific powers. He was assigned important defence and foreign-policy powers. These included his position as commander-in-chief of the armed forces and his ability to negotiate treaties with other countries. However, his domestic powers were more limited. He had a responsibility to ensure that the laws were carried out. He was also given the right to veto bills. This was included as a further check on the populist and impulsive tendencies of the House of Representatives. A vice-president was also to be elected. He was to take the president's place in the event of death or incapacity, but his powers were otherwise ill-defined and unspecified.

Article III: the Supreme Court

In contrast with the preceding Articles, Article III says relatively little. It simply states that 'the judicial power of the United States shall be vested in one Supreme Court'. It also allowed Congress to establish 'inferior' courts.

The Constitution also assigned the federal courts a number of specific powers and responsibilities. Their jurisdiction included legal disputes between the national government and other institutions and the resolution of conflicts between state governments. It was only later, through a process of evolution, that the Supreme Court established the power of *judicial review* and the right to declare a law or action undertaken by the federal or a state government unconstitutional.

Article IV: federalism

Although it also extended some assurances to them, the principal purpose of Article IV was to encourage closer co-operation between the individual states. For example, it laid down in the 'full faith and credit clause' that each state should recognise court rulings made in other states. Article IV also allowed for the admission of new states to the USA, and guaranteed that every state should have a republican – or representative – form of government.

Article V: amending the Constitution

The process of changing – or *amending* – the Constitution was made intentionally difficult. It is dependent upon 'supermajorities'. An amendment must be proposed by either a two-thirds majority in both houses of Congress or by a special constitutional convention that would have to be convened by two-thirds of the state legislatures. Any amendment arising from Congress or the convention has then to be ratified by three-quarters of the states. Congress has generally imposed a seven-year deadline for this, although the period allowed for the ratification of the Equal Rights Amendment – which would have entrenched legislation prohibiting discrimination on the basis of sex by government agencies – was extended for a further three years. However, despite this, the proposed amendment did not gain the necessary two-thirds majority.

No constitutional convention has been held since the Framers met in 1787. Nonetheless, over 10,000 amendments to the Constitution have been proposed in Congress. However, of those, only 33 gained the required Congressional supermajority, and a mere 27 have been ratified by the states. The first ten of these – forming the Bill of Rights – were adopted just four years after the Constitution was written. They are widely regarded as a part of the original constitution. Other, subsequent amendments extended the right to vote, added to civil rights, increased the power of the federal government, and made limited alterations to the institutions of government:

1 The amendments forming the Bill of Rights were intended to offer greater protection to individual citizens and the states against the power of the federal government. By limiting the actions of government and recognising liberties, they are based on a negative conception of rights. The first amendment is widely known. It protects freedom of speech and religion. The second amendment guarantees the right to 'bear arms', and is, today, the subject of controversy.

2 A series of later amendments established that the right to vote could not be denied on grounds of race (15th), and granted the vote to women (19th), the citizens of Washington DC (23rd), and those over eighteen (26th). The 24th amendment – which was adopted in 1964 – prohibited laws that tied the right to vote in federal elections to the payment of poll taxes. Such taxes had been used in a number of southern states to deny the right to vote to African-Americans.

3 Civil rights were extended in the aftermath of the Civil War (1861–65) with the abolition of slavery (13th), and the assertion that all citizens were entitled to 'the equal protection of the laws' (14th). However, the protections offered by the 'equal protection' clause were – in practice – systematically denied to African-Americans for a century after its passage. Furthermore, the way in which it was understood shifted during the latter half of the twentieth century. The fourteenth amendment was initially understood as a means by which the rights of citizenship would be extended to those who had long been excluded from it. However, 'equal protection' was increasingly redefined so that equality was represented in terms of outcome. If the outcome of a particular policy was unequal, this was regarded as a breach of the clause. This had implications for the role of government. It was

---

Box 3.2 The Bill of Rights: summary

Amendment I: limits on Congress

Congress shall not make any law establishing a religion or limiting freedom of religion, speech, and assembly.

Amendments II, III and IV: limits on the executive

The executive branch shall not limit the right to bear arms (II), place soldiers in people's homes (III), or search and seize for evidence without a warrant (IV).

Amendments V, VI, VII and VIII: limits on the judiciary

In serious cases, a grand jury must determine where there is sufficient evidence to bring an individual to trial. No one should be required to provide testimony against themselves. An individual cannot be prosecuted for the same offence more than once (V). The courts shall provide a speedy and public trial (VI). Juries are to determine guilt or innocence (VII). The courts may not impose excessive bail nor 'cruel and unusual' forms of punishment (VIII).

Amendments IX and X: limits on the national government

The provision of rights in the Constitution should not be taken to imply that these are the only rights the people have or to otherwise curtail liberties (IX). Powers not explicitly assigned by the Constitution to the federal government remain with the states or the people (X).

---

increasingly argued that it had an obligation – through the policy-making process – to ensure that there was greater social equality.

4 The sixteenth amendment, adopted in 1913, allowed the federal government to raise an income tax. The eighteenth amendment prohibited the sale of alcohol across the US, but, after thirteen years of Prohibition, it was repealed in the twenty-first amendment. These amendments added to the powers of the federal government.

5 Other amendments have reformed the institutions of government. The most significant of these – the seventeenth amendment – established that all Senators should be directly elected by the people, thereby extending popular participation in the process of government. The twenty-second amendment was introduced in the wake of Franklin Roosevelt's long period of tenure. It restricted the president to only two terms of office.

During the 1990s, conservatives put forward and campaigned for a series of proposed constitutional amendments. These included the Flag Desecration Amendment – which sought to protect the US flag – the Balanced Budget Amendment, a Term Limits Amendment, and a School Prayer Amendment. None, however, were successful. The only amendment to be incorporated into the Constitution was passed in the wake of public resentment about congressional privileges. The twenty-seventh amendment states that Congressional pay increases cannot take effect immediately; instead, members of Congress must wait until after the next election, so that voters have the opportunity to pass judgement.

Table 3.2 *Proposals to amend the US Constitution, 1989–99*

Congress	Number of proposed amendments
106th (1999)	60
105th (1997–98)	103
104th (1995–96)	158
103rd (1993–94)	156
102nd (1991–92)	165
101st (1989–90)	214

Source: adapted from C-SPAN.org, *Congress*, www.c-span.org/questions/weekly54.asp.

Box 3.3   Freedom of speech: *The People v. Larry Flynt* (1996)

Director: Milos Forman
Starring: Woody Harrelson, Courtney Love, Edward Norton

How far should freedom of speech, guaranteed under the First Amendment, extend? Does 'speech' extend to all forms of expression? *The People v. Larry Flynt* explores these themes.

Larry Flynt publishes pornographic magazines. The film traces his battles in different state courts where he faced obscenity charges. It also reconstructs his biggest confrontation with the law. This came when *Hustler*, one of his magazines, printed an article ridiculing the Reverend Jerry Falwell, a leader of the Christian right. Falwell sued, and was awarded substantial damages for 'emotional distress'. As the film shows, the case eventually reached the Supreme Court. The Court ruled that if such damages were allowed, freedom of speech and the First Amendment would be in jeopardy.

Website: movieweb.com/movie/flynt/.

Assessing the Constitution

The goal of the founders was to create a government that would be effective but limited. It would be efficient in undertaking its responsibilities, but would at the same time respect and protect the rights of both the citizen and the states. Subsequent debates around the Constitution have examined the extent to which these goals have been achieved. Whereas some assert that the federal government is relatively powerless, others claim that it has become overbearing.

Too weak

Liberals and radicals argue the case for more activist forms of government, although, despite some calls to extend statehood to Washington DC and, in the wake of the 2000 presidential election, for the abolition of the Electoral College, few have put forward proposals for Constitutional amendments. They assert that the system of government established by the Constitution prevents the successful resolution of the many pressing economic and social problems facing the nation. These include the needs to close the gap between rich and poor, to constrain the activities of the large corporations, and to address environmental issues. However, it is said, the system of government has developed in such a way that the 'energy in the executive' required by Alexander Hamilton has been crushed. The critics make three principal claims.

1 In practice, checks and balances have created *gridlock*. Decisions cannot be made, because there is insufficient agreement between the different branches of government. In contrast with the countries of western Europe, the US has, many liberals argue, been unable to impose effective gun control or to establish comprehensive healthcare provision, because decision-making requires such a widely-shared consensus. The system is structured around mechanisms that prevent reform; and although Congress considers a wealth of legislative proposals, they are rarely enacted.
2 The weakness of the American political parties has added to the obstacles that reformers face, even when they have the backing of public opinion. Although there were significant shifts during the 1990s, the parties can only play a limited role in co-ordinating the work of Congress and easing the tensions between Congress and the White House.
3 By distributing power among the three branches of government and between the national (or federal) government and the states, the American system of government lacks accountability. Power is so widely distributed that it is difficult for citizens to identify who is responsible for any particular action or decision. Although the No Child Left Behind Act was signed into law in January 2002, the US education system has been criticised for its long-term failure to address the needs of those at the lower end of the income scale. In part, it is said, this can be attributed to the dispersal of responsibility between local boards of education, state governments and the Department of Education in Washington DC.

In 1987, the Committee on the Constitutional System, which seeks comprehensive constitutional reform, claimed that:

> The separation of powers, as a principle of constitutional structure, has served us well in preventing tyranny and the abuse of high office, but it has done so by encouraging confrontation, indecision and deadlock, and by diffusing accountability for the results. Because the separation powers encourages conflict between

the branches and because the parties are weak, the capacity of the federal government to fashion, enact and administer coherent public policy has diminished and the ability of elected officials to avoid accountability for governmental failures has grown. (Committee on the Constitutional System 1987: 3)

This critique has led to calls for the adoption of the parliamentary model of government. In a parliamentary or prime ministerial system – such as that used in Britain – the government is formed by a party leader who can command majority support in the legislature. Unless there is a 'hung Parliament', in which no single party has an overall majority in the legislature, or serious unrest within the governing party, the leader – who becomes prime minister – will have few difficulties when his or her legislative proposals are considered. They are more or less certain to become law. In contrast, the US president faces a separately elected legislature and – even when his own party has a majority – his legislation may be lost or amended beyond recognition. Those who believe that the political system is too weak have put forward a number of proposed solutions. In the US, reformers have put forward four proposed reforms that would establish a quasi-parliamentary system.

1 The president should be able to appoint members of Congress to the cabinet so as to establish a closer and less confrontational relationship between the two institutions.
2 The president should have the power to dissolve Congress and demonstrate through an election whether the people endorse him or his congressional opponents. This would allow a particular issue to be resolved in a decisive way.
3 There should be one six-year term for the President. He would not, then, have to think in terms of immediate electoral popularity, and this would strengthen his bargaining position.
4 The president and Congress should be elected together on the same ticket in every district. Voters in national elections would therefore no longer be able to vote for candidates from different parties. This would ensure that a single party had control of both Congress and the White House.

Too strong

There are those, however, who have asserted that government has become too powerful and intrusive. They are mostly conservatives. They argue that the federal government is now much more interventionist than the founders intended. They point to high levels of taxation, the federal government's role in regulating business, and its progressive involvement in state responsibilities such as education and social policy. In simple terms, the federal government has become too big, too expansive and too expensive. In contrast to liberals, conservatives assert that the federal government does too much rather than too little. Why has the Constitution failed to check the growth of federal government? From a conservative perspective, there are three factors:

1 'Special interests' have come to dominate the decision-making process. Many political decisions therefore reflect narrow sectional interests and are not for the public good. Some conservatives point, in particular, to the way in which some groupings have been able to secure legislation, such as the minimum wage or other barriers to entry in a particular trade, that excludes newcomers and confers monopoly privileges.
2 The federal government has, through financial incentives and legislation that led to an expansion of its role, gained control and influence over many responsibilities that were the traditional prerogatives of the states. The tenth amendment, which appeared to circumscribe the powers of the national government and offer assurances to the states, has been forgotten.
3 The federal judiciary has abused judicial review. It has enlarged its own powers at the expense of elected institutions. In the interests of social equality, the Court has also allowed government interventionism and curtailed individual freedom of action. It has colluded in destroying the powers and prerogatives of the states.

Many conservatives have therefore proposed a number of amendments to the Constitution. They also seek the appointment of federal judges who would establish a different understanding of the Articles and amendments.

1 They back an amendment which would impose term limits on members of Congress. In most of the proposals, federal legislators would be restricted to twelve years. This represents six terms in the House and two Senatorial terms. Such a reform, they assert, would begin to recreate a 'citizen legislature' that would be much more closely tied to the people it purports to represent.
2 The Balanced Budget amendment would require the federal government to balance its revenues and expenditures. It would only be able to borrow in times of war or other emergencies.
3 The Tax Limitation amendment would limit the amount that the federal government could tax as a proportion of the Gross National Product (GNP) or require a *supermajority* of 60 per cent if taxation levels were to be raised.
4 There would be a stronger emphasis upon the Tenth Amendment and greater recognition of *states' rights*.
5 Some conservatives have also called for curbs on the role of the federal courts. For example, Patrick Buchanan, who sought the Republican presidential nomination in both 1992 and 1996, has argued that federal judges should be subject to reconfirmation by Congress every eight years. Buchanan also calls for a Constitutional amendment allowing Congress to set aside Supreme Court rulings if there is a two-thirds majority in both houses and the president is in agreement (1990: 356).

There is, however, a twist in the conservative argument. Although they believe that the federal government has often been interventionist in a way that threatens rights and liberties, particularly within the economic sphere, some hope to amend the Constitution so as to reverse particular Supreme Court rulings and codify their understanding of the US as a 'Christian nation'. There have been calls for amendments to prohibit 'flag desecration' and to authorise school prayer. This would compel the authorities to allow 'prayer or other religious expression in circumstances in which expression of a non-religious character would be permitted'.

If successful, such amendments would, liberal critics assert, jeopardise liberties and undermine the federal courts that – through judicial review – interpret and apply the Constitution. As Kathleen M. Sullivan argued in *The American Prospect*:

> Increasing the frequency of constitutional amendment would undermine the respect and legitimacy the Court now enjoys in this interpretive role. This danger is especially acute in the case of proposed constitutional amendments that would literally overturn Supreme Court decisions, such as amendments that would declare a fetus a person with a right to life, permit punishment of flag burning, or authorize school prayer. Such amendments suggest that if you don't like a Court decision, you mobilize to overturn it. (Sullivan 1995)

Conclusion

Although the US Constitution is sometimes hailed as a model, few other countries have adopted all of its provisions. Indeed, as Robert Dahl has noted, 'among the countries most comparable to the United States . . . and where democratic institutions have long existed without breakdown, not one has adopted our American constitutional system' (quoted in Scialabba 2002). Few nations, in particular, have adopted constitutions that offer such a degree of independence to the executive branch, a 'first-past-the-post' electoral system that almost always discriminates against minor parties, and an upper chamber based upon highly unequal representation.

Nonetheless, the US Constitution has survived over two hundred years without being fundamentally altered. It has adjusted to the diversity and complexity of contemporary American society. It is striking that few commentators believe that the Constitution requires radical change, and even those most critical of the current political system still claim that the principles it embodies remain valid.

The Constitution's resilience can, in part, be explained by the relevance of the principles associated with constitutional democracy to both agrarian and industrial societies. It can also be attributed to the amendments that have been adopted. The most important amendments modernised those sections that were most deeply rooted in late eighteenth-century thought. The survival and strength of the Constitution can also, however, be explained by the Supreme Court's role in reinterpreting it, often in the light of changing social and economic circumstances. The Court is surveyed in Chapter 4.

References and further reading

Buchanan, P. J. (1990), *Right from the Beginning*, Washington DC, Regnery Gateway.

Committee on the Constitutional System (1987), *A Bicentennial Analysis of the American Political Structure*, Washington DC, Committee on the Constitutional System.

Foley, M. (1991), *American Political Ideas*, Manchester, Manchester University Press.

Henretta, J. A., W. E. Brownlee, D. Brody and S. Ware (1993), *America's History*, New York, Worth Publishers.

Neustadt, R. E. (1991), *Presidential Power and the Modern Presidents: The Politics of Leadership from Roosevelt to Reagan*, New York, The Free Press.

Scialabba, G. (2002), 'Democracy-proof', *The American Prospect*, 1 July, www.prospect .org/print/V13/12/scialabba-g.html.

Sullivan, K. M. (1995), 'Constitutional amendmentitis', *The American Prospect*, 6:23, 21 September, www.prospect.org/print/V6/23/sullivan-k.html.

Wills, G. (1999), *A Necessary Evil: A History of American Distrust of Government*, New York, Simon and Schuster.

4

The US Supreme Court

Constitutions require interpretation. This is partly because particular words and phrases have an ambiguous or subjective character. Is, for example, the right to 'bear arms' – assured in the second amendment – conditional upon individuals serving in the 'well regulated militia' specified in the first part of the sentence? What does the 'equal protection of the laws', guaranteed in the four-teenth amendment, mean in practice? What conditions must be met if an indi-vidual accused of a crime is to be afforded 'due process of law', as required by the fifth and fourteenth amendments? However, difficulties also arise because the commonly accepted meaning of particular words and phrases has changed over time. What, today, constitutes the 'cruel and unusual punishment' that is prohibited by the eighth amendment? The provisions of the Constitution also have to be applied to specific and inevitably complex issues. Does, for example, the random checking of bags on a bus in a search for drugs – by feeling their contents from the outside – breach the fourth amendment's prohibition of 'unreasonable searches and seizures'?

Furthermore, how should the Constitution be read? Should it be understood in narrow, literal terms? Should its words and phrases be examined in terms of the original meaning put upon them – in so far as it can be discerned – by their authors? Should the broader spirit of the Constitution's provisions be applied to the standards of the modern age? Should the implications of particular terms be considered? Do, for example, the different Articles and amendments imply a 'right to privacy', as some suggest? Should the constitutionality of particular measures be judged on the basis of their intent or of their outcome?

Although all these questions are of far-reaching political importance, they are determined by the federal courts rather than the elected branches of government. Their role is drawn from their power of *judicial review*. Although the Constitution assigned the Supreme Court – and the lower federal courts – other functions, including that of ruling on disputes involving the United States government, resolving controversies between states, and hearing cases arising under federal law, the courts can – if an appropriate case is brought forward –

Table 4.1 *The US Supreme Court, June 2003*

	Date appointed	President
Chief Justice		
William Rehnquist	1971/1986	Nixon/Reagan
Associate Justices		
John Paul Stevens	1975	Ford
Sandra Day O'Connor	1981	Reagan
Antonin Scalia	1986	Reagan
Anthony Kennedy	1987	Reagan
David Souter	1990	Bush
Clarence Thomas	1991	Bush
Ruth Bader Ginsburg	1993	Clinton
Stephen Breyer	1994	Clinton

The US Supreme Court: political opinion

liberal		<	<	centre	>	>		conservative
Stevens		Breyer		O'Connor		Rehnquist		Thomas
	Ginsburg		Souter		Kennedy		Scalia	

Source: adapted from Robert J. McKeever (1997), *The United States Supreme Court: A Political and Legal Analysis*, Manchester, Manchester University Press, p. 29.

assess the *constitutionality* of any law passed, or action undertaken, by either the federal government or the state governments. Laws and actions can be declared null and void – or *struck down* – if the courts conclude that they are unconstitutional. Although judicial review is not specifically identified in Article III of the Constitution, Supreme Court Chief Justice John Marshall (who held the office from 1801 to 1835) claimed the right when ruling in the case of *Marbury v. Madison* (1803). He asserted: 'It is emphatically the province and duty of the judicial department to say what the law is.' The Court's power of judicial review has been accepted and unchallenged ever since.

Nine judges sit on the Supreme Court. Most of the cases that it considers will have first been heard by a lower federal court, although it sometimes considers appeals that have been brought directly from the state courts if constitutional issues are involved. The lower federal courts – which hear cases arising under both the Constitution and federal law – consist of the circuit courts of appeal and, on a lower tier, US district courts. There are twelve regional circuits, each of which has a court of appeals. They all consider appeals from the US district courts located within their particular circuit. Furthermore, the Court of Appeals for the Federal Circuit has national jurisdiction to hear appeals in highly technical cases, such as those involving patent laws.

For their part, the states have their own judicial systems that interpret and apply state laws. Their courts have jurisdiction over almost all divorce and child custody matters, probate and inheritance issues, and property questions. They also decide upon most criminal cases, contract disputes, traffic violations, and personal injury cases.

This chapter considers the role of the US Supreme Court and the lower federal courts. It surveys the appointments process, and assesses the significance of the Court's powers. It asks whether the US has 'government by judiciary' or if the Court is, as some have claimed, 'the least dangerous branch'? It also looks at other debates. What approaches should judges on the Supreme Court bench adopt in making their rulings? Some call for judicial activism, and argue that the Court should use its powers in a pro-active way to change American society. Others, however, favour judicial restraint. The chapter also asks whether the Court should be considered a judicial or a political institution?

Appointing the judges

Federal judges are appointed by the president with 'the advice and consent of the Senate' (Article II section 2). Although there are no official criteria, a number of considerations have emerged:

1 An appointee is almost always associated with the same political party as the president. As Robert McKeever notes: 'An examination of the history of presidential nominations to the Supreme Court reveals one overwhelming fact . . . In only a handful of almost 150 nominations to the Court has the President gone outside of his party for a Supreme Court nominee. This tradition was firmly established by George Washington.' (McKeever 1997: 122)
2 The president will appoint those who he believes broadly share his political and judicial philosophy. The judges nominated during the Reagan era were either moderate or more 'hardline' conservatives. Their ranks included Antonin Scalia, while William Rehnquist was elevated to become Chief Justice. Both were markedly unsympathetic towards affirmative action programmes and the rights of criminal suspects. Their rulings have had a consistently conservative character. For his part, President Bill Clinton selected Stephen Breyer and Ruth Bader Ginsburg who were – like Clinton – moderate liberals.
3 Judges are expected to be legally qualified, to have practised law, and to have had judicial experience. Traditionally, the American Bar Association (ABA), the professional body for lawyers, was assigned a quasi-official role. For about fifty years, the administration sent the names of nominees to the ABA for scrutiny before they were publicly announced. Through its Standing Committee on Federal Judiciary, the ABA assessed the qualifications of, and assigned ratings for, potential appointees. Each was rated well qualified, qualified or not qualified. This was decided – in the words of the Committee

– on the basis of 'the professional competence, integrity, and judicial temperament of candidates'.

However, in March 2001 the Bush administration ended this practice. The White House announced that, from then on, the ABA was to lose its special role. Instead, it would invite comments on its nominees from a broad range of individuals and organisations (*New York Times* 2001). The administration's decision reflected longstanding conservative criticism of the ABA. Despite its claim to be non-partisan, the Association is, they assert, guilty of liberal bias. Conservative nominees, they claim, have not been awarded the ratings that their judicial accomplishments merited. In particular, Clarence Thomas, who was nominated by President Bush in 1991, was deemed only to be 'qualified'.

Republican administrations have instead depended much more on the Federalist Society. The Society – which draws its membership from among conservatives and libertarians – is committed to a literal – or *strict constructionist* – interpretation of the Constitution. It is suspicious of attempts to discern implied rights that are not specifically stated in the seven Articles and twenty-seven amendments. In the Bush White House, Federalist Society members include the Attorney General John Ashcroft, who has direct responsibility for selecting federal judicial nominees. Many of the administration's nominees for the district and appeals courts have been drawn from its ranks.

4 It is now accepted that there should be a degree of diversity on the Supreme Court bench. Thurgood Marshall, the first African-American, was appointed in 1967. Sandra Day O'Connor, appointed by Reagan in 1981, was the first female Justice on the Supreme Court. Between 1916 and 1969, there was a 'Jewish seat' on the Court (McKeever 1997: 124).

5 Abortion has become a pivotal or 'litmus test' issue. In practice, although other issues are also considered, a nominee's attitude towards abortion is critical. Although Republican presidents will – when making appointments – have to consider the composition of the Senate, their nominees will – at the least – be broadly sympathetic towards 'pro-life' arguments. A Democratic president's nominee will have 'broadly pro-choice' attitudes.

Confirmation

Presidential nominations have traditionally been accepted by the Senate, but confirmation cannot be assured. Since the founding of the US, eleven nominations to the Supreme Court have been rejected and others have had to be withdrawn or postponed. However, only five of these rejections were in the twentieth century (Ragsdale 1996: 422–3). In 1969 and 1970, the Senate opposed two of Nixon's nominees, Clement F. Haynesworth and G. Harrold Carswell, who were accused of ethical violations and segregationist sympathies respectively. In 1987, Reagan nominated Robert Bork, a former law professor, a justice on the DC Court of Appeals and a leading advocate of judicial restraint. A widespread public campaign was organised against him, spearheaded by liberal pressure groups, and the Senate defeated the nomination by 58 to 42 votes. A further nominee for the post, Douglas H. Ginsburg, withdrew his nomination in 1987 after admitting to having smoked marijuana. President Bush won a narrow victory in 1991 when he nominated Clarence Thomas, a conservative black judge, to replace Thurgood Marshall. There was strong opposition on ideological grounds, echoing the arguments against Bork, and there were also claims of sexual harassment by a former assistant, Anita Hill. Thomas described his televised interrogation by the Senate Judiciary Committee as a 'high-tech lynching', but he was narrowly endorsed by 52 to 48 votes. Clinton had little trouble in his nominations of centrist liberals, Ruth Bader Ginsburg and Stephen G. Breyer, who were appointed in 1993 and 1994 respectively.

Lower federal court nominations should also be considered. During both the Clinton and Bush administrations, there were accusations that the Senate was using delaying tactics so as to obstruct nominations to the district and appeal courts. During the latter half of the 1990s, the Republicans, it was said, used their majority to delay President Clinton's nominees. A study found that in 1992 the Democrat-controlled Senate took an average of 92 days to hold hearings on the Republican President George Bush's nominations for district judges. However, by 1998, the Republican Senate took an average of 160 days to hold hearings on Clinton's nominees (Ohio State University 1999). In turn, there were claims that the Democrats – who won back control in mid-2001 – had obstructed President George W. Bush's appointments.

Table 4.2 *Federal court confirmations, 1995–2002*

Year	District court confirmations	Circuit court of appeal confirmations	Total
1995	45	11	56
1996	17	0	17
1997	29	7	36
1998	51	13	64
1999	26	7	33
2000	31	8	39
July–Dec. 2001	23	5	28
2002	60	12	72

Source: adapted from US Senator Patrick Leahy (2002), *Judicial Nominations Update – Final Numbers For 107th Congress . . . As Senate Confirms 100th Bush Judicial Nominee*, www.senate.gov/~leahy/press/200211/112002b.html.

However, although the Democrats could justly claim to have confirmed rather more nominees than the Republicans had during the mid-1990s (Table 4.2), these statistics need to be set against the needs of the federal courts. There were growing numbers of vacancies. At the end of October 2002, there were

79 vacancies, a 9 per cent vacancy rate. Furthermore, caseloads grew significantly during this period. In response, President Bush put forward a plan. He asked federal judges to give notice if they intended to leave the federal bench at least a year in advance. The administration would then submit a nomination to the Senate within 180 days. The Senate Judiciary Committee would have a further 90 days to hold a hearing. The full Senate would act within 180 days of the president submitting the nomination.

Guerrilla warfare between the parties continued despite the Republicans' recapture of the Senate in the 2002 mid-term elections. Although the Democrats were relegated to minority status after the elections, they may still be able to block judicial appointments. In early 2003, claiming that the administration had failed to release sufficient information, they threatened the use of a *filibuster* to obstruct the nomination of Miguel Estrada to Washington's US Circuit Court of Appeals. They may have also been fearful that the White House would use 'stealth tactics' and appoint – when a Supreme Court vacancy opened up – a little known nominee whose background could be hidden.

Apart from Senate opposition, there are other constraints upon the president's leverage over the federal judiciary. His appointee may not act in a way that was expected. President Eisenhower nominated Earl Warren. As a former governor of California, he was regarded as a cautious moderate. However, to Eisenhower's chagrin, he proved to be a judicial liberal. Indeed, the Warren Court spearheaded the 'civil rights revolution'. Similarly, today, although Republican nominees are in a majority on the Court, the rulings made by moderate conservatives such as Sandra Day O'Connor are at times more centrist in character than the right would wish.

Furthermore, once appointed, judges are insulated from both presidential pressure and public opinion. This is because – under the terms of the Constitution – they are appointed for life subject only to 'good behaviour'. They can only be removed in the most exceptional circumstances, through impeachment and conviction by Congress of 'Treason, Bribery, or other high Crimes and Misdemeanors'. To protect the Court from political pressure further, the salaries of federal judges cannot be reduced during their period of office.

Hearing cases

In a limited number of areas the Supreme Court has *original jurisdiction*. It can consider cases that are brought before it without having been earlier considered by a lower court. These areas are specified in the Constitution, and include 'controversies between two or more states' or cases involving the US government. However, the majority of cases are *appellate* cases, in which the Court may, at its discretion, consider appeals against decisions made by lower courts, US Courts of Appeal, state supreme courts and the US Court of Military Appeals.

In a year, the Court receives over eight thousand petitions asking the

Supreme Court to review a case – or to grant a writ of *certiorari* ('cert') – on a case originally heard by a lower court. The judges – or Justices – themselves decide on the granting of 'cert' at weekly meetings. Under the 'rule of four', if at least four of the nine justices wish to consider a particular case, it is heard. Despite suggestions that – in practice – the clerks who assist the Justices play a pivotal role in determining which cases are considered, Robert McKeever argues that they do not impose their views: 'most see their role as carrying out the wishes of their Justice. Thus, when they have learned their Justice's tendencies with regard to grants of review, their recommendations will follow suit . . . It seems unlikely, then, that clerks are in a position to substitute their own views for those of the Justices' (McKeever 1997: 79).

These deliberations rarely lead to a case being reviewed. Since the mid-1990s, fewer than a hundred cases have been considered annually.

Table 4.3 *The Supreme Court caseload, 1980–97*

Year	Cases submitted	Cases heard
1980	5144	154
1985	5158	171
1990	6316	125
1995	7565	90
1996	7602	90
1997	7692	96
1998	8083	90

Source: adapted from J. W. Wright (ed.) (2000), *The New York Times Almanac 2001*, New York, Penguin, p. 126.

What factors determine the granting of 'cert'?

- Some issues have a long-term significance for American society or the political process. This may have persuaded the Court to hear cases in recent years that addressed the relationship between the federal government and the states, the constitutionality of affirmative action programmes, and the counting of votes in the 2000 presidential election.
- A Justice may seek to deny 'cert' despite the importance of a case, if she or he fears that if the case is heard a ruling will be made with which she or he disagrees.
- There are sometimes tensions between the circuit courts of appeal when they have made different rulings about similar cases. The Supreme Court may see it as its responsibility to resolve this by hearing the cases.
- The Court is more likely to hear a case if the federal government – represented by the Solicitor General – is seeking the review of a particular case.
- There are legal rules governing which cases may be heard. A case may, for example, be 'moot' if the circumstances that gave rise to it no longer hold.

Those bringing a case must have 'standing', in so far as they must have been personally disadvantaged by a denial of constitutional rights and therefore be seeking redress.

Although oral arguments are put forward, and lawyers for each of the parties to the case are granted thirty minutes to present their case, they may play only a marginal role. It is also difficult to determine the role of *amicus curiae* briefs that may have been submitted by pressure groups that are lobbying for particular outcomes. The more important deliberations take place in private both before and after the oral hearings. Case conferences are held. These are presided over by the Chief Justice; but his powers are limited and he is not always in the majority.

Court decisions require only a simple majority, and 5–4 rulings – such as that made in *Bush v. Gore* (2000) – are common. When the decision is announced, written opinions are also published. These outline and explain the legal reasoning underpinning a vote. Opinions can take three forms: the *majority opinion*, which explains the basis for the Court's decision; a *concurring opinion*, which agrees with the decision but bases it on different legal grounds; and a *dissenting opinion*. This allows a minority to express its reasoning for opposing the decision. All the opinions are subject to considerable examination and debate. Between 20 and 30 per cent of cases are unanimous.

How much power?

Some commentators believe that the courts are too powerful. Raul Berger made this claim in *Government by Judiciary*, originally published in 1977. He asserts that the Supreme Court has been engaged – particularly through its rulings on the Fourteenth Amendment – in a 'continuing revision of the Constitution, under the guise of "interpretation" that has subverted our democratic institutions'. (1997). Others argue that the federal courts have more limited powers. They echo the words of *The Federalist 78*: 'The Judiciary is beyond comparison the weakest of the three departments of power' (Hamilton 2002).

Those who stress the powers of the Court point to the scope and scale of its judgements. They have reshaped American society and the political process. Much of its history has been associated with three broad and often intertwined constitutional questions. These are the relationships between government and the economy, federalism and equality, and government and individual liberties.

'Necessary and proper'

During the early years of the US, there was uncertainty about the role of the national government and the rights of the states. Under Chief Justice John Marshall, in *McCulloch v. Maryland* (1819), the Court established the principle of national supremacy over the states by recognising the right of Congress to create a national bank with a degree of authority over the states' banks. This had implications for relationship between the national government and the states. However, the importance of the ruling goes beyond this. Lawyers for the state of Maryland had maintained that – because it was not specified in the Constitution – the federal government did not have the constitutional power to establish a national bank. In rejecting this and making their ruling, the Justices drew upon the final sentence of Article I, Section 8. After listing the specific or 'enumerated' powers of Congress, it stated that Congress could 'make all laws which shall be necessary and proper for carrying into execution the foregoing powers, and all other powers vested by this Constitution in the government of the United States.' The 'necessary and proper' clause of the Constitution thereby provided a basis for assigning the federal government implied powers that went beyond the wording of the Constitution.

Government and the economy

As the US became an industrial society, there were increasingly vocal calls for government intervention in economic affairs. The federal and state governments, it was said, should alleviate poverty and urban problems. Monopolies should be restricted. Working hours should be regulated. The slums and tenement blocks should be cleared.

What role does the US Constitution assign to government? During the late nineteenth and early twentieth centuries, Court decisions reflected the view that it was severely limited. In *Lochner v. New York* (1905), the Court ruled that the state of the New York did *not* have the power to regulate working hours for bakery workers. Their ruling rested on the principle of 'substantive due process' in the fourteenth amendment. It was understood to protect the right of an employer to hire workers without external interference.

This limited, *laissez-faire* interpretation of the government's role was challenged by the activist interventionism of the New Deal era. The Roosevelt administration sought – through a programme of government action, economic reform and public works – to ensure that the country recovered from the depression. Initially, the Court challenged the constitutionality of key elements in President Franklin Roosevelt's programme. They were struck down. In May 1935, in *Schechter Poultry Corporation v. United States*, the Court declared that the National Recovery Administration (NRA) which had been created under the National Industrial Recovery Act had acted unconstitutionally by taking action against a Brooklyn business that had been selling diseased chickens. Under the Constitution, the federal government only had the power to regulate interstate, not intrastate, commerce. By defining 'interstate commerce' in a narrow way, the Court placed much of the New Deal in jeopardy. Similarly, Roosevelt's agricultural programme – the 1933 Agricultural Adjustment Act – which imposed a tax on food-processing businesses – was deemed in *US v. Butler*

(1936) to be an unconstitutional extension of the federal government's powers to intervene in the economy.

Roosevelt responded in 1937 by seeking to enlarge the Court beyond the existing nine members to fifteen. He proposed adding one new Justice to the Court for each existing Justice aged over seventy. Although presented as a means by which the Court's workload could be eased, Roosevelt's 'court packing' plan would have enabled him – through the new appointments – to have gained a majority which would have been sympathetic to the New Deal. However, the proposal met firm resistance in Congress. It was seen as a crude attack on the separation of powers. However, in the wake of the Roosevelt plan, the Court modified its approach and began to consider New Deal legislation in more positive terms. In April 1937, it ruled that the 1935 National Labor Relations Act which had required employers to negotiate with trade union representatives was constitutional. Similarly, Washington state's minimum wage legislation was upheld. The Court's apparent change of heart was described as 'a switch in time that saved nine'.

In the decades following the New Deal era, the Court was cautious in challenging presidential and Congressional actions in the economic field. Indeed, some conservatives suggested that the Court had thus surrendered its obligations under the Constitution by failing to limit the federal government to its enumerated powers. However, the Rehnquist Court's increasingly circumscribed understanding of the interstate commerce clause at the end of the 1990s seems to suggest a shift back towards earlier forms of constitutional interpretation (see below).

Equality, race, gender and sexuality

For much of the nineteenth century, the Court backed the denial of basic rights of citizenship to African-Americans. In 1857, in *Dred Scott v. Sanford*, the Court, headed by Chief Justice Roger Taney, declared that the Missouri compromise, an Act of Congress that had allowed former slaves to be free in the new border territories created by westward expansion, was unconstitutional. The Court insisted that the slave, Dred Scott, who had been taken to a free state and had claimed his liberty, be returned to his former owner. The ruling endorsed the legitimacy of slavery and curtailed the rights of the federal government. The outrage that it created among those committed to the abolition of slavery contributed to the election of Abraham Lincoln as president in 1860 and the outbreak of the Civil War.

In 1896, the Court accepted the constitutionality of segregation. In the closing decades of the nineteenth century, whites had – despite the South's defeat in the Civil War – progressively reasserted its power. Segregation laws were introduced across the southern states that relegated blacks to separate and invariably inferior public facilities. Segregation extended to education, shops, restaurants, transport, and even the graveyards. The Supreme Court declared in *Plessy v. Ferguson* that the segregation laws were a matter for the states. They 'have been generally, if not universally recognized as within the competency of state legislatures in the exercise of their police powers' (Tindall and Shi 1989: 476).

It was 58 years before the Court took a different view. In September 1953, President Eisenhower appointed the former Governor of California Earl Warren as Chief Justice. Despite expectations that it would pursue a conservative course, the Warren Court brought about a judicial revolution. The Court's rulings were pervaded by a spirit of judicial activism. In 1954, in *Brown v. Board of Education (Topeka, Kansas)*, the Court reversed the *Plessy* judgement and declared that segregated schooling was unconstitutional. The relegation of black children to separate schools conveyed a message of inferiority and caused psychological damage. It was a denial of the 'equal protection' required by the fourteenth amendment. A year later, the Court demanded that the desegregation of southern schools should proceed 'with all deliberate speed'.

Earl Warren was succeeded as Chief Justice by Warren E. Burger. While in some respects more cautious than the Warren Court, the Burger Court (1969–86) extended the 'civil rights revolution'. Although the southern states were finally desegregated a decade after the Brown ruling, the US remained a racially divided and unequal society. In both the south and the north, blacks and whites lived in different areas and districts. Even in the absence of restrictive laws, neighbourhood schools were predominantly white or black. Furthermore, blacks were under-represented in higher education, business and the professions. In 1971, in *Swann v. Charlotte-Mecklenburg Board of Education*, the Court ruled that school students should be taken by bus to different schools across a city so as to ensure a broad racial balance in each school. The Court also considered affirmative action. Such programmes are derived from a conception of equality based not on opportunity but on outcome. Their supporters assert that disparities of income and achievement between the races, ethnic groupings and genders are, in themselves, evidence of institutionalised discrimination. In their most rigorous form, affirmative action programmes include numerical admissions quotas so as to increase minority representation in a certain field of employment or on a particular educational course. In *Griggs v. Duke Power Company* (1971), the Court outlawed selection tests that were not obviously job-related and produced different pass rates between the races. In making the judgement, Chief Justice Warren Burger focused on 'the *consequences* of employment practices, not simply the motivation' (Thernstrom and Thernstrom 1997: 430). In *Regents of the University of California v. Allan Bakke* (1978), the Court did not accept the full affirmative action argument. Nevertheless, it ruled, albeit by a narrow majority, that although concerns for racial equality were not to be the only consideration, educational institutions could include race as a factor when recruiting students. Subsequently, in 1980, in *Fullilove v. Klutznick*, the Court accepted the constitutionality of *set-asides* that awarded a fixed proportion of federal government construction contracts to minority-owned firms.

The civil rights era created the conditions for the emergence of the women's movement. Feminism established itself on the political and judicial agenda. Against this background, the Burger Court ruled in *Roe v. Wade* (1973) that a woman had an unfettered right to an abortion in the first three months of a pregnancy. States were allowed to impose only limited restrictions in the second trimester so as to protect the mother's health. In the final trimester, when the fetus may be viable outside the mother's womb, states may introduce laws restricting abortion, except when the woman' s life or health is at risk. Prior to *Roe*, abortion regulations varied greatly between the different states, and this ruling circumscribed their ability to make their own laws. The ruling was based – at least for some of the Justices – on an implied right of privacy. Individuals, it was said, had the right to determine certain matters – particularly issues relating to their children – themselves, and the authorities should respect their personal autonomy. Although the concept of privacy is not to be found in the Constitution, the right was drawn, in the words of Justice William O. Douglas, from the 'penumbras and emanations' of the Constitution (McKeever 1997: 15). The ruling had important consequences. Confirmation hearings increasingly focused on a nominee's attitude towards abortion. Many evangelical Christians were drawn still further towards the political process, creating the preconditions for the emergence of the 'religious right' as a significant political force during the 1980s and 1990s. *Roe* also led an intensification of pressure group activity and the mass mobilisation of both the pro-life and pro-choice movements.

Although the overall character of the Court is shaped by other variables apart from the politics of the Chief Justice, the Rehnquist Court (1986–) has been much more conservative in its thinking. Indeed, some have spoken of a judicial 'counter-revolution' or the 'rolling back' of the judgements made by the Warren and Burger Courts. Rehnquist and other judicial conservatives favour a 'strict constructionist' approach to the process of constitutional interpretation. The Constitution, they assert, should be read narrowly and literally. Attempts to discern implied rights or apply the spirit of the Constitution to the modern era inevitably lead to the making of public policy on the basis of the judges' personal desires and prejudices. They argue for a much more restrictive conception of discrimination than that employed during the Warren and Burger years, one based upon individual instances of unfair treatment rather than on generalised claims that entire groups such as African-Americans have suffered institutionalised disadvantage. Judicial conservatives also emphasise the importance of 'states' rights' and the limits that the Constitution imposes upon the powers of the national government.

However, although the Rehnquist Court had a broadly conservative stamp, its rulings have not had an entirely consistent or predictable character. Instead, the composition of the majority and the minority changed to some extent according to the issue under consideration. Why was this? While Rehnquist, Antonin Scalia and Clarence Thomas formed an important faction on the bench, conservatives failed to gain a clear majority during the Reagan and Bush era. Indeed, some of the moderate conservatives appointed in this period turned out to be 'swing votes' who sometimes sided with the more liberal members of the Court. Then, in the 1990s, President Clinton had the opportunity to appoint Stephen Breyer and Ruth Bader Ginsburg to the bench. This dashed conservative hopes of full-blown 'counter-revolution'.

This is evident in the rulings on abortion. There has been a partial, but limited, pull-back from the assertion of abortion rights in *Roe v. Wade*. The basic framework established by the *Roe* ruling has, however, remained intact. In July 1989, in *Webster v. Reproductive Health Services*, the Court upheld the constitutionality of a Missouri law prohibiting the use of state facilities and personnel in the performance of an abortion. Three years later, in June 1992, *Planned Parenthood of Southeastern Pennsylvania v. Casey* permitted states to impose a waiting period before an abortion is carried out, and to require unmarried women, aged under eighteen, to gain the consent of a parent or judge (Hinkson Craig and O'Brien 1993: 329–41). In 2000 (*Stenberg v. Carhart*), the Court overturned Nebraska's ban on so-called 'partial-birth' abortion. The Nebraska law, the Court asserted, included 'overly broad' language that threatened the continued availability of legal abortions.

The Court's judgements on the constitutionality of affirmative action programmes have also had an uneven character. Although the circumstances in which such programmes can be applied have been progressively circumscribed since the *Griggs, Bakke* and *Fullilove* rulings, the Court has not, however, ruled that they are unconstitutional. In 1989, the Court ruled in *Richmond v. J. A. Croson* that state and local governments could only adopt a system of minority set-asides for contracts if they were addressing specific instances of discrimination. They were to be 'strictly reserved for remedial settings' (Thernstrom and Thernstrom 1997: 437). Other Court rulings imposed further constraints on affirmative action programmes. *Wards Cove Packing Company v. Antonio* (1989) looked again at company employment policies. It narrowed the grounds on which discrimination could be claimed, but at the same time broadened the basis on which employers could justify the use of particular selection tests and hiring practices. In 1995, *Adarand v. Pena* applied the arguments that underpinned the *Croson* ruling to the award of federal government contracts, and permitted minority set-asides in only narrowly prescribed circumstances. The Court had similar concerns about racial redistricting. In some states, the boundaries between electoral districts had been drawn so as to ensure that there were black or Hispanic majorities. This was intended to increase the overall level of minority representation in Congress. In *Shaw v. Reno* (1993) and *Miller v. Johnson* (1995), the Court rejected redistricting plans in which race was the 'predominant factor'.

However, despite predictions that affirmative action programmes would be 'rolled back', the Court maintained its commitment to diversity as a goal and an acceptance that race could be used as a factor – albeit alongside many others –

in the making of recruitment policies. In June 2003, in *Gratz v. Bollinger* and *Grutter v. Bollinger*, the Court reaffirmed the spirit of the *Bakke* ruling. It struck down the University of Michigan's undergraduate admissions policy – which assigned additional points to minority applicants – but allowed the University's Law School to continue considering race and diversity in its recruitment procedures, because these took a relatively flexible and pragmatic form.

Gay and lesbian rights have also come to the fore since the 'sexual revolution' of the 1960s and 1970s. In 1986, in the case of *Bowers v. Hardwick*, the Court denied that the right to privacy that some asserted was implied in the Constitution extended to homosexuality. Instead, the legality of homosexual acts was left to the state legislatures. However, in a June 2003 ruling (*Lawrence et al. v. Texas*) that has wide-ranging implications, the Court reversed this. It decided that the right to privacy was broader than had been earlier understood and did include homosexual acts. The Texas law – which had outlawed gay sex – was thereby struck down. As Justice Anthony Kennedy argued: 'The petitioners are entitled to respect for their private lives. The State cannot demean their existence or control their destiny by making their private sexual conduct a crime' (*Washington Post* 2003).

Individual rights

The Bill of Rights establishes the basic liberties of the individual. However, the federal courts have also played a role in determining the practical meaning of those rights. A succession of cases focused on the rights in suspects in criminal cases. *Gideon v. Wainwright* (1963) laid down that all defendants had a right to an attorney. To ensure this, the states would pay the expenses for those on a low income. Three years later, *Miranda v. Arizona* (1966) established that criminal suspects must be read their rights upon arrest. This ruling was derived from the protection of the right against self-incrimination in the Fifth Amendment.

Since the days of the Warren Court, there has been much less of a readiness to extend the rights of the accused. Instead, the ability of the authorities to secure a conviction has been much more of a consideration. In 1991, in *Fulminante v. Arizona*, the Court ruled that even if a confession is obtained by coercion, that fact does not necessarily invalidate a conviction based upon it.

The rights of the convicted have also been circumscribed. In two 1989 cases (*Penry v. Lynaugh* and *Stanford v. Kentucky*), the Court ruled that it was constitutional to extend capital punishment to the mentally retarded and to those who committed murder as juveniles (McKeever 1995: 283). The ability of the Court to consider appeals based on an alleged denial of constitutional rights by the state courts was also reined in. The most conservative judges on the Court, Antonin Scalia and Clarence Thomas, have taken the view that the Constitution, and therefore the Supreme Court, could not forbid 'the execution of an innocent man who has received, though to no avail, all the process that our society has traditionally deemed adequate' (quoted in Roberts 1995: 155).

However, the Court has also imposed limits upon the powers of the federal authorities. In *US v. Bond* (2000), the Court held that the fourth amendment's prohibition of 'unreasonable searches and seizures' had been breached when a bus passenger's carry-on luggage was squeezed from the outside by a federal border agent in Texas, leading to the discovery of a 'brick' of methamphetamine.

The Court' s rulings on freedom of speech and the first amendment also had an uneven character. Some have extended the boundaries of the First Amendment. In June 1997, in *Reno v. the American Civil Liberties Union (ACLU)*, the US Supreme Court struck down the Communications Decency Act (CDA). The Act, which sought to prohibit 'indecency' on the internet, was deemed to be an unconstitutional restriction on free speech. Five years later, in April 2002, the Court also invalidated the Child Pornography Prevention Act of 1996 (*Ashcroft v. The Free Speech Coalition*), which had outlawed computer-generated images of children. However, the Court has also asserted that there are limits on speech. In a 2003 ruling (*Virginia v. Black*) made by 6 to 3, the Justices ruled that the burning of a cross – a ritual act undertaken by the Ku Klux Klan – may be prohibited by states if the purpose of it is to intimidate others. Although he offered a concurrent opinion in the case, Justice Clarence Thomas spoke for the majority when he asserted that the message of a burning flag was one of terror and lawlessness. It should not therefore be regarded as a form of protected expression: 'Just as one cannot burn down someone's house to make a political point and then seek refuge in the First Amendment, those who hate cannot ter-rorize and intimidate to make their point' (*New York Times* 2003).

Federalism

Many of the Court's rulings on cases involving the economic role of govern-ment, the position of minorities, or individual rights had implications for the relationship between the national government and the states. During the Warren and Burger years, most of these judgements seemed to constrain the decision-making powers of the states. White southerners felt that they had lost the right to protect and preserve their 'way of life'. Once abortion had been established as a constitutional right through the *Roe* ruling, the state legisla-tures lost their ability to frame their own abortion laws.

Although the Reagan administration was committed to the restoration of states' rights (see Chapter 8), the Court maintained the centralising trend. In *Garcia v. San Antonio Metropolitan Transit Authority* (1985) the Court allowed the federal government to regulate the wages paid by the city authorities to local bus workers. However, by the 1990s there had been a significant shift in attitude on the part of the Court. In 1995, the Court stressed the constitutional limits on the role of the federal government. In *US v. Lopez*, the Court declared the Gun-Free School Zones Act unconstitutional. Washington, the Court argued, did not have the power that it had claimed under the interstate commerce clause of the Constitution to restrict the possession of a gun within 1,000 feet of a school (McKeever 1997: 45). Appropriate legislation was, the judges asserted, a matter for the individual states. The commitment to 'states' rights' that underpinned the *Lopez* ruling also informed a series of subsequent judgements such as *Kimel v. Florida Board of Regents* and *United States v. Morrison* (2000) (see Chapter 8).

Sources of power

The Supreme Court has – through its rulings – had a far-reaching impact on American politics and society. There are a number of factors that have added to its importance:

1 The Court has wide jurisdiction. Article VI of the Constitution established the Constitution and the laws of the US as the supreme law of the land. This was confirmed through the evolution of judicial review, permitting the Court to apply its judgement to any federal law. By 1995, the Court had declared more than 125 acts of Congress unconstitutional (Wetterau 1995: 201). Its interpretations have reshaped and changed the accepted meaning of many others.

Table 4.4 *Laws struck down as unconstitutional, 1960–96*

	Federal laws	State and local laws
1960–69	16	149
1970–79	20	193
1980–89	16	162
1990–96	10	45

Source: adapted from H. W. Stanley and R. G. Niemi (1998), *Vital Statistics on American Politics 1997–1998*, Washington DC, CQ Press, p. 282.

2 Judicial review extends beyond law to the actions of government. The president, Congress, executive departments, and government agencies can be overruled. The Supreme Court's 1974 ruling that President Richard Nixon's *executive privilege* did not protect the tape recordings of his conversations in the White House led to his resignation.

3 *Fletcher v. Peck* (1810) established that the principle of judicial review also extended to state law and the actions of state officials. Furthermore, the protections – such as the prohibition of 'unreasonable searches and seizures' and 'cruel and unusual punishments' – included in the Bill of Rights were progressively extended. They were initially understood to constrain the federal government alone. However, during the course of the twentieth

---

Box 4.1   Factors influencing Supreme Court rulings

Attempts to assess the factors shaping Supreme Court rulings must inevitably be speculative. Although both majority and minority opinions are published, and sometimes read from the bench, the Court's proceedings are confidential. Nonetheless, some tentative conclusions can be drawn.

A number of influences are evident. Firstly, there are internal factors. As has been noted, the justices regard their role in legal, not political terms. They are bound by the wording of the Constitution. They are guided by past precedent – the principle of *stare decisis*. For example, the 1973 *Roe* ruling was shaped, in part, by an earlier judgement, *Griswald v. Connecticut* (1965), which established that the Constitution incorporated an implied right to privacy. The justices' understanding the judicial process is also important. Whereas some are strict constructionists, others argue that the Constitution should be interpreted and reapplied to twentieth-century conditions. Federal judges, they argue, should be more concerned with the spirit than the text of the Constitution.

External factors should, however, also be considered. Although members of the Court are not subject to election, and are therefore sealed off from the other branches of government and public opinion, they do appear to be swayed by wider opinion.

1 When a case is being considered, interest groups submit *amicus curiae* briefs to the Court. These argue in support of a particular outcome. In 1978, the *Bakke* case, which considered the constitutionality of affirmative action, attracted 58 such briefs (McKeever 1997: 83).

2 The Administration also 'lobbies' the Court. It is represented by the Office of

---

century – in cases such as *Wolf v. Colorado* (1949) and *Louisiana ex rel. Francis v. Resweber* (1947) – the Supreme Court increasingly asserted that they also limited and bound the actions of the states. The Bill of Rights was thereby 'nationalised' (McKeever 1997: 31–2).

4 The Court's judgements can only be reversed through the process of constitutional amendment. This requires a *supermajority* in Congress and among the states. As a consequence, only five amendments have been passed so as to overrule Supreme Court decisions (Wetterau 1995: 201).

5 The Court has immense authority and prestige. Although the southern states obstructed the implementation of the *Brown* ruling, the Court's right to decide on constitutional questions is almost always unchallenged even by those who disagree with its decisions.

6 Because Supreme Court judges serve for life, or until they chose to retire, they are – in contrast with those who are subject to periodic re-election – protected from the pressures of public opinion. They can therefore make rulings that are profoundly unpopular with some groups, such as the *Brown* or *Roe* judgements, without fear of electoral consequences.

the Solicitor General, which is located in the Department of Justice. The Office will ask the Court to review particular cases, and also itself submits *amicus curiae* briefs. It has a high success rate, both because its staff will have more expertise than other litigants and because they have a relatively close working relationship with the Court. When, during the Reagan years, *amicus curiae* briefs were submitted, the Court concurred with the opinion stated in them in 67.5 per cent of cases (Ragsdale 1996: 434).

3 The Court has shifted its ground in response to changes in the public mood. In 1942, it backed the internment of Japanese-Americans as a necessary wartime measure. The *Brown* ruling (1954) should be seen against a background in which the armed forces had already been integrated and groupings such as the NAACP had begun to campaign against segregation. Similarly, *Roe v. Wade* (1973) emerged at a time when the women's movement and feminist arguments were beginning to gain acceptance. The impact of public opinion – particularly where there is a broad consensus around an issue – has been acknowledged by Justice Sandra Day O'Connor. In her 2003 book, *The Majesty of the Law*, she noted that courts: 'are mainly reactive institutions . . . change comes principally from attitudinal shifts in the population at large . . . rare indeed is the legal victory – in court or legislature – that is not a careful byproduct of an emerging social consensus' (quoted in Greenhouse 2000).

References and further reading

Greenhouse, L. (2003), 'Context and the court', *New York Times*, 25 June.

7 The federal courts have a wide range of remedies available to correct wrongs. One federal judge ordered that improvements be made to prisons in Alabama, at a cost of $40 million per annum, arguing that the conditions in them constituted a 'cruel and unusual' form of punishment prohibited under the Eighth Amendment.

8 The federal courts also play an important role in American life because America is a *litigious* society. Americans readily resort to the courts to resolve conflicts and to protect what they regard as their rights. Many issues are taken to court, providing countless opportunities for judicial decision-making. Even in the first half of the nineteenth century, Alexis de Tocqueville remarked: 'Hardly any question arises in the United States that is not resolved sooner or later into a judicial question' (quoted in Bickel 1986: 199).

9 The courts offer an access point for interest groups. Groups that have failed to achieve their goals in the political arena will frequently seek to achieve them in the courts. Interest groups have, furthermore, backed individuals who have acted as petitioners and have brought cases. The civil rights

movement and the pro-choice groups have both used this strategy success-fully. When not directly involved, interest groups will also submit *amicus curiae* ('friend of the court') briefs to the courts in support of a particular ruling. In some years, there have been over three thousand of these (Wetterau 1995: 206).

10   As government has become more and more involved in every aspect of life, the range of issues considered by the federal courts has been extended. They have, in particular, been increasingly involved in judging the consti-tutionality of growing government intervention in the economy.

11   Other institutions may have avoided resolving particularly difficult contro-versies, and they thereby assign responsibility for the issue to the courts. When the two houses of Congress and President Clinton could not agree how to proceed with a balanced budget amendment to the Constitution, it was worded in a loose and imprecise way so as to maximise support for the measure. If it had been added to the Constitution – and it failed to gain the necessary two-thirds majority in both chambers – it would undoubtedly have had to be considered by the courts.

Constraints on power

Although some observers argue that the federal courts play an immensely influential role, others emphasise the limits and constraints on their powers. They are limited in their ability to enforce their rulings. As Alexander Hamilton was to assert in *The Federalist Papers*, they are – in practice – dependent upon the compliance of those whom the ruling affects or the backing of the executive branch: 'The judiciary . . . has no influence over either the sword or the purse . . . and can take no active resolution whatever. It may truly be said to have neither FORCE nor WILL, but merely judgment; and must ultimately depend upon the aid of the executive arm even for the efficacy of its judgments' (Hamilton 2002). The events that followed *Brown v. Board of Education* in 1954 confirm the validity of Hamilton's critique. Although the ruling called for the desegregation of public schooling, the process of implementation required the use of troops. There was hostility from white crowds, and the state authorities in the south pursued a strategy of non-compliance. In 1957, President Eisenhower had to send troops to the Central High School in Little Rock, Arkansas, so as to ensure that nine black students could attend classes along-side whites. Segregation and the Jim Crow laws only came to an end once Congress agreed to the 1964 Civil Rights Act and the 1965 Voting Rights Act.

The Supreme Court has no power of initiative, and cannot consider a hypo-thetical legal question. It is an appeals court, and can therefore only react to cases that are submitted to it. It cannot identify a law or action that it considers uncon-stitutional and express an opinion. Instead, it must await an appellant with 'standing' who claims that his or her constitutional rights have been denied.

Congress has powers over the federal courts. It has the ability to alter the number of judges, both on the Supreme Court and in the lower courts. Although the number of Supreme Court Justices has been stable at nine since 1869, there have been substantial increases in the overall number of federal judges. Congress can also broaden or restrict the jurisdiction of lower courts and create new courts. Furthermore, although it cannot circumvent the requirements of the Constitution, if Congress feels that the laws that it has passed have been misinterpreted by the courts, it can amend its own statutes so as to clarify its intentions and wishes.

Congress also has the power of impeachment, but this is very rarely used. Since the founding of the US, sixty-one federal judges have been investigated, Of these thirteen were impeached, and seven subsequently convicted. Furthermore, in almost all these cases, Congress was responding to accusations of personal misconduct. Its actions were not a challenge to judicial rulings. In 1989, for example, two US district judges were impeached, convicted, and – as a consequence – removed from office. Judge Alcee Hastings of Florida was charged with perjury and conspiring to obtain a bribe. Walter L. Nixon of Mississippi was charged with lying to a federal grand jury.

Although the process is fraught with political difficulty, Congress and the states can initiate a constitutional amendment if they oppose a ruling by the Supreme Court. In 1895 the Supreme Court declared a federal income tax unconstitutional. The Sixteenth Amendment was then ratified in 1913, specifically authorising such a tax.

The Court cannot, in the long run, disregard public opinion. Its legitimacy depends upon its popular credibility. In 1972, in *Furman v. Georgia*, the Court declared all existing death penalty laws unconstitutional, largely because of the arbitrary, random and chance way in which the death penalty was imposed. Chief Justice Warren Burger concluded from the *Furman* ruling that capital punishment had been abolished in the US (McKeever 1997: 145–46). However, there is widespread backing for the death penalty in the US. This led many state legislatures to pass revised death penalty legislation that had a less random character. In *Gregg v. Georgia* (1976), the Court retreated from its original position and accepted the constitutionality of the amended legislation. The overwhelming majority of states now include the death penalty in their statutes.

In some instances the judges exercise a degree of self-restraint. They are reluctant to enter 'the political thicket'. As appointees, they should, in most circumstances, defer to the elected branches of government. According to rules laid down by Justice Louis D. Brandeis in 1936, the Court should interpret a statute so as to avoid ruling it unconstitutional 'even if a serious doubt of constitutionality is raised' (Witt 1993: 216). Notions of self-restraint have been particularly evident in times of war and during periods of national crisis. During the First World War, Congress passed legislation prescribing fines and imprisonment for opponents of the War – principally socialists – who sought to interfere with the recruitment of troops or campaigned against the war effort. Despite claims that such measures contravened the First Amendment's assurance of free speech, Supreme Court Justice Oliver Wendell Holmes wrote that 'in many places and in ordinary times' the Socialists would be within their constitutional rights. But the Bill of Rights does not protect words creating a 'clear and present danger' of 'evils that Congress has a right to prevent'. Eighty years later – in the aftermath of the 11 September attacks – Congress passed the Patriot Act, which, critics asserted, curtailed individual liberties. However, there was an expectation that if it came before the Supreme Court it would pass muster under the now established doctrine of 'clear and present danger'.

The Courts are constrained by precedent. Decisions are guided by previous rulings or those reached in the lower courts. This is known as the principle of *stare decisis*. The importance attached to precedent is evident in the Supreme Court's reluctance to overturn *Roe v. Wade*, even though a majority of current judges on the Court would almost certainly not have decided the case in the same way as the Burger Court.

Federal courts deal with only a relatively small proportion of cases. They consider about 2 per cent of all the cases brought in the US. Most criminal cases involve breaches of state rather than federal law.

Judicial philosophies

On what basis should judges make their decisions? There are two schools of thought about the principles that should guide the way in which judges reach their rulings. These are known as 'judicial activism' – which is broadly associated with liberalism – and 'judicial restraint', which is tied to conservative thinking.

Judicial activism

One of the most famous judges associated with judicial activism was Thurgood Marshall (1967–91). A leading contemporary academic advocate is Professor Laurence Tribe. The school is sometimes called non-interpretivist. Supporters talk of a 'living Constitution' that can adapt over time without requiring amendment.

Those associated with judicial activism interpret the Constitution through loose constructionism. They suggest that the federal courts should apply the spirit of the Constitution to the modern era and – where the elected branches of government and the state governments appear to have failed – address social needs. In some accounts, judges should go beyond the mere interpretation of the Constitution. They have a role to play as independent 'trustees' serving society and, in particular, oppressed minorities. The advocates of judicial activism put forward five principal arguments.

1 Justice rather than textual fidelity is the proper basis for determining what is right and wrong. The basic purpose of the courts is 'to do right'.
2 The courts should provide a check on government. The actions of the president and Congress – in, for example, condoning and sometimes endorsing segregation – have at times been both flawed and unjust. This has been because the executive and legislative branches of government have to think of electoral considerations. It is the responsibility of the Court to compensate for the failures of elective institutions.
3 The federal courts have an anti-majoritarian purpose. Judges have a particular responsibility to protect the poor and minorities, because such groups have little political influence, and unless the courts take action, their interests will be neglected.
4 Decisions should be measured in terms of their outcomes and consequences. The methods by which the decision is reached are less important. The *Brown* ruling should be celebrated, because it led to the desegregation of schools.
5 Although some judges and legal scholars argue that rulings should be based on the doctrine of *original intent*, and assessing the thinking of those who wrote the Constitution and the later amendments that were adopted, supporters of judicial activism assert that intent cannot be identified. The Founders are dead, and furthermore, legislators often have inherently contradictory aims and purposes.

Judicial restraint

Others believe that the courts should not over-reach themselves. They point out that the founders of the nation believed that the role of the Supreme Court should be limited. Thomas Jefferson warned that otherwise 'the Constitution . . . [would be] a mere thing of wax in the hands of the judiciary which they may twist and shape into any form they please'. He also declared: 'To consider the judges as the ultimate arbiters of all constitutional questions [is] a very dangerous doctrine indeed, and one which would place us under the despotism of an oligarchy. . . . The Constitution has erected no such single tribunal' (quoted in Barton 2002).

Advocates of judicial restraint argue that the courts should simply interpret the words and phrases in the Constitution. Judges should adhere – as closely as possible – to the literal text. There is a deep suspicion towards those who seek out the 'penumbras and emanations' of the Constitution that Justice William O. Douglas discerned in establishing a Constitutional right of privacy. Some also assert that the role of the Court is, where the text of the Constitution is unclear, to identify the original intent of the founders of the Constitution or the legislators who introduced later amendments. One source would, for example, be the speeches of the founders at the Philadelphia convention. Furthermore, it is said, judges have no popular mandate and – so long as policy-makers remain within the parameters of the Constitution – should therefore defer to the decisions of the elected branches of government and to the states. The most prominent contemporary advocate of judicial restraint is Robert Bork, whom the Senate refused to confirm as a member of the Supreme Court bench in 1987. Supporters of restraint emphasise six arguments.

1 As the federal judiciary is unelected, judicial activism assigns power to an elite institution which is not democratically accountable to the people. It thereby takes power from democratically elected institutions. Critics of activism talk of an 'imperial judiciary'.
2 Justices who base their rulings on judicial activism are inevitably imposing their own values. However, in many cases, their beliefs and preferences are unrepresentative of American opinion. For example, the Burger Court ruled against capital punishment in *Furman v. Georgia* (1972). At the time, however, opinion polling suggested that over 80 per cent of Americans supported the death penalty. Critics of the 'right to privacy' which formed the basis of *Griswold v. Connecticut* (1965) – which struck down a state law prohibiting the prescription and use of contraceptives – and *Roe v. Wade* (1973) assert that it has no basis in the Constitution and was based instead on the personal wishes of those serving on the Supreme Court at the time.
3 Judicial activism has expanded the number and scope of constitutional rights. The Court rulings that created these rights are applied across the entire nation. However, the US is a diverse country with many different local and regional traditions. Attitudes towards abortion, for example, differ between the larger cities, the suburbs and more rural areas (Table 4.5). However, by imposing absolute rulings that apply across the US, the Supreme Court does not allow for regional and local diversity.

Table 4.5 *Attitudes towards abortion, 1994 (% of population)*

	Large cities	Suburbs	Towns and rural areas
Strong agree / agree	50.9	51.0	28.8
Neither agree nor disagree	8.2	8.5	13.1
Strongly disagree / disagree	40.9	40.6	58.2

Question text: 'Do you agree or disagree . . . A pregnant woman should be able to obtain a legal abortion for any reason whatsoever, if she chooses not to have the baby.'
Source: adapted from General Social Survey (2003), *1972–2000 Cumulative Datafile –
ABCHOOSE / XNORCSIZ*, www.icpsr.umich.edu:8080/GSS/rnd1998/merged/cdbk/abchoose.htm.

4 The courts lack the specialised knowledge or experience to make decisions. Federal judges have to rule on very complex cases, such as school administration or environmental protection, which involve subjects about which they have little or no knowledge. They are therefore making judgements without fully understanding the consequences. As Judge Robert Bork has argued, judicial activism has led the courts towards the making of social policy. However, he claims, this is not only an illegitimate usurpation of

power, but the judges have also imposed poorly devised and ill-considered forms of policy.

5 Activism reduces the credibility of the federal courts in the eyes of the public. The legitimacy of the courts depends on the acceptance of their rulings by the people. When decisions are made that the public does not accept – such as *Furman v. Georgia* (1972), which struck down all the existing death penalty laws – this undermines the legitimacy of government institutions.

6 Legal systems are structured around stability, dependability and continuity. When judges overturn earlier decisions or precedents that have been established and disregard the principle of *stare decisis*, they undermine confidence in constitutional law. The Supreme Court has reversed its own judgements on at least 150 occasions (Wetterau 1995: 200).

Judicial activism and restraint are frequently described as liberal and conservative theories respectively. However, although this description corresponds with the realities of the Warren and Burger eras, it can be misleading. During the mid-1930s – at the time when the Supreme Court struck down core components of the New Deal – it was liberals rather than conservatives who favoured restraint. Liberals claimed that Franklin Roosevelt had a popular mandate for the New Deal economic polices, and the Court should not seek to abrogate the people's verdict. For their part, conservatives emphasised the right – and duty – of the Court to defy the other branches of government.

In the 1990s and at the beginning of the new century, there were again suggestions that the Court was characterised by notions of conservative activism. The Rehnquist Court has not, some note, shrunk from challenging the authority of the legislative and executive branches of government. Indeed, Jeffrey Rosen compares the Rehnquist and Warren courts, arguing that both sought the aggrandisement of judicial power: 'Both combine haughty declarations of judicial supremacy with contempt for the competing views of the political branches' (Rosen 2000: 16). Furthermore, for the Court's critics, the conservative majority has substituted its own prejudices for the rule of law. From this perspective, the 5–4 ruling in *Bush v. Gore* (2000) exemplified these trends.

The *Bush v. Gore* ruling was issued six weeks after the 2000 presidential election. There had been a very close result in Florida – upon which the outcome of the entire nationwide election depended – and a bitter dispute about the validity of some of the votes that had been cast in the state. In its ruling, the Supreme Court cited the Fourteenth Amendment and ruled that the manual recount of votes that had been undertaken in some counties represented a form of unequal treatment, since the validity of those votes rested, at times, on a subjective assessment of a 'chad' (or punched hole in the voting card). Five of the justices also asserted that shortage of time precluded further recounts. Although the Court's supporters argue that the judgement simply applied the Fourteenth Amendment, critics assert that it was an overtly political decision that handed the presidency to the Republicans. As John Paul Stevens – who was, ironically, a Republican appointee – remarked in a dissenting opinion that was also signed by Stephen Breyer and Ruth Bader Ginsburg: 'One thing, however, is certain. Although we may never know with complete certainty the identity of the winner of this year's Presidential election, the identity of the loser is perfectly clear. It is the nation's confidence in the judge as an impartial guardian of the rule of law' (quoted in Greenhouse 2000).

Activism and restraint are not, then, the property of liberals and conservatives respectively. For much of the Rehnquist era, conservatives have backed judicial activism in cases involving states' rights. However, they have opposed the activism of the Court when it has addressed individual rights. Many, for example, were very critical of rulings such as *Reno v. the American Civil Liberties Union (1997) and Ashcroft v. The Free Speech Coalition* (2002), which prohibited attempts to restrict the availability of pornography on the internet. At the same time, liberals have condemned the activism of the Court in cases involving states' rights, but have endorsed it in matters concerning individual rights.

Politicial or judicial?

Should the Supreme Court be regarded as a judicial body with a significant impact on politics, or a political institution that has a judicial edge to its deliberations? In other words, are the judges merely 'politicians in robes'?

Robert McKeever argues that the Court is a 'political institution whose legal characteristics make it different from other political institutions' (1995: viii). Richard Hodder-Williams talks in similar terms (Hodder-Williams 1992). Five points can be used to support their claims. Firstly, the judiciary is involved in the political process. Pressure groups lobby the federal courts by backing litigants or by submitting *amicus curiae* briefs urging the judges to resolve a case in a particular way. Secondly, the Justices are involved in bargaining processes between themselves both in deciding which cases should be heard and in agreeing a ruling. Bargaining is an inherently political process. Thirdly, mid-century judicial activism and theories of loose constructionism – which are based upon a flexible and expansive understanding of the Constitution – led the Justices towards an emphasis upon the outcome of a ruling and away from the text of the Constitution. If – many conservatives suggest – the courts work in this way, they are making public policy. Fourthly, by rulings on issues such as abortion or police powers, the courts have set the political agenda, compelling candidates and office-holders to respond. Fifthly, as Sandra Day O'Connor has acknowledged, the courts – like legislatures – respond to shifts and changes in public opinion. Lastly, many critics assert, the judges vote along political lines. *Bush v. Gore* (2000) is often cited as an illustration. Most of the Republican nominees on the Court voted to end the recounts in Florida, thereby awarding the presidency to George W. Bush.

However, Richard Maidment emphasises the judicial and legal characteristics of the Court: 'it cannot avoid a political role. But that does not mean that judges are politicians' (Maidment and Tappin 1990: 40). It is a court in so far as it can only act through litigation. Secondly, decisions are often determined by technical and legal factors. Thirdly, precedence constrains the rulings that are made. Fourthly, the spirit or ethos of the court is non-political. Fifthly, the judges do not act or perceive themselves as politicians. Nor – in contrast with at least some legislators – do they follow popular opinion. Because they are appointed for life, they are largely 'insulated' from the other branches of government and public pressures. Sixthly, judges are compelled to distinguish between their personal preferences and the requirements of the legal process. In June 1989, for example, the Supreme Court ruled that the burning of the US flag as a form of political protest was a constitutional right under the First Amendment. Laws in 48 states prohibiting flag-burning were thus judged unconstitutional. The majority in *Texas v. Johnson* included two conservatives, Antonin Scalia and Anthony Kennedy. They undoubtedly regarded the burning of the flag as an act of wanton disloyalty. However, they felt that, given the wording of the Constitution, they had little choice but to allow such actions.

Conclusion

Chapter 3 noted that the US Constitution had weathered all the upheavals and transformations of the past two centuries in a basically unaltered form. The Supreme Court provides a reason why it could do this. The Court's ability to reinterpret concepts such as equality ensured that although many of the words in the Constitution remained unchanged, they were understood and applied very differently. In the 1890s, the Court granted constitutional legitimacy to segregation and, sixty years later, to desegregation. Although the legal methodology underlying this shift in thinking has continued to attract criticism from strict constructionists, the Court thereby gave the Constitution an adaptability that enabled it to survive social, political and economic change.

References and further reading

Barton D. (2002), *Wallbuilders – Impeachment of Federal Judges*, www.wallbuilders.com/resources/search/detail.php?ResourceID=69.

Berger, R. (1997), *Government by Judiciary: The Transformation of the Fourteenth Amendment*, Indianapolis, IN, Liberty Fund.

Bickel, A. M. (1986), *The Least Dangerous Branch: The Supreme Court at the Bar of Politics*, New Haven, CT, Yale University Press.

Greenhouse, L. (2000), 'By single vote, justices end recount, blocking Gore after 5-week struggle', *The New York Times*, 13 December.

Hamilton, A. (2002), *Federalist No. 78 – The Judiciary Department*, www.foundingfathers.info/federalistpapers/fed78.htm.

Hinkson Craig, B. and D. M. O'Brien (1993), *Abortion and American Politics*, Chatham, Chatham House.

Hodder-Williams, R. (1992), 'Six definitions of political and the US Supreme Court', *British Journal of Political Science*, 22:1.

Maidment, R. and M. Tappin (1990), *American Politics Today*, Manchester, Manchester University Press.

McKeever, R. (1995), *Raw Judicial Power? The Supreme Court and American Society*, Manchester, Manchester University Press.

McKeever, R. (1997), *The United States Supreme Court: A Political and Legal Analysis*, Manchester, Manchester University Press.

Ohio State University (1999), *Study Finds Unprecedented Delay in Appointing Federal Judges*, 25 April, www.acs.ohio-state.edu/units/research/archive/fedjudg htm8/ 25/99.

Ragsdale, L. (1996), *Vital Statistics on the Presidency: Washington to Clinton*, Washington DC, Congressional Quarterly Inc.

Roberts, R. S. (1995), *Clarence Thomas and the Tough Love Crowd: Counterfeit Heroes and Unhappy Truths*, New York, New York University Press.

Rosen, J. (2000), 'Pride and prejudice', *The New Republic*, 10 and 17 July, 4,460 and 4,461, 16–18.

Thernstrom, S. and A. Thernstrom (1997), *America in Black and White: One Nation Indivisible*, New York, Simon and Schuster.

Tindall, G. B. and D. E. Shi (1989), *America: A Narrative History*, New York, W. W. Norton and Company.

Wetterau, B. (1995), *Desk Reference on American Government*, Washington DC, Congressional Quarterly Inc.

Witt, E. (1993), *Congressional Quarterly's Guide to the US Supreme Court*, Washington DC, CQ Press.

Supreme Court websites

The Court's website is at www.supremecourtus.gov/. However, the text of US Supreme Court rulings and opinions can be found at www.law.cornell.edu/ supct/.

For more general information about all the US federal courts – including the US Supreme Court – see www.uscourts.gov/. The website answers frequently asked questions (FAQs), and provides a news service, links to related websites and a listing of publications for further research.

5

Congress

The US Congress is, according to the Constitution, the first branch of government. It has a *bicameral* structure and its powers include the passage of legislation, declarations of war, the ratification of treaties, the formulation of the annual budget, consent to major political appointments, and the oversight of executive departments and agencies. Although the president can – at times – play a pivotal role in shaping Congressional decisions, it is always far from certain that his thinking will prevail.

This chapter will consider a number of questions. What are the powers of Congress? How effective is the oversight process? What are the differences between the House of Representatives and the Senate? How are laws made? What determines congressional voting behaviour? How important is party leadership? Should we think, as some argue, in terms of 'two Congresses' that play contrasting political roles and should be judged in different ways? Does Congress require reform?

Congress and the Constitution

The character of Congress – and its powers – were established and shaped by Article I of the Constitution, subsequent Supreme Court rulings, and the tensions between the different branches of government.

1 Congress is the national legislature and, as such, it is responsible for the making of federal law. The legislative role of Congress stems from the powers assigned to it by the Constitution. There are *enumerated* powers, such as the control of trade 'among the several States', the regulation of foreign trade, and the raising of an army. However, as Chapter 4 established, the elastic character of some clauses in the Constitution – such as the 'necessary and proper' clause in Article I, Section 8, allowed the Supreme Court to establish that Congress also had *implied* powers (see p. 60). Furthermore, the scope of

certain powers specified in the Constitution – such as the power to regulate trade and business that crosses state lines – or 'interstate commerce' – has been extended. This has been partly because society has changed in character. In the late eighteenth century, most forms of trade and commerce were small-scale in character. They served a local market. A modern economy rests instead upon national and global markets. Most contemporary firms – beyond the most basic forms of small business – produce, distribute and sell their products across the nation or internationally. At the same time, another factor 'stretched' the interstate commerce clause. For about sixty years, between the 1930s and the 1990s, the Supreme Court understood the clause in loose and expansive terms, enabling Congress to regulate almost every aspect of economic and social life.

Congress not only makes law, but also has the ability to pass resolutions. Concurrent resolutions are used to make or amend rules or express Congressional sentiments. A joint resolution, passed by both houses, and signed by the president – such as the 1964 Gulf of Tonkin resolution that provided the pretext for large-scale US intervention in Vietnam – has the force of law. Congress can, furthermore, propose constitutional amendments, although, to be adopted, they require a two-thirds majority in both houses and the assent of at least three-quarters of the states. In March 1997, an amendment requiring a balanced federal budget – so that expenditure would have to match revenue – was killed in the Senate by one vote.

2   Congress has the *power of the purse*. Article I, Section 8 of the Constitution specifically empowered Congress to raise taxes and impose duties. Furthermore, it asserted that bills 'for raising revenue' should originate in the House of Representatives, although they must – like other legislation – also be passed by the Senate. The budget is now, as Robert Singh has noted, of pivotal political and economic importance: 'The budget is the supreme political document, determining national priorities, shaping congressional and election debates, and allocating benefits to national, state and local interests' (Singh 2003: 249). The president submits a proposed budget to Congress at the beginning of each year. It covers the coming Fiscal Year that begins on 1 October. His proposals are drawn up by the Office of Management and Budget (OMB) within the White House on the basis of expenditure plans and projections submitted during the preceding year by the departments, agencies and bureaux within the executive branch. Once under consideration within Congress, the budget is shaped by competing pressures and interests. The Senate and House Appropriations Committees and their associated subcommittees play a particularly significant role. The budget is broken down into thirteen spending – or appropriations – bills. Each of these bills corresponds to one subcommittee on the Appropriations Committees. Such is the power of these subcommittees – in so far as they decide how much government funding is allocated to, for example, defence, agriculture, or urban development – that the House subcommittee chairmen have become traditionally

known as the 'Cardinals'. As Paul Hilliar records: 'Mostly unknown outside of Washington Beltway, these "Cardinals" control the flow of hundreds of billions of dollars, which makes them some of the most powerful men in America' (Hilliar 2002).

3 As the 1946 Legislative Reorganization Act confirmed, Congress has *oversight* powers. It reviews and monitors the executive departments and agencies that constitute the federal bureaucracy. Oversight or 'watchdog' work is undertaken through Congress's committee structure. Many of the standing committees that have legislative responsibilities also 'shadow' a particular executive department. Others oversee a less defined area of policy. The Senate, for example, has an armed services committee, a foreign relations committee, and an agriculture committee. The House too has an agriculture committee, but also a small business and science committee. While the standing committees exist on a permanent basis, select committees may also be created by either chamber or jointly on an *ad hoc* basis, so as to look at matters that fall outside the jurisdiction of the standing committees or in order to conduct a specific investigation.

Oversight takes a number of forms. It includes formal and informal communication with administrators, committee hearings, the evaluation of a particular programme by congressional support agencies, or a requirement that an agency issue a report outlining and explaining aspects of its work.

Observers are divided about the extent to which members of Congress pursue their oversight responsibilities and the effectiveness of their work. Peter Woll suggests that scrutiny of the executive branch offers relatively little to the individual members of Congress, the district or state that they represent, and their chances of re-election (1985: 146). In the same vein John Hart concludes that oversight is 'negligible'. Congress, he asserts, 'has neither the will nor the interest nor the incentive to reverse a half century of significant institutional development in American government' (1995: 237). There have also been assertions that partisanship plays a role, and that members of Congress are reluctant to subject a president who is drawn from their own party to extensive or critical scrutiny. Although he argues that Congress regards its 'watchdog' role in serious terms, Ross English notes that: 'too many committees approach oversight with a "fire-fighter" approach, responding when a problem with the executive branch comes to light, rather than maintaining a more systematic style of surveillance' (English 2003: 121). However, Joel D. Aberbach argues that oversight work became much more important from the mid-1970s onwards (1990: 19, 72). As public unease about the federal government grew, the political 'payoffs' for oversight work increased. Some members of Congress sought to eliminate waste. Others attempted to highlight policy failures in response to disquiet among those they represented. Furthermore, oversight activity has at times made a significant impact upon the executive branch and the political process.

- From 1965 to 1970, the Senate Foreign Relations Committee – under Senator J. William Fulbright – subjected the White House's military operations in South-east Asia to serious, and increasingly bitter, criticism.
- The Senate Select Committee on Presidential Campaign Activities, which was chaired by Senator Sam Ervin, played a pivotal role – along with newspapers such as the *Washington Post* – in uncovering the Watergate scandal.
- In 1983, the head of the Environmental Protection Agency was censured and thereby compelled to resign after refusing to supply Congress with documents.
- In 1987–88, select committees drawn from both the House and the Senate unravelled the Iran–Contra scandal. Colonel Oliver North – who had worked for the National Security Council – was among those compelled to provide testimony.

The ability of Congress to oversee and influence the actions of the bureaucracy was strengthened by the *legislative veto*. From 1932 onwards, legislation often included a provision that particular decisions and actions undertaken by the executive branch should be referred back to Congress. The first legislative veto permitted President Herbert Hoover to reorganise the executive agencies, but established a ninety-day delay before any changes would take effect. During this period, the legislation allowed Congress to veto the organisational changes he had made. The overall effect of the legislative veto was to give Congressional committees authority over day-to-day decisions by sections of the executive branch. In the 1950s, for example, a Congressional committee – the Joint Committee on Atomic Energy – decided where the Atomic Energy Commission should locate power stations and what forms of technology would be adopted.

In June 1983, however, the US Supreme Court declared that the legislative veto was unconstitutional. In *Immigration and Naturalization Service v. Chadha* the Court found that by giving Congress a power that was not subject to presidential concurrence, this form of veto breached the separation of powers. However, the overall impact of *Chadha* appears to have been limited. The status of laws passed between 1932 and 1983 that included a legislative veto remains uncertain. They have not been repealed and, furthermore, as Louis Fisher argues, more than 140 laws passed since 1983 have included a legislative veto (*Congressional Quarterly* 1997: 18).

4 The Senate has 'advice and consent' powers. It can confirm or reject the appointment of senior federal officers such as Cabinet Secretaries, federal judges, and Ambassadors. The Senate's 'advice and consent' powers also extend to the ratification of treaties signed by the president with foreign powers. Under the Constitution, these require a two-thirds majority. Although the president generally gains the assent of the Senate to his appointments and proposed treaties, there have been important exceptions. These are recorded in Chapter 6.

5 Congress has the power to remove leading officials of the executive, includ-

ing the president. However, *impeachment* proceedings that may – if there is a conviction – lead to removal from office have only ever become a consideration in the most exceptional circumstances. The process begins with a vote of the House to conduct an inquiry. The results of the inquiry, undertaken by the House Judiciary Committee, are presented to the full House. If the official is *impeached* by the House (and this requires only a majority vote), a trial is then conducted before the Senate. The Senators constitute a jury. A two-thirds majority (67 votes) is required if a public official is to be removed from office. The House of Representatives has only seriously considered the impeachment of eighteen officials since the founding of the US, and only seven of these were convicted.

A president can only be impeached for 'high crimes and misdemeanours'. The first president to be impeached was Andrew Johnson in 1868. In the aftermath of the Civil War, radical Republicans felt that he was over-sympathetic to the south, although Johnson's dismissal of his Secretary of War – in contravention of the Tenure of Office Act – offered the pretext. However, Johnson was acquitted. His accusers failed by a single vote to gain the required two-thirds majority in the Senate. In 1974, impeachment proceedings were initiated against President Richard Nixon, although he resigned before the matter was considered on the floor of the House. Nixon had been accused of obstructing justice by hiding White House involvement in an illegal break-in at Democratic Party offices. In December 1998, the House voted to impeach President Bill Clinton following claims that the President had – through his alleged sexual conduct and his later actions – committed acts of perjury and obstructed justice. The Senate eventually acquitted Clinton by 55 to 45 and 50 to 50 on the two charges.

6   The Constitution endows Congress with the power to declare war (Article I, Section 8). However, while US forces have been sent into action much more often, Congress has only declared war in five wars (see p. 104). As a *Congressional Quarterly* study records: 'Presidents have ordered the armed forces to protect settlers from Indians, repel bands of foreign outlaws, punish nations and groups for belligerent or criminal behavior, rescue US citizens abroad, support friendly governments and train their armies, fight pirates and terrorists, warn potential enemies against taking aggressive action, deliver humanitarian aid, and secure disputed lands' (*Congressional Quarterly* 1997: 204). Congress sought to constrain the president with the War Powers Resolution of 1973. This stipulated that Congressional approval must be given for medium- and long-term military actions overseas.

Comparing chambers

The US legislature is *bicameral*. In other words, it has two chambers. There are a number of similarities between them. Both senators and members of the House devote extensive resources to addressing the problems and concerns of

Box 5.1   Congressional standing committees, 2003

House of Representatives
Agriculture
Appropriations
Armed Services
Budget
Economic and the Workforce
Energy and Commerce
Financial Services
Government Reform
House Administration
International Relations
Judiciary
Resources
Rules
Science
Small Business
Standards of Official Conduct
Transportation and Infrastructure
Veterans' Affairs
Ways and Means

Senate
Agriculture, Nutrition, and Forestry
Appropriations
Armed Services
Banking, Housing, and Urban Affairs
Budget
Commerce, Science, and Transportation
Energy and Natural Resources
Environment and Public Works
Finance
Foreign Relations
Governmental Affairs
Health, Education, Labor, and Pensions
Judiciary
Rules and Administration
Small Business and Entrepreneurship
Veterans' Affairs

Source: adapted from US House of Representatives (2003), *Committee Offices*, www.house.gov/house/CommitteeWWW.html and US Senate (2003), *Committees*, www.senate .gov/pagelayout/committees/d_three_sections_with_teasers/committees_home.htm.

constituents. All legislation must be passed by the House and the Senate. Both chambers have oversight responsibilities. Furthermore, the working life of both chambers is organised around a committee structure. Standing committees exist on a permanent basis, and consider both legislation and the actions of the executive branch. Some Senate committees also hold hearings and make recommendations when the president puts forward nominees for either the administration or the federal courts. In 2003, if joint committees are excluded, there were nineteen committees in the House and seventeen committees in the Senate. Each committee has a large number of affiliated subcommittees.

Both houses of Congress can draw upon the support of an extensive number of staff. An average member of the House has a staff of fourteen. A Senator has – on average – 34 aides. Most are involved in the everyday work of an office, such as the answering of letters. Others advise on policy matters. Some are also employed in district and state offices. Congress itself employs about 26,000 people. They mainly staff the different committees. There are also specialists working in the Congressional Budget Office (CBO), which monitors and evaluates the annual budget. The Congressional Research Service (CRS) provides an independent assessment of all legislation. The General Accounting Office (GAO) investigates the executive branch to ensure honesty and efficiency

However, although there are similarities, there are also important differences between the chambers. The House of Representatives and the Senate have their own distinct identities. They differ in their terms of office, constituencies, size, minimal qualifications, rules, partisanship and collective identity. There are often differences of opinion, and there can be competition for power, between them.

The House of Representatives

The House is directly elected by the people in single-member constituencies drawn up on the basis of population. Those who serve have to be twenty-five years old or more, and have been a US citizen for at least seven years. Although the number is not specified in the Constitution, and is determined instead by law, the House has, since 1911, had 435 members. Each represents – following the 2000 census – an average population of 646,952. The House is a large and heterogeneous chamber. Its members face re-election every two years, and they therefore have to be district-oriented. Although members break ranks with their party on particular issues to a much greater extent than in, for example, the British House of Commons, there is – in contrast with the Senate – a sense of *partisanship*.

House rules are detailed, formal and comprehensive. House members tend to specialise in a limited number of policy areas and serve on only one or two standing committees. There will almost always be an association between a member's area of specialisation and the district that she or he represents. A Congressman from a rural district would, for example, seek a place on the Agriculture committee.

The size of the institution has tended to give more power to party leaders, and it is thus more centralised. It is a *majoritarian* institution in so far as decision-making is based upon decision-making by a simple majority rather than a shared consensus or a 'super-majority'. Furthermore, the rules of debate in the House have a fairly restrictive character. Amendments, for example, can be ruled out of order if not relevant – or germane – to the bill.

The leader of the majority party in the House takes the post of Speaker. Although the Speaker will often preside, particularly on important occasions, the Speakership is not, in contrast with its British counterpart, a ceremonial role. Instead, the Speaker of the House is an active and influential partisan.

The Senate

The Senate has been, since 1913, directly elected by the people of the different states. Each state elects two Senators, regardless of its size. California has two Senators, representing an estimated population of 34,501,130 in 2001. Wyoming's two Senators speak for only 494,423 people. Therefore, there are – in total – 100 Senators. The senator elected first in a particular state is referred to as the 'senior' Senator. The other is described as the 'junior' senator. If a Senator dies or resigns during his or her term of office, the governor of the state may – in most states – appoint a successor until the next election.

The Constitution stipulates that senators must be thirty years old or more, and have been citizens for nine years or more. One-third are elected every two years for terms of six years. Political change in the Senate, because elections are staggered in this way, is a more gradual and less abrupt process than in the House.

Although the vice-president is – according to Article I of the Constitution – 'president' of the Senate, he takes the chair only if a tied vote seems likely. In these circumstances, he holds a casting vote. The Constitution also allows the appointment of a President *pro tempore*, customarily the majority-party Senator with the longest continuous service. Between 2001 and 2003 – as control switched between the parties – the position was occupied in turn by Strom Thurmond (Republican), Robert Byrd (Democrat) and Ted Stevens (Republican). Although the post is regarded as an important honour – and the President *pro tempore* is third in the line of succession to the Presidency after the vice-president and the Speaker of the House – he is also a committee chairman, and only presides in the Senate on an occasional basis. In practice, the President *pro tempore* appoints junior first-term Senators to preside on a rotating basis throughout the day.

The comparatively small size of the Senate allows for a relatively intimate atmosphere in which friendships and personal relationships develop, many of which stretch across party lines. The Senate see itself as more deliberative and thoughtful than the House. Senators tend to be more concerned with national and international interests and affairs than Congressmen. Their numbers do not allow for specialisation, and Senate members tend to have a more *generalist* approach. They serve on two or three standing committees. The Senate also has fewer formal rules. Senators are, for example, allowed more latitude than members of the House when bills are being considered on the floor of the chamber, and non-germane amendments can be permitted.

The customs of the chamber ensure that each Senator has much more influence than an individual House member. Party pressures are fewer, and the leaders have less leverage. In place of the House's majoritarianism, there is a tradition of consent, co-operation and *individualism*. More is discussed on the Senate floor, and the chamber is less committee-based than the House. In the absence of unanimous consent agreements (see below), its deliberations are often slower. Indeed, a determined Senator can attempt to block legislation by speaking – or threatening to speak – until a bill is dropped, in a process known as a *filibuster*. In 1957 Senator Strom Thurmond, then a committed segregationist, spoke for twenty-four hours and eighteen minutes so as to block a civil rights bill. Under Senate rules, debate can only be curtailed – and a filibuster thus be prevented – if there is a three-fifths majority of the full Senate. This *closure* procedure was introduced in 1917 for legislation and in 1949 for nominations (*New York Times*, 5 June 2003). Eric Schickler has captured the cumulative effect of these rules and traditions: 'Regardless of party, individual senators continue to insist on asserting their prerogatives under the Senate's rules and procedures. In addition to the right of unlimited debate, numerous senators use "holds" (threats of a filibuster) to delay – sometimes indefinitely – legislation and nominations they oppose. When legislation does reach the floor, individual senators typically resist limitation on amendments' (Schickler 2002: 104). Although the House and the Senate have been described as co-equal institutions – and the Constitution shares out responsibilities by assigning the House primacy in considering government finances and the Senate the principal responsibility for foreign affairs – the Senate has greater status. This stems, in part, from the smaller size of the Senate. A Senator usually represents a larger number of people. She or he serves longer terms of office, faces re-election less often, and has a more of a national profile. The Senate can thereby offer a more effective starting-point for those considering a presidential bid. It is significant that a member of the House will give up his or her seat so as to capture a Senate seat. A Senator would not, however, abandon his or her seat in pursuit of a place in the House.

How are laws made?

The legislative process is long, complex and difficult. The overwhelming majority of bills never become law. In 1996, for example, 6,808 bills were introduced, but only 337 were adopted (Davidson and Oleszek 1998: 278). Many proposals are killed off in committee and are never considered by the chamber as a whole.

The bills that survive only emerge in a heavily amended form. A bill has to pass through a seven-stage obstacle course to become law.

1 All bills are initiated or sponsored by members of Congress, who are described as the 'sponsors' of the measure. However, in the modern era, the 'executive communication' often provides a basis for legislative proposals. This term refers to a message or letter from a cabinet secretary, the head of an agency, or the President himself. Many of these 'communications' follow on from the President's State of the Union address. The chairman or the ranking minority member of the appropriate committee – the most senior member of the minority party on that committee – customarily introduces the bill.

   Bills may begin in either the House of Representatives or the Senate unless they are intended to raise revenue. (The Constitution specifies that revenue bills must originate in the House.) Bills are popularly known by the names of their principal sponsors. The 1985 measures progressively to reduce the federal government deficit were, for example, referred to as 'Gramm–Rudman–Hollings' after Representative Phil Gramm of Texas, Senator Warren Rudman of New Hampshire and Senator Ernest Hollings of South Carolina.

2 A bill will then be allocated – or *referred* – to a *standing committee* or commit-tees for consideration. In the House, the Speaker decides which committee is appropriate. In the Senate, the Majority Party Leader has the power of refer-ral. Sometimes a bill will be considered by more than one committee, when it involves multiple spheres of jurisdiction. Clinton's healthcare bill was, for example, considered by two Senate and three House committees. Most bills, about 95 per cent, are killed at this stage. There are four stages to committee deliberations.

   • The committee chairman decides whether the bill is to be referred to a subcommittee or 'pigeonholed'. If it is *pigeonholed* by the chairman, it cannot progress further. For this reason, the committees are sometimes described by political observers as 'gatekeepers'.

   • The subcommittee will hold hearings to consider the bill with witnesses and presentations from relevant government departments, experts and interest groups. The hearings allow participation in the legislative process and, as Ross English notes: 'The primary function of hearings is to allow the committee members to gain enough knowledge to determine whether a change in the law is necessary, and if it is, what the details of the new law should be' (English 2003: 67).

   • There will then be the consideration of the bill on a line-by-line basis. The writing of the detailed provisions is known as *mark-up*. Following a final vote, it will be reported to the full committee. There will be further mark-up and the bill is then *reported out*. If a House committee is reluctant to allow the bill to be reported out, the House can – in exceptional circumstances and if it can muster a majority – issue a discharge petition. This was used in 2002 to hasten the progress of the campaign finance reform bill (English 2003: 79–80).

3 Once a bill has been reported out, time must be found to consider it in the chamber. Decisions to provide a place in the calendar and opportunities for debate and amendment are made by the House Rules Committee and, to a lesser extent, the Senate Majority Leader. The Rules Committee has been described as the House's 'traffic manager' (Griffith 1976: 40). It determines the framework within which a bill is handled and the conditions under which amendments can be submitted. There are three types of rule. An *open rule* allows amendments, while a *closed rule* prohibits them. A *modified rule* allows amendments when some sections of the bill – but not others – are being considered. The process takes a different form in the Senate. Unanimous consent agreements place limits on amendments and debate, although – as their name suggests – they require unanimity. In the absence of this, legislation remains vulnerable to filibuster, amendment and delay.

4 The bill is then considered and debated by the chamber as a whole. This is known as *floor action*. A bill must obtain a majority in both chambers. Voting is conducted by voice vote, or there may be a recorded *roll-call* vote using an electronic system.

5 However similar the bills introduced in the House and the Senate, there will almost certainly be differences between the versions passed in the two chambers. If they are to become law, the bills must pass in an absolutely identical form. A *conference committee*, consisting of members from both houses, customarily drawn from the appropriate standing committees, will meet to seek a compromise between the different versions. This gives these members a pivotal role in shaping the final form of the legislation.

6 If a compromise is agreed by a majority of both delegations, the bill must return to both chambers in its revised form for final approval. This is usually forthcoming, although there is a danger that members of either house may feel that too much has been conceded in conference negotiations.

7 Once it has been passed by the two chambers of Congress, the bill is submitted to the president. He may sign it, or simply allow it to become law by allowing it to lie upon the table for ten days. However, under the terms of the Constitution, the president can *veto* a bill. A veto can only be overridden if members of Congress can muster a two-thirds majority in both houses. Faced by a Democratic Congress, President Bush (1989–93) cast twenty-nine vetoes and was overridden only once. The veto power should not, therefore, be underestimated, and the implicit threat of a veto may be sufficient in itself to force members of Congress to modify their original goals. The roles of the veto and the *pocket veto* are discussed further in Chapter 6.

Parties in Congress

Although there were – in 2003 – two independents in Congress, almost all members of the House and Senators belong to either the Republican or the Democratic Parties. The parties are organised – within Congress – through the Senate Republican and Democratic Conferences, the House Republican Conference, and the Democratic Caucus. The Democratic Caucus defines its role in these terms:

> The Caucus nominates and elects the House Democratic Leadership, approves committee assignments, makes Caucus rules, enforces party discipline, and serves as a forum to develop and communicate party policy and legislative priorities. It accomplishes these tasks through weekly Caucus Meetings, on-going Issue Task Forces, the yearly Caucus Issues Conference, periodic special events, and continual Member-to-Member communication. (Democratic Caucus – US House of Representatives 2003)

Three individuals play a key role in leading the majority party in the House. As was noted above, the Speaker is responsible for the planning and implementation of the House's legislative agenda. His ability to chair proceedings allows him to rule upon contested points of order. However, his administrative control extends far beyond this. He influences decisions about the committee to which a bill is assigned, and can place deadlines on committee action. He also has considerable powers of patronage, shapes the membership of select committees, and since 1975 has nominated majority party members to the all-important Rules Committee. Some Speakers have used the position to stamp their personality and politics upon Congress as a whole. Joe Cannon (1903–11), Sam Rayburn (1940–47, 1949–53, and 1955–63), and Newt Gingrich (1995–99) played a particularly noteworthy role (English 2003: 90). For his part, the House Majority Leader structures and co-ordinates debate on the floor of the chamber. At the same time, he directs the party's strategy, intervenes in disputes among party members, and negotiates agreements with the minority party. The Majority Whip acts as a conduit of information between the executive and party members in the House. He provides advice about the voting intentions of particular Congressmen and – together with a team of assistant whips – encourages colleagues to vote with the party. He also provides information to members about forthcoming votes and the floor schedule. Tom DeLay, the Republican Majority Leader, earlier served as the party's Whip, and is said to have played a particularly significant role in marshalling the votes so as to ensure the passage of landmark legislation.

The individualism of the Senate limits the degree of leverage exercised by the party leaderships. Nonetheless, the Senate Majority Leader has an important role to play in co-ordinating party activity, managing day-to-day business on the floor of the chamber, establishing priorities, and negotiating time agree-

Table 5.1 *Party leadership in the House of Representatives, 108th Congress, 2003–*

	Post	District
	Republicans	
Speaker	Dennis Hastert	Illinois 14th
House Majority Leader	Tom DeLay	Texas 22nd
House Majority Whip	Roy Blunt	Missouri 7th
	Democrats	
House Minority Leader	Nancy Pelosi	California 8th
House Minority Whip	Steny Hoyer	Maryland 5th

Source: adapted from the US House of Representatives, www.house.gov.

Table 5.2 *Party leadership in the Senate, 108th Congress, 2003–*

	Post	State
	Republicans	
Senate Majority Leader	Bill Frist	Tennessee
Assistant Majority Leader (Majority Whip)	Mitch McConnell	Kentucky
	Democrats	
Senate Minority Leader	Tom Daschle	South Dakota
Assistant Minority Leader (Minority Whip)	Harry Reid	Nevada

Source: adapted from the US Senate, www. senate.gov.

ments and unanimous consent agreements with the Minority Leader that will set a timetable for the consideration of legislation.

In most legislatures, the party is the most significant feature structuring voting decisions. MPs in the British House of Commons, for example, almost always follow the dictates of the whipping system. Although there were significant rebellions in Labour's ranks during the Blair government's second term, revolts are still comparatively rare. Indeed, the backbencher is sometimes dismissed as mere 'lobby fodder'. However, the parties are now much less influential in Congress than in most other national legislatures.

Party leadership plays a significant role in organising the procedures and the agenda of the chambers, but the leaders cannot command individual members to act. They can only seek to use their influence. Party group meetings, or caucuses, are rare and of relatively little importance. There are only a small number of 'party votes' that pitch the majority of one party against another. It is rare for all of one party to be against all of the other, except in elections for the leadership of the chamber. Even then, there is no certainty.

Why are the parties are weak in Congress? While the whips have some forms of patronage, including nominations for vacant committee assignments, participation in conference committees considering important bills, campaign contributions from leadership PACs (Political Action Committees established by prominent party figures so as to fund their own campaigns or those of others), or selection for foreign trips, they are – in contrast with their counterparts in the House of Commons – limited in the sanctions that they can impose upon dissidents. In contrast with Britain, where dissident MPs have – *in extremis* – been 'deselected' as party candidates, the party apparatus cannot prevent candidates who break ranks from gaining the party nomination. Instead, their fate depends upon their own ability to win and maintain the loyalty of primary voters. There are, however, other reasons why the parties play only a limited role.

1 The federal government – the executive – does not depend on votes in the legislature. In most *parliamentary* systems the chief executive is elected by, accountable to, and dependent upon votes in the legislature. The defeat of a major bill would, for example, lead to a vote of no confidence in the government, and if this were carried, a general election would almost certainly be called. In the US system, the executive – the president – is elected independently and retains office regardless of his performance or support in Congress. Legislators belonging to the same party can vote against their president without the fear that he may be forced to resign and the other party may gain office.

2 Congress itself offers a career structure. In a parliamentary system, promotion into and within the executive offers a way forward for those with ambition. Advancement, however, generally depends upon loyalty towards the party and its leaders. In Congress, those who are ambitious do not generally look towards the executive branch. Instead, they seek a more powerful position, such as a committee chairmanship or membership of a more important committee, within Congress itself.

3 Congress rests on a committee system. In the words of M. J. C. Vile: 'it is difficult to exaggerate the importance of these committees, for they are the sieve through which all legislation is poured, and what comes through and how it comes through, is largely in their hands' (quoted in Bennett 1991: 17).

   Although the authority and autonomy of committee chairs has fluctuated, power is largely decentralised. Indeed, from the early 1970s onwards, Congress became more fragmented as a plethora of subcommittees assumed greater powers. While the reforms that followed the 1994 elections partially reversed this by asserting the authority of party structures, shifting the locus of legislative activity to the full committee, and limiting the number of subcommittees, the committees and the associated subcommittees constitute an alternative power network that imposes limits upon the authority of the party leaders (Owens 1998: 51).

4 Committee chairmen are usually appointed on the basis of *seniority*. By tradition, the longest continuously serving majority party member of the committee takes the post. Similarly, membership of the most important and

prestigious committees has customarily been reserved for those with the greatest seniority. There have, however, been some significant modifications to this. In 1975, three House chairs were replaced, despite their seniority, by less senior Democratic colleagues. After winning the 1994 elections, the House Republican leadership was committed to ensuring that conservative policy proposals would be adopted. It by-passed the seniority principle in making appointments to the chairmanship of three of the most significant committees. At the same time, new – or 'freshmen' – members were appointed to prestigious committees such as Appropriations, Ways and Means, and Rules. However, seniority remains the customary method of selection. The most important positions in Congress are not, therefore, generally dependent on the party apparatus or loyalty to it.

5 There are caucuses and task forces which are organised independently of the parties and cut across party lines. These include groupings based around the needs and interests of a particular industry, such as the Steel Caucus. There are also state delegations. A Texan member of the House of Representatives has described the work of his delegation: 'we have a wide ideological spectrum . . . but we're able to close ranks and work together for any program that benefits any part of the state' (Woll 1985: 183). Weight of numbers can give some delegations significant political leverage. Political cohesion adds further strength. A large, organised state delegation may be able to help an individual Congressman gain committee assignments and leadership positions.

Although the parties have traditionally been weak, and power has rested with others – most notably the committee chairs or 'barons' – there have been efforts to increase the role and profile of the parties. In the 1980s, Democratic Speakers such 'Tip' O'Neill and Jim Wright began to play more of a role in deciding which committees considered important bills and the conditions under which legislation was debated on the floor of the House (Owens 1996: 16).

In the wake of Republican election victories in November 1994, the former House Speaker Newt Gingrich attempted to increase the power of both the Party and its Congressional leadership. He broke with the seniority rule by selecting the chairs for the Appropriations, Commerce and Judiciary Committees over the heads of more senior colleagues. Furthermore, those chairing committees were limited to a six-year period of tenure. He placed many of the newly-elected members of Congress ('freshmen' and 'freshwomen') – those who were most committed to conservative principles – on the most important committees.

At the same time, Gingrich and other leading Republicans structured the work of the committees around the policies outlined in the *Contract with America*, the assertively conservative platform upon which many of the House Republican candidates had stood in the elections. The Republican leadership ensured the passage of nearly all the proposals included in the *Contract*. All were considered within the first hundred days of the new House. Furthermore, despite the institutional obstacles that the US political system places in the way of legislative reform, 23 of the 40 items in the *Contract* were adopted. Most notably of all, the Personal Responsibility and Work Opportunity Reconciliation Act was passed and signed into law. It ended the system of welfare provision that had been initially established in the 1930s and created – in its place – the Temporary Assistance for Needy Families (TANF) programme. This imposed time-limits on public assistance and introduced work requirements for recipients.

There was a high level of party unity and voting discipline. In 1995, a majority of Republicans voted against a majority of Democrats on over 73 per cent of votes taken on the floor of the House. Against a background where many members of Congress were relatively inexperienced, but at the same time shared a commitment to radical conservative reforms, the Gingrich leadership could assert itself and the Republican Party as key players in Congressional proceedings.

Although the 'Gingrich revolution' took place in the House, there were echoes in the Senate. Over two-thirds of votes followed party lines, and there were attempts – led by Senator Rick Santorum of Pennsylvania – to remove the long-established chair of the Appropriations Committee. Republican Party discipline was strengthened through the appointment of additional whips, the adoption of measures curtailing the traditional autonomy of committee chairs, and a requirement that they promote legislation supported by the overwhelming majority of Republican senators.

However, despite all this, the Contract did not renew the conservative revolution in the way that its supporters hoped. Some of the most significant legislative proposals that it included were not enacted. More importantly, the Republican strategy of confrontation with the White House failed. It also created tensions and divisions among House Republicans. At the end of 1995, Congress passed a budget that reduced taxes, aimed to balance the budget within a seven-year period, and restructured some federal entitlement programmes. Clinton vetoed the budget reconciliation bill and a number of associated appropriations bills, arguing that the proposed budget threatened the future of education, Medicare and Medicaid. Instead, he offered compromise solutions. As Barbara Sinclair records:

> Republicans were convinced that Clinton would cave in under pressure from the public. When negotiations between them and the White House failed to produce an agreement they considered satisfactory, they several times let appropriations lapse and shut down the government, in one case for twenty-two days over Christmas. Not only did Clinton hold fast, but the public reaction was the opposite of what House Republicans had expected; the public blamed the Republicans, not the president, and Clinton's job-approval ratings went up. (Sinclair 2000: 86)

Public opinion – which backed the President by a two-to-one majority – compelled the Republicans to back down. In early January 1996, the

Republicans voted to allow federal employees to return to work and the government business continued on the basis of appropriations bills but without an overall budget agreement.

Although the 1996 elections returned Republican majorities in both houses, the 105th and 106th Congresses (1997–2001) represented a partial return to more traditional forms of Congressional government. There were few policy initiatives. As John E. Owens records:

> On issues like tobacco regulation, health reform and campaign finance, Republicans preferred a wait-and-see strategy, often delaying action, waiting for events to run their course and interest groups to determine the climate of opinion. Issues pursued by Republican leaders were largely of minor political importance, necessitated little political risk and required only small investments of political capital. (Owens 2000: 51)

Although chastened, Gingrich himself survived as House Speaker until the 1998 mid-term elections. These results represented a further setback for the Republicans. Traditionally, it is the president's party that suffers losses. However, the Republicans not only failed to make gains, but instead lost seats, reducing their majority to eleven. In the aftermath of the elections, Gingrich stepped down and the Republican Conference chose Dennis Hastert as House Speaker. While the House Republicans continued to pursue Bill Clinton and impeached him in 1998, and the sense of bitter partisanship continued, both Hastert's personality and politics epitomised the renewed sense of pragmatism and caution. He has, for example, broadened out the process of decision-making and allowed others to play a part in the selection of committee chairmen. Indeed, Hastert has – to some extent – been overshadowed by Tom DeLay, a more outspoken conservative partisan who served as Majority Whip and then Majority Leader (Schickler 2002: 100). Within the Senate, the Republicans were led by the Mississippi Senator Trent Lott from 1996 until the end of 2002. Although a southern conservative, Lott usually sought to broker compromises and was not regarded favourably by many activists on the right. He was succeeded by Bill Frist, who had close ties with the White House. Although committed to economic conservatism, he approached some social and cultural issues with a degree of moderation.

What factors determine Congressional votes?

European observers are accustomed to voting discipline in national legislatures. Backbench revolts are regarded as a comparative rarity. However, US parties are much less cohesive. This is evident in the number of party unity votes in which a majority of Republican members of Congress vote against a majority of Democrats (Davidson and Oleszek 1998: 260). This – it should be noted – is a relatively loose and undemanding definition. If a more vigorous definition – based up on 90 per cent of party members voting on opposite sides – is employed, only about 10 per cent of roll-call votes can be considered party unity votes.

Table 5.3 *Party unity votes in Congress, 1960–2002 (% of roll-call votes where a majority of Republican members of Congress vote against a majority of Democrats)*

Year	House	Senate
1960	55	48
1970	27	35
1980	38	46
1990	49	54
1991	55	49
1992	64	53
1993	65	67
1994	62	52
1995	73	69
1996	56	62
1997	50	50
1998	56	56
1999	47	63
2000	43	49
2001	40	55
2002	43	45

Source: adapted from *CQ Weekly* (2002), 60:48, 14 December, 3281.

Although Newt Gingrich's fall from power appears to suggest that attempts to establish more effective party structures within Congress must inevitably founder, the importance of partisan cleavages should not be underestimated. Although members' efforts will often be directed towards re-election, they also seek advancement in Congress. This depends – in part – on party loyalties and the character of a member's relationship with the party leadership. A degree of loyalty is expected. Furthermore, the parties have – in recent years – acquired greater ideologically coherence. For their part, the Republicans have established a more clearly defined conservative identity. At the same time, as they lost many of the conservatives from their ranks, the Democrats have defined themselves in more overtly liberal terms.

Other factors, however, also play a role in determining the outcome of Congressional votes. The district is significant. The votes of Congressmen will be shaped by views and opinions 'back home'. Re-election may depend upon a member's responsiveness to popular opinion in his or her own district or state. As the former Democratic Party Speaker Tip O'Neill stressed, 'all politics is local'. Congressmen from farm districts will, for example, be highly sensitive to the need for farm subsidies. Those representing districts where the oil industry is a major presence will concentrate their attention on energy policy. This is not, however, a straightforward process. On some issues there will no doubt where constituency interests and opinions lie. In these cases, the Congressman's or Senator's vote is highly predictable. On other issues, however, there is no clear constituency position or interest. In these instances, the Congressman will have more latitude in following his own preferences.

Ideology or political philosophy will influence voting behaviour. Since the 1930s, a conservative coalition of southern Democrats and Republicans has exercised considerable influence. In recent years, however, the parties have become more ideologically homogeneous. There are still, however, significant differences within the parties. Among the Democrats, about 35 moderates and conservatives – many of whom are drawn from the south and west – belong to the Blue Dog Coalition. They are committed to the balancing of the federal government budget and emphasise 'common sense, conservative economics and compassion' (Blue Dog Coalition 2003). For its part, the Congressional Black Caucus – which is wholly Democratic – has a different emphasis. It stresses the rights of labour, the need to assist minority-owned businesses, the provision of health care, and the iniquity of a penal system that imprisons 'whole masses of African-American men'.

Among Republicans, conservatives are brought together by the Conservative Action Team and moderates in the Tuesday Lunch Club. When party majorities are small, a minority faction within the majority party can exercise considerable influence.

Congressional 'staffers' may, in practice, also influence voting decisions. An average member of the House has a staff of seventeen, and a Senator will have about forty working on his or her behalf. They provide a counterbalance to the information and arguments advanced by the executive branch. John Kingdon has noted that 'a high probability exists that a congressman's vote will reflect his or her staff position' (Woll 1985: 189). The influence they exert stems in part from the volume of work and the number of issues facing the individual Congressmen or Senators. They will inevitably be guided by the recommendations of their aides.

The role of lobbyists and interest groups should also be considered. There are an estimated 14,000 lobbyists working in Washington DC on behalf of companies alone. They utilise a range of techniques. Some organisations will take advantage of the sense of affinity that party members traditionally feel towards a particular group. The trade unions held sway during the long years that the Democrats controlled Congress. Conversely, the Republican victories from 1994 onwards brought many business and conservative organisations into the political mainstream. In *Fortune* magazine's 1999 ranking of groups in terms of influence, the National Rifle Association was number two and the National Right to Life Committee – which campaigns against abortion – was placed at number eight.

Interest groups can – at least in some instances – mobilise a large constituency. The National Rifle Association – fearing further federal gun control legislation – ensured that Congressmen received three million telegrams in 72 hours. Following a call to its supporters by the American Association of Retired Persons (AARP), the former House Speaker, Jim Wright, received fifteen million postcards (Cigler and Loomis 1995: 395). In recent years, companies have also sought to mobilise members of the public in support of their interests. Individuals and groups are encouraged to write to or telephone members of Congress. According to Alison Mitchell, the tobacco companies spent $40 million organising a grassroots campaign against restrictive legislation in the spring of 1998. Companies, she asserts, are now attempting to put a 'public face on private interest'. There are other strategies. Instead of grassroots campaigns, some companies have pursued 'grasstops' initiatives. These are directed towards winning over those 'to whom a member of Congress cannot say no – his chief donor, his campaign manager, a political mentor' (Mitchell 1998).

The president's support for a bill may also influence the individual Senator or Representative. However, the 'chief legislator' will, in practice, take a formal position on only a small proportion of the bills considered by Congress. In 1996, for example, President Clinton adopted a definite stand on just 19 per cent of legislation. The role of the president is, however, intertwined with party loyalties. Partisanship ensures that presidents inevitably have most success with members of their own parties. In 1998, the average House Democrat supported President Clinton 78 per cent of the time, and the average Democrat Senator 86 per cent of the time. For Republicans the figures were 27 per cent for House members and 42 per cent for Senators (Ornstein, Mann, and Malbin 2000: 199). Because Congressional votes are often uncertain, the president may need to look for support beyond the ranks of those in his own party. President Clinton was only able to ensure the passage of the North American Free Trade Agreement (NAFTA) in 1993 by building a cross-party coalition of support.

Assessing Congress

Congress is understood in different ways. Opinion polls suggest that the American people are critical of Congress as an institution, but – paradoxically – respect their own Congressman (Hibbing and Theiss-Morse 1995). In 1992, 17 per cent of Americans expressed disapproval of Congress, while 54 per cent expressed approval of their own Congressman. Furthermore, sitting – or incumbent – members of Congress are almost always re-elected. The distinction between Congress as an institution and Congress as an aggregate of individual representatives has led some observers to talk of 'the two Congresses' (Davidson and Oleszek 1998).

To an extent, all national legislatures have to fulfil two functions. They represent diverse interests and constituencies across the nation, but they also collectively decide on issues facing the nation as a whole. The tension between the two functions of a legislature was identified by Edmund Burke in a celebrated address to the electors of Bristol in 1774. A parliament, he said, could be: 'a Congress of Ambassadors from different and hostile interests, whose interests each must maintain as an agent and advocate, against other agents or advocates [or] a deliberative assembly of one nation, with one interest, that of the whole, where not local purposes, not local prejudices, ought to guide, but the general good, resulting from the general reason of the whole' (quoted in Davidson and Oleszek 1998: 8). For his part, Burke favoured the latter approach. A legislature, he argued, had to stand above the immediate sectional or local wishes of constituents, and instead collectively to determine the fate of the nation.

Assessments and evaluations of Congress depend on which of these 'two Congresses' is under consideration. Congress can be judged as a mouthpiece of the districts and states. Seen this way, its performance is measured by its responsiveness to constituency pressures, its efficiency in assisting individual constituents with problems – such as claims for a higher level of veteran benefits – and the ability of members to attract government projects and businesses to their districts or states. From this perspective, Congress will *inevitably* be decentralised and individualistic. It will necessarily be characterised by both short-term thinking and weak party cohesion.

If, however, Congress is seen as a collective institution, it is measured by its ability to deliberate and make decisions on a long-term basis. It will also be judged on the nature of legislative–executive relations and the character of legislation that is passed. Such a Congress requires centralisation, a strong party system, and a sense of collective identity.

In practice, Congress is drawn towards notions of the representative as a constituency servant. Members often seek amendments to legislation that allocate funding, resources and the provision of employment to their own district or state. This has led to widespread criticism. 'Pork-barrel politics', it is said, distort legislation and corrupt government programmes. In the aftermath of the *Challenger* space shuttle disaster in 2003, Senator John McCain suggested that $167 million of 'pork' had been added to legislation funding the National Aeronautics and Space Administration (NASA) and that this may have had an impact on NASA's safety programmes. He cited spending in particular districts and states: $15.5 million for the Institute for Scientific Research in West Virginia, $7.6 million for hydrogen research by the Florida State University System, and $1.35 million for the expansion of the earth science hall at the Maryland Science Center in Baltimore (*Washington Post*, 15 May 2003).

The same process also encourages particularism. The making of public policy is biased towards local and special interests at the expense of the national interest. It places constituency service and campaigning before attention to legislation. It encourages symbolic acts, such as the proposing of bills that have no chance of success so as to gain publicity. Legislation will often not receive the attention that is required. As each legislator struggles to promote his or her own constituency, deliberations end in *gridlock*, fragmentation and incoherence. Elections become less competitive and are skewed towards the incumbent. Over

90 per cent of Representatives and Senators are re-elected. There are fewer and fewer marginal seats.

Congress is also subject to other forms of criticism. It has said that Washington politics are too distant from the voters. Although it was once a 'citizen-legislature', Congress is now failing to fulfil its representative function. Today, those who are elected have become self-serving professionals who are tied to a career structure. Within Congress, reforms have assigned too much power to the leadership. Furthermore, the strength of incumbency has encouraged arrogance and complacency.

Notions such as these acquired a particular strength during the early 1990s, although they are still heard. From this perspective, *term limits* offer a partial answer. If such a constitutional amendment was adopted, a representative could only serve in a chamber for a limited period. Reformers have suggested that an individual could be a member of the House for only three terms or six years, and of the Senate for two terms or twelve years. They claim that if term limits were introduced, Congress would attract candidates who were more closely tied to those who elected them. There would be fewer incumbents and more open, competitive elections. However, term limits have also been criticised. Opponents argue that they would exclude the most experienced representatives. This would inevitably increase the political leverage of the federal bureaucracy and the aides who staff the Congressional committees.

Conclusion

Despite the vigour with which criticisms such as these are made, they should not be overstated. Although Congress is skewed – to a greater extent than many other national legislatures – towards the representation of constituency interests rather than the 'national good', it has still been able to consider and pass important legislative measures. These have included welfare and educational reform as well as major tax reductions. Significantly, as the 1990s progressed, the bitterness that had been shown towards legislators at the beginning of the decade – and fuelled the calls for term limits – began to dissipate.

References and further reading

Aberbach, J. D. (1990), *Keeping a Watchful Eye: The Politics of Congressional Oversight*, Washington DC, The Brookings Institution.

Bennett, A. J. (1991), *American Government and Politics*, Godalming, the author.

Blue Dog Coalition (2003), *The Blue Dog Coalition*, baronhill.house.gov/bluedogs/

Cigler, A. J. and B. A. Loomis (1995), 'Contemporary interest group politics: more than "more of the same"', in A. J. Cigler and B. A. Loomis, *Interest Group Politics*, Washington DC: Congressional Quarterly Inc, pp. 393–406.

Congressional Quarterly (1997), *Powers of the Presidency*, Washington DC, Congressional Quarterly.

Davidson, R. and W. Oleszek (1998), *Congress and its Members*, Washington DC, Congressional Quarterly.

Democratic Caucus – US House of Representatives (2003), *What is the Democratic Caucus?*, dcaucusweb.house.gov/about/what_is.asp.

English, R. (2003), *The United States Congress*, Manchester, Manchester University Press.

Griffith, E. S. (1976), *The American System of Government*, London, Methuen.

Hart, J. (1995), *The Presidential Branch: From Washington to Clinton*, Chatham, Chatham House.

Hibbing, J. R. and E. Theiss-Morse (1995), *Congress as Public Enemy: Public Attitudes toward American Political Institutions*, Cambridge, Cambridge University Press.

Hilliar, P. (2002), *Caging the Cardinals, Citizens for a Sound Economy*, 3 December, www.cse.org/informed/issues_template.php/1192.htm).

Mitchell, A. (1998), 'A new form of lobbying puts public face on private interest', *The New York Times*, 30 September.

Ornstein, N. J., T. E. Mann, and M. J. Malbin (2000), *Vital Statistics on Congress 1999 – 2000*, Washington DC, The AEI Press.

Owens, J. E. (1996), 'A return to party rule in the US Congress?', *Politics Review*, 6:1, September, 15–19.

Owens, J. E. (1998), 'Congress and partisan change', in G. Peele, C. J. Bailey, B. Cain and B. Guy Peters, *Developments in American Politics*, pp. 42–70, Basingstoke, Macmillan.

Owens, J. E. (2000) 'Congress after the "Revolution": the continuing problems of governance in a partisan era', in A. Grant (ed.), *American Politics: 2000 and Beyond*, pp. 29–63, Aldershot, Ashgate.

Schickler, E. (2002), 'Congress', in G. Peele, C. J. Bailey, B. Cain and B. G. Peters, *Developments in American Politics*, pp. 97–114, Basingstoke, Palgrave.

Sinclair, B. (2000), The president as legislative leader', in C. Campbell and B. A. Rockman, *The Clinton Legacy*, New York, Chatham House – Seven Bridges Press, pp. 70–95.

Singh, R. (2003), *American Government and Politics: A Concise Introduction*, London, Sage Publications.

Woll, P. (1985), *Congress*, Boston, Little, Brown and Company.

Congress – websites

The Senate and the House of Representatives have their own websites. Both incorporate information about individual members, reports on current legislative work, opportunities to search for information on particular topics, voting records, and links to other federal government websites:

www.senate.gov/

www.house.gov/.

The Library of Congress offers THOMAS. Named after Thomas Jefferson, this offers searchable information, the text of bills, Congressional committee reports, and the Congressional Record.

thomas.loc.gov/home/thomas2.html.

Detailed coverage of developments in Congress can also be found at the *Roll Call* website: www.rollcall.com.

6

The president

The president is the most visible public representative of the American government. His powers are such that in the 1960s, some observers talked about the *imperial* presidency. However, his authority does not go unchallenged and, in practice, he is subject to a considerable number of constraints. This chapter surveys the president's powers and the limitations that the other branches of government impose upon him.

The Constitution and the presidency

The US Constitution assigns relatively few specific powers to the president. He is the head of state as well as head of government and, as such, undertakes ceremonial duties. He is Commander-in-Chief of the armed forces. He appoints senior government officials, Supreme Court Justices, and those who serve as US ambassadors abroad. He can grant pardons. He has – in the words of the Constitution – the 'Power, by and with the Advice and Consent of the Senate, to make Treaties, provided two-thirds of the Senators present concur.' He may also 'give to the Congress Information on the State of the Union, and recommend to their Consideration such Measures as he shall judge necessary and expedient'. He can, furthermore, veto proposed laws passed by Congress.

However, many of these powers are matched – or 'checked' – by those assigned to one or both of the houses of Congress. Only Congress can declare war. A significant proportion of a president's appointments have to be confirmed by the Senate. Treaties are subject to ratification by a two-thirds majority in the Senate. The making of law and financial control – known as the 'power of the purse' – remain the prerogative of Congress. Furthermore, the president's ability to veto bills passed by Congress can be overridden by a two-thirds majority in both houses. Lastly, Congress has the power of impeachment. The Constitution states that a president can be tried by the Senate for 'treason, bribery, or other high crimes and misdemeanors'. If convicted, he is removed from office.

Table 6.1 *US presidents, 1953–*

President	Party	Election(s)	Period of office
Dwight D. Eisenhower	Republican	1952 1956	1953–61
John F. Kennedy	Democrat	1960	1961–63
Lyndon B. Johnson	Democrat	1964	1963–69
Richard M. Nixon	Republican	1968 1972	1969–74
Gerald R. Ford	Republican		1974–77
Jimmy Carter	Democrat	1976	1977–81
Ronald Reagan	Republican	1980 1984	1981–89
George H. W. Bush	Republican	1988	1989–93
William J. Clinton	Democrat	1992 1996	1993–2001
George W. Bush	Republican	2000	2001–

The president and foreign policy

Although the Constitution was delicately constructed around a *separation of powers* and a system of *checks and balances*, the authority of the president progressively grew during the course of the nineteenth and for much of the twentieth centuries. By the late 1960s and early 1970s – when Richard Nixon occupied the White House – the president had undoubted primacy or *hegemony* in the handling of defence policy and national security matters. He was also, as critics observed, able to use the apparatus of government to pursue personal political goals. This was the era of the 'imperial presidency', as Arthur Schlesinger Jr., a distinguished historian, described it in a celebrated phrase. Congress – although sometimes vocal in its comments – seemed to play a subordinate role. The growth of presidential power was symbolised by US involvement in the Vietnam War. Despite the intensity of the conflict – which led to the loss of 58,000 American lives and embroiled neighbouring countries – there was never a declaration of war. Presidents Lyndon Johnson and Richard Nixon's only authority was the Gulf of Tonkin resolution passed by Congress in 1964, which backed retaliatory action in response to an alleged attack on American vessels by North Vietnamese forces. Why did presidential power grow?

Some words and phrases in the US Constitution have an 'elastic' character. Article II, for example, requires the president to 'take care that the laws be faithfully executed'. The meaning of these words has been progressively stretched, thereby allowing the president greater latitude and freedom of action.

Particular presidential styles or decisions by individual presidents set precedents that would be followed by their successors. Their actions enlarged the scope of the office and changed expectations about its nature. In 1803,

President Thomas Jefferson (1801–9), authorised the purchase of French Louisiana. Although this more than doubled the size of US territory, he made the decision without consulting Congress. In the Civil War, President Abraham Lincoln (1861–65), ordered the blockade of southern ports and increased the numbers enlisted in the army without Congressional assent. Under Franklin D. Roosevelt (1933–45), the size and scale of the executive branch grew dramatically during the period of the New Deal – the economic recovery programme of the 1930s – and the Second World War. In particular, although there was some shrinkage during the 1990s, the Executive Office of the President (EOP) – the president's personal staff – expanded in terms of both size and authority. From the Roosevelt era onwards, the presidency consisted not of one individual, but was instead structured around a large number of aides, decision-makers and administrators.

The president's constitutional role as commander-in-chief enabled him to dispatch US forces across the world without seeking a formal declaration of war from Congress. Although members of Congress retained the 'power of the purse', and could, where it disagreed with the president's objectives, threaten the withdrawal of funding, this could be seen – in periods of tension or conflict – as a betrayal of the country's armed forces. Congress has few other options. Although there have only been eleven declarations of war – in five separate wars – American forces were ordered into action abroad on 234 occasions between 1798 and 1993 (Collier 1993).

Table 6.2 US declarations of war, 1812–1942

Date	Antagonist
1812	Britain
1846	Mexico
1898	Spain
1917	Germany
1917	Austria-Hungary
1941	Japan
1941	Germany
1941	Italy
1942	Bulgaria
1942	Hungary
1942	Romania

Source; Adapted from Congressional Research Service (2001), Information Regarding Declarations of War, www.house.gov/burton/RSC/DeclarationofWar.PDF.

Congress has been poorly placed to determine or even influence the character of US foreign and defence policy, particularly in the years after 1945 when the nature of war had been transformed by the stationing of American forces around the world and the development of missile technology. The legislature is a slow and bureaucratic institution. As Clinton Rossiter asserted in a celebrated phrase: 'secrecy, dispatch, unity, continuity, and access to information – the ingredients of successful diplomacy – are properties of his [the President's] office, and Congress . . . possesses none of them' (1963: 26). The legislature has, furthermore, a parochial and inherently short-term character. In particular, members of the House of Representatives have their eyes on the next election, which will always be less than two years away. Their interests and concerns may not extend, therefore, beyond those of their home district. At the same time, it is the executive branch that takes the initiative in the making of foreign and defence policy. Through the military chain of command, the president orders troops into action. Congress can only respond to decisions taken within the administration. Congress has, furthermore, often held back and acquiesced in administration decisions. The reason for this lies partly in the status and authority that US political culture assigns to the presidency. However, it is also rooted in the extent and scale of the consensus on foreign and defence policy goals that lasted between the late 1940s and the demise of the Soviet Union at the beginning of the 1990s. Although there were disagreements – throughout the Cold War years – about the specific character of particular operations, only a small handful of individuals on the radical edges of American politics challenged the belief that the US had to lead the 'free world' in the battle to contain communism. There was, similarly, in the immediate aftermath of the terrorist attacks on 11 September 2001 a renewed consensus on the need to take military action in Afghanistan.

Although some judgements have reined in presidential authority, the Supreme Court has also played a role in bolstering presidential authority. In 1936, in the case of *US v. Curtiss-Wright Export Corporation*, the Court upheld a 1934 Act allowing the president to embargo arms shipments to foreign combatants in a South American war. Justice George Sutherland asserted that the president was 'the sole organ of the federal government in . . . international relations' (*Congressional Quarterly* 1997: 126).

'Presidential determinations' allow the commitment of forces, funds and assistance if, in the eyes of the president, it is essential for the security of the US. Congress does not have to give specific authorisation. For example, the president can use 'drawdown' authority to transfer military equipment from one country to another. He can also reallocate funding to another theatre of operations. In 1993, for example, President Clinton provided economic assistance to Mexico and supported peacekeeping forces in Liberia on this basis (Ragsdale 1996: 335).

Although the Constitution stipulates that treaties require the 'advice and consent' of the Senate, successive presidents have circumvented this by drawing up executive agreements with the heads of foreign governments. Although such agreements do not have the legitimacy or authority of treaties and may not be maintained by subsequent presidents, some have nonetheless had far-reaching international implications. In 1940, President Franklin Roosevelt used an executive agreement to 'swap' fifty destroyers for air bases in the British Empire. This assisted the British war effort against Germany, and strengthened US strategic might in the Americas. In 1973 an executive agreement signed between President Richard Nixon and South Vietnam promised that the US would 'respond with full force' to North Vietnamese violations of the Paris peace agreement that had ended American military intervention in Vietnam.

Although Congress passed the Case Act in 1972, requiring that the Senate and House Foreign Relations Committees be notified of all executive agreements within 60 days, this did nothing to stem their flow. Indeed, between 1985 and 1989, the Reagan White House signed 1271 international agreements, only 47 of which were treaties. Furthermore, as John Dumbrell records, 'even the reporting provisions of the Case Act have been evaded and undermined by persistent executive delay' (1997: 135).

After Vietnam

The US had to face the prospect of defeat in Vietnam, and this led Congress to impose constraints on the president's ability to deploy troops overseas. For a period, it seemed that there had been a fundamental shift in the balance of power between the executive and legislative branches of government. Nonetheless, by the early 1980s, commentators were talking of a 'resurgent presidency'. Under Ronald Reagan, the White House was again prepared – in at least certain circumstances – to intervene abroad and authorise the use of US forces.

Grenada is a small island in the Caribbean. Following a revolution, it aligned itself with Cuba and the Soviet bloc. In October 1983, a power struggle between different factions within the ruling New Jewel movement offered the US – and the Reagan administration – an opportunity to show that it was prepared to act against communism. In Operation Urgent Fury, US marines occupied Grenada, and the New Jewel movement was removed from power. However, Congress played a negligible role in all of this. Rapid military success, and widespread public support for the invasion, enabled the Reagan administration to keep Congressmen relegated to the sidelines.

In April 1986, following a terrorist attack against American servicemen and a clash between US and Libyan forces in the Mediterranean, the Reagan administration ordered American air attacks on Tripoli and other targets in Libya. These led to over 100 civilian deaths. Congressional leaders were invited to the White House only as the US bombers were approaching Libya. President Reagan argued that the action had been self-defence, and fell within his responsibilities as Commander-in-Chief.

The Reagan administration also fought a covert – and, critics asserted, illegal – war during this period. Although the Boland amendment had been passed by Congress in 1984 cutting off funding for military and paramilitary aid to the

---

Box 6.1   The Vietnam War

The Vietnam War consolidated presidential hegemony and contributed to the emergence of what Arthur Schlesinger Jr. termed 'the imperial presidency'. The conflict began by stealth. Following a war of independence against French colonial rule, the country was divided in 1954 between the north, under Communist rule, and the south, which had a Western-leaning, although authoritarian, form of government.

The government of South Vietnam found itself facing guerilla attacks by the National Liberation Front (or 'Vietcong'). The NLF had the support of North Vietnam and its armed forces. US policy-makers – who had, between 1950 and 1954, backed the French, began to provide large-scale military backing for the South Vietnamese government. They were fearful that if South Vietnam collapsed, other countries in the region would also fall – like a row of dominoes – to the Communists.

During the Kennedy years, US military advisers played an increasingly visible role in supporting South Vietnam. In August 1964, there were reports that US naval ships had come under fire from the North Vietnamese, although it has been subsequently claimed that no such attack took place. Whatever the true circumstances, the US Congress responded by passing – virtually unanimously – the Gulf of Tonkin Resolution. This authorised President Lyndon Johnson to take 'all necessary measures to repel any armed attack against the forces of the US and to prevent further aggression'. On the basis of the Resolution, the war escalated and the administration committed large-scale military resources to South-east Asia. For a decade, the US waged what has been described as a 'presidential war'. The increasingly vocal criticisms of the war made by the Senate Foreign Relations Committee had little effect.

Around 58,000 Americans lost their lives. These losses, and organised opposition to the war in the US, led to a policy of 'Vietnamization', whereby the fighting was progressively handed over to the South Vietnamese. At the same time, negotiations with North Vietnam were opened up. However, although a peace agreement was signed with the North Vietnamese, it lasted only for a short period. In April 1975, the NLF and the North Vietnamese forces captured Saigon, and South Vietnam surrendered. Vietnam was reunited under Communist rule. The US had been defeated.

Contras, a right-wing army seeking the overthrow of the radical leftist Sandinista government in Nicaragua, they were backed and directed by staff within the Reagan administration. They acquired funding for the venture from secret arms sales to Iran and private donations.

In December 1989, President Bush sent US troops into Panama. The attack – *Operation Just Cause* – followed a period of tension between the country's military ruler, General Manuel Noriega, who had been accused of involvement in the international drug trade, and the United States. Noriega was arrested by US forces at the beginning of January, and, after a trial in Miami, imprisoned.

President Bush ordered the withdrawal of the troops by the end of February 1990. The invasion took place while Congress was out of session.

President Clinton also deployed troops or took other forms of military action. From April 1994 onwards, there were – under NATO auspices – air strikes against Bosnian Serb forces in support of United Nations peacekeeping operations. Following the 1995 Dayton (Ohio) peace accord, 16,500 US troops were sent to Bosnia as part of a multinational force that was used to enforce the agreement. The numbers were progressively reduced.

In September 1994, Clinton also used US troops in Haiti, although following an agreement negotiated by the former US president, Jimmy Carter, the landings were unopposed. They were stationed as part of an operation to reinstate the country's elected president, Jean-Bertrand Aristide.

There were also periodic attacks on Iraq. In June 1993, for example, US forces launched a missile attack on Iraqi intelligence headquarters in Baghdad in retaliation for evidence linking the Iraqi government to an assassination plot against former President Bush. In December 1998, against the background of the impending impeachment drama in Washington DC, President Clinton ordered a four-day air and cruise missile campaign against Iraqi military targets. It was a response to Iraq's lack of co-operation with United Nations weapons inspectors.

During the same period, fears about Islamic terrorism were beginning to grow. In June 1996, a truck bomb exploded in Dhahran, killing nineteen US servicemen. Although the Clinton administration was later to be accused of negligence, attention increasing focused on the activities of the Al-Qaeda organisation and its leader, Osama bin Laden. In August 1998, cruise missile attacks were launched against suspected terrorist training camps in Afghanistan and the Sudan.

Towards the end of Clinton's presidency, in 1999, US forces played a leading part in NATO air attacks on Serbia in Operation Allied Force. Once Serbian forces had been compelled to withdraw from Kosovo, the province was controlled and administered by NATO forces.

11 September, Afghanistan and Iraq

The terrorist attacks by Al-Qaeda operatives on the World Trade Center and the Pentagon on 11 September 2001 transformed the presidency of George W. Bush and the character of US policy. Urged on by 'hawks' such as Donald Rumsfeld and Paul Wolfowitz at the Department of Defense, Bush committed the US to a broad war on terrorism. He emphasised that the US would 'make no distinction between the terrorists who committed these acts and those who harbor them'. Following this, US air strikes and a proxy army – the Northern Alliance – who were aided by US special forces, overthrew the ruling Taliban regime in Afghanistan.

In his January 2002 State of the Union address, Bush went further. He identified an 'axis of evil' involving Iraq, Iran and North Korea. In June 2002, he spelt out a new doctrine; the US would take military action against countries before they had the opportunity to attack or sponsor attacks on the US: 'Our security will require all Americans to be forward-looking and resolute, to be ready for preemptive action when necessary to defend our liberty and to defend our lives.'

This commitment to pre-emption led the Bush administration towards Iraq. Undeterred by its failure to win specific authorisation from the United Nations and the opposition of countries such as France and Germany, the US maintained its assertion that Saddam Hussein's regime held chemical and biological weapons, and – with allies such as Britain – invaded Iraq in March 2003. Military victory came within weeks and the US looked towards the political reshaping of the Middle East. Other 'rogue states', it was said, would recognise the 'new realities' of American might.

The president and domestic policy

Some observers also emphasise the role of the presidency in the making of domestic as well as foreign policy. Powers derived from the Constitution, Supreme Court rulings, and subsequent laws passed by Congress offer him extensive political leverage.

The president has the constitutional right to veto legislation passed by Congress. If he wishes to do this, Article I specifies that he must send a statement to Congress within ten days of a bill being passed, setting out his reasons for refusing to sign it. A presidential veto can only be overridden by a two-thirds majority in both houses, which is difficult to muster. President Woodrow Wilson regarded the veto as a very powerful weapon indeed. It 'is, of course, beyond all comparison, his most formidable prerogative' (Ragsdale 1996: 365).

It has, at times, been used extensively. For example, President Ford vetoed fifty-three bills. By the summer of 1990 – just eighteen months after taking office – President George Bush had vetoed thirteen bills. None of these vetoes were overridden. Indeed, a 1996 estimate suggested that since the founding of the US, only 0.7 per cent of vetoes had been overridden (Ragsdale 1996: 365).

The president can also employ the *pocket veto*. If the president does not sign a bill within a ten-day period, and Congress has, by the end of that time, adjourned, the bill does not pass into law. (Note that if Congress *is* in session, and the president takes no action, the bill becomes law at the end of the ten-day period. This mechanism can thus be used by a president to convey a lack of enthusiasm for a measure.) Since the early 1970s, it has been accepted that the pocket veto can only be used immediately before the end of a two-year Congressional term, rather than during the days preceding a recess. However, despite this, the pocket veto has been used extensively. For example, President

Table 6.3 *Presidential vetoes, 1953–*

Years in office	President	Regular vetoes	Vetoes overridden	Pocket vetoes
1953–61	Eisenhower	73	2	108
1961–63	Kennedy	12	0	9
1963–69	Johnson	16	0	14
1969–74	Nixon	26	7	17
1974–77	Ford	48	12	18
1977–81	Carter	13	2	18
1981–89	Reagan	39	9	39
1989–93	Bush	29	1	17
1993–2001	Clinton	36	2	1
2001–	Bush	0	0	0

Note: These figures do not include the line-item veto that was to be declared unconstitutional. There have been disputes about the use of the pocket veto and the circumstances in which it can be deployed.
Sources: adapted from H. W. Stanley and R. G. Niemi (2000), *Vital Statistics on American Politics 1999–2000*, Washington DC, CQ Press, p. 256 and N. J. Ornstein, T. E. Mann and M. J. Malbin (2002), *Vital Statistics on Congress 2001–2002*, Washington DC, The AEI Press, p. 151.

Reagan (1981–89) issued thirty-nine pocket vetoes as well as thirty-nine regular vetoes.

However, the use of the veto may be an indication of presidential weakness rather than strength. George Bush frequently threatened a veto so as to gain legislative concessions from the governing Democrats in Congress. At first sight, this appears to have been an effective strategy. Congressional leaders held back from committing themselves to legislation unless they felt that they had a two-thirds – or 'veto-proof' – majority in both houses (Mervin 1996: 116). There is, however, another perspective. President George Bush (1989–93) may have been compelled to adopt a confrontational approach because he lacked other political resources. The veto is, furthermore, a *negative* instrument. It offers a way of blocking legislation, but it cannot be used to create the type of legislation that a president wishes to see.

The president can issue executive orders. These stem from the powers assigned to the president under the Constitution, from legislation already passed by Congress, or from his role in heading the executive branch. He can require agencies or individuals to undertake acts not necessarily mandated by Congress. Until 1933, executive orders were generally confined to administrative matters; but while they are still used to shape and mould the federal bureaucracy, they have since acquired a greater significance. On taking office in the midst of economic depression, President Franklin Roosevelt ordered a four-day closure of the banks. In 1942, Executive Order 9066 interned Japanese-Americans living in California when it was feared that they might assist Japanese military actions against the US. In 1948, President Truman used an executive order to desegegrate the armed forces. In 1957, President

Eisenhower used an executive order to 'federalise' the Arkansas National Guard so as to allow black students to enrol at Little Rock Central High School. On coming into office in 1993, President Clinton cancelled the executive orders issued by his two predecessors that had imposed a 'gag rule' which had prevented counsellors at federally-funded family planning clinics discussing the possibility of an abortion with clients. For his part, George W. Bush issued 54 orders in 2001 and 31 in 2002.

From 1946 onwards, the number and text of all executive orders is published in the *Federal Register*, the official US government record of all executive branch announcements, proposals, and regulations. There are, however, some 'classified' executive orders dealing with national security issues. These appear in the *Register* by number only.

The 1946 Employment Act created the Council of Economic Advisers (CEA) within the Executive Office of the President and empowered the president to 'use all practicable means . . . to promote maximum employment, production, and purchasing power' (quoted in Ragsdale 1998: 255).

The modern presidency has also acquired emergency powers. These were rationalised and codified by the 1976 National Emergencies Act, which was passed during the post-Watergate period. The Act stated that if an emergency is declared, the president must specify the laws under which powers are being exercised. The emergency is automatically terminated after a year unless he notifies Congress to the contrary. The president's powers include the restriction of travel by individuals to particular countries, the suspension of *habeas corpus*, which prevents arbitrary arrest, and the ability to declare martial law.

The president is well placed to shape and mould the annual budget. This is because the process is initiated within the executive branch. As Plano and Greenberg note, the Budget's 'size and specificity tend to reduce legislative discretion' (1989: 163). Some presidents have had particular success. President Reagan co-ordinated the 1981 budget process with his supporters in Congress. In May of that year – the time when Congress adopts budget resolutions setting overall spending ceilings – Congressional committees were directed to impose large-scale reductions in expenditure. Even in October 1998, when President Clinton's authority was at a very low ebb following the House of Representatives' decision to initiate impeachment hearings, he was able to win significant concessions from the Republican majority in Congress. These included a $1.1 billion plan to employ 100,000 additional teachers. As the *New York Times* concluded, those who asserted that the president had been 'terminally weakened . . . underestimated the president's resilience and the inherent authority of the office' (16 October 1998).

Presidents have also gained informal powers through the evolution of custom and precedent. In particular, ever since Franklin Roosevelt assumed the presidency in 1933, it has been accepted that presidents should initiate and propose measures that they hope to see enacted into law. Harry Truman began the

---

Box 6.2   Executive Order 13234

Presidential Task Force on Citizen Preparedness in the War on Terrorism Executive Order

By the authority vested in me as President by the Constitution and the laws of the United States of America, and in order to support and enhance the efforts of the American public with respect to preparedness and volunteerism in the war on terrorism, it is hereby ordered as follows:

Section 1. Establishment.
There is hereby established the "Presidential Task Force on Citizen Preparedness in the War On Terrorism" (Task Force).

Section 2. Membership.
(a) The Task Force shall be composed of the heads of the following executive branch entities, who may designate representatives from within their respective entities to assist them in their duties in connection with the Task Force: the Office of the Vice President, the Office of Homeland Security, the Domestic Policy Council, the Office of Science and Technology Policy, the Office of Management and Budget, the Department of the Treasury, the Department of Justice, the Department of Labor, the Department of Health and Human Services, the Department of Housing and Urban Development, the Department of Transportation, the Department of Energy, the Department of Veterans' Affairs, the Environmental Protection Agency, the Federal Emergency Management Agency, and the Corporation for National and Community Service. The heads of other executive branch departments and agencies and other senior executive branch officials may participate in the work of the Task Force upon the invitation of the Co-Chairs.

---

practice of presenting an annual package of legislative proposals (Mayhew 1991: 6). From then onwards, the president was recognised as the nation's 'Chief Legislator'. For example, Ronald Reagan offered a conservative 'revolution', and his campaign for the presidency resting on a promise of decentralisation, military rearmament, tax cuts, and deregulation. He hoped to liberate business from what he regarded as restrictive government policies, and thereby generate economic growth. On taking office, Bill Clinton also had a specific series of reforms in mind. His plans included tax reductions for the 'middle class', an 'economic stimulus package' that would accelerate recovery from the 1990–91 recession, the balancing of the federal budget, and the reform of health care. For his part, George W. Bush promoted tax reductions, educational reform, and faith-based initiatives that would offer assistance through church organisations to those in need. These themes were drawn from his commitment to 'compassionate conservatism'.

(b) The heads of the Office of Homeland Security and the Domestic Policy Council, or their designated representatives, shall serve as Co-Chairs of the Task Force.

Section 3. Mission.
The Task Force shall identify, review, and recommend appropriate means by which the American public can:

(a) prepare in their homes, neighborhoods, schools, places of worship, work-places, and public places for the potential consequences of any possible terrorist attacks within the United States; and

(b) volunteer to assist or otherwise support State and local public health and safety officials and others engaged in the effort to prevent, prepare for, and respond to any possible terrorist attacks within the United States.

Section 4. Reporting Requirement.
The Task Force shall submit its recommendations to the President within 40 days from the date of this order.

Section 5. Termination of Task Force.
The Task Force shall terminate 30 days after submitting its report to the President.

GEORGE W. BUSH
The White House, November 9, 2001.

Federal Register page and date: 66 FR 57355, November 15, 2001
Amended by: EO 13284, January 23, 2003
Source: US National Archives and Records Administration (2001), *Federal Register – Executive Orders Disposition Tables – George W. Bush – 2001,*
www.archives.gov/federal_register/executive_orders/2001_wbush.html.

Limits and constraints

There is, however, another perspective on the US presidency. Despite his powers, some observers argue that the president remains subject to a number of severe constraints. Joseph A. Califano Jr., who served in both Lyndon Johnson's and Jimmy Carter's administrations, claimed that Congress had 'become the King Kong of Washington's political jungle, dominating an executive branch that can no longer claim the co-equal status that the Founding Fathers saw as crucial' (1996: 112). In another allusion to a work of fiction, the president has been likened to Gulliver, who was held down by tiny Lilliputian ropes in Jonathan Swift's classic satire. The ability of Congress to impose its will, and curtail presidential ambitions, was starkly illustrated in 1919–20 when President Woodrow Wilson submitted the Treaty of Versailles to the US Senate. Fearful of further entanglements in European affairs, the Senate put forward amendments, and following the rejection of these, refused ratification. In the wake of this, the US followed an isolationist course for two decades.

Fifty years after the Treaty of Versailles was defeated, the constraints on a US president were again graphically illustrated. The shock of military defeat in Vietnam was compounded by other blows to the credibility of the presidency. It became clear that the Nixon administration had used federal government agencies, such as the Internal Revenue Service, to harass its opponents. The Watergate scandal, which involved an attempt by the president and his aides to hide White House involvement in a bid to plant listening devices in a Democratic Party campaign office, finally led to President Nixon's resignation in August 1974. While the Nixon White House sought to save itself, Congress began to reassert its authority. Steps were taken to 'contain' the powers of the presidency. These measures encouraged some observers to talk in terms of the 'imperilled' or 'impaired' presidency.

The War Powers Resolution and after

The War Powers Resolution became law – despite a veto by President Richard Nixon – in November 1973. It sought to ensure that the US would not again become embroiled in a 'presidential' war such as Vietnam by involving Congress in decisions to deploy US forces in conflicts. This was represented as a reassertion of the Constitutional principle. The preamble to the Resolution stated that its purpose was:

> to fulfill the intent of the framers of the Constitution of the United States and ensure that the collective judgement of both the Congress and the President will apply to the introduction of U.S. armed forces into hostilities, wherein situations where imminent involvement in hostilities is clearly indicated by the circumstances, and the continued use of such forces in hostilities or in such situations.

The Resolution asserted that – unless Congress had declared war – it could require the president to withdraw US forces involved in overseas hostilities within a period of sixty days. A further thirty days was permitted if the president certified that further military action was necessary to disengage US military personnel from a conflict safely. The Resolution also called upon the president to consult with Congress 'in every possible instance' before deploying troops.

For President Richard Nixon, the War Powers Act removed 'authorities which the president had properly exercised under the Constitution for almost 200 years'. He, and subsequent presidents, denied its constitutionality. Henry Kissinger, President Nixon's National Security Adviser, also saw the Resolution, and the other measures adopted by Congress, as a fundamental shift in the character of the relations between the legislative and executive branches: 'The decade-long struggle in this country over executive dominance in foreign affairs is over. The recognition that the Congress is a co-equal branch is the dominant fact of national politics today' (quoted in Foley and Owens 1996: 372).

In 1983, the War Powers Act was applied, albeit in a loose form. President Reagan sent US forces to the Lebanon. Congress responded by 'starting the clock' established under the Act, although the President was given eighteen months rather than the ninety days specified by the Resolution. However, in the aftermath of a brutally effective terrorist attack, when a suicide bombing led to the deaths of 219 Americans, the President withdrew the troops. Congress took other steps – aside from the War Powers Act – to rein in the president in his handling of foreign and defence policy:

- The 1974 Jackson–Vanik Amendment inserted clauses into a trade bill explicitly linking the Soviet Union's trading status to levels of Jewish emigration. Although this was bitterly resented by Soviet leaders, the number of *émigrés* increased significantly following its passage.
- In 1980, President Jimmy Carter withdrew SALT-II – the Strategic Arms Limitation Treaty that he had concluded with the USSR – once it had become clear that, in the aftermath of the Soviet invasion of Afghanistan, the Treaty would be rejected by the Senate.
- In 1986, Congress imposed trade sanctions against South Africa, as a protest against the country's system of racial *apartheid*, despite a presidential veto.

Congress has also used its 'power of the purse'. In December 1970 it prohibited funding for combat troops in Cambodia and in June 1973, this was extended to the remainder of South-east Asia. In 1976, Cuban military forces were deployed in Angola so as to support the Soviet-aligned government against Western-oriented guerrilla armies. Although the US is traditionally fearful of Cuban operations, Congress was haunted by the prospect of another Vietnam, and specifically denied funding for military activities in the country.

The shadow of Vietnam was still evident in the 1990s. Presidents continued to pay heed to Congressional sentiment, and Congress sought to mould and often to curtail presidential initiatives. Although the War Powers Resolution was not invoked, President George Bush sought Congressional backing before hostilities began in the 1991 Gulf War. On the eve of war, the House backed military action against the Iraqi forces by 250 to 83 votes. The Senate agreed by 52 to 40 votes. Shortly before his presidency came to an end, President Bush launched *Operation Restore Hope* in response to events in Somalia. The people faced mass famine. The country was being torn apart by gangs and rival warlords. The mission was an attempt to secure an environment in which humanitarian relief could be distributed to those in need, and 28,000 US troops and 2,000 soldiers from other nations were sent. However, the difficulties were underestimated, and, within months, eighteen US servicemen had been killed in Mogadishu. Congress set a deadline of 31 March 1994 for the end of US military involvement. In September 1994 – foreseeing a quagmire – Congress sought to curtail US intervention in the central African state of Rwanda by again using the 'power of the purse': 'no funds provided in this Act are available for United States military participation to continue Operation Support Hope in or around Rwanda after October 7, 1994, except for any action that is necessary to protect the lives of United States citizens' (quoted in Grimmett 2001).

As John Dumbrell has argued, the Clinton administration's foreign policy was – at least in part – moulded by Congressional pressures. While emphasising that the president retained the power of initiative, Dumbrell records: 'Congress clearly has the ability to drive the executive in new directions. Congressional pressure was also important in influencing policy towards Haiti and Northern Ireland. It contributed to a virtual turnaround in Bosnia in 1995 and reset US policy towards Cuba in 1996' (Dumbrell 2000: 97).

- The 1994 landings in Haiti followed lobbying by the Congressional Black Caucus. However, amidst fears of embroilment, most members of Congress – and a majority of the public – were opposed to the deployment of US troops. There was talk of invoking the War Powers Resolution. These pressures may have fuelled a decision by the White House to accept the compromise whereby American troops met no opposition, while the Haitian military leaders were allowed to leave the island.

- In the period before the Northern Ireland peace process gained momentum and took a public form, the Clinton administration rejected British objections and gave Gerry Adams, president of Sinn Fein, a visa allowing him to visit New York. The decision was, in part, a response to lobbying by about forty members of Congress, including Senator Edward Kennedy of Massachusetts.

- The disintegration of Yugoslavia led to savage warfare, particularly in Bosnia. In 1995, members of both the House and the Senate sought the lifting of the arms embargo that had been placed on the Bosnian government – as well as the other combatants – so that they could defend themselves against attacks. Dumbrell suggests that this encouraged the Clinton administration to take the initiative. It led – in late 1995 – to the Dayton agreement that brought the war to a close.

- In 1996, Congress played a part in the active shaping of US foreign policy by passing the Cuban Liberty and Democratic Solidarity Act, also known – after the names of its initial sponsors – as Helms–Burton. The act strengthened the economic embargo on Cuba, ruled out negotiations with the Castro government, and imposed penalties on foreign companies investing in Cuba (Dumbrell 2000: 92).

- Even in the wake of September 11th, President George W. Bush felt obliged to seek Congressional backing. Three days after the attacks, Congress approved a resolution that was rather narrower in scope than that initially considered in the White House. It authorised the president to: 'use all necessary and appropriate force against nations, organizations, or persons he determines planned, authorized, committed, or aided the terrorist attacks that occurred on September 11, 2001, or harbored such organizations or persons, in order to prevent any future acts of international terrorism against the United States by such nations, organizations or persons.'

The votes for the resolution were 98–0 in the Senate and 420–1 in the House of Representatives. The lone dissenter was Barbara Lee, a black Democratic Congresswoman who represents the ninth district in California. Just over a year later, the consensus had begun to fray. In October 2002, the House of Representatives agreed to the use of force against Iraq by 296–133. The Senate vote was 77–23.

Loss of primacy

Why – from the perspective of those who stress the limits and constraints upon administrations – has the president lost much of his authority in the making of foreign and defence policy?

As the harsh realities of the Vietnam war became evident, public cynicism towards the White House grew. This – and the Watergate episode – led to a long-term shift in the character of public attitudes towards the political process, and the White House in particular, Although there was a limited recovery during the latter half of the 1990s, trust in government declined markedly. Against this background, presidents were unwilling to embark on military action unless it had narrowly defined goals and US casualties could be minimised.

Table 6.4 *Trust in government 1958–2000 (% of the population)*

	1958	1972	1980	1994	2000
None of the time	0	1	4	3	1
Some of the time	23	44	69	74	55
Most of the time	57	48	23	19	40
Just about always	16	5	2	2	4
Don't know, depends	4	2	2	1	1

Question text: 'How much of the time do you think you can trust the government in Washington to do what is right – just about always, most of the time or only some of the time?'
Source: adapted from National Election Studies (2003), *Trust the Federal Government 1958–2000*, www.umich.edu/~nes/nesguide/toptable/tab5a_1.htm.

The communications revolution of the 1980s and the emergence of policy units (or 'thinktanks') contributed to changes in the political atmosphere. Earlier, instinctive loyalties towards the president were undermined as internet 'bloggers' – who publish daily commentaries on public affairs – and the proliferation of news channels such as CNN, MSNBC, and Fox News broke down White House hegemony over information and analysis. As Michael Foley and John Owens note: 'Instead of a near monopoly of foreign policy information and reflexive Cold War deference to presidential judgement, presidents are now besieged by a multiplicity of groups and organisations not only with information sources and evaluation techniques of their own but with the means and willingness to challenge a president's foreign policy decisions on tactical, strategic, and ethical grounds' (1996: 380).

The end of the Cold War placed the foreign and defence policy consensus under considerable strain. It had begun to disintegrate during the Vietnam era. The removal of the Soviet threat finally allowed different opinions and strategies to flourish. During the 1990s, there were – in particular – significant tensions between those who sought a neo-isolationist course and others who were committed to what their critics derided as 'nation-building' in countries across the globe. The 2003 war in Iraq also provoked dissent. It was opposed by significant numbers of Democrats, and there were further divisions around the role that the United Nations should be permitted to play. Against this background, the foreign and military options pursued by the White House were subject to much more intense and critical scrutiny than in former years.

The president faces further obstacles in the making of foreign trade policy. The North American Free Trade Agreement (NAFTA) phases out trade restrictions between the US, Canada and Mexico. Under its provisions, all tariff barriers between the three countries are to be eliminated by 2000. When NAFTA came to a vote in November 1994, it passed in the House by a majority of 234 to 200, and gained a 61–38 majority in the Senate. However, it was only passed after protracted discussions had taken place and President Clinton had assembled a coalition of support within each house. Trade policy is subject to political bartering and negotiation because:

1 In other areas of defence and foreign policy, there are feelings of national loyalty towards the president in his role as commander-in-chief or as a statesman on the world stage. Such considerations are far less of a factor in the formulation of trade policy.
2 Some of the most effective pressure groups – including large-scale corporations and the labour unions – have much at stake in the future of trade policy. They are involved in lobbying activities. Whereas most business organisations endorse the principle of free trade, and believe that it will increase company profitability, many in the unions – and some businessmen in 'exposed' industries – fear that unrestricted trade with low-wage countries will destroy US jobs.
3 These lobbies are represented within both the major political parties. Sections of the Democratic Party – represented by, for example, the former House Minority Leader, Dick Gephardt – are closely tied to the trade unions, and are suspicious of unrestrained trade. For its part, the Bush administration responded to pressure from the steel industry and – in 2002 – imposed tariffs of between 8 and 30 per cent on imported steel over a three-year period.

While NAFTA was a success for the Clinton administration, there have been setbacks. The freeing up of trade – and the progressive elimination of tariff barriers – is largely dependent upon the ability of presidents to gain 'fast-track authority' from Congress. The process was established in 1974 but lapsed in 1994. It rests on an undertaking from Congress that they will consider trade agreements concluded by the administration with other nations under a procedure with compulsory deadlines, no amendments, and limited debate. Armed with fast-track authority, presidents can negotiate with other governments from a position of mutual confidence. NAFTA was considered on this basis. Without fast-track authority, any discussions with other countries have limited purpose or credibility.

In November 1997, President Clinton sought fast-track authority for further international trade deals. He had hoped to expand NAFTA to include Chile, and to create a Free Trade Area of the Americas by 2005. His longer-term vision rested on the construction of a free trade area stretching across the Pacific Ocean by about 2020. Clinton was, however, unable to win fast-track authority from Congress. In the House of Representatives, the vote was 180–243. Only about forty of the 205 Democrats in the House voted for the proposal. Many of the others feared that trade liberalisation would jeopardise the interests of US workers who would be threatened by low-wage competition from abroad. There were also concerns that foreign producers – who did not have to respect regulations protecting the environment – would have open access to the American market.

However, despite the fears of some producer groups – such as the textile industries – and the granting of concessions so that workers displaced by foreign competition are offered retraining programmes, President Bush gained fast-track authority in mid-2002.

Constraints on domestic policy

The decline in public trust in decision-makers and the pervasive character of contemporary news reporting have placed constraints upon the president's domestic policy making powers to an even greater extent than in the formulation of foreign policy. There are, however, further limits.

Although the president is 'manager of the economy', his administration has only limited authority over the country's monetary policy. The setting of the interest rate – which can determine a country's economic wellbeing – is the prerogative of the Federal Reserve Board.

While the federal government's annual budget is initially proposed by the president, and he is the key figure in shaping its character, it must be agreed by Congress. A budget is the product of prolonged negotiation and compromise (see Chapter 5). Indeed, as David Mervin notes, the eventual outcome 'may be quite at odds with the president's original intention' (1990: 104). President

George Bush (1989–93) learned this lesson in an episode that contributed to his loss of the presidency. His 1988 election victory owed much to the soundbite: 'Read my lips. No new taxes.' Faced, however, with spending commitments and an entrenched budget deficit, the 1990 Budget included both tax increases and expenditure cuts. Opposed by both conservative Republicans – who opposed the tax increases – and Democrats, who rejected cuts in welfare provision, the initial budget was defeated in the House of Representatives. The White House and Congress agreed to a revised version, increasing tax revenues by $140 billion over a five-year period, which was passed at the end of October 1990. Bush's opponents repeatedly cited his 'betrayal' in the 1992 presidential election.

There are other constraints upon the president's fiscal – or budgetary – powers. The 1974 Budget and Impoundment Control Act prevented a president withholding funds that had been allocated for a particular purpose by Congress. (President Nixon had, for example, cut about nine billion dollars from funds appropriated for the Environmental Protection Agency.) The Act specified that funds cannot be 'impounded' by the Administration unless both houses of Congress approve of the action within forty-five days. The Act also created the Congressional Budget Office (CBO). The CBO provides specialist economic analysis, and therefore enables members of Congress to take an independent look at the economic projections drawn up by the executive branch.

The president faces a further set of constraints. In contrast with those who lead nations that have a *unitary* structure – where political power is concentrated in the hands of the central government – the US has a *federal* structure. Power is distributed between Washington DC and the individual states. In a number of policy spheres, therefore, decision-making has to be a negotiated process between the president, Congress, state governors and state legislatures. This is explored in Chapter 8.

Although the president has the power to nominate ambassadors, cabinet members, other senior officials in the federal bureaucracy (see Chapter 7), and federal judges, his power of appointment is subject to Senate confirmation. This is not necessarily a straightforward process. In 1987, President Reagan nominated a well-known conservative jurist, Robert Bork, to the Supreme Court bench. The Senate Judiciary Committee – guided by prominent Democrats such as Edward Kennedy and Joseph Biden – asserted that Bork's views disqualified him from serving on the Court. He was rejected. Subsequently, in 1989, President Bush nominated a former Senator, John Tower, as Secretary of Defense. However, in March 1989, allegations about Tower's personal life and his relationships with companies seeking military contracts led Senators to reject the nomination by a 53–47 vote (Parmet 1997: 379). In 2001, Linda Chavez, a Latino conservative, was nominated by George W. Bush to be Secretary of Labor. However, in an echo of the 'nannygate' that the Clinton administration had faced eight years earlier, she was compelled to withdraw following claims that an illegal immigrant had lived in her home and undertaken household duties.

Recent presidents and their senior staff have been subject to investigation by independent counsel. Under the 1978 Ethics in Government Act – adopted in the aftermath of Watergate – special prosecutors are appointed to investigate allegations of law-breaking at the highest levels of government. They report to Congress. Between 1979 and 1998, there have been twenty independent counsel investigations, the most well-known of which was Kenneth Starr's inquiry into President Clinton's financial affairs, personal behaviour, and legal testimony. His report provided the basis for impeachment proceedings against Clinton. However, the law allowing for these investigations lapsed without renewal in mid-1999. The power to investigate alleged misconduct in government thereby reverted to the Attorney-General, a cabinet member and an appointee of the president.

Although the Supreme Court has played a role in strengthening the powers of the presidency, some rulings have curtailed the president's freedom of action. Significant components of the New Deal were struck down in rulings such as *Schechter Poultry Corporation v. US* (1935) and *US v. Butler* (1936). The Court regarded the government interventionism upon which the New Deal rested as a threat to individual liberties and rights. President Truman's Administration took control of steel mills when they were threatened by strike action (there were fears that industrial action would interrupt supplies destined for the Korean War effort). The Court ruled in *Youngstown Sheet and Tube Company v. Sawyer* (1952) that the president's action had been unconstitutional. He had exceeded his powers. In 1974, the Supreme Court played a role in the Watergate crisis. Its judgement in *US v. Richard M. Nixon* circumscribed the concept of 'executive privilege' by ruling that the president must release transcripts of the tape recordings that had been made of his conversations with aides. In the 1990s, the president's sphere of privacy was narrowed down still further. In a succession of court battles, arising from an allegation of sexual harassment against President Clinton and Kenneth Starr's investigations, it was established that civil proceedings could be brought against a sitting president and White House political and legal advisers could be questioned and compelled to answer under oath.

Appraising the arguments

Some observers distinguish between the powers of the president in the making of foreign and domestic policy. Indeed, the late Aaron Wildavsky suggested that there were 'two presidencies'. There is a presidency for managing foreign affairs and a separate presidency for domestic policy formation. Each of these offers distinct opportunities and constraints. Traditionally, although George W. Bush emphasised domestic policy until the 11 September attacks, presidents focus upon foreign policy, because they have greater freedom of action and are subject to fewer limits.

Box 6.3   Scoring presidential success: CQ ratings

In 1953, *Congressional Quarterly* – a respected Washington journal – established a system of measurement by which presidential success and failure could be evaluated. *CQ ratings* – as they became known – are based upon formal, 'roll-call' votes in Congress. The rating measures the proportion of these where the president 'took a clear position' and his position was subsequently endorsed in a roll-call vote in the House of Representatives and the Senate. It is expressed as a percentage.

Presidents Eisenhower and Johnson come out particularly well. In some years, they attracted CQ ratings of over 80 per cent. Others, however, have fared much less well. President Bush sank to 43 per cent in 1992. In 1973, Richard Nixon gained a rating of only just over 50 per cent. President Bill Clinton's 36.2 per cent score in 1995 represented an all-time low. However, Clinton recovered from this, and there was a dramatic improvement during the course of 1996. His rating reached 55.1 per cent, an increase of 18.9 per cent. This was the biggest one-year jump since *Congressional Quarterly* began its system of ratings.

Congressional voting in support of the president's position (%)

President	House and Senate
Eisenhower (average)	72.2
Kennedy	84.6
Johnson	82.6
Nixon	67.2
Ford	57.6
Carter	76.4
Reagan	61.9
Bush	51.6
Clinton	
1993	86.4
1994	86.4
1995	36.2
1996	55.1
1997	53.6
1998	50.6
1999	37.8
2000	55.0
Bush	
2001	87.0
2002	87.8

Source: adapted from *CQ Weekly* (2002), 60:48, 14 December, 3275.

President George W. Bush's ratings of 87 per cent and over overshadow those of his predecessors. CQ ratings have, however, been subject to criticism on methodological grounds. Some observers claim that they are misleading:

1 They treat all votes and legislative proposals equally. There is no attempt to include an assessment of the relative importance or unimportance of a particular measure.

2 Many important issues do not come to a roll-call vote. This is sometimes because a voice vote is taken. It may also be that opposition to the president's proposals is so overwhelming that they are dropped before being formally considered by Congress. In 1994, the plan to reform health-care provision drawn up by Hillary Rodham Clinton and Ira Magaziner, a key presidential aide, had to be abandoned once it became clear it had very little support. It was never submitted to any form of vote.

3 The legislation that the CQ rating measures is not necessarily representative. Since the 1960s, presidents have only taken a position on about a quarter of the legislation put to a roll-call vote in Congress. Arguably, they have been reluctant to adopt a formal position where defeat is a strong possibility or likelihood (Ragsdale 1996: 360).

4 CQ ratings make no attempt to distinguish between presidents who face a Congress dominated by the other party and those who do not. As David Mervin notes, this 'makes a mockery of simple comparisons between, say, Johnson and Nixon, or even Carter and Bush' (Mervin 1996: 112).

References and further reading

Congressional Quarterly Weekly, 21 December 1996, 3428.

However, the relationship between the president and the other branches of government is not static. Neither can it be defined in terms of a unilinear trend. For his part, Charles O. Jones suggests that the relationship between the president and Congress has a cyclical character. Looking back over the past century, he identifies periods of Congressional primacy, such as the 1920s, but records that there were phases – such as the 1930s and 1960s – when the president played a predominant role. There have also been periods of 'mixed government' in which power was balanced between the legislative and executive branches of government. However, the relationship took different forms. It could either be co-operative or adversarial in character (Jones 1995: 11).

Jones suggests that these cycles – and the extent of presidential power – are shaped by broad external circumstances. Against this background, the personality of the president is a secondary consideration. Presidents, Jones argues: 'face the challenge of governing under the contrary political conditions set by the American voters, the competitive institutional conditions created by a reformed Congress, and the policy conditions resulting from the huge post-Great Society self-generating agenda' (1995: 55–6).

From this perspective, the character of the relationship between the president and Congress is shaped by a range of variables. Observers stress different factors, but most include the nature of the preceding presidential election, the partisan composition of the Senate and the House of Representatives, the structures of Congress, public opinion, and the state of the economy.

Presidential elections and issue differences

Presidents can dominate the political process, but only in if they have unusual electoral advantages. They gain, in particular, if they have won the presidency in a contest structured around significant issue differences between the candidates. In 1964, Lyndon Johnson, the incumbent president, offered a message based upon compassion, moderation and reform, although much of it had been set in place before the election. His Republican opponent, Senator Barry Goldwater, a hardline conservative, appeared much more extreme in terms of both domestic and foreign policy. In a highly polarised contest, Johnson won a landslide victory and thereby gained considerable political leverage. There was also a stark contrast between the candidates in November 1980. Jimmy Carter, who was coming to the end of his first term, appeared to offer little to counter the US's relative weakness on the world stage – which had been vividly symbolised by the taking of US embassy personnel as hostages by radical Moslems in Iran – and the sense of economic malaise and national decline. In contrast, the Republican challenger, Ronald Reagan, talked in terms of rebuilding American military and economic strength. In both the 1964 and the 1980 election, the incoming president had a mandate. His legislative proposals therefore had a legitimacy that encouraged members of Congress to acquiesce in their passage.

Partisanship

Presidents are in an advantageous position – in terms of their bargaining abilities – if there has been a landslide gain for their party in Congressional elections. Correspondingly, political observers have customarily argued, they may face significant difficulties and be subject to severe constraint during periods of 'divided government'. This is when one party holds a majority on Capitol Hill and the other party occupies the White House. In these circumstances, many commentators suggest, a degree of *gridlock* – when the process of decision-making comes to a halt because the different branches of government have conflicting goals and priorities – is commonplace. As V. O. Key Jr. noted: 'Common partisan control of executive and legislature does not assure energetic government, but division of party control precludes it' (quoted in Mayhew 1991: 2).

The Democrats controlled Congress for almost all the period between 1933 and 1995, and Republican presidents faced hostile Congressional majorities. The US again had divided government after the November 1994 elections, when the Republicans won a majority in both houses of Congress, while President Clinton, a Democrat, occupied the White House. There were particular tensions because the House Republicans were committed to the *Contract with America*, a platform of measures that included welfare reform and a pledge to take action against crime. At the time, it was seen by observers as an attempt by the then House Speaker Newt Gingrich to usurp the president's role as 'Chief Legislator'. George W. Bush faced significant difficulties between May 2001 and the end of 2002 because the Senate was controlled – albeit narrowly – by the Democrats. He had to make concessions and reach compromises. Despite the administration's initial objections, for example, airport security was placed under the control of federal government employees. There was, furthermore, no ban on 'partial-birth abortion' and the 2001 No Child Left Behind Act – which sought to reform the nation's schools – did little to further longstanding conservative plans for school vouchers and parental choice. At the same time, two of the White House's nominations to the Circuit courts of appeal – Charles Pickering and Priscilla Owen – were blocked.

However, there is another perspective. In *Divided We Govern*, a study of Congress's legislative and oversight record between 1945 and 1990, David Mayhew has concluded that 'it does not seem to make all that much difference whether party control of American government happens to be unified or divided' (1991: 198). The desire of both branches of government to claim legislative accomplishments encourages compromise and accommodation. Furthermore, even when both the executive and legislative branches are controlled by the same party, there are no assurances of success for the president. Party discipline is weak, and some members of Congress may break ranks with their colleagues on a particular issue. Furthermore, the president and members of Congress have different constituencies to consider and face different electoral cycles. There are therefore always tensions between them, even in periods of 'unified government'. In 1979, President Jimmy Carter's plan for energy conservation was rejected despite a Democratic majority in both houses of Congress. Similarly, President Clinton had to abandon his 1993 plans for health care reform because of Congressional opposition. In March 2003, the Republicans controlled the White House and both chambers of Congress. Nonetheless, although President Bush was able to gain much of his policy agenda, his attempts to allow drilling for oil and gas in Alaska's Arctic National Wildlife Refuge were defeated in the Senate by 52 to 48 votes (*Washington Post* 20 March 2003).

Congressional structures

Some observers argue that changes in the structure and organisation of Congress have also had an impact on presidential–Congressional relations. From the 1970s onwards, the structures of Congress became much more decentralised and fragmented. Traditionally, power within Congress lay in the hands of the committee chairmen. Although the 'barons' still hold considerable authority, their position has been weakened by the devolution of power to subcommittees and measures such as the Legislative Reorganisation Act of 1970 that required committees to abide by formal rules of procedure rather than follow the, often arbitrary, rulings of the chairman. As John E. Owens has recorded: 'Once the bastions of congressional power, in the post-reform Congress of the 1980s and 1990s standing committees and their chairs found that their wings had been severely clipped. They were now obliged to heed the demands of ordinary rank-and-file members within the party caucuses and conferences' (Owens 1996: 16).

Although the parties correspondingly gained greater leverage and coherence, the growth of a more independent and assertive spirit among members of Congress made it more difficult for presidents to construct coalitions that would enable the legislation they favoured to pass into law.

Public opinion

Many commentators suggest that public opinion plays a pivotal role in either strengthening or weakening a president. Congress is, as James Q. Wilson has argued, reluctant to oppose a popular president: 'Other things being equal, the more popular the president, the higher the proportion of his bills that Congress will pass' (1992: 344). Although President Eisenhower (1953–61) was able to maintain relatively high approval ratings throughout his period of office, presidents generally enjoy a fairly brief 'honeymoon' with the US public. After a year or so, their popularity usually begins to slip.

President George W. Bush's ratings initially followed this pattern. Despite the circumstances of his election – and the prolonged battle to secure the Florida Electoral College Vote – he had a honeymoon period. However, perceptions of Bush and his presidency were transformed by the 11 September attacks. Indeed, his approval ratings were unprecedented. It was only then that they slowly sank back towards political normality, until they were revived by the swift conclusion to the 2003 Iraq war.

However, although commentators such as Wilson emphasise the role of public opinion, this conclusion can be challenged. Although Bush's popularity reached very high levels, and was at an unprecedented 89 per cent two months

Table 6.5 *President George W. Bush: poll ratings (%)* (Time/CNN *Opinion Poll conducted by Harris Interactive*)

	Favourable	Unfavourable	Not familiar	Not sure
March 2003	67	30	2	1
August 2002	69	27	2	2
November 2001	89	9	1	1
July 2001	58	36	5	1
March 2001	56	35	6	3
January 2001	58	32	5	5

Source: adapted from PollingReport.com (2003), *President Bush: Favorability Ratings*, www.pollingreport.com/BushFav.htm.

after the 11 September attacks, he still faced significant difficulties winning support for his legislation in the Senate. From June 2001 until the end of 2002, the Democrats had – following the defection of Senator Jim Jeffords (Vermont) from the Republicans – a one-seat majority in the upper chamber. Despite the emotional shock of the attacks, there was a strong sense of partisanship on Capitol Hill and Bush, therefore, had to make concessions and reach compromises. Despite his commitment to the private sector, many airport security personnel became federal government employees. The No Child Left Behind Act, an education bill that became law in January 2002, emphasised overall standards and testing rather than longstanding conservative proposals for tax credits or vouchers that would have allowed a measure of school choice. Furthermore, the president's nominations of Charles Pickering and Priscilla Owen to the Circuit Courts of Appeal made no progress.

Economy

There have been suggestions that the position of the president is – at least in part – dependent upon the state of the economy. From 1933 onwards, when President Franklin Roosevelt took office, presidents have been held responsible for the nation's economic progress and prosperity. This coincided with a change in economic thinking. The federal government budget was increasingly regarded as an instrument of macroeconomic policy. Spending and taxation were to be used so as to modify the business cycle and increase overall employment levels. The 1946 Employment Act confirmed the president's role as 'manager of the economy'. He was 'to avoid economic fluctuations [and] . . . maintain employment, production and purchasing power.'

To some extent, the 'Reagan Revolution' of the 1980s modified expectations that an administration could or should direct a nation's economy in this way. Nonetheless – as some elections seem to confirm – the president is still held largely responsible for the country's economic fortunes. President George Bush's loss of the 1992 presidential election is widely attributed to the recession that preceded it. In 1991, the economy contracted, and national output fell by 0.5 per cent. In the following year, unemployment rose to 7.5 per cent. Conversely, President Bill Clinton's re-election victory in 1996 owed much to relative economic prosperity. The *Wall Street Journal* talked in terms of the 'Goldilocks economy', in which both inflation and unemployment had been reduced to a minimum, and that was therefore neither too 'hot' nor too 'cold'.

Nonetheless, although the state of the economy ensured Clinton's re-election in November 1996, and may have contributed – through the medium of public opinion – to his acquittal when he was impeached two years later, there are difficulties with the claim that economic conditions can determine presidential power. Although he became the first two-term Democratic president since Franklin Roosevelt, Clinton was unable to promote a distinct policy agenda. Once the Congressional Republicans had been swept to power in the 1994 mid-term

Table 6.6 *Real economic growth, 1990–2002 (% change in GDP in constant 1996 dollars)*

Year	% change
1990	1.8
1991	−0.5
1992	3.0
1993	2.7
1994	4.0
1995	2.7
1996	3.6
1997	4.4
1998	4.3
1999	4.1
2000	3.8
2001	0.3
2002	2.4

Source: adapted from Bureau of Economic Analysis (2003), *National Accounts Data – Current Dollar and Real GDP*, www.bea.doc.gov/bea/dn/gdpchg.xls.

elections, he was compelled to accept measures – most notably welfare reform (the Personal Responsibility and Work Opportunity Reconciliation Act) – that had been initiated by them.

The craft of persuasion

Some scholars have a different emphasis. While acknowledging that external circumstances can impose constraints upon a president and that his position is, at least in part, a product of the formal powers bestowed upon him by the Constitution, they argue that a president's personal abilities can be pivotal. Drawing upon President Eisenhower's frustrations at the unresponsiveness of the government apparatus, Richard Neustadt concludes that much depends upon the skills of the individual office-holder:

> 'powers' are no guarantee of power . . . The President of the United States has an extraordinary range of formal powers, of authority in statute law and in the Constitution. Here is testimony that despite his 'powers' he does not obtain results by giving orders – or not, at any rate, merely by giving orders. He also has extraordinary status, *ex officio*, according to the customs of our government and politics. Here is testimony that despite his status he does not get action without argument. Presidential power is the power to persuade. (Neustadt 1991: 10–11)

What is persuasiveness? It incorporates, Neustadt suggests, charm and the ability to offer a reasoned argument based upon logic. However, it goes beyond this. It involves the strategic use and application of the president's status and authority. It also rests upon the employment of bargaining skills. Governing is a two-way relationship between the president and others who must anticipate his reaction if he is defied or obstructed. For his part, the president can 'trade' the resources of his office: 'With hardly an exception, those who share in governing this country are aware that at some time, in some degree, the doing of *their* jobs, the furthering of *their* ambitions, may depend upon the President of the United States. Their need for presidential action, or their fear of it, is bound to be recurrent if not actually continuous. Their need or fear is his advantage' (Neustadt 1991: 31).

From the perspective of Neustadt and his co-thinkers, there is, as Tim Hames records, 'almost no ceiling or floor to what a president might achieve. The incumbent may emulate Franklin D. Roosevelt or Warren Harding, depending on his political ability' (Hames 2000: 67). Lyndon Johnson is widely regarded as an effective 'persuader'. A former Senate Majority Leader, he used his personal ties and skills to build coalitions of support for his civil rights legislation and the 'war on poverty'. President Reagan also had a significant measure of success in the early years of his presidency. His administration mobilised interest groups behind particular measures and, at the same time, adopted a strategy based on the setting of inflated goals. As Martin Anderson, the President's chief adviser on domestic and economic policy issues, notes, Reagan 'almost always got more than he would have been willing to settle for, because in the beginning he instinctively asked for far more than he could reasonably expect to get' (1988: 241).

Jimmy Carter had, however, fewer skills. Although both chambers had a Democratic majority, he had a difficult relationship with Congress. As a former governor of Georgia, he was regarded as a Washington outsider. His staff lacked experience of Congress. He had only a limited strategic agenda, and there were difficulties establishing a sense of political direction. The House leadership was sidelined. The president's powers of appointment, which can be used to win allies within Congress, were largely squandered.

Observers do, not always agree. There are different assessments of President Clinton during the early phases of his period in office. John Owens sees the President's approach during his first year in office as 'skilful', and cites his 'hands on' style (1994: 8). Clinton was, Owens argues, an effective communicator who employed experienced staff in the all-important Office of Legislative Affairs, the Congressional liaison office that is located in the west wing of the White House. His skills ensured a number of important legislative successes, such as the passage of the 1993 budget, and the 'motor voter' bill that enables citizens to register as voters rather more easily. Clinton's skills in ensuring that Congress passed NAFTA have attracted particular praise. He not only constructed a bipartisan coalition in both houses, but: 'defined the issue, took the propaganda initiative, demonstrated considerable legislative finesse and made the necessary compromises and bargains to overcome opposition within his own party to win the vote' (Foley and Owens 1996: 305–6). Anthony Bennett adopts a very different perspective. He talks in terms of 'utter confusion' and failure (1994: 33). There were repeated setbacks. The fate of Clinton's health-care proposals has already been noted. Congress emasculated his economic stimulus package. Clinton was also committed to the early implementation of a campaign pledge to end the ban on open homosexuals serving in the armed forces. However, after facing opposition from within Congress and the armed forces, he had eventually to settle for an uneasy compromise structured around a 'don't ask, don't tell' policy.

Observers are rather more generous to Clinton in the later years of his pres-idency. Although his legislative accomplishments were sparse, he was able to mobilise public opinion so as to limit and circumscribe the ambitions of Congressional Republicans. The Republicans had won a majority in both houses of Congress in the November 1994 elections, and differences quickly emerged about the shape of the annual budget. In late 1995, the Republicans passed a continuing resolution that maintained funding for government pro-grammes until a budget had been agreed. However, it incorporated spending cuts that Clinton opposed, and he therefore vetoed it. Many government depart-ments and agencies were – as a consequence – shut down. Despite his earlier unpopularity, public opinion rallied behind the president rather than Congress. The Republicans were compelled to make a strategic retreat, and the crisis pro-vided a basis for Clinton's re-election victory in November 1996.

For his part, President George W. Bush has employed different strategies. He has been assertive about his legislative plans and priorities. In the early months of his presidency, he put forward a $1.6 trillion tax-cutting package. Although trimmed to $1.3 trillion, it was passed. This approach continued into the second half of the Bush presidency. From January 2003 onwards, David Hobbs directed the White House's lobbying efforts. The New York Times has commented on his style: '"The White House tends to shoot for the moon," said one Republican Senate aide who said he had watched, almost incredulous, as Mr. Hobbs and his legislative affairs staff had pushed policies that had little chance of making it into law. "Maybe it's a Texas thing: go into the room and play like you have four aces on every hand"' (New York Times 15 May 2003).

Other strategies have, however, also been employed. Although the White House was blamed by some for Senator Jim Jeffords's defection from Republican ranks in May 2001, the administration sought to strengthen its ties with the Congressional Republicans. Whereas some of his predecessors maintained a degree of distance, Bush successfully campaigned for Republican victories in the 2002 mid-term elections. A month later, the White House was said to have played an instrumental role in forcing the resignation of Trent Lott, the Senate's Republican leader, after he had made comments that seemed to evince a degree of nostalgia for the segregationist era. Indeed, such was the degree of administration involvement during the episode that Karl Rove, President Bush's principal strategist, was described as the 101st senator.

Furthermore, although Bush has employed public criticism, particularly when the Senate Democrats appeared to be obstructing his judicial nominations, he has held regular private meetings with Democratic as well as Republican leaders in Congress. He also accepted the 2002 Bipartisan Campaign Reform Act, a measure initiated in Congress that he believed was 'far from perfect'.

The role of the vice-president

Few vice-presidents have considered that the post they occupied had much overall significance. John Adams (1789–97), the first vice-president, noted that 'My country has in its wisdom contrived for me the most insignificant office that ever the invention of man contrived or his imagination conceived.' In another celebrated comment, John Nance Garner, one of Franklin Roosevelt's vice-presidents (1933–41), described the role as worth only 'a gamer of warm spit'.

The vice-president's principal role is to assume the presidency if the president dies or resigns from office. The character of the transition was, however, only clarified with the passage of the 25th Amendment. Until then, there was some ambiguity. It was unclear from the Constitution in its original form whether the vice-president became president or simply assumed the duties associated with the presidency. The Amendment surmounted the ambiguity by declaring that 'the Vice President shall become President'. It also established that the vice-president should serve as 'Acting President' when the president is undergoing surgery or is otherwise incapable of fulfilling his role. In 1985, President Reagan transferred his powers to Vice-President Bush for an eight-hour period while he was in the operating theatre.

Beyond that, the role involves few formal responsibilities. Although the Constitution states that the vice-president should serve as president of the Senate, he only takes the chair on ceremonial occasions or if there is likely to be a close vote. He has a casting vote in the event of a tie. Beyond this, there are barriers. Under the Constitution, 'executive power' lies solely with the president. There is no provision for 'power-sharing'. Furthermore, there is always the problem that Dan Quayle (vice-president 1989–93), identified: 'anything you do, you're going to be getting into somebody else's domain'. At the same time, the vice-president and president often had a distant relationship. The vice-president was traditionally nominated because he *balanced the ticket*. His background, politics and personality were therefore often different to those of the president and his inner circle of aides. As vice-president, Lyndon Johnson had a notoriously strained relationship with John Kennedy and his advisers.

The post of vice-president should not be, however, dismissed too lightly. Despite Johnson's sense of isolation, the role of the vice-president grew during the latter half of the twentieth century as a consequence of both changes in the law and presidential discretion. Since 1933, the vice-president has attended cabinet meetings. By law, he is a member of the National Security Council. By executive order, he serves on the Domestic Council (see Chapter 7). Presidents have also delegated some of their responsibilites. Vice-presidents took on some of the president's ceremonial tasks, such as attendance at the funerals of foreign dignitaries. Although elected on the Republican ticket, President Eisenhower (1953–61) regarded himself as 'above politics'. Nixon, his vice-president, therefore acted as *de facto* party leader. He also made highly publicised visits to the Soviet Union at the height of the Cold War.

President Ford named Vice-President Rockefeller to head a commission to investigate allegations against CIA officials. George Bush (vice-president 1981–89), chaired a number of inquiries, including the President's Task Force on regulatory reform, a study of responses to terrorism, and a South Florida Task Force on drug smuggling. Dan Quayle had agreed and specified functions as vice-president. These included liaison with Congress, organising the Party, and some foreign relations responsibilities. Quayle also chaired the White House Council on Competitiveness and the National Space Council.

In contrast with his predecessors, Al Gore (vice-president 1993–2001) was elected on an *unbalanced* ticket. He and Bill Clinton share a similar background, and Gore appeared to be part of the president's decision-making circle. Gore made his mark in different ways. He had responsibility for the National Performance Review. This was directed towards the reduction of federal government bureaucracy and waste. He was also involved in advising on environmental initiatives, promoting the 'information superhighway', and assessing airline safety. He has acted as a Democratic Party leader, standing in for the president at the Democratic National Committee and directing, amidst controversy, some fund-raising activities. Gore was also able to use his casting vote in the Senate to some effect. In June 1993, there was a tied vote on the Budget Reconciliation Bill (as the final version of the annual Budget is known), and Gore used his casting vote to allow the Budget, in a form endorsed by President Clinton, to pass. At a more informal and largely hidden level, Gore had a role in offering advice. He was ready to disagree with president in meetings and was said to have been heavily involved in developing a strategic response to the 1995–96 budget crisis.

Dick Cheney – George W. Bush's vice-president – has been described by Thomas Mann of the Brookings Institution as 'the most influential vice-president in history' (*The Guardian*, 8 May 2003). In contrast with Bush, who, despite his family background, had little Washington experience, Cheney is a consummate 'insider'. He was White House Chief of Staff in the Ford administration and, after that, a member of the House of Representatives. As Secretary of Defense under President George Bush (1989–93), he directed Operation Just Cause in Panama and Operation Desert Storm in the Middle East.

Although he has had a low public profile, his long experience was put into service from 2000 onwards. He was responsible for the transition in the weeks before Bush took office. He was then charged with planning a long-term energy policy for the country. After 11 September, his advice appears to have been crucial, and he played a major role – along with figures such as Defense Secretary Donald Rumsfeld – in steering the administration towards war with Iraq. His conservatism has sometimes seemed more full-blooded than that offered by Bush, and he has been able to shore up support for the White House among conservative hardliners.

Conclusion

The position of the president has been understood in different ways. Some observers emphasise the progressive growth of his powers. Others stress the problematic character of his relationship with Congress. Whereas British prime ministers can, almost always, command a disciplined majority in the House of Commons and are assured that their legislative proposals will pass into law, a president's plans may be rejected or amended beyond recognition.

This chapter has argued that the president's powers vary between the different areas of policy-making. They also depend upon external circumstances and, in some accounts, his personal abilities. There is, however, a further dimension to a discussion of presidential power. He not only has to contend with the other branches of government, but must also manage and co-ordinate the work of the executive branch. This offers opportunities and represents a political resource; but, at the same time, the difficulties that he encounters represent another constraint upon his powers. His role as 'Chief Executive' is considered in Chapter 7.

References and further reading

Anderson, M. (1988), *Revolution*, San Diego, Harcourt Brace Jovanovich.

Bennett, A. (1994), *American Government and Politics 1994*, Godalming, the author.

Califano, J. A. (1996), 'Imperial Congress', in B. Stinebrickner (ed.), *American Government 96/97*, Guilford, CT, Dushkin Publishing Group, pp. 91–3.

Collier, E. C. (1993), *Instances of Use of United States Forces Abroad, 1798–1993*, Washington DC, Congressional Research Service — Library of Congress, www.history.navy.mil/wars/foabroad.htm.

Congressional Quarterly (1997), *Powers of the Presidency*, Washington DC, Congressional Quarterly.

Dumbrell, J. (1997), *The Making of US Foreign Policy*, Manchester University Press.

Dumbrell, J. (2000), 'Foreign policy and foreign policy making', in A. Grant (ed.), *American Politics: 2000 and Beyond*, Aldershot, Ashgate, pp. 85–101.

Foley, M. and J. E. Owens (1996), *Congress and the Presidency: Institutional Politics in a Separated System*, Manchester, Manchester University Press.

Grimmett, R. F. (2001), *Congressional Use of Funding Cutoffs Since 1970 Involving U.S. Military Forces and Overseas Deployments*, www.fas.org/man/crs/RS20775.pdf.

Hames, T. (2000), 'Presidential power and the Clinton presidency', in A. Grant, *'American Politics: 2000 and Beyond*, Aldershot, Ashgate, pp. 65–83.

Jones, C. O. (1995), *Separate But Equal Branches: Congress and the Presidency*, Chatham, Chatham House Publishers.

Mayhew, D. R. (1991), *Divided We Govern: Party Control, Lawmaking and Investigations, 1946–1990*, New Haven, CT, Yale University Press.

Mervin, D. (1990), *Ronald Reagan and the American Presidency*, London, Longman.

Mervin, D. (1996), *George Bush and the Guardianship Presidency*, Basingstoke, Macmillan.

Neustadt, R. (1991), *Presidential Power and the Modern Presidents*, New York, The Free Press.

Owens, J. E. (1994) 'Clinton and Congress: An early assessment', *Politics Review*, February, 5–10.

Owens, J. E. (1996), 'A return to party rule in the US Congress?', *Politics Review*, September, 15–19.

Parmet, H. S. (1997), *George Bush: The Life of a Lone Star Yankee*, New York, Scribner.

Plano, J. and M. Greenberg (1989), *The American Political Dictionary*, Fort Worth, TX, Holt, Rinehart and Winston.

Ragsdale, L. (1998), *Vital Statistics on the Presidency: From Washington to Clinton*, Washington DC, Congressional Quarterly.

Rossiter, C. (1963), *The American Presidency*, London, Harvest.

Wilson, J. Q. (1992), *American Government: Institutions and Policies*, Lexington, MA, D. C. Heath.

Websites

The president and his administration have a website – www.whitehouse.gov/. This provides biographical information about the president, the vice-president and their families, a virtual tour of the building, an audio-visual library of speeches, and reports on recent initiatives. The site also allows access to federal government agencies and commissions.

Executive orders issued by the president are recorded and filed by the National Archives and Records Administration (NARA). Those issued by George W. Bush are at: www.archives.gov/federal_register/executive_orders/2001_wbush.html.

7

The president and the executive branch

The US president heads the executive branch of government. It is structured around an elaborate mosaic of departments, bureaux, corporations and agencies. The federal bureaucracy – as it is also known – has four principal functions:

1 *Policy implementation*   Sections of the federal bureaucracy – most visibly the Department of Justice – are responsible for the implementation of laws passed by Congress and policies decided upon by the president.
2 *The development and imposition of regulations*   Some laws have a loose or imprecise character. They state goals but do not specify the means by which they are to be achieved. Federal agencies such as the Environmental Protection Agency (EPA) and the Occupational Safety & Health Administration (OSHA) play a particular role in this.
3 *Interpretation, adjudication, and arbitration*   Agencies determine whether federal regulations have been breached, or may seek to resolve conflicts between particular groups.
4 *Information gathering*   The collection of data forms a basis for much of the federal bureaucracy's work. The Census Bureau, for example, undertakes an exhaustive study of the US population every ten years. These findings can provide a basis for policy formulation.

The classical or 'textbook' model of government suggests that there is a line of authority flowing downwards from the president in his role as 'Chief Executive'. In this ordered hierarchy, subordinates within the bureaucracy follow the directions that they are given by seniors, and have relatively little discretion in making decisions or applying federal government regulations.

These 'textbook' representations of the executive branch are pervasive. As Richard Neustadt has noted: 'Even Washington reporters, White House aides, and congressmen are not immune to the illusion that administrative agencies comprise a single structure, "the" executive branch, where presidential word is law, or ought to be' (Neustadt 1991: 33–4).

Many observers argue, however, that the classical model is a profoundly

135

misleading description. Successive presidents, they say, have in practice had profound difficulty controlling the work of the bureaucracy and imposing a sense of strategic direction upon it. McGeorge Bundy, who served as National Security Adviser in both the Kennedy and Johnson administrations, noted that the bureaucracy 'more nearly resembles a collection of badly separated principalities than a single instrument of executive action' (*Congressional Quarterly* 1997: 7). This chapter surveys the different perspectives on the character of the executive branch and assesses the evidence that is used to illustrate them.

Problems of control

Those observers who stress the resistance of the bureaucracy to presidential authority emphasise 'bureaucratic inertia'. Most of those who staff the departments, agencies, and bureaux are permanent employees and will have developed their own procedures and cultures. These can often be resistant to the demands of a particular president or his administration. At the same time, many forms of government activity are interdependent, and the process of policy implementation therefore requires the active co-operation of separate agencies, bureaux and departments, each of which has its own interests and outlook. Furthermore, the number of layers within the bureaucracy has progressively grown, again impeding the processes of centralised direction and co-ordination.

These obstacles are compounded by the structural character of the federal bureaucracy, in particular its size and organisation, the laws defining and regulating its actions, and the character of its relationships with both Congress and interest groups.

Size

The scale of the bureaucracy, in itself, impedes the co-ordination of its work. The numbers employed by the federal government began to build up during the nineteenth century, but then grew rapidly during the New Deal years. By 1940, it had reached 699,000. At this time, American citizens increasingly regarded the federal government as a guarantor of full employment and a provider of social assistance. Government interventionism was displacing *laissez-faire*, and the federal government was expected to play a progressively bigger part in the everyday lives of American citizens. President Franklin Roosevelt (1933–45) captured the shift in popular expectations:

> Of course we will continue to seek to improve working conditions for the workers of America . . . Of course we will continue to work for cheaper electricity in the homes and on the farms of America . . . Of course we will continue our efforts on behalf of the farmers of America . . . Of course we will continue our efforts for

young men and women . . . for the crippled, for the blind, for the mothers . . . Of course we will continue to protect the consumer. (quoted in Weisberger 1997: 49)

The Second World War and – twenty-five years later – President Lyndon Johnson's 'Great Society' programmes, which sought to end rural poverty in states such as West Virginia and urban deprivation in cities such as Chicago, fuelled a further period of growth. By 1970, the number of civilian federal executive branch employees had reached a peak of 2,203,000. Although there was a modest fall in numbers after this, 1,818,000 people were employed by the executive branch in 2002.

Table 7.1 *Executive branch employment (000s), 1940–2002 (excluding US Postal Service)*

Year	Employees
1940	699
1950	1,439
1960	1,808
1970	2,203
1980	2,161
1990	2,250
2000	1,778
2001	1,792
2002	1,818

Source: adapted from Office of Management and Budget (2003), *Table 17.1 – Total Executive Branch Civilian Employees: 1940–2002*, www.whitehouse.gov/omb/budget/fy2004/sheets/hist17z1.xls.

Organisation

The problems that arise in co-ordinating the work of the bureaucracy are not, however, a function of numerical size alone. The executive branch has a byzantine structure organised around interlocking and overlapping departments, bureaux, commissions, agencies and corporations.

Executive or cabinet-rank departments are responsible for broad areas of policy such as Defense, Commerce and Transportation. By 2003, there were sixteen such departments. The number has progressively grown since the country's early days. The Department of State, which is responsible for foreign relations, and the Treasury were established in 1789. Others – such as Education, Veterans' Affairs, Environment and Homeland Security – are of much more recent origin. They date from 1979, 1989, 1993 and 2003 respectively. Each department is headed – and represented at cabinet level – by a Secretary.

Bureaux have more focused and narrowly defined responsibilities. The most familiar is the Federal Bureau of Investigation (FBI), which gained national recognition during the gangster era of the 1920s. After the Second World War, the

FBI concentrated on the hunt for communist agents and spies. Through its efforts, two communist sympathisers, Julius and Ethel Rosenberg, were executed for espionage in June 1953.

The structural complexity of the bureaucracy is particularly evident when the position of the bureaux is considered. They are generally located *within* executive departments. There are, for example, eight bureaux within the Department of the Interior.

Box 7.1   Bureaux within the Department of the Interior (May 2003)

National Park Service

US Fish and Wildlife Service

Bureau of Indian Affairs

Bureau of Land Management

Office of Surface Mining

Minerals Management Service

US Geological Survey

Bureau of Reclamation

Source: adapted from United States Department of the Interior, www.doi.gov/bureaus.html.

Bureaux therefore create particular problems of command and control. The FBI is part of the Department of Justice, alongside other bureaux such as the Bureau of Alcohol, Tobacco, Firearms, and Explosives, the Bureau of Justice Assistance, and the Bureau of Justice Statistics. The FBI Director is therefore answerable to the Attorney-General, the cabinet secretary who heads the Justice Department. However, because the FBI plays a pivotal national role in crime-fighting, it has a direct relationship with the president.

Independent Regulatory Commissions (IRCs) have quasi-legislative and quasi-judicial functions. They monitor a particular sector of the economy or society, establish regulations, and make judgements about what may, or may not, be permitted. Those who violate IRC rulings are subject to prosecution. Some IRCs have a particularly high profile. The Federal Communications Commission (FCC) is responsible for the regulation of radio stations, together with terrestrial, satellite and cable television channels. The Interstate Commerce Commission (ICC), created in 1887, has responsibility for business operations and services that cross state lines. When the Constitution was written, this was only a small proportion of the American economy. As industry took on national, and increasingly global proportions, the role and responsibilities of the ICC have correspondingly grown.

There are also large numbers of other federal agencies, including the Central Intelligence Agency (CIA), the National Endowment for the Arts, and the National Aeronautics and Space Administration (NASA), which is responsible for the US space programme.

Government corporations are nationalised industries and enterprises. There are relatively few of these. Whereas European governments assumed ownership and control of strategic industries such as the coal and steel industries in the aftermath of the Second World War, *laissez-faire* traditions have a stronger hold in the United States. In general, the federal government relied upon the regulation of industries rather than ownership. Nonetheless, some industries and services have come under public ownership. The Tennessee Valley Authority is a government corporation responsible for the hydro-electric programmes. It was established in the southern states during the New Deal years. Long-distance railway services have, since 1970, been provided by Amtrak, the National Railroad Passenger Corporation.

The difficulties associated with the administrative structure of the federal bureaucracy are compounded by other factors. Often, the dividing line between the public and private sectors is blurred. There are significant numbers of 'quasi-bureaucrats' who work on government programmes, and are employed in firms and agencies that are supported by federal funding. They are not, however, directly answerable to senior civil servants. Furthermore, although the bureaucracy is widely seen as a distant Washington-based institution, a very large proportion of federal employees work in field-service offices outside the nation's capital. At the same time, many departments, agencies and commissions have overlapping spheres of jurisdiction. Anti-poverty programmes, drug control, and intelligence gathering are all, for example, the responsibility of different agencies. Their operations are not co-ordinated, and, against a background where each of the different departments and agencies has its own understanding of events and seeks to promote its own interests, there will be feuding. At the end of the 1960s, the Defense Secretary Robert McNamara clashed with the Secretary of State, Dean Rusk, about the conduct of the Vietnam War. During the Ford presidency, Secretary of State Henry Kissinger and Defense Secretary James Schlesinger were, in Hedrick Smith's words, 'seething adversaries' (Smith 1988: 784). During 2002–3, there were evident tensions between the two departments. The Department of Defense (the Pentagon) under Donald Rumsfeld – was scathingly dismissive of the United Nations and the countries of 'old Europe', most notably France and Germany, who opposed a pre-emptive war against Iraq. The Department of State – headed by Colin Powell – seemed more reluctant to distance itself from longstanding allies.

Statutory limits

A defining characteristic of the commissions, agencies and corporations is that, although located within the executive branch, they have a significant degree of operational autonomy. For example, the Federal Reserve System has jurisdiction over the formulation of monetary policy. This has far-reaching significance for the entire economy. A relatively high interest rate will curb inflation, but will have deflationary implications. Unemployment and bankruptcies are, for example, likely to rise. A relatively low interest rate will increase the level of purchasing power in the economy, leading to falling unemployment. It may, however, fuel inflation. However, despite the centrality of the Federal Reserve's economic role, the president's powers over the 'Fed' are strictly circumscribed. Members of its Board of Governors are appointed by the president, subject to Senate confirmation, but once in office cannot be instructed to adopt a particular course of action or set the interest rate at a specified level. They jealously guard their autonomy. Thus when President Reagan became president, Paul Volcker, the chairman of the 'Fed', refused to meet him in either the White House or at the Federal Reserve Board building, for fear of jeopardising his independence (Anderson 1988: 252).

Even where the law does not limit the president's ability to direct the work of government agencies, political considerations can play a role. It has been suggested that, for many years, the FBI escaped proper scrutiny by either presidents or Congress. It was, under its long-time director, J. Edgar Hoover, administered as a semi-independent empire.

The role of Congress

The president's difficulties are compounded by the bureaucracy's relationship with Congress. In practice, federal bureaucrats serve two masters. The president is the 'Chief Executive', but the departments, commissions, and agencies are also dependent upon Congressional authority. There are three principal reasons why Congress has a hold over the bureaucracy.

- Congress has to pass the legislation that establishes government programmes or creates agencies.
- Congress plays a pivotal role in determining the federal government's annual budget, which allocates funding and authorises spending commitments by departments and agencies.
- As Chapter 5 noted, the work of the bureaucracy is subject to *oversight* through Congress's committee structure.

Interest groups and 'iron triangles'

According to a number of accounts, the president's ability to co-ordinate the work of the bureaucracy is frustrated in another way. Some interest groups, particularly 'producer' organisations such as companies, trade unions or small business federations, have established close ties with departments and agencies. They are generally seeking protection from market forces or an advantage in terms of government funding, subsidies, and price guarantee mechanisms. For their part, departments, bureaux and agencies have an interest in either the expansion of federal government programmes or, at the least, their continued survival. Bureaucrats will wish to increase their salary, status, and sphere of responsibility. Members of Congress also have their own interests at stake. They will hope for an endorsement at election time from groups and lobbies, particularly those that are strongly represented in their state or district. The three institutions – the bureaucracy, an interest group, and a Congressional committee – are bound together in a symbiotic relationship. They form an 'iron triangle' in which they depend upon each other, and have a shared interest in the continued expansion and development of a particular federal government programme. The net effect is to detach sections of the bureaucracy from the hierarchy. They are pulled in other directions. As B. Guy Peters notes: 'Each functional area tends to be governed as if it existed in splendid isolation from the remainder of government' (1986: 22).

Accounts suggest that President Jimmy Carter was confronted by an 'iron triangle' when he sought to transfer the educational programmes offered to former servicemen by the Veterans Administration into the newly-created Department of Education. He encountered determined opposition from the Veterans Administration itself, veterans' organisations, and the Congressional committees associated with those who had served in the US armed forces. In the face of these forces, the president eventually had to withdraw his proposals.

Presidential resources

There is, however, another perspective. Despite the constraints, the president does have some powers and political resources that enable him to influence the character of the federal bureaucracy.

The power of appointment

The president has the power of appointment. He can attempt to co-ordinate and influence the character of the federal bureaucracy by appointing those who not only have particular forms of expertise, but will be sympathetic to his policies. His powers of appointment include those who head the departments and serve in the cabinet; but they extend far beyond this. In contrast to the UK, where nearly all senior civil servants are permanent employees whose responsibility is to serve the government of the day, whatever its political hue, the president nominates many of the most senior bureaucrats. With each incoming president, there is a turnover of personnel. If the White House staff, those who are placed in charge of the departments and agencies, members of the Senior Executive Service, and so-called Schedule C positions, are added together (including both full-time and part-time posts), the president – together with his aides and subordinates – appoints a total of about 5,200 individuals to positions in the executive branch (*Congressional Quarterly* 1997: 21). The president himself, however, will only be involved in the selection of the most senior three or four hundred of these appointees.

President Reagan, in particular, sought to ensure that those he placed in key positions shared his conservative policy goals. As Joel Aberbach has noted: 'whereas in past administrations, notables who had good relations with established interest groups or good connections with key people on congressional committees were likely to get the jobs, in the Reagan administration political ideology was the key' (Aberbach 1991: 227–8).

Although a president will always seek to ensure that his nominees have leadership skills and can undertake negotiations with Congress in an effective way, appointments can also be used to 'reward' core groups of supporters or to send 'signals' about policy intentions. For his part, George W. Bush has used his appointments – many of which had to be made in a compressed period of transition following the battle to secure Florida's Electoral Vote – to send distinctly mixed political signals. They included some hardline conservatives who were wedded to moral traditionalism. For example, he nominated John Ashcroft, a committed social conservative, as Attorney-General. He also put forward Jerry Thacker, an evangelical Christian who had described AIDS as the 'gay plague', to serve on the Presidential Advisory Commission on HIV and AIDS. Thacker later withdrew his name (*Washington Post* 24 January 2003). However, the administration broke new ground for the Republican Party by making openly gay appointments. Scott Evertz, a member of the Log Cabin Republicans – the principal gay organisation within the party – became director of the Office of National AIDS Policy.

However, the extent to which the power of appointment enables a president to co-ordinate the work of his administration and impose a sense of direction upon the federal bureaucracy should not be exaggerated. There are seven significant constraints.

1 Although a president and his subordinates can make over 5,000 appointments, this is, in practice, a relatively small-scale operation. When President Clinton entered the White House in January 1993, he could only appoint about a hundred individuals in the Department of Transportation, constituting less than 1 per cent of the total workforce. In the Department of Commerce, he was limited to 222 appointments from a total of 37,485 – again, less than 1 per cent (*Congressional Quarterly* 1997: 4, 21). These numbers may not provide a president with sufficient political and managerial leverage.

2 During the transition period between election day and inauguration, the president-elect will be besieged by applicants seeking a post in the new

administration. Many will have been campaign supporters and activists. As Robert Reich, who served as Labor Secretary during President Clinton's first term, noted in late November 1992: 'Thousands of twenty-somethings and thirty-somethings have descended on Washington – field organizers, precinct workers, advance teams, phone-bank volunteers – all with hopes of landing a job . . . The one large feverish campaign to elect Bill Clinton president has now disintegrated into thousands of intensely personal campaigns to work for President Bill Clinton' (Reich 1998: 21).

Against this background, however, there are time constraints. Because the transition period is only two months long, an incoming president will have to delegate a large proportion of sub-cabinet appointments to others. Furthermore, many of these appointees will not take office until many months later. The process cannot be easily managed or co-ordinated.

3 Despite the often frantic lobbying for jobs that follows a presidential election, there may be a shortage of individuals with the requisite skills and expertise. New administrations seek a balance between political loyalty and experience as a manager or policy expert. As the *Washington Post* observed, it is: 'valuable to have the stature of having run a private sector company or program of the same size and budget that would be under your control as the head of a federal sub-agency or program. Many executive level positions require that type of management experience' (Washingtonpost.com 2003). However, those with this form of managerial experience may be reluctant to abandon lucrative long-term posts in private companies for short-term service in Washington DC. Furthermore, others could be unwilling to disclose detailed information about their personal lives and financial affairs.

4 Many of a president's appointees will only serve for a relatively short period of time, will have little or no government experience, and may well be overwhelmed by the scale of their responsibilities. As Robert Reich noted:

> The Department of Labor is vast, its powers seemingly endless . . . I can barely comprehend it all . . . Every time a new president is elected, America assembles a new government . . . who only sometimes know the policies they're about to administer, rarely have experience managing large government bureaucracies, and almost never know the particular piece of it they're going to run . . . And they remain in office, on average, under two years – barely enough time to find the nearest bathroom. It's a miracle we don't screw it up worse than we do. (Reich 1998: 52)

5 Although temporary 'recess' appointments can be made by the president while the Senate is not in session, his senior appointments are subject to Senate confirmation. The Clinton White House had difficulties with its initial appointments. In January 1993, Zoe Baird, President Clinton's nominee to head the Justice Department, had to withdraw when it was revealed that she had employed an illegal immigrant as a nanny in her household. His replacement nomination, Kimba Wood, had to pull out for identical reasons. Three months after 'nannygate', President Clinton felt obliged to withdraw Lani

Guinier, his nominee to a post heading the civil rights division in the Justice Department, once it became clear that she had published articles calling for reforms to the voting system so as to guarantee greater minority representation. The views that she expressed were regarded as too radical. The Bush White House also encountered difficulties. Although Attorney-General John Ashcroft was, despite predictions, confirmed easily, George W. Bush faced some problems that recalled 'nannygate' eight years earlier. He put forward Linda Chavez to serve as Labor Secretary. However, following revelations that she had used an illegal immigrant as a household help, she withdrew her name.

6 Political appointees need to build a close working relationship with the permanent, career civil servants in their department. Norman C. Thomas and Joseph A. Pika suggest that this – in practice – leads them to distance themselves from the inner circles of the administration: 'Political executives in the bureaucracy are in a kind of twilight zone . . . They can best serve the president by winning the trust of the careerists who make up the permanent government, but to do so they find it expedient to maintain a considerable degree of independence from the White House' (Thomas and Pika 1997: 254).

7 A president may feel the need to ensure that his appointments are – in overall terms – broadly representative of American society. This will constrain his choices. Although the appointments process will be dominated by White Anglo-Saxon Protestant – or *WASP* – males, a president may seek to ensure that particular groups have a visible presence. For his part, President Clinton appears to have been guided by the so-called 'egg' formula, whereby appointments were structured, at least in part, around 'ethnicity, gender, [and] geography'. The Bush administration was less committed to diversity as a policy goal, although African-Americans served at the highest levels and unparalleled numbers of Asian Americans and Pacific Islanders were appointed. However, the proportion of women who were appointed at senior levels fell under the Bush administration when compared with the Clinton White House.

Presidents can also – within certain parameters – 'fire' staff by asking for their resignations. In December 2002, Paul O'Neill, the Treasury Secretary, was compelled to resign. This followed widespread claims that his performance in the job had been lacklustre. However, just as a president's appointments are subject to Senate confirmation, his ability to remove those he has appointed is constrained. Those who serve on the independent regulatory commissions are, in particular, protected from dismissal. Although a 1926 Supreme Court ruling, *Myers v. United States*, gave the president wide powers to remove executive branch employees, his authority was circumscribed by later judgements. In *Wiener v. United States* (1958), the Court ruled that if an official's sphere of responsibility included adjudicative functions (where judgements are made about individual cases or grievances) the president cannot remove the official for political reasons (*Congressional Quarterly* 1997: 29–30).

The power of reorganisation

The president has the power to reorganise and restructure the federal bureaucracy. However, although the 1949 Reorganization Act gave the president considerable discretion, this was not renewed after 1983, and restructuring therefore depends upon the president's ability to reach agreement with Congress. President Richard Nixon was concerned, to a greater extent than other modern presidents, that his administration would encounter 'disloyalty and obstruction', particularly from career civil servants who had been appointed during the Kennedy and Johnson years. Therefore, in 1971, he proposed that eight existing cabinet-rank departments should be merged so as to form four larger 'super-departments': Natural Resources, Community Development, Human Resources and Economic Affairs. He believed that this would facilitate more centralised direction. Congress, however, would not accept the proposals, and they had to be abandoned.

Nonetheless, there has been some restructuring of the bureaucracy. It has, however, been an incremental process. In 1988, the Department of Veterans' Affairs was created. It was – cynics contended – a political response to the growing strength of the senior citizens' vote. In 1994, Congress agreed to President Clinton's proposal that the Department of Agriculture should be rationalised (*Congressional Quarterly* 1997: 21). There were also some personnel reductions following the National Performance Review undertaken by Vice-President Al Gore. Then – in the wake of the 11 September attacks and amidst fears that the hijackers had evaded controls upon visitors to the US – President Bush proposed a cabinet-level department of homeland security. It was, as *USA*

Box 7.2   The Homeland Security Department

In the wake of the 11 September attacks – and amidst fears that the hijackers had evaded controls upon visitors to the US and slipped between the different security agencies, Bush proposed a cabinet-level Department of Homeland Security. It was, as *USA Today* noted, 'the biggest reshuffling of the federal bureaucracy in 55 years' (*USA Today*, 7–9 June 2002).

The creation of the Department brought together twenty-two disparate agencies from existing departments such as the Immigration and Naturalization Service (INS), the Customs Service, and the Coastguard. According to initial projections, there would be 169,154 employees. The former Pennsylvania Governor, Tom Ridge, was appointed as the first Secretary of Homeland Security.

Department of Homeland Security website: www.dhs.gov.

Today noted, 'the biggest reshuffling of the federal bureaucracy in 55 years' (*USA Today* 2002). The Department brings together all or part of twenty-two agencies that played a security role, such as the Immigration and Naturalization Service (INS), the Customs Service, and the Coastguard. Initial estimates suggested that it would have over 169,000 employees. Tom Ridge, the former governor of Pennsylvania, was appointed to head the department.

The cabinet

At first sight, the cabinet appears to offer a means by which the work of the executive branch can be drawn together and co-ordinated. Its membership includes those who head the executive departments – such as the Secretary of State and the Secretary of Defense. Other figures such as the United Nations Ambassador, the Chief of Staff, and the head of the Office of Management and Budget (OMB) are generally given cabinet status. Bill Clinton extended cabinet-rank to eleven officials. For his part, President George W. Bush accorded cabinet-level rank to the vice-president, his Chief of Staff, the Administrator of the Environmental Protection Agency, the Director of the Office of Management and Budget, the Director of National Drug Control Policy, and the US Trade Representative.

It is tempting to draw parallels with the British cabinet. They both have a membership of just over twenty. However, such comparisons do not extend very far. In the UK, many of the most important decisions are – despite the growth of prime ministerial power – taken by the cabinet on a collective basis. Furthermore, a prime minister's authority is derived, at least in part, from the degree to which she or he enjoys cabinet support. Indeed, a prime minister will be unable to stay in office if cabinet support is lost. In November 1990, for example, it was the cabinet that played a decisive role in persuading Margaret Thatcher that she had no option but resignation.

The US picture is, however, different. Some presidents – most notably Dwight Eisenhower – sought to establish a cabinet that would work on the basis of collective decision-making. However, in practice, the cabinet is only as important or unimportant as a president chooses to make it. Although the great majority of presidents have begun their periods of office by declaring that the cabinet would become a principal forum for decision-making, almost all have – within a short period – abandoned this as a goal.

At times, the sidelining of the cabinet has gone further. During the Nixon presidency, most of those serving in the Cabinet did not have regular access to the president. Only John Mitchell, the Attorney-General, was able see the president freely. The others were unable to get beyond the president's aides (Cunliffe 1987: 306). The cabinet also tends to meet infrequently. Only about six cabinet meetings were held in the first year of the Clinton presidency (Bennett 1996: 213). In their place, Leon Panetta, the White House Chief of Staff, gave 'briefings' to cabinet members. Many decisions are made by the president meeting with cabinet members on a *bilateral* (or one-to-one) basis.

This pattern seems to have continued during George W. Bush's administration. Despite some tensions between the Secretary of State, Colin Powell, and Donald Rumsfeld, the Secretary of Defense, the Bush cabinet gained a collective sense of direction in the wake of the September 11th attacks. Nonetheless, it was reported – in January 2003 – that only fifteen cabinet meetings had been held during the preceding two years. Although the president sometimes asked cabinet members for impromptu presentations on events, cabinet meetings had only a limited role: 'he uses them to review his political and policy goals – and to boost team spirit'. Decisions are not generally announced but passed back later to the heads of the departments through Andrew Card, the President's Chief of Staff (*National Journal* 2003: 236–7).

While some cabinet members have at times played an important role in shaping policy, this was not because they served in the cabinet. Instead, their influence rested on other considerations. As Attorney-General, Robert Kennedy played a pivotal role because he was the president's brother. James Baker, Secretary of State between 1989 and 1993, had a close personal relationship with President Bush, and this gave him a degree of influence as a policy adviser. As Anthony Bennett notes: 'they were not important because they were in the cabinet, but in spite of being in the cabinet' (1996: 164).

There are five principal reasons why the cabinet has relatively little overall importance as a policy-making body.

1 The president is the sole source of political authority. As William Howard Taft put it: 'The Cabinet is a mere creation of the president's will. It exists only by custom' (quoted in *National Journal* 2003: 232). While the British cabinet consists largely of MPs, although some members may be drawn from the House of Lords, US cabinet members are not elected representatives. Few will hold positions of influence within the president's party. Indeed, they may be *non-partisan*, or even belong to the opposing party. William Cohen, Secretary of Defense during President Clinton's second term of office, was a Republican. Norman Mineta, a Democrat, served as Secretary of Commerce during the final months of the Clinton administration, and was then appointed Transportation Secretary under George W. Bush. The influence and role of cabinet appointees is entirely dependent upon presidential discretion. Indeed, the cabinet can be over-ruled by the president at any time. In a classic phrase, uttered at the end of a cabinet discussion, Abraham Lincoln declared: 'Seven noes, one aye – the ayes have it.' He himself was the one 'aye'.

2 Because the cabinet has no formal or established role, it is not respected or trusted by presidents. As Martin Anderson, Reagan's chief adviser on domestic and economic policy, records, only a small number of issues can usefully be discussed in cabinet meetings. Many only concern one or two cabinet members, and others are too confidential to be considered in a large meeting.

3 Although presidents have sometimes appointed close associates to certain positions, such as that of Attorney-General, most of the officials who head cabinet-level departments may not have been selected by the president because of their ability to co-operate with him in shaping policy. Instead, they may have been appointed for other reasons. They may have experience as Washington insiders, and a particular form of technical expertise. Furthermore, the cabinet can play a role in sending political signals or in acknowledging the significance of a particular grouping. As has been noted, a president may seek diversity by applying the 'egg' formula. In 1992, President Clinton declared that his cabinet would 'look like America'. His initial cabinet choices fell far short of this, but included three African-Americans and two Hispanics.

4 Successive presidents have felt that cabinet members were drawn too closely towards their departments and the interest groups active in their area of policy. There is often a sense in which the departmental secretaries have seemed almost disloyal to the Chief Executive. As President Lyndon Johnson (1963–9) put it: 'When I looked out at the heads of my departments, I realized that while all of them had been appointed by me, not a single one was really mine . . . I felt like a football quarterback running against a tough team and having his own center and left guard throwing rocks at him' (Mervin 1993: 103).

5 The Executive Office of the President and its component bodies – most notably the National Security Council (NSC) – are better placed to offer the president advice and expertise, particularly in times of national crisis. The cabinet is too unwieldy, and few of its members are in a position to contribute constructively. In the 1962 Cuban missile crisis, President Kennedy relied upon ExComm, the Executive Committee of the NSC. President Bush turned to the NSC on 11 September 2001. It – and less formal meetings of key individuals – mapped out the US response to the terrorist attacks.

The cabinet does, however, serve some purposes. It can be used to emphasise the president's commitment to the interests of particular groupings. It may also be employed as a means of rallying and mobilising support for a certain set of policies. President Reagan is said to have used his cabinet meetings to pull the administration behind particular goals, most especially the cutting of budgets. There was no discussion. Instead, the president or his senior advisers would simply outline developments and strategy (Anderson 1988, 223 and 232).

Cabinet councils

President Ronald Reagan was elected to office by promising a conservative revolution, resting on 'small government' and the deregulation of the economy. He wanted to ensure that the entire administration shared these goals, and that in particular, cabinet members would not be sidetracked or drawn away by the inherent inertia of the federal bureaucracy.

Therefore, instead of leaving the process of policy implementation to Cabinet secretaries who were regarded as potentially fickle, the Reagan team established Cabinet councils. Modelled upon the National Security Council (NSC), they brought together personnel from the bureaucracy and the White House staff, and had a responsibility to develop, implement and monitor policy. Five were established in April 1981, and two further councils were set up in 1982. The principal council was the Cabinet Council on Economic Affairs. It held fifty-seven meetings in the first year of its existence (Anderson 1988: 231).

President Reagan was the nominal chairman of each, but he did not, in practice, attend every meeting. These were, however, always held in the White House. As Martin Anderson recalls: 'Just the act of having to leave their fiefdoms, get into a car, and be driven to the White House was a powerful reminder to every member of the cabinet that it was the president's business they were about, not theirs or their department's constituents' (1988: 226).

The system of cabinet councils was rationalised during President Reagan's second term, and two broader bodies, the Domestic Policy Council and the Economic Policy Council, were created. These brought some cabinet secretaries and agency administrators together with staff from the Executive Office of the President such as the Director of the Office of Management and Budget. Although there were some structural changes, particularly when President Clinton took office in January 1993, these councils were maintained by successive presidents after Reagan left office.

As well as the National Security Council, the Bush administration (2001–) had four cabinet councils: the Domestic Policy Council, the Council on Environmental Quality, the Council on Homeland Security, and the National Economic Council. Their membership includes department and agency heads, and the councils are staffed by policy specialists from within the White House. The Director is drawn from within the Executive Office of the President (EOP). The Domestic Policy Council is responsible for policy formulation and implementation in areas such as education, health, welfare, justice, federalism, transportation, environment, labour, and veterans' affairs. A number of White House units are affiliated to it: the Office of National AIDS Policy, the Office of National Drug Control Policy, and the Office of Faith-Based and Community Initiatives. The Council on Environmental Quality reports to the President on the state of the environment, oversees the process of environmental impact assessment, and acts as a referee when there are disagreements between agencies. For its part, the National Economic Council co-ordinates economic policy advice for the President and seeks to ensure that policy decisions and programmes are in line with the President's economic goals.

The Executive Office of the President (EOP)

As the scale and responsibilities of the federal government bureaucracy grew, the president appeared to be an increasingly isolated figure. On coming to office, President Franklin Roosevelt brought in a significant number of personal advisers. Then, in 1936, the Brownlow Committee of Administrative Management was established. It studied the position of the president within the executive branch, and concluded that 'The President needs help.'

From these beginnings, the EOP has grown. Congress and successive presidents added further units, so that it has, as David Mervin records, assumed pivotal significance: 'Presidents have the gravest difficulties as it is in gaining control of a notoriously fractious political system; without the expertise and assistance of the EOP they would be helpless and the United States would be truly ungovernable' (1993: 78).

The contemporary EOP employs over 1,600 people. Although some subject specialists hold permanent positions, many of the EOP's staff are appointees. It is divided into a number of different components, including the National Security Council, the other cabinet councils and their affiliated offices (see above), the Council of Economic Advisers, and the White House Office.

National Security Council (NSC)

The NSC was formed in 1947 at the beginning of the Cold War. Its membership includes the president himself, the vice-president, the secretaries of defense, state and the treasury, the Central Intelligence Agency director, and the chairman of the Joint Chiefs of Staff. The NSC has a staff, headed by the National Security Adviser.

Different presidents have used the NSC, and the National Security Adviser, in different ways. Henry Kissinger – who served as National Security Adviser during the Nixon years – spearheaded foreign policy initiatives, most notably the American *rapprochement* with China at the beginning of the 1970s. Although the State Department's advice on Northern Ireland was sometimes ignored, President Clinton's National Security Advisers were eclipsed by his Secretaries of State, Warren Christopher and Madeleine Albright. However, some earlier National Security Advisers were predominant figures. George W. Bush's National Security Adviser, Condoleezza Rice – a specialist in Soviet and east European affairs and a confidante of the Bush family – has played a major part in the development of foreign and defence policy.

There is considerable potential for tension between the National Security Adviser and cabinet officials. There were, for example, frequent battles, during the Carter presidency, between the Secretary of State, Cyrus Vance, and the National Security Adviser, Zbigniew Brzezinski. In the Bush administration, Rice is said to be the last person that the president consults before reaching a final decision. Nonetheless, her role in policy formulation may be limited. As the

---

Box 7.3   The Executive Office of the President: some offices

Council of Economic Advisers

National Security Council

Office of Administration

Office of Faith-Based and Community Initiatives

Office of Homeland Security

Office of Management and Budget

Office of National AIDS Policy

Office of National Drug Control Policy

Office of Science & Technology Policy

Office of the United States Trade Representative

President's Critical Infrastructure Protection Board

President's Foreign Intelligence Advisory Board

USA Freedom Corps

White House Military Office

Source: adapted from The White House (2003), The Executive Office of the President, www.whitehouse.gov/government/eop.html.

2003 war with Iraq approached, policy-makers at the Pentagon – most notably the Secretary of Defense, Donald Rumsfeld and Paul Wolfowitz, Assistant Secretary at the Defense Department – seemed to be mapping out and directing the most important policy initiatives.

Office of Management and Budget (OMB)

The OMB has a staff of over five hundred and a number of important functions. It has a significant career civil service staff as well as political appointees.

The OMB draws up draft executive orders, screens legislation passed by Congress before it is submitted to the president, and monitors the rules and regulations issued by the federal bureaucracy. The OMB also evaluates the effectiveness of agency programmes and oversees the purchasing – or procurement – process. Most significantly of all, the OMB draws up the federal government budget on behalf of the president. It assesses the budget requests of the different departments, and ties them together within the overall framework of the president's political and economic strategy.

These proposals are then submitted to the lawmakers on Capitol Hill.

Box 7.4   The Iran–Contra affair

Some of the difficulties associated with the EOP – and the ability of the executive branch to evade the will of Congress – were graphically illustrated by the Iran–Contra affair. In November 1986, it was revealed that President Reagan had secretly authorised the selling of antitank missiles and other weaponry to Iran. The shipments were worth about $600 million. There were shocked reactions. Iran was a rigid Islamic state thought to be behind acts of international terrorism and involved in the holding of Western hostages in the Lebanon. The White House appears to have hoped that, although the covert sales were in breach of the Arms Control Export Act, they might strengthen the position of more moderate elements within the Iranian leadership circles and lead to the release of the hostages.

There were, however, further revelations. The National Security Adviser, Vice-Admiral John Poindexter, and his deputy, Lieutenant-Colonel Oliver North, used about $16 million taken out of the profits obtained from the transactions with Iran to purchase weaponry for the *Contras*. The Contras were right-wing guerrillas engaged in a war against government forces in Nicaragua, a small central American nation. The Nicaraguan government was aligned with Cuba and the Soviet bloc. However, the transfer of funds to the Contras broke US law. Congress had, through the 1985 Boland Amendment, prohibited the giving of military aid to the Contras. As North and his supporters saw it, Congress had abandoned freedom fighters in the field of battle.

It has never became clear exactly how much President Reagan knew about the diversion of funds to the Contras. The Tower Commission, which was appointed to examine the decision-making process within the National Security Council, concluded that the president had not subjected the actions of his staff to sufficiently close scrutiny, thereby allowing NSC personnel to pursue what constituted an independent foreign policy.

However, although Congress – aided by those who staff the Congressional Budget Office – will introduce a substantial number of amendments, the political initiative in the budget debates generally remains with the president.

The White House Office (WHO)

The four hundred or so staff in the WHO are those who work most closely with the president. They organise his day-to-day work. Some presidents, such as Franklin Roosevelt and John F. Kennedy, adopted a circular model of organisation in the WHO. A considerable number of senior policy advisers reported directly to the president. The Clinton administration followed this pattern in its early days. It had an open, informal, almost casual style, in which large numbers had access to the president.

In contrast, other presidents – particularly Republicans – have established a system based upon a hierarchy of authority. Only a few senior advisers have a close relationship with the president. The White House Chief of Staff – who is responsible for other staff members and acts as 'gatekeeper' by regulating both access and flows of information to the president – generally plays a pivotal role. The post was established in 1953, when President Eisenhower appointed Sherman Adams, although both Kennedy and Johnson had no chief of staff. They feared that they might be walled off from aides. Some who have held the position are felt to have been over-powerful. President Richard Nixon's Chief of staff, H. R. Haldeman, was part of a 'Berlin Wall' of advisers. Nixon was disproportionately dependent upon their advice, and other senior figures were limited in terms of their access to the president.

Andrew Card, George W. Bush's Chief of Staff, is seen in less authoritarian terms. Nonetheless, he has said that his role was 'about making sure the right people get access to the president at the right time and on the right issue' (Texas A&M University 2002). Meetings between departmental secretaries and the president must, for example, be scheduled. They cannot see him on an impromptu basis. Card also plays a further role in co-ordinating the work of the administration. Together with Dick Cheney – the vice-president – he chairs the Budget Review Board. This considers appeals from departmental secretaries if – when the budget proposals are being assembled – they wish to appeal against decision by the Office of Management and Budget (OMB) (*National Journal* 2003: 237).

Alongside Card and Condoleezza Rice, Bush also relies heavily upon the advice of Karl Rove, his principal domestic policy strategist, who guided Bush's presidential election campaign in 2000.

Office of Legislative Affairs

President Harry Truman had one aide dealing with Congressional relations. Since then, there has been a significant increase in the numbers employed in promoting the president's legislative agenda. There were six professional staff under Kennedy and thirteen during the Reagan era. Other aides may also play a role in the process of lobbying members of Congress. David Hobbs, who headed the Office in George W. Bush's administration from January 2003 onwards, is said to be part of a broader effort: 'Mr. Hobbs, legislators said, is often the nice guy part of an administration good-cop, bad-cop routine in which Karl Rove and Mr. Bush's other political advisers take on the role of the heavies' (*New York Times* 15 May 2003).

The significance of the EOP

Presidents have almost invariably placed greater trust in the EOP than in those who head the federal bureaucracy. Indeed, it has been suggested that the president's staff 'constitutes a "presidential branch" of government distinct from the larger executive branch' (Thomas and Pika 1997: 171). Anthony Bennett identifies four reasons why the EOP plays a pivotal role:

- The 'staffers' who are assigned positions in the EOP are more likely to be long-term associates of the president and will therefore have a much closer relationship with him. They are *his* people. In contrast, as has been noted, Cabinet members may be virtual strangers who have been appointed because they bring expertise to the post or simply because they have symbolic significance.
- Staff members are likely to maintain their personal loyalty to the president. Cabinet members are, however, torn between their loyalty to the president, the attitudes and views of the department they head, and interest groups who have a close association with their department.
- Although the State Department is only about a mile from the White House – in the Foggy Bottom neighbourhood of Washington DC – the EOP is in much closer physical proximity to the president. These distances are important when decisions are being made.
- A cabinet member will inevitably be preoccupied with managing his or her department. As Bennett puts it: 'He may be closeted in some top-level departmental meeting. He may be on Capitol Hill appearing before a congressional committee. He may be in California or Texas or Michigan giving a speech or attending a conference. He may not even be in the United States at all' (1996: 169).

However, despite the importance of the EOP's role, there are difficulties.

1 Those who staff the EOP are simply advisers to the president. Although some posts in the EOP are subject to Senate confirmation, they do not have executive powers, and cannot give instructions to those who work in the federal bureaucracy. In contrast, Cabinet members are empowered by legal authority and have a legitimacy that the White House staff inevitably lack (Bennett 1996: 179).
2 Despite their lack of formal power, the tensions and rivalries that sometimes arise between those in the EOP and cabinet members can be destabilising for the administration and the implementation of policy. The stresses between Cyrus Vance and Zbigniew Brzezinski during the Carter presidency have already been noted. During the Reagan era, there were conflicts between the Secretary of State, George Shultz, and the National Security Adviser, Vice-Admiral John Poindexter.
3 The EOP can, in practice, constitute a 'mini-bureaucracy', presenting problems of management, direction and control (Foley and Owens 1996: 214–15). Presidents have responded to this by increasing the size of the White House Office. However, as Lyn Ragsdale notes, this did not represent a solution: 'presidents could not control cabinet departments, so they increased the size of the EOP. Because the EOP was itself too big and too diverse to control, presidents then expanded the WHO' (1996: 255).

Considerations such as these lead James Pfiffner to conclude that the term 'Executive Office of the President' is a misnomer. It has a sprawling structure and lacks the power to direct events: 'The EOP is not really a single office, but rather a collection; and it is not really executive, since it contains units that are primarily advisory rather than executing' (Pfiffner 2000: 87).

Conclusion

Pfiffner suggests that the problems that an administration faces in co-ordinating the work of the federal bureaucracy can be exaggerated: 'The vast majority of career professionals believe in the Constitution and respect the outcome of elections. Political executives have the necessary managerial tools to motivate career civil servants' (Pfiffner 2000: 126). Nonetheless, aside from the problems that arise from bureaucratic inertia, size and organisational character, the bureaucracy is torn between loyalty to the president, its own perceptions, and its obligations to Congress and particular interest groups. There are, however, mechanisms that enable the president to go some way in imposing a sense of direction on the executive branch. The president has the power of appointment to senior posts. The cabinet and the EOP offer possibilities. However, these are limited by the inherent weaknesses of both institutions. The federal bureaucracy therefore has considerable influence, and may be considered a *political actor* in its own right.

References and further reading

Aberbach, J. D. (1991), 'The president and the executive branch', in C. Campbell and B. A. Rockman, *The Bush Presidency: First Appraisals*, Chatham, Chatham House.

Anderson, M. (1988), *Revolution*, San Diego, CA, Harcourt Brace Jovanovich.

Bennett, A. J. (1996), *The American President's Cabinet: From Kennedy to Bush*, Basingstoke, Macmillan.

Congressional Quarterly (1997), *Powers of the Presidency*, Washington DC, Congressional Quarterly.

Cunliffe, M. (1987), *The Presidency*, Boston, Houghton Mifflin.

Foley, M. and J. E. Owens (1996), *Congress and the Presidency: Institutional Politics in a Separated System*, Manchester, Manchester University Press.

Mervin, D. (1993), *The President of the United States*, New York, Harvester Wheatsheaf.

National Journal (2003), 25 January, Special Report, pp. 236–7.

Neustadt, R. (1991), *Presidential Power and the Modern Presidents*, New York, The Free Press.

Peters, B. G. (1986), *American Public Policy: Promise and Performance*, Basingstoke, Macmillan.

Pfiffner, J. (2000), *The Modern Presidency*, Boston, Bedford/St Martin's.

Ragsdale, L. (1996), *Vital Statistics on the Presidency: Washington to Clinton*, Washington DC, Congressional Quarterly.

Reich, R. B. (1998), *Locked in the Cabinet*, New York, Vintage Books.

Smith, H. (1988), *The Power Game: How Washington Works*, London, Fontana.

Texas A&M University (2002), *White House Chief Of Staff Andrew Card Speaks At Texas A&M*, 18 November, rev.tamu.edu/stories/02/111802–13.html.

Thomas N. C. and J. A. Pika (1997), *The Politics of the Presidency*, Washington DC, CQ Press. *USA Today* (2002), 7–9 June.

Washingtonpost.com (2003), *Executive Branch Career Opportunities*, www.washington-post.com.

Weisberger, B. A. (1997) 'What made the government grow?', *American Heritage*, September, 34–52.

Executive branch websites

The Federal Web Locator (www.infoctr.edu/fwl/), hosted by the Chicago-Kent College of Law, Illinois Institute of Technology offers links to all government departments, agencies, commissions, and bureaux. It is intended to be 'the one stop shopping point for federal government information on the World Wide Web [and to] . . . bring the cyber citizen to the federal government's doorstep'.

8

Federalism: the role of the states

The US is a federal country. Political power is distributed between the national (or federal) government and the individual states. As Jack C. Plano and Milton Greenberg put it, the US has: 'a system of government in which power is divided . . . between a central government and regional or subdivisional governments. Both governments act directly upon the people through their officials and laws. Both are supreme within their proper sphere of authority' (Plano and Greenberg 1989: 37).

There are many broad similarities between the fifty states. Each has its own constitution and a system of government structured around a separation of powers between the executive, judicial, and legislative branches. All but one of the state legislatures has a bicameral structure. Nonetheless, there are also significant structural differences. Some state constitutions assign considerable power to the legislature. The governor has only limited authority. Others bolster the position of the governor by offering a line-item veto so that particular clauses in a bill can be deleted. Many states – particularly in the west – provide a degree of direct democracy. They allow citizens to vote upon initiatives and referendums and – in certain circumstances – to recall public officials so that their term of office is curtailed.

However, despite these differences, there has been – over the past two centuries – a process of *centralisation*, and political power has progressively shifted from the individual states to the federal government in Washington DC. The states' 'sphere of authority' – to which Plano and Greenberg refer – has been increasingly circumscribed. Indeed, some suggest that the US is now – to all intents and purposes – a unitary state in which sovereignty and power resides – as in Britain – in a single institution. However, others dissent from these claims. They suggest that, despite centralisation, power is still shared between the federal government and the individual states. This chapter outlines and explains the arguments.

Federalism and the Constitution

The 'Founding Fathers', who drew up the Constitution, were divided among themselves about the character that federalism should take. For some the US was an agreement – or *compact* – between semi-sovereign states. They believed that the federal government should have only limited authority. From their perspective, the states existed *before* the federal government and the US came into being. The national government should, therefore, be considered the servant of the states rather than their master. There was, however, determined opposition to this argument. Alexander Hamilton and those around him emphasised the economic weakness and military vulnerability of a country that lacked national direction. They called for a central government that would have authority and an ability to respond to both domestic and external challenges. There were also claims – which took a more developed form as the years progressed – that the US rested upon – and owed its allegiance to – the American people rather than the states. The Constitution sought to reconcile these tensions by approaching *intergovernmental relations* in three ways:

1 It emphasised the essential unity of the US in its relationships with other nations. Foreign policy powers were to be the sole prerogative of the federal government. According to Article I of the Constitution, states may not conclude treaties with other countries, impose taxes on imports and exports, or maintain their own troops in times of peace. These stipulations were intended to ensure that the US came together as a single diplomatic, economic, and military entity.

   Alongside these limitations, other clauses of the Constitution also inhibited the decision-making powers of the states. Article I specifies that the US Congress has the authority to pass laws for the 'general welfare of the United States'. It also, in what became known as the 'interstate commerce' clause, permitted Congress to regulate trade and business between the states. The wording of these phrases – and the *expansive* interpretation that the Supreme Court subsequently put upon them – provided a basis for the growth of the federal government and its role in American society.

2 The Constitution offered certain specific assurances to the states. Article II assigned a formal role – through the Electoral College – to the states in the choosing of a president. In Article IV, the states are assured that they will be defended from invasion, that their boundaries will not be changed without their consent, and that they will be given equal representation in the US Senate. Article V specifies that the Constitution can only be amended with the assent of three-quarters of the states.

   However, the rights of the states extend beyond these guarantees. The Tenth Amendment, which formed part of the Bill of Rights, and was added in 1791, was intended to ensure that these states, rights were not subsumed by the national authorities. It states that 'the powers not delegated to the

United States by the Constitution, nor prohibited by it to the States, are reserved to the States respectively, or to the people'. In other words, those decision-making powers not specifically assigned to the federal government are the prerogative of the individual states. The states can make their own laws in these areas.

There are, as a consequence, significant differences between the states. Levels of health care vary considerably. Regulations regarding marriage and divorce differ. Vermont, for example, allows same-sex couples to enter into 'civil unions' that have some of the attributes of marriage. Restrictions on gambling and alcohol depend upon state law. The sales tax that is paid on retail goods and services varies between the states. States also have their own income taxes. Driving is subject to a range of laws and regulations. Legal punishments also differ. The majority of states, for example, have the death penalty on their statute books. Twelve, including, for example, Vermont, do not. Some, most notably Texas, carry out executions on a regular basis. In most other states, they are a very rare occurrence. Euthanasia is also a matter for state policy-makers. Following a referendum in 1994, Oregon passed the 1997 Death with Dignity Act, allowing doctors to prescribe drugs so that the terminally ill can end their own lives.

3 The Constitution also established that the states have duties and obligations towards each other. A fugitive who has been charged with an offence in one state, and flees to another, must be extradited and returned to the original state. 'Full faith and credit' has to be given by each individual state to the laws and court rulings made in other states. In other words, one state cannot undermine another by refusing to recognise the validity of its laws and court judgements. This caused concern in some states when the Hawaii Supreme Court considered the statutory recognition of same-sex marriages.

The growth of the federal government

In the early years of the United States, the provisions of the Constitution relating to federalism were generally understood to mean that the federal government and the states had their own separate and distinct spheres of responsibility. The federal government had authority over foreign policy, defence, and some other specifically identified domestic responsibilities such as the regulation of interstate commerce. However, most forms of domestic policy-making remained the prerogative of the states. As James Madison, one of the most prominent of the 'Founding Fathers' put it, the authority of the individual state would 'extend to all objects which, in the ordinary course of affairs, concern the lives, liberties, and properties of the people'. This has been described as *dual federalism* or *layer-cake federalism*, in so far as the federal and state governments were engaged in separate and distinct spheres of activity.

Although there are those who have questioned whether dual federalism ever

---

Box 8.1 Layer cake and marble cake federalism

Morton Grodzins devised a metaphor to convey the changing character of American federalism. He described dual federalism – the model of relations between the national government and the states that was accepted from the founding of the US until the early twentieth century – as *layer-cake federalism*. This suggests that the two forms of government each had their own separate spheres of responsibility. The authority of the national government extended to tariff policy, defence, and foreign relations. The state governments had responsibility over matters not specifically cited in the US Constitution, such as education, unemployment, law and order, and transportation. In the Grodzins model, the functions provided by the two tiers of government were as distinct as the layers in a layer-cake.

However, the growth of grants-in-aid and the New Deal led to a reconceptualisation of federalism. The national government became involved in the provision of education, work creation projects, transportation, and welfare provision. Increasingly, it was recognised that the efforts and responsibilities of the different governments within the US were intertwined and intermeshed. They no longer had their own separate spheres. Some described this as 'co-operative federalism'. Grodzins talked about *marble-cake federalism*. The two tiers of government were now intermixed.

Further reading

Grodzins, M. (1966), *The American System*, Chicago, Rand McNally.

---

existed in the pure form that has been depicted, the character of American federalism undoubtedly changed dramatically over the next century and a half. During the nineteenth and twentieth centuries, central government gained in terms of both authority and resources. Four processes and developments made a particular contribution to the shift.

The Civil War

As the nineteenth century progressed, tensions between the north and the southern states grew. As the north industrialised, the economic differences between the regions became more pronounced. At the same time, slavery came to the fore. While the abolitionist cause won many adherents in the north, the southern states insisted that African-Americans should remain the legal property of their owners. These tensions led many southerners to place a stress on the rights of the states and the constraints that, as they saw it, the Constitution imposed upon the powers of the national government. The US was, they insisted, a voluntary compact between the states, and the states therefore remained sovereign. Against this background, John C. Calhoun of South Carolina asserted that the states could, within their territory, *nullify* – or refuse to accept – laws passed by Congress. Increasingly, secessionist voices were also heard, arguing that the southern states should abandon the US and construct their own independent nation.

The Civil War (1861–65) began when the southern states seceded and established the Confederate States of America. The Confederacy was founded in an attempt to ensure the preservation of slavery and to resist northern commercialism. Its eventual defeat by northern forces established that the federal government directly represented the American people as a whole. The US was not simply a loose agreement between semi-sovereign states that could be dissolved. Instead, it was a single country. Some observers have noted that a significant shift in popular terminology took place at the time. It matched the changing realities of politics. Before the Civil War, the US was a plural concept. People commonly said 'the United States *are* '. After 1865, references to the US took a singular form ('the US *is*').

Constitutional amendments

The defeat of the south was followed by the passage of amendments to the Constitution that sought to give a measure of protection to the former slave population. Under the Fourteenth Amendment, every state had to ensure that all those living within its jurisdiction were accorded 'the equal protection of the laws' and that no person could be deprived of 'life, liberty, or property, without due process of law'. The Fifteenth Amendment required that the right of US citizens to vote could not be denied 'on account of race, color, or previous condition of servitude'.

However, despite these amendments, white rule was re-established in the southern states by the 1880s, and the black population progressively lost the limited rights that it had won in the aftermath of the Civil War. A system of racial segregation – a form of institutionalised racism under which blacks were consigned to separate and inferior public facilities – and the voting 'tests' that kept the right to vote in white hands made a mockery of the Fourteenth and Fifteenth Amendments until the 1960s.

Nonetheless, despite continuing racial injustice, other Constitutional amendments – which sought to establish uniform standards across the nation – did increasingly limit the authority of the individual states. A national system of income tax collection came into being when the Sixteenth Amendment was ratified by the states in 1913. This gave the federal government an independent and very large-scale source of revenue. Almost sixty years later, the Twenty-Sixth Amendment reduced the voting age to eighteen.

Supreme Court rulings

As Chapter 4 noted, a number of Supreme Court rulings had a profound impact on relations between the federal government and the individual states. In the early years of the US, the Court legitimised the expansion of the federal government's powers. In 1810, in the case of *Fletcher v. Peck*, the Court established that it had the right to declare a state law unconstitutional. Nine years later, the Court bolstered the position of the federal government. In the case of *McCulloch v. Maryland* (1819), the Court asserted that the federal government not only had *enumerated* powers – those specifically identified in the Constitution – but also had *implied* powers. Its prerogatives stemmed, in the words of Chief Justice John Marshall, from both 'the letter and spirit of the Constitution'.

However, as the nineteenth century progressed, the Court became increasingly suspicious of federal government authority, and protective of 'states' rights'. Its rulings rested on notions of *dual federalism*. In the closing years of the century, this led the Court to acquiesce as white southerners regained much of the authority that they had held in the years preceding the Civil War, and imposed a system of segregation across the south. The Court accepted the 'separate but equal' doctrine, that underpinned segregation, in the case of *Plessy v. Ferguson* (1896).

By the middle of the twentieth century, judicial attitudes had shifted. The activism of the Warren and Burger Courts (1953–86), represented a sustained attempt to impose uniform standards of justice and citizenship across the nation. *Brown v. Board of Education (Topeka, Kansas)* (1954) declared segregated schooling to be unconstitutional. Although the southern states initially resisted the ruling, and used 'states' rights' as a rallying call, *Brown* eventually came to be accepted. *Baker v. Carr* (1962) established that the electoral districts for state legislatures had to be drawn on the basis of population. There had to be, the Court argued, periodic reapportionment to reflect population shifts. *Roe v. Wade* (1973) asserted that abortion was a constitutional right. In *Furman v. Georgia* (1972), the Court ruled that existing death penalty laws were unconstitutional because sentences were imposed in an arbitrary and random way. All these judgements reined in the decision-making powers and jurisdiction of the state legislatures.

Economic and social developments

The growing scope and scale of the federal government also contributed to the changing character of the relationship between Washington DC and the individual states. In the 1930s, the New Deal established that the executive branch had a national role as 'manager of the economy'. The economic prosperity of the states came to depend upon judgements made in the nation's capital. Measures such as the 1935 National Labor Relations Act laid down national standards for both capital and labour. Employment projects – most notably the Tennessee Valley Authority, which brought hydroelectricity to the rural south – cut across state lines.

At the same time, the states became increasingly financially dependent upon the federal government. Washington DC had begun giving *grants-in-aid*

– or financial transfers – in 1887 so as to assist the states in the development of agricultural research, education, and highway programmes. The number and size of these transfers increased dramatically during the 1930s. In 1925, grants-in-aid amounted to $114 million. By 1937, this had risen to nearly $300 million. Under the 1935 Social Security Act, Washington DC used grants-in-aid to provide the beginnings of a rudimentary welfare state. There was material assistance for some dependent children, the elderly and the unemployed. V. O. Key has recorded the consequences of these measures: 'The federal government . . . had been a remote authority with a limited range of activity . . . Within a brief time, it became an institution that affected intimately the lives and fortunes of most, if not all, citizens' (quoted in Conlan 1988: 5).

The process of centralisation went further during the Great Society years of the 1960s. President Lyndon Johnson committed the federal government to ending poverty in both the inner-city neighbourhoods and the rural areas. In a 1964 speech that reflected the ambition and optimism of the early 1960s, he called for a 'Great Society': 'For in your time we have the opportunity to move not only toward the rich society and the powerful society, but upward to the Great Society. The Great Society rests on abundance and liberty for all. It demands an end to poverty and racial injustice, to which we are totally committed in our time. But that is just the beginning.' On the basis of this vision, the federal government committed large-scale financial resources to this, and its economic and social role expanded dramatically. Despite his 1968 election pledges, the growth of 'big government' continued during President Nixon's period of office. In 1970 alone, grants-in-aid to the states rose by 19.3 per cent on the previous year.

Centralisation

In the 1960s, some observers talked in terms of *creative* federalism. This was an admiring description of the shift in relationships that had accompanied the Great Society programmes. The different tiers of government were – it was said – collaborating together so as to construct a national system of education, social security and housing. While the national government provided the bulk of the funding, the states and localities supplied the administrative staffing and the workforce. The complex intermixing of national and state responsibility for the programmes has been dubbed 'marble-cake federalism'. This, as the programmes' critics emphasised, had three political consequences.

1 It increased the degree to which the states were finally dependent upon the federal government.
2 The financial transfers from the federal government to the states increasingly took the form of *categorical* rather than block grants. A categorical

---

Box 8.2   The case for decentralisation

Those who favour the decentralisation offered by a federal system of government put forward a number of claims. Firstly, in a diverse and heterogeneous
society such as the US, different regions, states, and communities will have
different preferences. Some in – for example – the south, will lean towards
moral and cultural traditionalism. They will not want their children exposed to
what they see as harmful or damaging influences. They will want religious
beliefs to be upheld and respected. Other areas in a diverse society will, however,
think in more liberal or 'progressive' terms. They will seek a secular or non-
denominational upbringing for children. Decentralised structures allow communities to follow their own wishes. Inevitably, in a centralised system of
government, these communities will be compelled to adopt policies that they
bitterly resent.

Secondly, those committed to 'states' rights' have geographical objections to
centralised government. Washington DC is 2,294 miles from Los Angeles, 991
miles from Baton Rouge, and 2,323 miles from Seattle. Whatever the merits of
national government, these distances prevent effective governance from the
nation's capital.

Thirdly, state governments are said to be more responsive to those they
purport to represent. State capitals such as Richmond (Virginia) and Atlanta
(Georgia) are relatively accessible. Furthermore, the state legislator will generally
have fewer constituents than the US Congressman or Senator. For example, in
New Hampshire, each state legislator represents only 2,500 people.

Fourthly, as Louis D. Brandeis, a celebrated Supreme Court justice, asserted in
1932, decentralised systems of government offer opportunities for policy experimentation and innovation: 'It is one of the happy incidents of the federal system
. . . that a single courageous state may, if its citizens choose, serve as a laboratory;

---

grant is provided for a narrow, specified purpose. By contrast, a block grant
allows the individual state much more discretion in determining the character of its spending plans. Alongside this, state decision-making was increasingly subject to federal government regulations.

3 Under many of the Great Society programmes, state governments were often
   bypassed as relationships were established and grants given directly to localities, city authorities, neighbourhood agencies and voluntary groups.

Citing points such as these, the opponents of creative federalism – who were
drawn largely from the conservative right – argued that it undermined the
power and authority of the states. Thomas R. Dye asserts that the US had
become 'indistinguishable from a centralized government. State and local
governments are viewed as administrative instruments of the national government. If flexibility is permitted at all, it is only better to implement national goals
in a local environment' (1990: 8).

and try novel social and economic experiments without risk to the rest of the country' (quoted in Tabarrok 2001).

For example, the deregulation of the airline industry – allowing open competition between different carriers – began at the state level. It was adopted across the country once it became evident that flights within the larger states were significantly cheaper than trips of the same distance that crossed state lines. Similarly, the reform of welfare provision – by limiting the period for which assistance is given and imposing work requirements on recipients and school voucher systems that allow a measure of parental choice, also began at the state level. The conclusions drawn from states pursuing different strategies enabled legislators to draw conclusions about the most effective policy options.

Fifthly, as libertarians stress, decentralisation adds to individual liberty. If decision-making is at the state or local level, individuals who dislike the policies that are adopted can move elsewhere. Gays and lesbians can, for example, move to cities such as New York and San Francisco where there are vibrant gay sub-cultures and neighbourhoods. If, however, policies are adopted and implemented across the entire country, it is – in practical terms – much more difficult to counter a policy through mobility.

Fifthly, state governments can balance out the actions of the national government. They can prevent the legislators and bureaucrats in Washington DC from becoming excessively powerful. Together with the separation of powers dividing out the three branches of the national government, the states provide a check against tyranny.

References and further reading

Alexander Tabarrok (2001), *Arguments for Federalism*, The Independent Institute, www.independent.org/tii/Presentations/Federalism.html.

New Federalism

From the late 1960s onwards, there was a political and cultural backlash against *creative federalism*. Conservative criticisms of centralisation and large-scale government expenditure gained increasing credibility and acceptance. The right was committed to reversing what they saw as the usurpation of state powers by the federal government. They argued that:

1 The federal government had become unresponsive to local and regional needs. Those inside the 'Beltway' (the interstate highway encircling Washington DC), were not only remote, but were in the grip of lobbyists and special interests. Legislators, it was said, had become detached from the electorate they were supposed to represent. Instead, they had been 'bought off' by elite groupings. A succession of ethics and corruption cases at the end of the 1980s and in the early 1990s, gave such claims added potency.

2 The policies imposed upon the states by the federal government were – it was said – derived from liberal fallacies. For example, the critics charged, federal administrators were responsible for the introduction of fashionable, 'pupil-centred' learning methods in the nation's schools. As a consequence, educational standards had fallen, discipline was no longer imposed, and essential skills such as literacy and numeracy were no longer being properly taught.

3 Observers also claimed that federal government projects were administered by a cumbersome and impersonal bureaucracy. Programmes were often frustrated by duplication, fragmentation, and overlap. Furthermore, they had killed off the charitable work that had traditionally been undertaken by voluntary and church organisations.

4 The expansion of federal government had economic, as well as political and social consequences. According to supply-side economists – who gained particular influence in the 1980s – increasing tax demands and the imposition of bureaucratic regulations stifled individual effort and deterred entrepreneurship. Government borrowing fuelled inflation and 'crowded out' private sector investment. Deregulation and a low tax regime, would, it was argued, lead to significantly higher levels of economic growth.

Richard Nixon's election as president in November 1968 was an early expression of the conservative backlash. He was committed to a system of *New Federalism*, which he depicted as a means through which the states would regain some of their former authority. His proposals were structured around *revenue-sharing*. Tax revenues, collected by the federal government, would be handed down to the individual states, and then spent as the states chose. The federal government would insist only upon proper auditing procedures and assurances that there would be no racial discrimination in the allocation of funds. In 1972, Congress agreed to a limited Revenue Sharing Act. However, revenue sharing did not survive for long. The Reagan Administration saw *all* forms of government spending – whether administered by federal, state, or local government – as frequently wasteful and inefficient. The Administration's scaled down revenue-sharing programmes in 1980, and they were finally abandoned in the Budget of 1986.

However, although he opposed revenue-sharing, President Reagan also talked in terms of *New Federalism*. His January 1981 inaugural address seemed to resurrect earlier assertions about the character of the US itself: 'the federal government did not create the states, the states created the federal government'. A year later – in his 1982 State of the Union message – Reagan promised a major effort to 'restore American federalism'. His proposals rested on four principal elements. Firstly, there was to be a 'swap' whereby the states would assume responsibility for welfare provision (*Aid to Families with Dependent Children* and food stamps), which in total cost about $24 billion a year, while the federal government would fund *Medicaid*, a $30 billion programme providing limited medical assistance to about 22 million people on low incomes. Secondly,

Box 8.3　Arguments against decentralisation

The claims of those who talk in terms of 'states' rights' should be set against a number of counter-arguments. Firstly, decentralisation can be the beginning of a process that goes much further than its designers had originally intended. Indeed, it can trigger demands for separatism, leading to the break-up of the nation. In Canada, decentralisation fuelled rather than dampened demands for the independence of Quebec, leading to fears of fragmentation.

Secondly, the threat posed by terrorism and the need for 'homeland security' requires a centralised response. A patchwork of different policies at state and local level would leave the US vulnerable to attack.

Thirdly, centralised forms of government do not necessarily prevent experimentation and the adoption of different forms of policy in particular areas. Even if the decision-making process is centralised, the processes of implementation and administration can be decentralised.

Fourthly, Americans are citizens of the US and, as such, are entitled to the *nationally-set* minimum standards of justice and social provision laid out in the Bill of Rights, codified in federal legislation and established in Supreme Court rulings. These standards are of particular importance because many states have a history of deeply undemocratic practices. As William Bennett, a well-known conservative commentator, notes, the devolution of power to the states 'has often meant reducing the Federal Government's capacity to monitor and correct'. Under the banner of 'states' rights', the southern states adopted racially discriminatory policies up until the 1960s. Federal government action – such as the 1964 Civil Rights Act and the 1965 Voting Rights Act – was required to ensure equality and justice. At the same time, a significant proportion of state legislatures were unrepresentative because electoral boundaries between districts did not reflect population movements. The rural areas were over-represented. This was only resolved by the US Supreme Court in *Baker v. Carr* (1962).

Fifthly, although state capitals may be physically closer to the citizen, there is little evidence of widespread public identification with state governments. Indeed, surveys have repeatedly found that few citizens even know the names of their state legislator. It is therefore difficult to sustain the claim that state government is 'closer to the people' than the decision-makers in Washington DC.

Lastly, although 'states' rights' are often depicted as a check on the power of the national government, Martha Derthick argues that federalism has, in practice, enlarged the role of the federal courts. This is because the division of power between national and state governments has inevitably created uncertainty. Responsibilities and jurisdictions overlapped or were subject to dispute. In such circumstances, the intervention of an umpire – the federal judiciary – was required.

References and further reading

Derthick, M. (1992), 'Up-to-date in Kansas City: reflections on American federalism', *PS: Political Science and Politics*, 25:4, December, 671–5.

there would be a relative reduction in the level of federal grants-in-aid. Thirdly, a number of categorical grant programmes would be merged into nine *block* grants, thereby giving the states leeway in deciding between different spending options. Lastly, certain federal regulations that curtailed state discretion would be eliminated.

The Reagan Administration had some successes in implementing these goals. Grants-in-aid shrank. Attempts were made – through executive orders – to reform the maze of federal regulations that circumscribed state and local governments; but these orders had a broad character. In October 1987, Executive Order 12614 instructed federal government agencies to 'recognize the distinction between problems of national scope . . . and problems that are merely common to the states'. The order asserted that the former required action by the federal government, but the latter should be left to the collective or individual efforts of the states. Some new block grants were created through the merging together of separate categorical grants. In the 1981 Omnibus Budget Reconciliation Act (the annual budget as it is finally agreed), seventy-seven were brought together as nine block grants (King 1989: 35–8).

However, the overall significance of these reforms should not be overstated. They fell short of the hopes raised by President Reagan's initial rhetoric. The proposed 'swap' had to be abandoned altogether. The National Governors' Association insisted that welfare provision should remain a national responsibility. There was also insufficient support within Congress. David R. Beam has noted the widely shared perception of the Reagan initiative: 'The impression was created that federalism was nothing more than a code word for stringent expenditure cuts' (Benda and Levine 1988: 123). Furthermore, there were – during the same period – centralising measures that cut across the goals associated with New Federalism. In 1984, following lobbying by the Christian right and groupings such as MADD (Mothers Against Drunk Drivers), the president supported an Act that raised the minimum drinking age to twenty-one. States that failed to implement the measure lost 10 per cent of federal highway funds. They all complied.

The revival of the states

Although many of the specific proposals associated with New Federalism were lost or passed only in a modified form, there was a shift in the character of state–central relations during the 1980s and 1990s. Although it would be fanciful to talk in terms of a return to dual federalism, there was a limited swing of the pendulum and a partial reassertion of 'states' rights'. This can be attributed to three developments.

1 The Supreme Court made a number of significant rulings. Although the *Garcia* ruling (1985) enhanced the powers of the federal government by limiting the scope of the Tenth Amendment and – seemingly – circumscribing the

role of the Court in adjudicating between the national and state governments, and *U.S. Term Limits, Inc. v. Thornton* (1995) prevented the states imposing statutory constraints upon their members of Congress, other Court rulings have bolstered the position of the individual states.

- In *New York v. United States* (1992), the Court struck down a statute requiring states to establish sites for the disposal of radioactive waste generated by businesses. In 1995, in *United States v. Lopez*, the Court restricted the interpretation of the interstate commerce clause of the Constitution. It said that it could not be used – as it was in the 1990 Gun Free School Zones Act – to prohibit the possession a gun within 1,000 feet of a school. By reading the clause narrowly, the Court was limiting the powers constitutionally assigned to the federal government.
- In *Seminole Tribe of Florida v. Florida (1996)*, the Court ruled that the Indian tribes – many of whom promote gambling on their lands as a source of revenue – could not, under the terms of the Eleventh Amendment, take legal action against state governments in the federal courts.
- The shift towards states' rights was confirmed in *Kimel v. Florida Board of Regents* (2000). This established – a 5–4 ruling – that states are protected from lawsuits alleging age discrimination. The states, the Court asserted, have sovereign immunity. The judgement struck down the Age Discrimination in Employment Act. The Court was stating, in effect, that state employees hoping for the redress of a grievance should seek a remedy under state discrimination laws rather than federal law.
- *United States v. Morrison* (2000) continued the trend. In a 5–4 decision, the Court struck down a core provision of the 1994 Violence Against Women Act, which stated that '(A)ll persons within the United States shall have the right to be free from crimes of violence motivated by gender' and allowed women to sue their attackers in federal court. The Constitution, the Court asserted, did not permit the federal government to make laws on matters – such as sexual violence – that were the prerogatives of the states. As Chief Justice William Rehnquist asserted: 'We accordingly reject that argument that Congress may regulate non-economic, violent criminal conduct based solely on that conduct's aggregate effect on interstate commerce. The Constitution requires a distinction between what is truly national and what is truly local.'

2 The reductions in the size and scale of grants-in-aid that the Reagan Administration introduced had consequences. Federal government aid fell as a share of state and local outlays. In 1980, federal aid accounted for 26.3 per cent of state and local outlays. By 1995, such aid represented only 22.2 per cent of the total. At first sight, this might be a reason to conclude that the decision-making abilities of the states were constrained yet further. Certainly, many of Reagan's opponents feared that this would happen. However, the progressive withdrawal of federal funding compelled the states to become more financially self-reliant.

3 Following the Republicans' 1994 election victories, the Republican majority in Congress developed policies that extended the states' decision-making powers. The 1996 Unfunded Mandates Act sought to curb federal laws and regulations that require the state and local governments to adopt a particular policy that has to be funded by state and local taxes. The measure stated that – with some exemptions – any federal regulation costing $50 million or more had to be funded by Congress.

   The 1996 Personal Responsibility and Work Opportunity Reconciliation Act also represented a decentralising shift. The essence of the Act was that the individual states would assume responsibility for welfare provision. It brought to an end a federal guarantee – established as part of the New Deal – that eligible mothers with dependent children would receive assistance. Under the 1996 Act, federal funding is given in the form of block grants. Although there is a broad national policy framework – intended to ensure that welfare is only a short-term prop – the states themselves have some discretion in determining the level at which, and the conditions under which, assistance is given to individual claimants. States were, for example, given the option of denying welfare to unwed parents under eighteen and to those who had further children while on welfare.

Box 8.4   'Death with dignity' in Oregon

In November 1994, the citizens of Oregon voted to permit doctor-assisted suicide by 51 to 49 per cent. A 1997 attempt to overturn this was rejected by 60 to 40 per cent. Under the law, a doctor can – on request from a terminally ill patient – prescribe a lethal medication. The legislation does, however, require a fifteen-day waiting period and a second medical opinion regarding the patient's mental state. The dose is to be self-administered. In 1998, the first full year in which euthanasia was legal, 15 people died after taking lethal medications.

The states responded to the changing political environment by becoming more assertive, imaginative and innovative. They began to promote their own interests more forcefully. They acted as pressure groups within the broader political system through organisations such as the National Governors' Association, the US Conference of Mayors, the National League of Cities and the National Council of State Legislatures. During the 1990s, these bodies had an increasingly visible profile and held frequent meetings with national legislators. The states themselves employed lobbyists to work on their behalf in Washington DC. They also experimented with different methods of raising revenue and found ways of administering their responsibilities that reduced or, at least, restrained costs. Some – frustrated by what they saw as federal inaction – attempted to develop policy alternatives. To an extent, a *culture of innovation* emerged at state level.

Firstly, a number of governors – mainly Republicans who were influenced by supply-side theories – pursued radical tax-cutting policies during the mid-1990s. They believed that these would lead to greater investment, stimulate entrepreneurship, and encourage individual effort. New York – under Governor George Pataki – cut the state income tax by 20 per cent. In 1995, earlier tax increases were reversed in California. Top income tax rates were cut in Arizona. The former New Jersey Governor, Christine Todd Whitman, reduced income taxes by 30 per cent. According to the Cato Institute, a libertarian thinktank, the average middle-class family paid $300 less a year in taxes (The Cato Institute 1996).

Secondly, many states have adopted new education policies that encourage initiative, allow greater parental choice and promote experimentation. Supporters argue that steps such as these can act as an engine of educational improvement. By 2001, 27 states and the District of Columbia had enacted a charter school law. A charter school has much greater freedom and autonomy than the traditional public school. However, the 'charter' – which is in essence a contract – is only granted for a 3–5 year period. The school is accountable to the public authorities and parents for its examination results and overall per-formance, and the charter may be terminated. Other states have considered or implemented 'school choice' programmes that permit a degree of competition between schools. From 1990–91 onwards, the Milwaukee Parental Choice Program provided an opportunity for some students to attend – free of charge – private schools. Florida offers 'opportunity scholarships' to students in schools that fail state assessments in two out of four years. These allow them to attend other schools. By 2001, 36 states offered limited or statewide choice pro-grammes (Moffit and Kafer 2001).

Thirdly, some states were in the forefront of efforts to impose more severe penalties on offenders. Although the public mood subsequently shifted away from capital punishment, and Illinois declared a moratorium on executions in 2000, New York reintroduced the death penalty in 1995. Texas continues to implement its death penalty laws to a greater extent than all the other states added together.

The states also took the initiative in adopting community notification laws that opened up registers of sex offenders to the public. The first such law – widely known as 'Megan's Law' – was passed in New Jersey in 1994. Some States impose a financial penalty on parents if their children are punished. Laws passed in Florida, Idaho, Indiana, North Carolina, and Virginia require parents to reim-burse the state authorities for the costs associated with the care, support, deten-tion, or treatment of their children while under the supervision of state agencies. Some states have also adopted measures requiring both children and their parents to participate in community service activities if a son or daughter has been in trouble with the law. New laws in Arizona, Florida, Indiana, Kansas, Kentucky, North Carolina, North Dakota, and Oregon require parents to attend counselling or other court-prescribed treatment programmes. Recent legislation

Table 8.1 *Executions by state, 2002*

State	No. of executions
Texas	33
Oklahoma	7
Missouri	6
Georgia	4
Virginia	4
Florida	3
South Carolina	3
Ohio	3
Alabama	2
North Carolina	2
Mississippi	2
California	1
Louisiana	1

ReligiousTolerance.org (2003), *Capital Punishment: The Death Penalty – Summary of the Year 2002*, www.religioustolerance.org/executd.htm.

in Arkansas, Colorado, Texas, and Wisconsin requires adult participation in parent training and responsibility courses (Office of Juvenile Justice and Delinquency Prevention 1996).

Some states have addressed juvenile crime by establishing boot camps. In Michigan, some young offenders were sentenced to a 90– to 180-day term of military training, study, and counselling, followed by a 4-to 6-month period of aftercare. In New Mexico, a 1995 law provided for work camps based around forestry and conservation. By the late 1990s, however, there were growing doubts about the value of boot camps in curbing criminality. Maryland closed its juvenile boot camp in March 1996 after just two years. Other States – such as Tennessee and Nevada – have introduced laws that seek to clamp down on gang membership. These measures provided further penalties for offences committed by someone in furtherance of a gang activity (Office of Juvenile Justice and Delinquency Prevention 1996).

The Bush administration and federalism

During the latter half of the 1990s, relative economic prosperity allowed states to reduce tax rates and at the same time increase spending, albeit modestly. At the beginning of the new century, however, the economy faltered. The stock market slumped, growth levels tailed off and business confidence fell, particularly after the psychological trauma of 11 September. The overall revenue collected from income, sales and corporate taxes dropped dramatically. Indeed, the fall in 2001–2 was about twice as steep as in the recession of the early 1990s. As a consequence, the states faced soaring budget deficits. Against this back-

Box 8.5   Same-sex marriage and the states

The period since the 1960s has been marked by the growth of new social movements. The gay and lesbian movement has been among the most visible and influential of these. Its growing strength has been reflected in calls for the legal recognition of same-sex marriages. These calls have, however, been forcefully opposed by cultural conservatives who regard homosexuality as pathological and emphasise the importance of traditionalist moral values.

Same-sex marriages are not currently legal in any state. However, in April 2000 the Vermont legislature responded to a state supreme court ruling by passing legislation that permitted 'civil unions' between same-sex couples. This granted them almost all the benefits, protections and responsibilities that married couples have under Vermont law. Furthermore, there are domestic partnership laws in California, the District of Columbia, Hawaii and Connecticut. In California, for example, same-sex couples can register their partnership. This offers some of the legal features of a marriage by enabling a partner to give authority for the other to receive medical treatment or to inherit in the absence of a will.

Set against this, 36 states have passed legislation specifically prohibiting same-sex marriages. Drawing on the 1996 Defense of Marriage Act, these laws also denied recognition of same-sex marriages that might be entered into elsewhere in the US. Following the Supreme Court's *Lawrence* ruling in 2003 – which seemed to expand the 'right to privacy' – cultural conservatives feared that this could be used as a basis for same-sex marriage. Some – including the Senate Majority Leader Bill Frist – backed calls for a Constitutional amendment entrenching the notion of marriage as a union between a man and a woman.

ground, many states are now considering cuts in spending levels and revenue-raising measures. These include tax increases on items such as alcohol, cigarettes, long-distance phone calls and gambling, and the broadening of the sales tax base so that taxes are levied on a broader range of goods and services. However, some state constitutions require a supermajority in the legislature if taxes are to be raised; and lawmakers were, furthermore, fearful of the potential electoral consequences of such a step. They looked towards Washington DC for assistance.

Furthermore, although a number of Supreme Court rulings appeared – by broadening the circumstances in which the eleventh amendment could be applied – to strengthen the position of the states, initiatives taken by the Bush administration and Congress imposed a number of 'unfunded mandates' upon them. The states had to play a major part in developing and implementing 'homeland security' measures. At the same time, the No Child Left Behind Act, passed by Congress in 2001, required the states to introduce recognised standards and testing, and to adopt new forms of teacher training.

Box 8.6   State legislatures

The fifty state legislatures consider approximately 150,000 bills annually. Of these, about 25 per cent will become law. This is more than 75 times the number of laws enacted by Congress each year.

- All but one state legislature is bicameral. The two chambers are generally known as the House and the Senate.
- Most of those elected to state legislatures serve on a part-time basis. Only nine – including California and Illinois – have full-time legislators.
- Sixteen states – including Arizona, California, and Missouri – have term limits. Legislators can only serve for a specified number of years.

State	Legislator service	House members	Senate members
Alabama	Part-time	105	35
Alaska	Part-time	40	20
Arizona	Part-time	60	30
Arkansas	Part-time	100	35
California	Full-time	80	40
Colorado	Part-time	65	35
Connecticut	Part-time	151	36
Delaware	Part-time	41	21
Florida	Part-time	120	40
Georgia	Part-time	180	56
Hawaii	Part-time	51	25
Idaho	Part-time	70	35
Illinois	Full-time	118	59
Indiana	Part-time	100	50
Iowa	Part-time	100	50
Kansas	Part-time	125	40
Kentucky	Part-time	100	38
Louisiana	Part-time	105	39
Maine	Part-time	151	35
Maryland	Part-time	141	47
Massachusetts	Full-time	160	40

Conclusion

There has been a limited and partial reassertion of 'states' rights'. In the 1980s, the US became a more diverse and pluralistic nation than it was in the 1960s and 1970s. Furthermore, there is a consensus – bringing together both liberals and conservatives – around the need to ensure a steady extension of state decision-making. At the same time, the Bush administration includes – within its ranks – many former state governors, most notably the president himself, who have long spoken in terms of an enlarged role for the states. Optimists trust that

State	Legislator service	House members	Senate members
Michigan	Full-time	110	38
Minnesota	Part-time	134	67
Mississippi	Part-time	122	52
Missouri	Part-time	163	34
Montana	Part-time	100	50
Nebraska	Part-time	*	49
Nevada	Part-time	42	21
New Hampshire	Part-time	400	24
New Jersey	Full-time	80	40
New Mexico	Part-time	70	42
New York	Full-time	150	61
North Carolina	Part-time	120	50
North Dakota	Part-time	98	49
Ohio	Full-time	99	33
Oklahoma	Part-time	101	48
Oregon	Part-time	60	30
Pennsylvania	Full-time	203	50
Rhode Island	Part-time	100	50
South Carolina	Part-time	124	46
South Dakota	Part-time	70	35
Tennessee	Part-time	99	33
Texas	Part-time	150	31
Utah	Part-time	75	29
Vermont	Part-time	150	30
Virginia	Part-time	100	40
Washington	Part-time	98	49
West Virginia	Part-time	100	34
Wisconsin	Full-time	99	33
Wyoming	Part-time	60	30

Note: * Nebraska has a unicameral legislature.
Source: adapted from OMBWatch (2001), *Overview of State Legislatures*,
www.ombwatch.org/ npadv/2001/stlg/stlgovrvw.html.

these developments may provide a basis for the beginnings of what Thomas R. Dye calls 'competitive federalism', in which federal, state, and local governments will compete with each other to provide the services that citizens demand (1990: 175–99).

However, none of this should be exaggerated. Federal financial aid to the states is still channelled through categorical grants, and the states have very little discretion in deciding how the funding is used. In 1993, there were only fifteen block and 578 categorical grants. Criminal law – traditionally a state responsibility – has been increasingly 'federalised', and federal law now includes over three thousand offences (Grant 1998: 4). Most importantly of all, the fiscal crunch at the beginning of the new century and the Bush administration's commitment to the adoption of national policies in both education and anti-terrorism began to cut across the rhetoric of state sovereignty.

References and further reading

Benda, P. M. and C. H. Levine (1988), 'Reagan and the bureaucracy: the bequest, the promise, and the legacy', in C. O. Jones (ed.), *The Reagan Legacy: Promise and Performance*, pp. 102–42. Chatham, Chatham House.

Bureau of the Census (1997), *Statistical Abstract of the United States 1997*, Washington DC, US Department of Commerce.

Cato Institute (1996), *Cato Fact Sheet – Tax Cuts and Balanced Budgets: Lessons from the States*, www.cato.org/pubs/wtpapers/taxcuts2.html.

Conlan, T. (1988), *New Federalism: Intergovernmental Reform from Nixon to Reagan*, Washington DC, The Brookings Institution.

Dye, T. R. (1990), *American Federalism: Competition Among Governments*, MA, Lexington, Lexington Books.

Grant, A. (1998), 'Reshaping American federalism', *Politics Review*, September, pp. 2–6.

King, D. S. (1989), 'US federalism and the Reagan administration', *Contemporary Record*, November, 35–8.

Moffit, R. E. and K. Kafer (eds) (2001), *School Choice 2001: What's Happening in the States*, www.heritage.org/research/education/schools/.

Office of Juvenile Justice and Delinquency Prevention (1996), *Juvenile Justice Reform Initiatives in the States 1994–96*, ojjdp.ncjrs.org/pubs/reform/ch2_d.html.

Plano, J. and M. Greenberg (1989), *The American Political Dictionary*, Forth Worth, TX, Holt, Rinehart and Winston.

Websites

The National Conference of State Legislatures is committed to the exchange of information between the legislatures, the promotion of policy innovation, and to 'ensure state legislatures a strong, cohesive voice in the federal system' (www.ncsl.org/).

The National Governors Association website offers news and data for those serving in the executive branch at state level, (www.nga.org/).

9

Political parties

Political parties have been defined as organised groupings 'sharing common policy preferences' that 'seek, or have, political power' (Robertson 1985: 252). They have traditionally had eight principal functions:

1 They have a nomination or recruitment function, because they put forward candidates for public office and generally offer the only secure route for individuals seeking political advancement.
2 They direct and organise election campaigns on behalf of candidates. These, and other forms of party activity, require substantial funding.
3 By providing a conduit between the citizen and the decision-making process, the parties have a communication function. Traditionally, they organised meetings and gatherings allowing the electorate to hear the views of candidates and, in what was a process of dialogue, put forward their own opinions.
4 Parties have a mobilisation function. Activists would traditionally ensure that all the party's grassroots supporters cast a vote.
5 They bring together diverse political views and fuse them so as to construct an agreed platform. The role of parties in uniting divergent interests and structuring compromises has been described as an integration or 'brokerage' function.
6 They have a co-ordination function. Without parties, legislatures would be anarchic and unwieldy. Every vote would involve the construction of fresh alliances and voting blocs. Parties offer a degree of leadership and discipline, and they thereby structure the passage of legislation. They can also provide ties between public officials in the different branches and tiers of government.
7 Parties have a policy or issue development function. They are compelled by the process of electoral competition to generate new proposals and policy options within a broad framework set by their core values. As Clinton Rossiter argued, the parties 'are perhaps best fitted of all agencies to convert formless hopes or frustrations into proposals that can be understood, debated, and, if found appealing, approved by the people' (1964: 50).
8 Parties offer a basis for political identification and choice. The voter can swiftly

recognise the political leanings and allegiances of candidates. This simplifies the electoral process and makes it accessible to those who have only limited political knowledge. As Martin Wattenberg has observed: 'it would probably take an individual approximately the amount of time required for one or two college-level courses a year in order to cast a completely informed vote for all of these offices in all of these elections. Therefore, voters need shortcuts, or cues, such as partisanship to facilitate their decision-making' (1996: 14).

Although political parties across both Europe and North America share these defining characteristics, there are significant differences between the European parties and those found in the US. Firstly, the American parties have also been broad coalitions drawing upon different regional and sectional interests. In contrast, the European parties emerged – or were formed – on the basis of adherence to particular political principles such as conservatism or socialism. Secondly, as a consequence of this, the US parties encompass broad and sometimes irreconcilable spans of opinion. Votes in Congress and the state legislatures cannot be predicted with certainty. As Clinton Rossiter put it: 'They are creatures of compromise, coalitions of interest in which principle is muted and often even silenced. They are vast, gaudy, friendly umbrellas under which all Americans, whoever and wherever and however-minded they may be, are invited to stand for the sake of being counted in the next election' (1964: 20).

Thirdly, the American parties are not membership-based. In contrast with Europe, where party membership rests upon payment of an annual subscription and adherence to rules, the term 'party member' is applied in the US to all those who register as party supporters. Fourthly, the US parties have traditionally been decentralised. In Rossiter's words, they have been 'loose confederacies' (1964: 21). The national party leaderships have always been relatively weak, and there has instead been an emphasis upon the autonomy of state parties and localism. Fifthly, the parties – particularly the Democrats – were for long periods associated with 'bossism'. Many larger cities were dominated by the 'machine politics' of party bosses – such as Mayor Richard Daley of Chicago – who often maintained their position through their ability to offer municipal employment to the immigrant communities.

Lastly, the US parties have always operated within a political context defined by the separation of powers. They traditionally provided a bridge between the different branches of government, offering a mechanism enabling the White House and members of Congress to work together in co-ordinating the passage of legislation.

Origins and party systems

The American parties had their origins in the small groups and factions created by politicians seeking office at both state and federal level. Those around Thomas

Jefferson established the Democratic-Republicans. They put forward a vision of a decentralised nation, and sought support from craftsmen and farmers. Alexander Hamilton's supporters, known as the Federalists, were backed by commercial interests and argued for stronger forms of national government. They were, however, only partially recognisable as political parties:

> They were neither deeply rooted in the political soil nor all-encompassing in their influence and importance. To be sure, some coordinated efforts were made to select candidates, manage campaigns, attract voters, and bring legislators and other officeholders under the discipline of a party . . . Nevertheless, there was always an intermittent, *ad hoc* quality to all of these efforts and a casual attitude toward the partisan forms. There was little coordination between the national level and the political battles in the states of party warfare. (Silbey 2002: 3)

Mass parties, extending beyond caucuses of elected officials, grew with the broadening out of the right to vote, or *franchise*. President Andrew Jackson was elected in 1828 through the efforts of the newly established Democratic Party. Although it drew on the backing of agricultural interests, Jacksonianism also rested on the opportunities that westward expansion offered to the ordinary citizen. At the same time, Jackson's critics came together and coalesced to form the Whigs.

The modern party system, based around Democrats and Republicans, emerged on the eve of the Civil War as slavery came to dominate national political debate. Those who opposed the extension of slavery into the newly created states and territories that westward expansion had created, formed the Republican Party or GOP (Grand Old Party). The Republican candidate, Abraham Lincoln, was elected to the presidency in 1860. Over the century that followed, the white south – as well as the waves of newly arrived immigrants from Europe – remained loyal to the Democratic Party.

The 1828 and 1860 elections had, therefore, a particular significance. Each ushered in a new party system based upon the demise and the rise of particular political parties. These have been dubbed *critical* or *realigning* elections. They were generally the result of tensions and conflicts that built up over a number of years and could not find expression in the existing parties.

Although the US political process has – since 1860 – been dominated by the Republicans and Democrats, there have been significant shifts in the character of the relationship between them. From 1896 – which is regarded as a further realigning election – onwards, the Republicans were predominant. They were the party of industrial capitalism and Protestantism. Despite the growing numbers of immigrants from southern and eastern Europe, the Republicans occupied the White House for twenty-eight of the years between 1897 and 1933.

The 1932 election inaugurated a period of Democratic hegemony. Although there were interruptions when the GOP seemed on the edge of a long-run recovery, the Democrats remained predominant for forty years. Their election

victories were constructed around a broad alliance of economic, racial, religious, and regional interests. The 'New Deal coalition' embraced blue-collar
industrial workers, Jews, Roman Catholics, African-Americans and white
southerners. It was held together between the 1930s and 1960s by the promise
of basic welfare provision, government employment projects, and a degree of
acquiescence towards the white south's efforts to maintain segregation. The
coalition was, however, subject to inherent strains. As the civil rights movement asserted itself in the 1950s and 1960s, the Democratic Party had to
choose between the political goals of African-Americans and those of the white
south. In the 1960 and 1964 elections, the Party chose the former, and blacks
now represent the Democrats' most loyal constituency. In the 2000 presidential election, for example, Al Gore won 90 per cent of black votes. However,
white southerners – and those, such as Senator Strom Thurmond of South
Carolina, who served as their political representatives – responded to the party's
growing identification with the civil rights movement by defecting to the
Republicans. Although the shift to the GOP took an uneven form, and
Democratic public officials continued to be elected at the sub-presidential level,
its extent and scale should not be underestimated. In 2000, just 26.1 per cent
of white southerners described themselves as Democrats, compared with 46.2
per cent in 1972 (General Social Survey 2003b).

The New Deal coalition suffered other losses during the 1960s and 1970s.
The Vietnam War proved increasingly divisive. At the same time, the rise of new
social movements – such as the women's movement and post-civil rights 'black
power' organisations – provoked hostility among the party's more traditional
blue-collar supporters. Their feelings were compounded by resentment against
'big government' and the taxation levels required to maintain it. From a blue-
collar perspective, the Democratic Party seemed to have been 'captured' by
intellectuals and radicals with whom they had little in common. The success of
George McGovern, a liberal, anti-war candidate, in winning the party's presidential nomination in 1972 confirmed their fears. He gained just 38 per cent of
the vote in the November election when he faced the incumbent president,
Richard Nixon.

Realignment

Those who spoke in terms of realigning elections argued that they took place
every thirty or forty years. There was, therefore, an expectation of realignment
from the late 1960s onwards. At times, it seemed that the Republicans had
become predominant. Certainly, the Democratic Party's difficulties proved to be
the Republican Party's opportunity. Both Richard Nixon and Ronald Reagan
were able to bring disaffected Democratic Party supporters – particularly blue-
collar workers – into the Republican camp. The GOP emphasised issues that
would solidify the divide between them and the liberalism that held sway

among many Democratic Party activists. They held out the promise of tax reductions, small government, traditional cultural values, opposition to race and gender-based policies, and a reassertion of US national interests on the world stage. Although President Nixon never fully embraced these themes, they increasingly became the political basis of Republicanism. From the 1980s onwards, the GOP had become a conservative party, and the few remaining liberals had been relegated to the sidelines. This is evident in partisan identification data. In 2000, for example, 70.1 per cent of Republicans defined themselves as conservatives, compared with only 53.6 per cent in 1975 (General Social Survey 2003a).

The policies adopted in the Reagan years reflected the drift towards conservatism. During his period of office (1981–89), there were tax cuts, a sustained attempt to reduce the scope and size of the federal government, and a pull-back from policies structured around gender and race. Cold War hostilities intensified until the USSR began a process of reform. While the Bush presidency (1989–93) marked a partial return to a more pragmatic political style, the Republican Party remained tied to conservatism. The party's candidates for the House of Representatives in the 1994 Congressional elections fought under the banner of the Contract with America, a national platform based upon conservative measures including tax reductions and strengthened law and order. Although George W. Bush talked in terms of 'compassionate conservatism', he also stressed the importance of tax cuts and deregulation.

However, although the closing decades of the twentieth century were dominated by Republican victories and the hegemony of the conservative policy agenda, only some observers are willing to embrace the concept of a realignment. Despite Republican successes in, for example, 1972, 1980 and – if Congressional elections are considered – 1994 and 2002, there has been no realigning election that can be compared with 1896 or 1932. Furthermore, there have been two Democratic occupants in the White House and – had it not been for the mathematics of the Electoral College – they would have been joined by Al Gore in 2000. Commentators speak – with some justice – of a 'fifty-fifty America' in which the parties are finely balanced.

The minor parties

Although the Democrats and the Republicans dominate studies of the American party system, the US is a heterogeneous nation, and there has always been, as a consequence, a plethora of minor or 'third' parties. In a classic study – first published in 1960 – Clinton Rossiter divided them into six categories, although some of the labels that he applied had a distinctly pejorative character (1964: 14). There were, he asserted, 'one-issue obsessionists', such as the Prohibition Party, which has long opposed the manufacture, sale and consumption of alcoholic drink. He also identified 'left-wing splinter parties', such as the Socialist Party, the Socialist Workers' Party, and the former Communist Party of the USA. At the same time, there are one-state parties. Wisconsin had a Progressive Party in the 1930s. There was a Farmer–Labor Party in Minnesota during the inter-war years. However, although the party won both the state governorship and its seats in the US Senate, it progressively lost support and merged with the Democrats in 1944. New York still has its own Conservative and Liberal Parties. Some minor parties, Rossiter notes, are 'the personal following of the dissident hero'. He cites the Bull Moose movement of 1912 – which was organised around the former president Theodore Roosevelt – as an example of this. There are also minor parties that have emerged from the dissident wing of a major party. In 1948, the 'Dixiecrats' – who drew their support from white southerners seeking to maintain the system of racial segregation – deserted the Democratic Party and put forward South Carolina Governor Strom Thurmond as their presidential candidate. Similarly, in 1968, the Alabama Governor George Wallace broke with the Democrats so as to form the American Independent Party. Lastly, there are those who Rossiter describes as 'true minor parties' that, he suggests, have the potential – in certain circumstances – to win major party status. He points to the People's Party – or *populists*. In the closing decades of the nineteenth century, they campaigned for currency reform and against the railroad companies and other 'trusts' that had, they asserted, a monopoly hold over a sector or market. The populists won particular backing in the agricultural areas in the West and South that had been ravaged by economic depression during those years. In 1890, the party won control of the Kansas state legislature. However, they were increasingly divided between those who hoped to use the party so as to change the political character of the Democrats and those who sought to maintain the party's independent identity.

Most contemporary third parties can be considered 'true minor parties'. The Libertarian Party (LP) was founded in December 1971. It is committed to 'a world of liberty; a world in which all individuals are sovereign over their own lives, and no one is forced to sacrifice his or her values for the benefit of others' (Libertarian Party 1996). The LP puts forward a platform based around free market economics, the abolition of welfare provision, and minimal government. However, the Party distances itself from others on the right by calling for the legalisation of all victimless 'crimes' – for example drug taking – and an end to restrictions on all consensual sexual activity. It supports gay rights and the legalisation of prostitution. Although the Greens may appear to be 'one-issue obsessionists', they have raised a range of issues associated with radicalism and feminism. During the 2000 election, when Ralph Nader stood as their candidate, they campaigned against the large corporations. The Reform Party could also be included within this category, although there is a case for adopting James Q. Wilson's typology and categorising it as an economic protest party (*Congressional Quarterly* 1997: 117). The party – which emerged in the wake of Ross Perot's 1992 presidential bid – drew upon the discontent that accompanied the recession at the beginning of the 1990s. It called for reforms to the political process – such as the imposition of term limits on federal lawmakers – and the adoption of protectionist policies so as to protect American jobs. However, by the end of the decade – against a background of relative economic prosperity – the party disintegrated.

Table 9.1 *Minor party and independent challenges, 1980–2000*

Election	Leading minor party candidate	Total % share of the vote gained by minor parties and independents
1980	John B. Anderson (Independent)	8.3
1984	David Bergland (Libertarian)	0.6
1988	Ron Paul (Libertarian)	1.0
1992	H. Ross Perot (Independent)	19.6
1996	H. Ross Perot (Reform Party)	10.1
2000	Ralph Nader (Green)	3.7

Source: adapted from H. W. Stanley and R. G. Niemi (1998), *Vital Statistics on American Politics 1997–1998*, Washington DC, Congressional Quarterly, 26–7 and Federal Election Commission (2001), *2000 Presidential Popular Vote Summary for All Candidates Listed on at Least One State Ballot*, www.fec.gov/pubrec/fe2000/prespop.htm (accessed 2003).

Barriers facing minor parties

Table 9.2 *The 2000 presidential election: minor party candidates*

Candidate (party)	No. of votes	% of vote
Ralph Nader (Green)	2,882,955	2.74
Patrick J. Buchanan (Reform)	448,895	0.42
Harry Browne (Libertarian)	384,431	0.36
Howard Phillips (Constitution)	98,020	0.09
John S. Hagelin (Natural Law)	83,714	0.08
James E. Harris, Jr. (Socialist Workers)	7,378	0.01
L. Neil Smith (Libertarian)	5,775	0.00
David McReynolds (Socialist)	5,602	0.00

Note: Only those gaining over 5,000 votes have been included. Six further candidates – whose votes ranged between 161 and 4,795 – have been excluded from the table.
Source: adapted from Federal Election Commission (2001), *2000 Presidential Popular Vote Summary for All Candidates Listed on at Least One State Ballot*, www.fec.gov/pubrec/fe2000/prespop.htm.

Minor – or third – party candidates attracted only a handful of votes in the 2000 presidential election. Indeed, although minor parties have sporadically attracted significant numbers of votes, no minor party has made a sustained electoral breakthrough since the Republican Party established itself in the years before the Civil War. Why have they failed?

1 Many of the attempts to build alternatives to the Republicans and Democrats have been made by groupings associated with the political fringes. Their thinking is far removed from the mainstream. In 2000, the Reform Party nomination was captured by Pat Buchanan. He was associated with an abrasive form of conservatism that emphasised moral traditionalism and opposition to immigration. The Constitution Party talks in similar terms. The Libertarian Party seeks minimal government and calls for the legalisation of drugs and prostitution. The Natural Law Party stresses the importance of meditation.

2 Many minor parties have been ridden by factional rivalries and internal tensions. The disintegration of the Reform Party is instructive. It was torn between different ideas. These included 'progressive' calls for the 'cleaning up' and modernising of government institutions, conservative fiscal theory, and populist demands for the protection of American economic interests against those of outsiders. A further ingredient was added when – in November 1998 – Minnesota elected Jesse Ventura, a Reform Party member, as state governor. He backed the legal availability of abortion and supported the legalisation of cannabis and same-sex marriage (Sifry 2002: 25).

   Against this background, the party began to fall apart. Ventura and his faction left the party in the Spring of 2000. Supporters of Patrick J. Buchanan – the hard right commentator who had sought the Republican presidential nomination in 1992 and 1996 – joined the party and promoted his candidature. They won, but only after a bruising and bloody battle with Perot loyalists. In the wake of all this, Buchanan gained just 448,895 votes.

3 There are particular problems facing leftist parties. In striking contrast with the countries of Europe, socialist and social-democratic thinking never took root in the US. Some attribute this to the hold of individualistic thinking and the material prosperity of the American working class. In a celebrated phrase, Werner Sombart, a German observer, wrote that America was 'Canaan, the promised land of capitalism' where 'on the reefs of roast beef and apple pie socialistic utopias of every sort are sent to their doom'.

4 There are administrative and legal obstacles. Many states require that candidates gain a certain number of signatures before their names can be placed on the ballot. The principal parties need only submit a limited number (Davies 1992: 134). The regulations for third parties are, however, much more demanding, and they require many more names. If Pennsylvania's 1997 rules for third parties had been adopted in the 1996 presidential election, they would have had to have collected 99,000 signatures in fourteen weeks (Bibby and Maisel 1998: 62). There are also 'sore loser' laws in some states that prohibit those who were defeated in the primaries entering the general election contest. Although the 2000 Green Party nominee – Ralph Nader – had widespread name recognition, he was unable to secure a place on the ballot in seven states. Although the obsta-

cles are not always insurmountable, they compel minor parties to devote their energies and financial resources to ballot access. The principal parties can, in contrast, concentrate their efforts on campaigning.

5 Congressmen represent single-member districts. There is a simple plurality – or 'first-the-the-post' – electoral system, and few people will vote for a small party that they believe has no realistic prospect of success. Presidential elections still rest on the Electoral College (see Chapter 10). This also works on a winner-takes-all basis. In 1992, Ross Perot attracted 19 per cent of the popular vote across the US, yet gained no Electoral College Votes at all.

6 There are also financial difficulties. Modern election campaigns depend upon television commercials and direct mail. They are therefore capital-intensive. However, with some notable exceptions, most independents and minor parties have only limited financial resources. Under the Federal Election Campaign Act (FECA), candidates contesting the Republican and Democratic presidential primaries are awarded matching funds by the federal government. Furthermore, the Democratic and GOP national conventions each attracted a subsidy from the taxpayer. In the November election campaign, the major party candidates have their costs paid in full. Minor parties must be on the ballot in at least ten states and gain at least 5 per cent of the poll to receive taxpayer funding. If they are a new party, these funds are only provided retrospectively rather than when they are most needed.

7 For many individuals and campaigns, interest group activity offers a more effective avenue of influence than the formation of a party. As Chapter 11 argues, the US political system offers countless access points that enable organised interests to reach decision-makers at both a federal and a state level.

8 Although some commentators have pointed to the growing number of people defining themselves as 'independents' and argue that this offers a basis for the birth and development of minor parties, significant numbers are still identifiers with the principal parties. In other words, loyalties to the Republicans and Democrats remain entrenched.

Table 9.3 *Partisan identification, 1952–2000 (% of respondents)*

	1952	1962	1972	1982	1992	2000
Democrat (including leaners)	57	54	52	55	50	50
Independent	6	8	13	11	12	12
Republican (including leaners)	34	35	34	32	38	37

Question text: 'Generally speaking, do you usually think of yourself as a Republican, a Democrat, an Independent, or what?'
Source: adapted from National Election Studies (2003b), *The NES Guide to Public Opinion and Electoral Behavior – Party Identification 3-Point Scale 1952–2000*, www.umich.edu/~nes/nesguide/toptable/tab2a_2.htm.

9 The development of primaries opened up the Democrats and Republicans. Individuals from a broad range of political backgrounds have the opportunity to campaign for support within the two principal parties, and there is therefore less of a likelihood that they will establish alternative party organisations. A strategy of 'burrowing from within' is likely to prove more successful (Bibby and Maisel 1998: 58). David Duke, a former Ku Klux Klan leader, initially attempted to break into politics as the presidential candidate of the Populist Party. He abandoned the Party and contested the 1988 Democratic Parties. In 1989, after success in the primary, he became a Republican nominee for the Louisiana state legislature, to which he was elected. In 1992, he entered the Republican Party presidential primaries, winning 11 and 9 per cent of the poll in Mississippi and Louisiana respectively.

10 Although some of those most committed to political activism see a process of ideological convergence between the parties and stress the similarities between successive administrations, much of the American public do see differences. Indeed, in 1995, John H. Aldrich concluded 'this perception of party differences has grown, especially over the past decade, to truly significant levels' (Aldrich 1995: 174). His claim is supported by findings from the National Election Studies.

Table 9.4 *Perceptions of differences between the Democrats and Republicans (% of respondents)*

	1952	1960	1972	1980	1990	1996	2000
Yes – a difference	50	50	46	58	45	64	64

Question text: 'Do you think there are any important differences in what the Republicans and Democrats stand for?'
Source: adapted from the National Election Studies (2003a), *The NES Guide to Public Opinion and Electoral Behavior – Important Difference in What Democratic and Republican Parties Stand For 1952–2000*, www.umich.edu/~nes/nesguide/toptable/tab2b_4.htm.

11 The character of the principal parties has denied opportunities to the construction of minor parties. In Europe, the principal parties were structured around ideological differences and social class. In contrast, the principal US parties have always had much more of a 'catch-all' character. They have drawn together strikingly different groups and interests. They have therefore had an integrative character and absorbed new social movements – that might have otherwise established parties – in a way that was precluded in Europe. As Clinton Rossiter has noted: 'One of the most persistent qualities of the American two-party system is the way in which one of the major parties moves almost instinctively to absorb (and thus be somewhat reshaped by) the most challenging third party of the time' (Rossiter 1964 15).

12 Minor party votes are often a function of voter discontent. At other times,

there is little to sustain their protests against 'establishment' politicians. Ross Perot's 1992 vote reflected disillusionment with Washington DC and anger at the recession. However, the issues that fuelled the anger of the early 1990s lost much of their former salience as the decade progressed.

However, although these barriers limit the ability of minor parties to gain votes, they should not be dismissed or disregarded. In the 1992 presidential election, Ross Perot – a Texan billionaire – won almost one in five of the votes. It was the most successful performance for a third-party candidate since Theodore Roosevelt – the former president – gained 27.4 per cent of the vote in the election of 1912. Perot's showing led to the formation of the Reform Party. Perot stood again – as the Party's 1996 presidential candidate – but only won 8.5 per cent of the vote.

The importance of minor parties also rests upon their ability to remould and restructure the political agenda. For example, many of the ideas around which Ross Perot campaigned were later adopted by major party candidates. These included the need for a balanced federal government budget, the importance of imposing term limits on lawmakers, the elimination of government waste, and the reform of campaign finance.

The role of minor parties, however, goes beyond agenda setting. As John B. Anderson, a former Congressman who received six million votes when he stood as an independent in the presidential election of 1980, argues, minor parties also ensure that the Republicans and Democrats do not lose touch with the American electorate: 'New parties offer voters better choices and bring important perspectives to political debate. They provide a check on any drift of major parties away from substantial numbers of people' (National Commission on Federal Election Reform 2001).

Furthermore, the 2000 election illustrated that the role of minor parties could – in certain circumstances – be decisive. As embittered Democratic Party activists observed in the aftermath of the 2000 election, Ralph Nader – the Greens' candidate – probably contributed to Al Gore's defeat. Although Gore won a narrow majority of the votes across the country, the outcome of the entire election came to depend upon the casting of Florida's 25 Electoral College Votes (ECV). In the end – after recounts and a challenge heard by the US Supreme Court – George W. Bush was finally deemed to have won in Florida by 537 votes. On this basis, he was assigned the state's ECV and gained the presidency (Federal Election Commission 2003). For his part, Ralph Nader attracted 97,488 votes in Florida. Although the claim has been challenged, analysts have asserted that many of these ballots would have been cast – in the absence of Nader – for Al Gore.

The Green campaign put the Democrats under pressure in another way. Gore was compelled to yield campaign resources – in terms of both staffing and finance – into states where Nader appeared to be garnering support, such as Wisconsin, Minnesota, and Iowa (McSweeney 2002: 38). Furthermore, as

Washington commentators such as Andrew Sullivan have noted, the Nader campaign shifted the political agenda. Gore was compelled to tack leftwards. His campaign speeches assumed a populist tone as he criticised powerful companies – such as those in the pharmaceuticals industry – for exploitative practices. This rhetoric, Sullivan has suggested, alienated moderate voters and propelled them towards the Republican camp.

Some observers have spoken of minor party votes as the harbingers of electoral realignment. The successes, it is said, presage a fundamental shift in the balance of power between the parties (Mayhew 2002: 77–8). The electoral statistics do not, however, provide much to sustain such a view. Their role is more modest. Richard Hofstadter, a celebrated historian, offers a more fitting epitaph. Minor parties, he once claimed, were destined 'to sting like a bee and die' (National Commission on Federal Election Reform 2001). In other words, while they make a significant impact, it is invariably short-lived.

Party decline

The party decline thesis – which was spelt out in David Broder's 1971 book, *The Party's Over* – suggested that if trends continued the principal parties would no longer perform many of the functions outlined at the beginning of this chapter. The thesis has been succinctly summarised:

> the two parties are in full retreat in all the areas that they have traditionally dominated. No matter whether it is selecting candidates, fundraising, running campaigns, mobilising voters, or co-ordinating government, the argument is that the parties have become less and less relevant. In short, the parties are no longer doing the things which parties are even minimally expected to do. (Bailey 1990: 12)

Nominating candidates and campaigning

The rise of primaries and caucuses, which enabled ordinary voters to select the parties' candidates, began as an attempt to dislodge the party 'bosses' and 'machine' politicians who had offered rewards – principally municipal employment – to those who backed them. However, as a long-term consequence, the nomination function was progressively transferred from the parties to the broader public.

The first primary was held in Wisconsin in 1905. By 1912, 32.9 per cent of the delegates attending the Democrats' national convention, which formally chooses the Party's presidential candidate, had been selected in primaries. By 1976, the proportion of delegates selected in the Democratic primaries had risen to 72.6 per cent, although old-style political leaders were able to influence or even dictate the primary results in some states until the 1960s (Hays

Lowenstein 1992: 67). Many of the delegates will have been 'pledged' or mandated to vote for the candidate who won in their state's primary.

In the past – particularly for the Democrats – the primaries were a drawn-out process. In 1988, for example, Michael Dukakis only secured victory over Jesse Jackson after the New York primary, which was held towards the end of the primary 'season'. In recent years, those who lose in the primaries have generally conceded defeat many months before the convention, often in the early stages of the process. Even if they wish to continue, their financial resources will almost certainly dry up and compel their withdrawal. The outcome of the nominating process is thereby determined in advance of the national convention. The convention now simply provides a formal endorsement of the voters' choice, and has been reduced from a decision-making forum to a stage-managed media event.

Table 9.5 *Primaries 1912–2004*

Year	Democratic Party		Republican Party	
	No. of primaries	% of delegates from primary 'states'	No. of primaries	% of delegates from primary 'states'
1912	12	32.9	13	41.7
1932	16	40.0	14	37.7
1960	16	38.4	15	38.6
1972	23	66.5	22	58.2
1980	35	81.1	36	78.0
1992	40	88.0	39	85.4
1996	35	70.9	43	85.9

Source: adapted from H. W. Stanley and R. G. Niemi (1998), *Vital Statistics on American Politics 1997–1998*, p. 62, Washington DC, Congressional Quarterly.

The role of the primary was entrenched by the McGovern–Fraser reforms. These were drawn up by the Commission on Party Structure and Delegate Selection that was established by the Democrats in the wake of the 1968 presidential election. In 1968, the Democratic nominee was former Vice-President Hubert Humphrey, a late entrant into the race, who, although backed by party leaders, had not stood in the primaries. It was a 'top-down' selection process, and there were allegations from supporters of Senator Eugene McCarthy – who had contested the primaries on a platform opposing America's military intervention in Vietnam – that the system by which national convention delegates were selected had been rigged to deny them proper representation.

The Commission's report and the basis for the reforms – *Mandate for Change* – was published in 1970. It led to amendments to state law, and thereby compelled both the parties to make rule changes. Caucuses – meetings which are held by some state parties to decide on candidate selection – were made more open. In the Democratic Party, the proportionality rules, which ensured that the delegation's voting at the national convention reflected the votes cast in the primary, were introduced. The Commission also stipulated that delegations should become more socially representative by including women, minorities and young people 'in reasonable relationship to their presence in the population of the state'. The reforms were put into effect at the 1972 national convention. They placed strict limits on the influence of party organisers and made primaries pivotal in delegate selection. A mere 1.1 per cent of the delegates were elected by the state party committees (*Congressional Quarterly* 1997: 28). The institutionalisation of the primary in the selection of candidates has had important consequences for the political character of the parties:

1 The primary system is liable to impose candidates upon the parties who may have extensive campaigning skills, but more limited governing abilities. As Anthony King notes:

> To win the nomination, a person needs to be able to attract media attention, to be able to communicate easily with ordinary citizens, above all to be able to project an attractive image of himself on the small screen . . . to win a presidential nomination in the age of caucuses and primaries, a person no longer has to do business with others, to build coalitions, or to bargain with people who possess things that he should acquire if he is to achieve his goals. It is enough that he be a supersalesman of himself. (King 1981: 323–4)

King cites the 1980 presidential election – which pitted the incumbent president, Jimmy Carter, against the Republican challenger, Ronald Reagan – as an example of this. Both, according to King, were flawed.[1] He notes the comment made in Britain's *Daily Telegraph* as the election approached, 'One sighs for a man of stature' (quoted in King 1981: 303).

2 The primaries also often lead to disunity within the parties, which can contribute to election defeat. Disputes are magnified as the candidates establish their own personal profiles and distinguish themselves from others in the field. All this inevitably takes place in the public arena. In 1976, President Gerald Ford was challenged in the Republican primaries by the former California governor, Ronald Reagan. Ford held off the challenge, but it damaged his political credibility. In 1980, Jimmy Carter's re-election prospects – which were already uncertain – were further damaged by divisions among Democrats. Although Carter was victorious in 24 of the primaries, the nomination was contested, and Senator Edward Kennedy won in 10 states. In 1992, Pat Buchanan's savage attacks on President George Bush during the early primaries contributed to Bush's defeat in the November election. In 2000 – during the Republican primaries – there were stresses as George W. Bush's backers sought to ensure the defeat of Arizona Senator, John McCain.

3 Primaries lessen a party's hold over its elected officials. They have led to candidate-centred forms of politics, because those who are electorally victorious owe their success to the campaign organisations that they established during the primaries rather than to the party apparatus. In 1972, for example, President Nixon's successful bid to win a second presidential term

was organised around the Committee for the Re-election of the President (CREEP). In 1992, Bill Clinton's election campaign was directed from Little Rock in Arkansas, not from the Democratic National Committee's headquarters in Washington DC, by his personal appointees, most notably George Stephanopoulos and James Carville. Indeed, in many elections, the campaign literature issued by candidates does not include references either to a party label or to fellow candidates from the same party.

Fundraising

The parties are also said to be losing their role as fundraisers. Presidential candidates are eligible for taxpayer funding under the provisions of the amended Federal Election Campaign Act (FECA) of 1974. In the 2000 presidential election, the major party candidates – Al Gore and George W. Bush – were each assigned $67,560,000 by the Federal Election Commission (FEC). The figure was based on a spending limit of $20 million – which was set in 1974 – and has subsequently been increased as the cost of living has risen (Federal Election Commission 2000).

Parties are being outflanked in another way. Following passage of the Bipartisan Campaign Reform Act (BCRA) in 2002, limits have been imposed on

Table 9.6 *The 2000 Congressional elections: sources of candidate funding (%)*

	Individual donors	PACs	Party contributions and spending	Self (contributions and loans)	Other
Senate 2000					
Democrats	40	19	3	43[a]	6
Incumbents	56	20	6	12	5
Challengers	43	8	1	41	8
Republicans	68	19	18	6	1
Incumbents	60	27	5	2	7
Challengers	70	9	8	3	10
All	53	13	4	24[a]	6
House of Representatives 2000					
Democrats	50	34	1	9	6
Incumbents	48	45	1	0	7
Challengers	57	17	2	19	4
Republicans	52	29	2	13	4
Incumbents	54	39	1	1	5
Challengers	56	13	4	23	4
All	51	31	2	11	5

[a] Without Jon Corzine, the Democratic candidate in New Jersey, the figure for the Senate Democrats would be 20 per cent and 10 per cent for all senatorial candidates.

Source: adapted from N. J. Ornstein, T. E. Mann, and M. J. Malbin (2002), *Vital Statistics on Congress 2001–2002*, Washington DC, The AEI Press, pp. 104–5.

Box 9.1   Political Action Committees

Political Action Committees (PACs) are organisations that are formed for the purpose of raising and distributing money so as to elect candidates. Most PACs represent business, labour or ideological interests.

The number of PACs has mushroomed since the early 1980s. In 1974 there were 608, but by 1996 the number had risen to 4,079 (*Congressional Quarterly* 1997: 51). In 1991–92, they gave a total of over $394 million to presidential and Congressional candidates. The leading donors are PACs established by companies and the trades unions. Whereas corporate interests and professional associations divide up their donations between the parties, union-based PACs give a very large proportion of their funds to the Democrats.

Top 20 PAC contributors to federal candidates, 2001–02

PAC Name	Total amount ($)	Proportion given to Democrats (%)	Proportion given to Republicans (%)
National Association of Realtors	3,648,526	47	53
Association of Trial Lawyers of America	2,813,753	89	11
Laborers Union	2,809,700	88	12
National Auto Dealers Association	2,578,750	34	66
American Medical Association	2,480,972	39	61
American Federation of State/County/ Municipal Employees	2,423,500	96	3
Teamsters Union	2,366,503	86	14
United Auto Workers	2,339,000	99	1
International Brotherhood of Electrical Workers	2,249,300	96	4
Carpenters & Joiners Union	2,243,000	77	22
Machinists/Aerospace Workers Union	2,200,350	99	1
National Beer Wholesalers Assn	2,065,250	21	79
Credit Union National Association	1,951,933	44	56
National Association of Home Builders	1,924,600	38	62
Service Employees International Union	1,886,662	89	10
National Education Association	1,833,000	91	8
United Food & Commercial Workers Union	1,726,474	98	2
Communications Workers of America	1,722,300	100	0
Ironworkers Union	1,656,000	88	12
United Parcel Service	1,621,291	31	69

Source: adapted from the Center for Responsive Politics (2003), *Top 20 PAC Contributors to Federal Candidates 2001–2002*, www.opensecrets.org/pacs/topacs.asp?txt=A&Cycle=2002.

their campaign expenditure. Interest groups are, however, assuming a more visible role in the electoral process. They can establish '527 committees'. Although such committees cannot be affiliated with a party or a candidate for federal office, they can spend 'soft money' (see Chapter 10). In early 2003, the trades unions set up the Partnership for America's Families, a 527 committee that will pay for 'issue-ads' and get-out-the-vote efforts. It will target non-union members as well as those who have joined their ranks. The Partnership's campaigns will stress the ways in which – from its perspective – the Bush administration has undermined the rights of employees (Edsall 2003).

Although Congressional candidates are not eligible for financial assistance from the Federal Election Commission, the parties contribute only a small proportion of their overall campaign funding. The 1998 mid-term elections offer an example of this. Although spending by the parties was skewed towards challengers, it still represented only a small proportion of total campaign funding for Congressional candidates. Instead, they built their campaigns around contributions from individual donors, their own resources, and money given by political action committees.

Communication

Modern technology has undermined another traditional function of the parties. Traditionally, they would hold meetings and organise processions in support of their candidates, particularly in the close-knit urban neighbourhoods. However, many of these neighbourhoods have been displaced by suburbs. At the same time, the press, radio and then television 'supplanted the political party as the main conduit between candidate and voter' (Ceasar 1990: 106). They offer the opportunity – through paid commercials – to present an unmediated message. This requires large sums. Indeed, spending on political advertisements has increased steadily over a twenty-year period, from $90,570,000 in 1980 to $498,890,600 in 1998 (Lewis 2000).

The role played by the mass media has however had consequences for the parties. Whereas party meetings were a two-way process, TV and radio are a one-way medium. Furthermore, some observers argue, a candidate's prospects have come to depend upon the way in which he or she is represented by the media, particularly television. As Anthony King recorded in the aftermath of the 1980 contest: 'the great majority had never been in the physical presence of any of the candidates . . . Instead they were forced to form their own impressions from what they could read in the printed media or see on television . . . the performances that mattered were not in high office but on the small screen (King 1981: 316).

Mobilisation

The role that the parties traditionally played in 'getting out the vote' has been assumed by interest groups. Increasingly, organisations have coalesced around one or other of the major parties. They concentrate their attention on campaigning activities intended to back the party and maximise turnout levels among those sections of the population most likely to support their aims and objectives.

In the 2000 elections, the campaigns to elect Al Gore to the White House and ensure that Democratic candidates were victorious in Congressional and state contests were boosted by groups representing minorities and organised labour.

- The National Association for the Advancement of Colored People formed a new organization – the NAACP National Voter Fund – with a $9 million budget to target black voters in twelve states that were crucial for the Democrats.
- The Human Rights Campaign – a gay and lesbian group – organised the 'Equality Rocks' concert.
- The National Abortion and Reproductive Rights Action League – which is 'pro-choice' – spent more than $5 million in fifteen target states.
- People for the American Way, a broadly liberal organisation campaigning for rights and freedoms, concentrated on the US Supreme Court appointments that might arise during the next presidential term. It targeted twelve states, distributing leaflets, phoning voters, and holding public forums (Associated Press 2000b).
- The American Federation of Labor–Congress of Industrial Organizations (AFL–CIO), which brings together the US trades or labour unions, had committees in seventy-one Congressional districts in twenty-five states to distribute literature and make individual approaches to union members. The evidence suggests that tactics such as these can be effective. According to the AFL–CIO, 76 per cent of union members who received election leaflets from them voted for the union-backed candidate in 1998, compared with 58 percent among those who did not receive information.

Other organisations, particularly those representing business interests and the 'religious right', are more closely associated with the Republican Party. They also undertook 'get-out-the-vote- activities, hoping to ensure GOP victories.

- The US Chamber of Commerce, the nation's largest business lobby, sent out mailings to three million business owners with mailings promoting its endorsed candidates.
- The Christian Coalition has, since its inception, canvassed churchgoers through phone calls, direct mail, and the production of voter guides. These guides list candidate attitudes towards the issues that the Coalition regards as pivotal. The preferred candidate – almost always a Republican – is readily evident. In 2000, seventy million voter guides were distributed (Associated Press 2000c).

Studies of British politics draw attention to backbench revolts. The coverage they receive in press reports and academic surveys is testimony to their lack of frequency. For the most part, the House of Commons is a disciplined institution, and MPs almost always follow the dictates of party leaders and whips. However, as Chapter 5 noted, party discipline and consensus has never been a feature of US politics. Indeed, there have always been significant divisions within both parties. This is evident in the relatively low proportion of 'party unity' roll-call votes in which a majority of voting Republicans has opposed a majority of voting Democrats.

The lack of voting discipline is not only a function of the candidate-centred politics generated by the primary system. It also stems from the breadth of the coalitions that the parties represent. From the 1930s until the 1970s, the Democratic Party embraced both northern blacks and white southerners, many of whom were seeking to maintain segregation laws in their own states.

Today, although there has been a growth in *partisanship*, there are significant differences within both of the parties. There are at least three distinct factions in the Republican Party:

1 The 'religious right' was spurred into the political arena by developments during the 1970s such as the shift in women's social and economic roles, the secularisation of education, successive Supreme Court rulings (particularly *Roe v. Wade*), and the emergence of the 'gay lobby'. Against this background, evangelical Christians sought the adoption of policies structured around moral traditionalism and family values. In particular, they hoped to outlaw abortion and counter efforts to represent homosexuality and heterosexuality as moral equivalents. The Christian Coalition, which was established in the aftermath of the Reverend Pat Robertson's attempts to secure the 1988 Republican presidential nomination, is the most influential of the organisations associated with the Christian right. By late 1995, it claimed 1.7 million members and supporters who were spread across all 50 states and organised in 1,700 local chapters.

   However, although Christian conservatives were well represented in the 2000 Republican presidential primaries through the candidacies of Gary Bauer, Alan Keyes and Steve Forbes, the Christian right lost ground towards the end of the 1990s. Indeed, in the 2000 elections, there was evidence that some grassroots Christian conservatives were pulling back from the political arena. According to Karl Rove, Bush's chief political adviser, only 15 million of the 19 million religious conservatives who should have voted went to the polls in the 2000 election. Even before this, some reports suggested that the Christian Coalition's earlier membership figures had been overstated and that it had been financially over-committed.

2 A number of Republican state governors had a different emphasis. Although they believed in cutting taxes, many also increased spending on education, the environment and the infrastructure. They stressed the need for the restructuring and modernisation of government services. At the same time, they distanced themselves from the strident moral traditionalism of the

Christian right. While their ranks included some in both the pro-life and pro-choice camps, neither sought to proselytise. Instead, issues such as gay rights and abortion were downplayed as they sought to fashion a form of Republicanism that did not prescribe a rigid moral code for others to follow. There were also systematic attempts to court the minority vote. George W. Bush, who was then governor of Texas, actively sought to reach out to the Latino communities. As Boris Johnson, editor of *The Spectator*, recorded in February 1999: 'Not only does he sloganise in Spanish. He speaks it . . . He makes long speeches full of the test score of Texan African-Americans; he calls in Hispanic adolescents who have learned to read successfully, and uses them as props for his orations' (Johnson 1999). Against this background, and from the early stages of his presidential campaign, Bush began to talk of 'compassionate conservatism'. In contrast with the anti-government rhetoric that had characterised Republicanism during the first half of the 1990s, it envisaged a limited but positive role for government. Government resources were to be used to assist churches, synagogues and mosques in helping the socially disadvantaged.

3 A further strand also emerged during the latter half of the 1990s. It initially crystallised around the Hudson Institute, the Project for Conservative Reform, and the *Weekly Standard*. Although there were few in its ranks, its emergence reflected a shift in mood among some on the right. Its adherents called for limited but, at the same time, 'energetic' forms of government. In the domestic sphere; this was to be tied to the strengthening of civic life alongside the market.

In the foreign policy sphere, those who talked of 'national greatness conservatism' or defined themselves as 'neoconservatives' looked back towards Theodore Roosevelt's presidency. They called for an assertion of American leadership across the globe based upon 'benevolent hegemony'. It would not be based upon business needs, a narrow understanding of the national interest, or the amoral calculus of *realpolitik*. Instead, it was to be informed by moral considerations and the 'export' of American values.

This form of thinking led some towards the candidacy of Senator John McCain in the 2000 Republican presidential primaries. After the 11 September attacks, however, it gained greater currency. It increasingly seemed that American national security could only be maintained if the wider world shared the values upon which the US was built upon, most notably democracy, liberty, and the free market. 'Neoconservative' voices – including that of Paul Wolfowitz at the Department of Defense – appeared to be predominant within the Bush administration and, it is said, contributed to the US's decision to invade Iraq in 2003.

Although the dividing lines are sometimes blurred, there are also tensions and cleavages among Democrats. Both Bill Clinton and Al Gore were associated with the Democratic Leadership Council (DLC). Formed in the aftermath of the

Democratic defeat in the 1984 presidential election, the DLC was formed as an attempt to 'modernise' the party. It talked – in a phrase that was to be adopted by some European social democrats – of a 'third way'. In this spirit, the DLC's *New Democrat Credo* draw on themes associated with both liberalism and conservatism: 'We believe that economic growth generated in the private sector is the prerequisite for opportunity . . . We believe that government programs should be grounded in the values most Americans share: work, family, personal responsibility, individual liberty, faith, tolerance, and inclusion' (New Democrats Online 2001).

In policy terms, the DLC called for the abolition of tariffs and unrestricted international trade. Government intervention, the DLC asserted, should be confined to certain specific sectors of the economy such as education. The leadership team includes Senator Evan Bayh of Indiana and Ellen Tauscher, who sits in the House of Representatives on behalf of California's 10th Congressional district.

However, the New Democrats of the DLC have not gone unchallenged. Indeed, they have been compared with the 'Boll Weevils' – the white conservative southerners – who, in earlier years, held the balance of power in Congress. According to Jeff Faux of the Economic Policy Institute: 'Their program cannot hold together. It is a tired mixture of conservative intention watered down with liberal tinkering in the hope that it will fill in the crack in the center' (1995: 173).

Although the scale and extent of their radicalism is limited, Democratic Party traditionalists instead stress the importance of government, particularly in the provision of health care and education. They are committed to policies that conservative critics have derided as 'tax and spend'. They seek to maintain the loose association between the Party and trade (or 'labor') unionism.

The tensions between the traditionalists and the New Democrats were brought into sharp relief in the 2002 mid-term elections. For traditionalists, the party lost Congressional seats because it failed to motivate some of its most committed supporters. To their dismay, many leading Democrats sought to avoid alienating the suburban 'swing' voter by backing the Republicans on controversial issues. In particular, they voted to allow President Bush the option of war against Iraq. For their part, however, 'New Democrats' believed that the party had lost the moderate vote because some in its ranks had opposed both the war effort and Bush's tax-cutting proposals. The election of Nancy Pelosi as House Minority Leader seemed to suggest that traditionalist arguments continued to hold sway. The conservative interest group, Citizens for a Sound Economy, was bitter in its criticisms of her:

Every Congress, CSE tracks key votes on the issues of lower taxes, less government, and more freedom. This Congress, Nancy Pelosi scored a Big Fat Zero. 0%. Null. That means on the twenty key votes for economic liberty in the 107th Congress, Nancy Pelosi voted the wrong way every single time. She voted for higher income taxes. She voted for the death tax. She voted to keep the trial lawyers fat and happy. She even voted against repealing the marriage tax penalty! (Kinnan 2002)

There is a third theme in the Democrats' thinking, although it overlaps and interweaves with other strands of thought within the Party. For some, 'identity politics' are pivotal, and they emphasise the importance of addressing the social and economic disadvantages faced by women and minority groupings. This leads to backing for policy proposals that include abortion rights, affirmative action, and measures to encourage black entrepreneurship.

Policy development

Policy development is increasingly undertaken by interest groups or 'think-tanks' rather than the parties. Conservative 'thinktanks' such as the American Enterprise Institute (AEI), the libertarian Cato Institute, and the more broadly based Heritage Foundation have, for example, been influential in Republican Party circles. Heritage was founded in February 1973 amidst concerns that the Republican Party was being pulled towards the pragmatism of centre-ground politics. The Foundation publishes *Policy Review*, a bimonthly journal, offers handbooks for candidates, briefing documents, research papers, and conferences, and supports a website that acts as a clearing-house for a broad range of conservative organisations and campaigns.

There are, however, liberal counterweights to conservative foundations such as Heritage. The Economic Policy Institute was founded in 1986 and has ties to the trades unions. It 'seeks to broaden the public debate about strategies to achieve a prosperous and fair economy'. The Progressive Policy Institute – which is closely associated with the Democratic Leadership Council – studies policy options that will 'foster a more inclusive, more democratic capitalism'. In June 2003, a number of prominent Democrats – including the former White House Chief of Staff, John Podesta – announced the creation of the American Majority Institute, which will develop 'progressive' thinking and challenge what its backers regard as Republican dominance of the media (*New York Times*, 5 June, 2003).

Party identification

There are also grounds for arguing that the parties play a less significant role in the voting process. There has been, it is said, a process of *partisan dealignment*, and the parties have failed to retain the loyalty of voters. As Martin Wattenberg puts it: 'for over four decades the American public has been drifting away from the two major political parties' (1996: ix).

These sentiments are reflected in the decline in the proportion of the electorate who can be regarded as 'party identifiers' and are committed to the party of their choice. In 1952, 47 per cent of the electorate regarded themselves as either 'strong' or 'weak' Democrats'. By 2000, the figure had fallen to 34 per cent. The party had, in particular, lost support among men, blue-collar workers, and white southerners. Although much less marked, there was a also a process of detachment among Republicans. At the same time, the numbers calling themselves 'independents' (which includes those who are 'independent' but 'lean' towards either the Democrats or Republicans) has grown steadily, increasing from 23 per cent in 1952 to 36 per cent in 2000. The reasons for these shifts are considered in Chapter 10.

Table 9.7 *Strong and weak party identifiers, 1952–2000*

	1952	1960	1970	1980	1990	1992	1994	1996	1998
Strong and weak Democrats	47	45	44	41	39	36	34	37	37
Strong and weak Republicans	28	30	24	23	25	25	30	27	26
Independents	23	23	31	34	34	38	36	35	36

Source: National Election Studies, Center for Political Studies, University of Michigan, *The NES Guide to Public Opinion and Electoral Behavior – Party Identification 7-Point Scale 1952–2000* (www.umich.edu/~nes/nesguide/toptable/tab2a_1.htm), Ann Arbor, MI: University of Michigan, Center for Political Studies [producer and distributor], 1995–2000. These materials are based on work supported by the National Science Foundation under Grant Nos.: SBR-9707741, SBR-9317631, SES-9209410, SES-9009379, SES-8808361, SES-8341310, SES-8207580, and SOC77-08885. Any opinions, findings and conclusions or recommendations expressed in these materials are those of the authors and do not necessarily reflect those of the National Science Foundation.

Consequences

According to those who talk in these terms, party decline has had significant consequences. The parties traditionally acted as agencies of political socialisation and offered a link between the citizen and the political process: they encouraged political participation. The low level of turnout in US elections can be tied to the weakness of the party system. The *individualisation* of politics has also restructured the character of the legislative process: 'In our era of debilitated political parties, Washington is run by 536 individual political entrepreneurs – one president, 100 senators and 435 members of the House – each of whom got here essentially on his own. Each chooses the office he seeks, raises his own money, hires his own pollster and ad-maker and recruits his own volunteers' (Wattenberg 1991: 165).

Why does this matter? It is important because voting in Congress has become individualistic, and members are now much more subject to the pressures applied by lobbyists. This – it is said – has allowed the 'buying' of Congressional votes by outside interests. It has also made the process of building coalitions that allow the passage of legislation more difficult. This has contributed to 'gridlock', thereby impeding the progress of much-needed reforms.

Anthony King goes further. He suggests that – as a consequence of party decline – it is now more difficult for those in Congress and the state legislatures to resist pressures and make decisions that may be unpopular, but are – nonetheless – in the national interest: 'Lack of party cover in the United States means that elective officeholders find it hard to take tough decisions partly because they lack safety in numbers . . . congressmen and senators are always in danger of being picked off one by one' (King 1997).

Survival and renewal

The party decline model has, however, been challenged. It rests, by implication, on the premise that there was a past 'golden age' when parties flourished. The accuracy of this is open to question. A 1956 study of Detroit revealed that less than one-fifth of local organisations were operating at their full potential. As a Congressman noted, two years later: 'if we depended on the party organization to get elected, none of us would be here' (quoted in Wattenberg 1996: 108).

The extent to which the parties are in decline has also been exaggerated. Despite dealignment, almost two-thirds of adult Americans still identify – either strongly or weakly – with one of the principal parties. Furthermore, although the proportion of 'independents' has grown, the political character of those who describe themselves in this way should be carefully considered. In practice, there are relatively few 'pure' independents. Instead, most 'lean' towards either the Democrats or Republicans. Indeed, there are still strong and secure partisan loyalties. As Bruce E. Keith *et al.* noted in 1992:

> They display an impressive tendency to vote for the candidate of the party they feel closer to; indeed, in presidential elections *they are generally more loyal to their party than weak partisans.* In seven of the ten presidential elections since 1952, Independent Democrats gave a higher proportion of their vote to the Democratic presidential candidate than did Weak Democrats . . . On average, since 1952, 89 percent of Independent Republicans have voted for the Republican presidential candidate, compared to 87 percent of Weak Republicans. (Keith *et al.* 1992: 65–6)

At the same time, if other forms of data are closely scrutinised, there are further grounds for questioning the dealignment thesis. The proportion of ticket-splitters has, for example, fallen since 1980.

It should also be noted that much of the dealignment process has been confined to the voting blocs associated with the Democrats. As was noted above, the party disproportionately lost support among white southerners, men, and blue-collar workers. The picture is, however, very different for the GOP. Indeed,

Table 9.8 *Split ticket voting: votes for the president/House of Representatives, 1952–2000 (% of voters)*

	1952	1960	1980	1992	1996	2000
President/House	19.3	26.1	32.8	23.0	25.3	19.8

Source: adapted from N. J. Ornstein, T. E. Mann, and M. J. Malbin (2002), *Vital Statistics on Congress 2001–2002*, Washington DC, The AEI Press, p. 78.

as Table 9.4 suggests, there was higher level of Republican partisanship in 2000 than in 1952.

Those who endorse the party decline thesis also fail to recognise the extent to which legislative politics are still dominated by the Republicans and Democrats. Of the 535 members of the House of Representatives and Senate, only two are independents. Senator Jim Jeffords of Vermont defected from the Republicans in mid-2001, handing overall control of the chamber to the Democrats. Congressman Bernie Sanders of Burlington in Vermont is also an independent. Although a 'progressive', he is, in practice, closely aligned with the Democrats.

The parties have also made sustained attempts to recapture the nomination process. Within the Democratic Party, there was a steady retreat from the McGovern–Fraser reforms that circumscribed the role of party officials and committees. The Commission on Presidential Nomination and Party Structure chaired by the former Michigan Party Chairman, Morley Winograd, between 1975 and 1980 recommended that party leaders, elected officials and 'add-ons' should also serve as convention delegates. In contrast with the delegates chosen on the basis of the primary and caucus results, these 'superdelegates' are unpledged, and can choose a candidate freely. Furthermore, their political experience reintroduced a degree of peer review into the nomination process. The Winograd proposals were built upon in 1982, when a commission chaired by Governor James B. Hunt of North Carolina recommended a significant increase in their numbers (*Congressional Quarterly* 1997: 27–31). As a consequence of these changes, 'superdelegates' generally represent about 18 per cent of the total delegate count. In 2000, for example, of the 4,336 convention delegates, 799 'superdelegates' were due to attend.

In the race to secure the 2000 Democratic presidential nomination – when vice-president Al Gore was challenged by former senator Bill Bradley – the Gore campaign made sustained efforts to win the 'superdelegate' vote. They reaped rewards. By early March, an Associated Press survey found that – of those contacted – 418 had pledged their support to Gore. Bradley – who was later compelled to withdraw – had 29 backers; and 117 delegates said they were uncommitted or had no preference (Associated Press 2000a).

For their part, the Republicans established two committees examining their rules for presidential selection. However, although they had to make changes because of amendments to state law, established party leaders did not lose control to the same degree as the Democratic hierarchy. The GOP also had less sympathy with claims that particular groups – such as blacks or women – should be allocated 'quotas' in the way that had been introduced in the Democratic Party following the McGovern–Fraser Commission's deliberations. Furthermore, the selection procedure had long been skewed towards the states that voted for the Republican nominee in the preceding election or elected Republicans in sub-presidential contests, and also assigned party officials as delegates on an *ex officio* basis. Furthermore, the Party's elected officials are said to play a role in influencing the outcome of the nomination process. Party elites allegedly played a role in ensuring that Bob Dole and George W. Bush won the Republican presidential nomination in 1996 and 2000 respectively. In both contests, for example, there were allegations that primary challengers were being unfairly excluded from the ballot in New York State. In 1996, Steve Forbes was compelled to take legal action against the New York Republicans. In 2000, it is alleged that the Republican Governor George Pataki was instrumental in attempts to challenge the petition drawn up by Senator John McCain's staff so as to ensure that his name was included on the ballot (CNN.com 2000).

A number of US Supreme Court rulings have also strengthened the position of parties. Following the 1972 Democratic national convention, the Court ruled in *Cousins v. Wigoda* (1975) that state courts cannot interfere with the right of national parties to decide who will be seated at their national conventions. This was confirmed in *Democratic Party of the United States v. LaFollette* (1981) (Plano and Greenberg 1989: 64). In 1986, in *Tashjian v. Republican Party of Connecticut*, the Supreme Court established that states could not prevent a party holding an open primary that allowed voters of all political persuasions – rather than simply those who were registered as party supporters – to participate in the election (Plano and Greenberg 1989: 81). Three years later, in *March Fong Eu v. San Francisco County Democratic Central Committee* (1989), the Court declared that the parties had the right to endorse a particular candidate in the primaries (Hays Lowenstein 1992: 8). In 2000, *California Democratic Party v. Jones* confirmed and further extended the rights of parties to control their nomination procedures.

State and national leadership

The parties began to establish more pro-active forms of national leadership during the 1970s. John F. Bibby has charted the ways in which the state parties – which had traditionally been organisationally ramshackle – adapted to changing circumstances. They established permanent headquarters, comprehensive databases of supporters, and websites. A 1999 study revealed that – on average – in an election year, state parties had a budget of $2.8 million and a headquarters staff of nine. They also became part of a more developed national infrastructure. As Bibby records: 'State parties in the first decade of the new century are substantially changed and stronger than they were in the 1960s and 1970s. They have adapted to the challenges posed by candidate-centered campaigning and the emergence of PACs as a major campaign funding source. They have also become more closely integrated into the national parties' campaign structures' (Bibby 2002: 45).

There have been parallel changes at a national level. For the Republicans, they began in the aftermath of the Watergate crisis. The Democratic Party took similar steps following the presidential and Congressional election defeats of 1980.

- There was party-building activity and infrastructural development. Bill Brock, who was Republican Party Chairman between 1977 and 1981, developed a direct-mail programme. By the early 1980s, the Party had attracted contributions from two million people and had raised almost $78 million (Bailey 1990: 13). In 1992 alone, it raised $254.8 million (*Congressional Quarterly* 1997: 106). The Republican National Committee (RNC) gained a permanent headquarters a block away from Capitol Hill, and by 1984 the number of staff it employed reached six hundred, a threefold increase from 1976 (Ceasar 1990: 105). It offers candidate training, a cable TV service (GOP-TV), and directs officials who are responsible for outreach work among young people and minorities, and fundraising activities.

    The Democrats' party-building activities lagged behind those of the GOP. The Democratic National Committee (DNC) acquired a permanent headquarters, owned by the Party itself, in 1984. The number of staff grew. In 1976, it employed only 30 but, by 1984, this had risen to 130 (Ceasar 1990: 105).
- The parties also became much more involved in fund-raising activities. Although the net effect of the Federal Election Campaign Act (FECA) – as amended in 1974 – was to weaken their financial role, the Act did in some respects assist the principal parties. Their national conventions were subsidised and they were allowed to make larger donations to election campaigns than PACs or individuals. Despite the limits on spending imposed by the FECA, amendments passed in 1979 permitted local and state parties to spend money on 'party-building' and 'get-out-the-vote' activities. Although this was subsequently to be restricted by the Bipartisan Campaign Reform Act, which the president signed into law in March 2002, *Colorado Republican Federal Campaign Committee v. FEC* (1996) established that the parties could spend unlimited sums on 'independent' campaigns in support of their candidates. This led to a proliferation of 'issue-advocacy' ads. Although these are broadly similar to the television advertisements issued on behalf of candidates, there are differences:

    They focus on individual candidates, emphasize the candidate's campaign themes, are frequently aired on prime-time TV and radio, and use compelling visuals, music, and scripts. They are distinct in their financing, in that they cannot expressly advocate the election or defeat of a federal candidate, and in

that they tend to be more negative or comparative than are candidate ads.
(Herrnson 2002: 57)

Alongside this, the national committees and other party committees have
played an increasingly assertive role in fund-raising activities. The National
Republican Senatorial Committee and the National Republican Congressional Committee and their Democratic counterparts – the Democratic
Senatorial Campaign Committee and the Democratic Congressional
Campaign Committee – have publicised their work in the two houses of
Congress, but also, more importantly, co-ordinate and direct the distribution
of funds to party candidates. They target, in particular, close contests and
open seats in which there is no incumbent.

- The parties have also sought to influence the promotion and selection of
  candidates in Congressional and state-level contests. Although the nomination process for nominees is open to the voting public through primaries and
  caucuses, Paul S. Herrnson records: 'They actively recruit some candidates
  to enter primary contests and just as actively discourage others from doing
  so . . . Party leaders and staff use polls, the promise of party campaign money
  and services, and the persuasive talents of party leaders, members of
  Congress, and even presidents to influence the decisions of potential candidates' (Herrnson 2002: 63).

Co-ordination and partisanship

There are other ways in which the parties have assumed a more coherent and
organised form. Since the 1960s, white voters in the south shifted in large
numbers from the Democrats – the party they had supported since the Civil War
– to the Republicans. The changed allegiance of the most conservative element
in the Democrats' New Deal coalition had long-term consequences. Arguably,
it removed some of the checks and restraints on the Democratic Party's liberalism. During the 1970s and, to a lesser extent, the 1980s, liberals within the
party had to make fewer compromises. This laid the basis for George
McGovern's presidential campaign in 1972 and Jesse Jackson's attempts to win
the Democratic nomination in 1984 and 1988.

At the same time, although many of the Republican Party's supporters and
public officials in the metropolitan regions, particularly the north-east, adopt
relatively liberal attitudes towards cultural issues, the GOP's conservatism was
reinforced and 'southernised' . While there are – as was noted above – GOP
moderates in Congress such as those who belong to the Tuesday Lunch Club,
little is now left of the Republican Party's once-influential liberal wing. Both of
the parties have come to assume increasingly different and polarised ideological identities. This is evident in data from the General Social Survey. As Table
9.9 suggests, by 2000, about two-thirds of Democratic Party supporters
regarded themselves as either 'liberal' or 'slightly liberal'. However, only about
a quarter of Republican backers described themselves in these terms.

Table 9.9 *Political attitudes and party identification, 2000 (%)*

	Strong, not strong Democrats and Democratic 'leaners'	Independents	Strong, not strong Republicans and Republican 'leaners'
Extremely–slightly liberal	64.4	50.6	25.8
Moderate	17.7	23.0	13.9
Slightly–extremely conservative	18.0	26.4	60.4

Source: adapted from General Social Survey (2003), *Cumulative Datafiles – Partyid / Polviews / Year(2000)*, www.icpsr.umich.edu:8080/GSS/homepage.htm.

There is other evidence of a resurgent partisanship. In the November 1994 mid-term elections, the Contract with America – a nationally agreed manifesto – was signed by over three hundred of the Republican candidates for the House of Representatives. The Contract promised that a Republican-controlled Congress would – within a hundred days – vote on measures such as welfare reform, an anti-crime package, and a balanced budget amendment (Ashford 1998).

Against this background, Newt Gingrich who – as House Speaker – led the Republican 'revolution' of 1994–96, attempted to ensure that, despite the decentralised character of Congress, the Republican Party leadership occupied a dominant position. He himself nominated committee chairs, and the seniority tradition, by which the longest-serving member of the majority party takes the chair, was modified. As Philip John Davies concluded a year after the 1994 Republican victory: 'the House now has a command structure more unified than anything seen in Congress for almost a century' (1996: 15).

Although much of the sense of momentum that the Contract unleashed was lost, the sense of partisanship remained – albeit in a weakened form – throughout the remainder of the decade. This was evident in 1998–99, when President Clinton was subject to impeachment proceedings. Nearly all the votes in the House reflected party divisions, as Republicans sought his removal from office while Democrats defended him. The same division was also apparent in the Senate.

Conclusion

The 'party decline thesis' should, therefore, be substantially qualified. Although the meaning of particular words and phrases is always hard to discern, substantially numbers still identify with the major parties. While primaries appeared to deprive the parties of their role in putting forward election nominees, the extent and scale of behind-the-scenes activity in promoting particular candidates – and disparaging others – should not be underestimated. Furthermore, the parties have in some ways been strengthened. Although they were, traditionally, loose confederations of state parties, there is a growing sense of both organisational and ideological identity. While the notion of a mass party rooted in the city neighbourhoods, and structured around the ward and precinct, has been undermined by demographic shifts, another model of party activity – based upon the provision of resources for candidates – is emerging in its stead. As John H. Aldrich concludes: 'They have become more truly national parties, better financed, more professionalized, and more institutionalized, with greater power to shape the actions of their state and local organizations' (Aldrich 1995: 260).

Note

1 Later judgements on Reagan, particularly those made by conservatives, have been much more generous. For his admirers, he is associated with economic revival, the country's growing stature in the world, and the demise of the Soviet Union.

References and further reading

Aldrich, J. H. (1995), *Why Parties? The Origins and Transformation of Parties in America*, Chicago, The University of Chicago Press.

Ashford, N. (1998), 'The Republican Party agenda and the conservative movement', in D. McSweeney and J. Owens, *The Republican Takeover of Congress*, London, Macmillan, pp. 96–116.

Associated Press (2000a), *'Superdelegates' firmly behind Gore*, 5 March, quest.cjonline .com/stories/030500/gen_supergore.shtml.

Associated Press (2000b), *Groups Working to Get Out the Vote*, 21 September, quest .cjonline.com/stories/092100/gen_0921006066.shtml.

Associated Press (2000c), *Interest Groups Try to Get Out Vote*, 7 October, quest.cjonline .com/stories/100700/gen_groups.shtml.

Bailey, C. (1990), 'Political parties', *Contemporary Record*, February, 12–15.

Bibby, J. F. (2002), 'State party organizations: strengthened and adapting to candidate-centered politics and nationalization', in L. S. Maisel (ed.), *The Parties Respond: Changes in American Parties and Campaigns*, Boulder, CO, Westview Press, pp. 19–46.

Broder, D. S. (1971), *The Party's Over: The Failure of Politics in America*, New York, Harper and Row.

Ceasar, J. W. (1990), 'Political parties – declining, stabilizing, or resurging', in A. King (ed.), *The New American Political System*, Washington DC, American Enterprise Institute for Public Policy Research.

Ceasar, J. W. and A. E. Busch (1997), *Losing to Win: The 1996 Elections and American Politics*, Lanham, MD, Rowman and Littlefield.

CNN.com (2000), *McCain Fights Own Party to Be on New York Ballot*, 20 January, edition.cnn.com/2000/ALLPOLITICS/stories/01/20/ny.mccain/.

Congressional Quarterly (1997), *Selecting the President: From 1789 to 1996*, Washington DC, CQ Press.

Davies, P. J. (1996), 'The legislative process in the USA', *Politics Review*, 5(3): 10–15.

Edsall, T. B. (2003), 'Labor targets nonunion voters', *Washington Post*, 27 February, A04.

Faux, J. (1995), 'The myth of the new Democrat', in W. D. Burnham (ed.), *The American Prospect Reader in American Politics*, Chatham, Chatham House, pp. 162–73.

Federal Election Commission (2000), *FEC Announces 2000 Presidential Spending Limits*, 1 March, www.fec.gov/press/preslimits2000.htm.

General Social Survey (2003a), *Cumulative Datafile – Partyid / Polviews / Year*, www.icpsr .umich.edu:8080/GSS/homepage.htm.

General Social Survey (2003b), *Cumulative Datafile – Partyid / Race / Region*, www.icpsr .umich.edu:8080/GSS/homepage.htm.

Hays Lowenstein, D. (1992), 'American political parties', in G. Peele, C. J. Bailey, and B. Cain (eds), *Developments in American Politics*, pp. 63–85, Basingstoke, Macmillan.

Herrnson, P. S. (2002), 'National party organizations at the dawn of the twenty-first century', in L. S. Maisel (ed.), *The Parties Respond: Changes in American Parties and Campaigns*, Boulder, CO, Westview Press, pp. 47–78.

Johnson, B. (1999), 'Hague seeks out Texan Bushman for magic formula', *Daily Telegraph*, 13 February.

Keith, B. E. (1992), *The Myth of the Independent Voter*, Berkeley, CA, University of California Press.

King, A. (1981),'How not to select presidential candidates: a view from Europe', in A. Ranney (ed.), *The American Elections of 1980*, Washington DC, American Enterprise Institute for Public Policy Research, pp. 303–28.

Kinnan, C. (2002), *Who is Nancy Pelosi?* Citizens for a Sound Economy, www.cse.org/ informed/issues_template.php/1172.htm.

Lewis, C. (2000), 'Media money: How corporate spending blocked political ad reform and other stories of influence', *Columbia Journalism Review*, September–October, www.cjr.org/year/00/3/mediamoney.asp.

New Democrats Online (2001), *The New Democrat Credo*, www.ndol.org/ndol_ci .cfm?kaid=86&subid=194&contentid=3775.

Plano J. C. and M. Greenberg (1989), *The American Political Dictionary*, Fort Worth, TX, Holt, Rinehart, and Winston.

Robertson, D. (1985), *The Penguin Dictionary of Politics*, Harmondsworth, Penguin.

Rossiter, C. (1964), *Parties and Politics in America*, New York, Signet.

Silbey, J. H. (2002), 'From "essential to the existence of our institutions" to "rapacious enemies of honest and responsible government": The rise and fall of American political parties, 1790–2000', in L. M. Maisel (ed.), *The Parties Respond: Changes in American Parties and Campaigns*, Cambridge, MA, Westview Press, pp. 1–8.

Wattenberg, M. P. (1991), *The Rise of Candidate-Centered Politics*, Cambridge, MA, Harvard University Press.

Wattenberg, M. P. (1996), *The Decline of American Political Parties 1952–1994*, Cambridge, MA, Harvard University Press.

Websites

All the principal political parties (and many minor organisations) have their own websites. Most offer links to the individual state parties and related campaigns:

Democratic National Committee – www.democrats.org.
Republican National Committee – www.rnc.org.
Green Party of the United States – www.gp.org.
Libertarian Party – www.lp.org.

10

Elections and campaigns

The US electoral system is, at first sight, open and democratic. Public offices, at federal, state and local level are subject to competitive election. Positions that in other nations would be assigned through an appointments process – such as judgeships or school board membership – are contested. Furthermore, party candidates are chosen by the voters themselves in primaries, not by party leaders or committed activists alone. Any citizen can run for office, as neither previous party membership nor a record of political activity is required. At the same time, in some states, issues may be decided directly by the voters themselves in referendums.

However, despite these features, the US electoral system has been subject to sustained criticism. Money and the media, it is said, play too much of a role. The length and complexity of the system discourage people from voting, contributing to low levels of turnout. Furthermore, those who are elected are – all too often – empty mediocrities. This chapter considers and assesses these questions.

Electing the president

The president is elected every four years. Since the twenty-second amendment was adopted in 1951, no president can be elected to serve more than two full terms. Candidates for the office face a two-stage system structured around the race to secure their party's nomination and the general election contest.

Candidates

Article II of the US Constitution establishes three basic requirements for those who serve as president. An individual must be at least thirty-five years old, born in the US, and a resident for fourteen years or more. In practice, however, a further qualification is required. Since March 1853, presidents have been drawn from either the Democratic or the Republican Party. However, although it is usual, individuals do not require a record of party activism or commitment. President Dwight Eisenhower (1953–61), who commanded the victorious allied forces during the Second World War, was courted by both parties before standing as a Republican.

In 2003–4, nine Democrats sought their party's nomination for the presidential race. Five were – or had been – members of the US Senate, two sat in the House of Representatives, and one was a state governor. This represented a shift. Four of the past five presidents served as governors before being elected to the White House. There have been suggestions, however, that the national focus on foreign affairs and 'homeland security' following the 11 September attacks has made members of Congress – particularly those in the Senate – who have, through their role, some experience of foreign policy deliberations, more credible candidates. State governors, however, will only have a record of involvement in domestic policy-making.

Box 10.1   Candidates seeking the 2004 Democratic presidential nomination (June 2003)

Howard Dean	Governor of Vermont
John Edwards	US Senator – North Carolina
Richard Gephardt	Former Minority Leader – House of Representatives
Bob Graham	US Senator – Florida
John Kerry	US Senator – Massachusetts
Dennis Kucinich	House of Representatives
Joseph Lieberman	US Senator – Connecticut
Carol Moseley Braun	Former US Senator – Illinois
Al Sharpton	Civil rights activist

An incumbent president may be unopposed within his own party. At the end of their first terms, Ronald Reagan, Bill Clinton, and George W. Bush faced no serious or credible challengers at the primary stage. However, this is not assured. In 1968, Eugene McCarthy and Bobby Kennedy ran against President Lyndon Johnson – before he withdrew – in the race to become the Democratic Party's nominee. In 1976, Ronald Reagan almost took the Republican nomination from President Gerald Ford.

The 'invisible primary'

The one- or two-year period preceding an election year has been dubbed the 'invisible primary'. Although it has not proper or well-defined status, it is the informal race to secure campaign funds and establish a lead in the public opinion polls. It plays a critical role in determining who will eventually secure the party's nomination. As William Mayer – who coined the term – observes: 'In seven of the 10 cases . . . the nominee-to-be had opened up a sizable lead over every other eventual candidate by, at the latest, one month after the preceding midterm election—more than a year, in other words, before the start of the actual delegate selection activities' (quoted in Schneider 2002).

In other words, although the formal selection procedure only begins in January of election year, the parties' presidential nominees are often becoming evident over twelve months before this. How can candidates build up the 'sizable lead' in the polls to which Mayer refers? Observers stress the initial winning of name recognition, the creation of an exploratory committee, the process of attracting campaign workers, participation in debates, success in the 'straw polls' organised by some of the state parties, the gaining of endorsements from well-known supporters, and inclusion in lists of credible presidential hopefuls considered by newspaper 'op-ed' columnists and TV commentators. During 2003, the Democrats' presidential hopefuls devoted much of their time to attending forums and debates organised by interest groups – such as the National Association for the Advancement of Colored People, NARAL Pro-Choice America and the Human Rights Campaign (a gay and lesbian organisation) – that are closely aligned with the party.

However, as Mayer emphasises, a candidate's financial resources are equally critical. A campaign cannot be sustained nor can a candidate secure credibility without a 'war chest'. Its importance is such that some commentators refer to the 'invisible primary' as the 'money primary'. Primary candidates can – if they adhere to specified conditions – obtain matching funds from the Federal Election Commission (FEC). These funds, which provide dollar-for-dollar assistance, are taken from those taxpayers who have agreed – on their annual income tax returns – that a proportion of the tax that they have paid may be used for this purpose. To qualify for matching funds – and deter marginal or eccentric candidates – a candidate must raise a total of at least $100,000 in twenty or more states, of which $5,000 must be raised in each state; and there is a ceiling of $250 on donations from any one individual (*Congressional Quarterly* 1997: 46).

It is usual for candidates – or those who have expressed a cautious interest – to fall away during the 'invisible primary'. They might not have found sufficient support, could not raise the funds required for an effective campaign, or have decided that they are not able to devote such a long period of time to a probably unattainable goal. For example, in December 2002 – at an early stage in the 2004 'invisible primary' – the Democrats' 2000 presidential candidate, Al Gore, announced that, despite his earlier intentions, he would not, after all, seek the 2004 nomination.

ABC News has taken the 'invisible primary' further. So as to assess the electoral potential of the different Democratic candidates for 2004 (and thereby influencing the course of the contest as well as reporting upon it) they produced a scorecard rating six of the candidates on a score of between

Table 10.1 *Democratic presidential candidate spending, until 31 March 2003*

Candidate	Expenditure ($)
John Edwards (D)	7,418,568
John Kerry (D)	7,010,242
Dick Gephardt (D)	5,951,721
Joe Lieberman (D)	3,013,842
Howard Dean (D)	2,639,209
Bob Graham (D)	1,124,186
Dennis Kucinich (D)	178,080
Al Sharpton (D)	82,656
Carol Moseley Braun (D)	19,960

Source: adapted from Opensecrets.org (2003), *2004 Presidential Election*, www.opensecrets.org/presidential/index.asp.

Table 10.2 *ABC News: the invisible primary, February 2003*

ABC 2004	Howard Dean	John Edwards	Dick Gephardt	John Kerry	Joe Lieberman	Al Sharpton
Money potential	5	3	3	1	1	6
Message/bio	3	2	5	1	3	6
Message/issues	2	4	1	3	4	6
Spouse	4	2	4	2	1	6
Iowa	3	3	1	2	5	6
New Hampshire	3	3	2	1	5	6
Other states	5	2	1	2	2	5
Perceived electability	5	3	4	1	2	6
In-person campaigning skills	4	1	6	4	3	2
TV campaigning skills	6	4	3	1	2	5
National Security credentials	5	4	3	1	2	5
Media coverage	4	2	5	1	3	6
Buzz/momentum	3	2	6	1	5	4
The Clinton factor	4	2	4	1	3	4
Polling/name ID	6	4	3	2	1	5
Fire in the belly	1	3	4	1	5	5
Endorsements	5	4	1	2	3	6
Labor	3	4	1	2	5	6
African-Americans	6	1	5	3	1	3
Un-Gore	2	1	5	3	4	6
Staff	5	2	2	1	4	6

Source: adapted from M. Halperin, E. Wilner, and M. Ambinder (2003), ABC 2004: *The Invisible Primary*, 21 February, i.abcnews.com/sections/politics/DailyNews/TheInvisiblePrimary_February2003.html.

12 and 1. Twenty-one variables were considered, including their fund-raising abilities, the attitudes of the former President Bill Clinton and Senator Hillary Clinton towards them, their standings in key primary states, and the extent to which they were different from the defeated 2000 candidate, Al Gore, as well as their overall skill and personality. A low number reflects a candidate's strength on a particular variable. A high number indicates weakness. By February 2003 (Table 10.3), Senator John Kerry appeared to be taking a lead.

Primaries (January–June)

The presidential candidate is formally chosen by majority vote at a party's national convention. Candidates therefore seek to maximise the number of their supporters among the state delegations. Delegates to national party conventions, which decide who will serve as the party's presidential candidate, were traditionally chosen by political 'bosses' and activists at a state party convention. However, although there are significant procedural differences between states, the primary election has become the norm. The direct primary allows members of the public, who are registered supporters of a particular party, to participate in the nomination process. They can decide who they wish their state party delegates to back as the candidate when the national nominating convention is held. The primary 'season' is therefore a race to win delegates.

The proportion of convention delegates chosen on the basis of the primary results in their states grew during the course of the twentieth century. By 1996, 65.3 per cent of Democratic national convention delegates and 84.6 per cent of Republican national convention delegates were selected in primaries (Congressional Quarterly 1997: 141). Of these, some were closed primaries that restricted voting to those who had registered earlier in the year as Democrats or Republicans. Others were open primaries that do not require pre-registration. In some states, voters are allowed to register with a party on the day that the primary is held. In others, they are offered a choice of ballots.

The growth of the direct primary is closely associated with the Progressive movement at the beginning of the twentieth century. It sought to modernise the political process by breaking the power of the party 'bosses'. Some states still, however, use caucuses and state party conventions. Caucuses are small-scale meetings. In Iowa, for example, although there are differences between the Democratic and the Republican procedures, meetings are held in each of the state's 1,997 precincts. They can often last over several weeks, allowing discussion of the different candidates' strengths and weaknesses. Participation inevitably tends to be limited to the more committed party activists. On the basis of deliberations in the caucuses, delegates are sent to county conventions, which, in turn, elect delegates to congressional district and state conventions. These choose the national convention delegates.

In the Democratic Party, the national convention delegates are elected on a proportional basis. Candidates receiving a minimum of 15 per cent of the vote obtain a share of national convention delegates in that congressional district that is proportional to the vote they received (Polsby and Wildavsky 1996: 120). Among the Republicans, some states adopt proportionality, while others have a 'winner takes all' system whereby the candidates with the most votes win all the delegates from that state. The overall size of a state party's delegation depends upon factors such as the state's population, its past support for that party's candidates in federal elections, and the number of elected officials belonging to the party. The Democratic convention is significantly larger in terms of delegate numbers.

Although preceded by the Iowa caucuses, the first state to hold a primary is, by tradition, New Hampshire. In the past, it was described as pivotal. By winning New Hampshire, it was said, candidates could gain a sense of momentum that would enable them to win in the later primaries. However, the state has rarely chosen the eventual winner. The 1992 Democratic primary was won by the late Paul Tsongas. It was Bill Clinton who secured the presidential nomination. In 1996, the maverick conservative commentator Patrick J. Buchanan won in the New Hampshire Republican primary, but was decisively beaten in the race for the nomination by the former Senate Majority Leader, Bob Dole. In 2000, the New Hampshire Republican primary was won by the Arizona Senator John McCain. Later primaries, however, gave victory to George W. Bush.

The primary 'season' traditionally lasted between February and June. It is, however, shifting forwards and becoming increasingly 'front-loaded' as the states jostle for an early date and party officials seek an early and conclusive victory so that the party can concentrate its efforts on winning the White House. Front-loading has consequences. The states that still hold their primaries on a later date are consigned to the political sidelines. Relatively obscure candidates can no longer hope to create a sense of momentum in New Hampshire – which has traditionally been the first primary state – and then attract the financial backing and endorsements that enable them to go on and secure later victories. Jimmy Carter's successful presidential bid in 1976 is often cited as an example. Furthermore, front-loading compels candidates to campaign in a significant number of states at the same time. This requires large amounts of money and increases the importance of the 'invisible primary' – the eighteen-month period before election year – as candidates seek to ensure that they are leading in the opinion polls by the time the primaries begin.

The Iowa caucuses and the New Hampshire primary are the initial tests. The primaries that are held in early March are decisive, although – as noted above – their net effect is often to confirm the results of the 'invisible primary'. The South Carolina primary has become increasingly critical. In 2000, George W. Bush's defeat of John McCain (53–42 per cent) established that he would prove to be the overall victor. Where significant numbers of states hold primaries or caucuses on the same day, the results acquire particular significance. In 2000

Box 10.2   Selected presidential primaries and caucuses, 2004

19 January	Iowa caucuses
27 January	New Hampshire primary
3 February	Arizona primary
	South Carolina primary
	Missouri primary
	Virginia primary
24 February	Hawaii caucus
	Idaho caucus
	Utah primary
2 March	California primary
	Connecticut primary
	Georgia primary
	Maryland primary
	Massachusetts primary
	Ohio primary
	Rhode Island primary
	Vermont primary
9 March	Florida primary
	Louisiana primary
	Texas primary

Source: adapted from www.nytimes.com

'Super Tuesday' – as it is dubbed – was held on 7 March. Sixteen states and the American territory of Samoa participated in this.

At this point, there is a snowballing effect. Funds and offers of backing flow towards the front-runner, who will almost certainly secure the nomination and may win the presidency. For their part, candidates who perform poorly in these early primaries may decide to withdraw. Indeed, they may be compelled to, because they may have lost much of their backing from donors. Furthermore, taxpayer funding – administered through the FEC – is restricted to those who gain at least 10 per cent of the vote in at least one of the two final primaries that they contest. This also encourages candidates who perform poorly to withdraw at an early stage. They fear that if they stay in the race they will lose their eligibility for matching funds (*Congressional Quarterly* 1997: 46). In the 1992 Democratic primaries, both Senator Tom Harkin of Iowa and Senator Bob Kerrey of Nebraska had pulled out of the race by early March. In 2000, the former New Jersey Senator, Bill Bradley, withdrew from the race in the aftermath of 'Super Tuesday', leaving the field to Al Gore.

The development of primaries opened up the nomination process, shifted power from party leaders to the ordinary voter, increased participation, and tested the stamina of potential candidates. In a study of the 1992 primaries, Pippa Norris concluded: 'if it ain't broke, don't fix it' (Norris 1992). However, the primary system has been subject to severe criticism.

1 The primary election 'season' is said to be too long. It stretches from January until June, and the length of the campaign imposes unnecessary 'wear and tear' upon candidates (King 1981: 317).

2 Although the Federal Election Commission offers matching (dollar for dollar) funds to candidates fulfilling a set of conditions, increasingly large sums of money are involved. As was noted above, the 'front-loading' of the primaries required high levels of spending at an early stage. In the 2000 Republican contest, John McCain had spent $21 million by the end of January. For his part, George W. Bush – who did not accept FEC funding and was not therefore bound by the spending limits set under the law – had spent $50.1 million, the most ever spent in a primary contest (Salant 2000).

3 The early caucuses and primaries matter most. Traditionally, Iowa and New Hampshire hold the first caucuses and primary respectively. Although, as noted, the eventual winner often loses in New Hampshire, candidates must, at the least, gain a respectable showing in the state if they are to be considered serious contenders. Critics of the process contend, however, that although Iowa and New Hampshire are accorded a significant role in deciding the fate of presidential hopefuls, they are unrepresentative of the nation in so far as they are largely rural, white and Protestant. It should, however, be noted that both states are losing their significance in determining the eventual outcome. The 'decline' of New Hampshire has already been noted. The Iowa caucuses have also rather less importance than they are sometimes accorded in commentaries. Although George H. W. Bush won the Republican caucuses in 1980 and claimed that his campaign had gained a sense of momentum – which he dubbed the 'Big Mo' – he was decisively beaten by Ronald Reagan. As William Mayer noted in an interview: 'I characterize momentum as a bit like a roller-coaster ride. It provides a lot of excitement. But in the end, it pretty much takes you back to where you started' (quoted in Schneider 2002).

4 In the early primaries a candidate is judged on his or her electoral performance in relation to the expectations that have been set. In February 1992, Bill Clinton gained only 26 per cent of the vote in the New Hampshire primary. He was 9 per cent behind the victor, Paul Tsongas. However, Clinton could call his result a victory and dub himself the 'comeback kid' because his vote exceeded expectations. However, such expectations are largely set by media predictions. The newspapers, radio stations and TV channels thereby gain undue influence.

5 As has been noted, some states have open primaries in which any voter can

take part. Critics claim that these encourage wrecking tactics. Supporters of an opposing party may participate, and could deliberately back a weak candidate. However, the number of 'crossover' voters is probably small. In the 2000 Republican primary in South Carolina, which was open, John McCain's strategy rested on the deliberate courting of Democratic voters. However, exit polls suggested that only 9 per cent of his vote came from Democrats. Indeed, McCain's overt appeal to Democrats may have encouraged many conservatives to turn out against him (Boston.com 2000)

6   The primary system eliminates peer review from the nomination process. Presidential candidates are generally state governors or serve in Congress. They should, it is said, be judged as candidates by their colleagues rather than by members of the public who will inevitably have little detailed knowledge about their record or suitability. Writing before reforms that extended the franchise in party leadership elections were introduced, Anthony King described the strengths of peer review in Britain:

> The candidates were assessed and voted upon exclusively by their fellow politicians . . . Most of them were on first-name terms with the people they were voting for; they were in an excellent position to know their strengths and weaknesses. More than that, they had a powerful incentive to arrive at the right decision since they personally would have to live with the consequences. They would have to work with the new leader; if they made the wrong decision, they would suffer electorally and possibly also in career terms. (King 1981: 310)

Because these features are absent in the US primary system, it encourages the election of mediocrities who often lack substantial political experience. Drawing on the 1980 contest, King saw Ronald Reagan and Jimmy Carter in these terms.

7   The system of primary elections has weakened the American political parties. Firstly, they have removed the parties' ability to nominate their own candidates, thereby causing candidates to become 'public property'. Secondly, the primaries have encouraged the creation of personal campaign organisations built around the candidates rather than the party (see Chapter 9). Thirdly, the primaries often lead to public disunity. The 2000 Republican primaries created bitter divisions between supporters of George W. Bush and Senator John McCain. The tensions engendered by the Democratic contest between Jimmy Carter and Edward Kennedy in 1980 contributed to the party's defeat later in the year. As Martin Wattenberg notes, even if a popular candidate eventually wins the party nomination, this can be 'insufficient to heal the wounds of the primary season' (1991: 59).

8   The turnout is often relatively low. The *Committee for the Study of the American Electorate* estimates that only 16.86 per cent of those eligible voted in the early 1998 primaries. There has been a process of steady decline since 1970, when turnout reached an all-time high of 32.22 per cent. There is usually a higher level of turnout for Democratic primaries. As a consequence, a

Box 10.3   The primaries: looking to the future

Should the primary system be reformed? There has been some discussion within both of the major parties. The Democratic National Committee (DNC) asked the party's Rules and Bylaws Committee to examine the scheduling of the presidential primaries and caucuses. However, in a report issued in April 2000, the Committee simply called for negotiations with the Republican National Committee to ensure that the two parties' primary timetables coincided with each other.

The debate within the GOP has been much more far-reaching. In 1999, the Republican National Committee (RNC) established an Advisory Commission on Presidential Nominating Process chaired by the former Senator and GOP Chairman Bill Brock. It published its final report in May 2000. Under the Brock proposals – sometimes dubbed the Delaware plan – a number of the least populous states would vote first. They would be followed by the intermediate states. Lastly, the most populous states would cast their votes. The plan, Brock asserted, would make it difficult for any candidate to win a majority of delegates until a relative late stage. This would increase participation because – at present – the contest is all but over after the first few weeks (Sperling 2000). However, the plan was defeated by 66 to 33 at a RNC Rules Committee meeting.

An alternative proposal, put forward by the Massachusetts Secretary of the Commonwealth, Bill Galvin – and endorsed by the National Association of Secretaries of State – would keep Iowa and New Hampshire as the initial contests, but then divide the country into four regions (East, South, Midwest and West). Each of the regions would vote first once every four elections and therefore gain an equal voice in the nominating process.

According to their supporters, both plans would spread the primaries out over a number of months, and ensure that candidates visited a broader range of states, and engaged in genuine debate rather than mere whistle-stop visits. The proposals would also end the jostling by states and parties to hold early primaries. As the California Secretary of State noted:

> No one benefits when states play the quadrennial game of presidential primary leapfrog . . . We must impose order on the process, but we also need to protect the early elections in small states like New Hampshire and Iowa so that under-funded and less widely known candidates will still have an opportunity to compete through retail one-on-one politics rather than the costly media-driven campaigns that are required in larger states. (South Dakota Secretary of State 1999)

However, the proposals would have to be approved by each of the state legislatures. The chances of implementation are therefore limited.

References and further reading

South Dakota Secretary of State (1999), *Secretary of State Joyce Hazeltine Supports Rotating Regional Presidential Primaries in 2004*, 28 July, www.state.sd.us/sos/Releases/regional_presidential_primaries_.htm.

Sperling, G. (2000), 'Quit the grumbling, reform primary system', *CSMonitor.com*, 28 March, www.csmonitor.com/durable/2000/03/28/fp11s2–csm.shtml.

Republican candidate could win with less than 5 per cent of the eligible vote (Committee for the Study of the American Electorate 1998). There have been some attempts to address this. In 2000, Arizona allowed internet and postal voting in the Democratic primary, raising the total number of votes to about 76,000, double those cast in earlier elections (Thomsen 2000).

9 The primary electorate is not fully representative of the American public. It is often said to include disproportionate numbers of strong party identifiers. V. O. Key suggested, for example, that it was better-educated and more ideologically extreme than the general population (Geer 1993: 353). The *New York Times* surveyed voters in the 1996 Republican primaries: 'Over all, people who voted in the [Republican] primaries were more male than female. They were wealthier, better educated and older than those who will probably vote in the general election and Americans over all. And they were more conservative' (quoted in Bennett 2000: 4).

For these reasons, Republican candidates have tended to stress their conservatism in the primaries and then moderated their tone later in the year. Democratic candidates are often advised to talk in broadly liberal terms during the primaries and then shift rightwards – so as to secure the middle-ground voter – in the general election campaign. However, recent research has cast doubt on the efficacy of these strategies. In contrast with Key's assertion, John G. Geer argues that the primary electorate has lower income and education levels than those who vote in the November elections. It is not, he concludes, ideologically extreme (Geer 1993: 359).

National party conventions (July–August)

Presidential candidates are formally chosen by the Democratic and Republican parties at their national nominating conventions. These are held during the summer months.

Historically, delegates chose the nominee from a number of candidates. This would follow a succession of ballots, compromises and deals in 'smoke-filled

Table 10.3 *National party conventions, 1980–2004*

	Democrats	Republicans (GOP)
1980	New York	Detroit
1984	San Francisco	Dallas
1988	Atlanta	New Orleans
1992	New York	Houston
1996	Chicago	San Diego
2000	Los Angeles	Philadelphia
2004	Boston	New York

Source: adapted from H. W. Stanley and R. G. Niemi (1998), *Vital Statistics on American Politics 1997–1998*, Washington DC, Congressional Quarterly, p. 68.

rooms.' In recent years, however, the candidate is invariably known months before the convention even begins, because most of the convention delegates are pledged to back the candidate who won their state primary or was selected in the caucuses. Furthermore, in most cases, the other candidates will have decided to withdraw although – within the Democratic Party – both Jesse Jackson (1988) and Jerry Brown (1992) stayed in the race and insisted that a formal convention vote be taken. However, since 1956, every presidential nominee has won on the first ballot. Conventions therefore simply crown an already anointed candidate. Since the Second World War, only two nominees – Thomas Dewey (Republican) in 1948 and Adlai Stevenson (Democrat) in 1952 – failed to secure a majority of delegate votes on the first ballot.

The convention also considers and agrees upon the party's platform. Its role is limited because – in an era of candidate-centred politics – the nominee will not feel bound by it. Furthermore, in contrast with Britain's parliamentary system, he cannot – if elected to the presidency – be assured that proposals will be enacted as law. Legislation is generally a compromise between the White House and Congress. However, the words and phrases in the platform may be a battleground between the party factions, who seek to adopt certain positions or 'planks'. Attitudes towards abortion have proved particularly divisive in the Republican Party.

In the past, the nominee also announced his choice of vice-presidential candidate or 'running mate' at the convention, who would then be confirmed by ballot. However, the announcement is nowadays made once the overall result of the primaries has become evident. Although there are few polling data to suggest that the vice-presidential candidate wins or loses significant numbers of votes, traditional wisdom suggests that the ticket should be 'balanced'. In other words, the running mate should be drawn from a different part of the country or a different wing of the party. In 1960, John F. Kennedy, a relatively young Catholic from Massachusetts, selected Lyndon Johnson, who was older, a Protestant, and from Texas. In 1988, the Democratic candidate, Governor Michael Dukakis, picked Senator Lloyd Bentsen as his vice-presidential candidate. Dukakis was from Massachusetts and a relatively liberal figure. In contrast, Bentsen was much more conservative and a Texan. There have, however, been the beginnings of a shift. Increasingly, the running mate is selected so as to compensate for a perceived weakness in the personality or politics of the presidential nominee. In 2000, George W. Bush selected Dick Cheney. Bush – who was serving as Governor of Texas – had, despite his family background, little experience of Washington politics or foreign policy. He was widely regarded as weak and perhaps even unqualified in dealing with these matters. Cheney, however, was a consummate Washington 'insider', having formerly served as White House Chief of Staff and Secretary of Defense. For his part, Bill Clinton picked Al Gore in 1992. It was an unbalanced ticket. Gore was from the neighbouring state of Tennessee, and he shared Clinton's moderate politics. However, he compensated for Clinton's failure to develop ties with organised labour and the environmentalist groupings within the Party, which were cautious towards, or perhaps even suspicious of, Clinton.

The convention has further functions. It is the only opportunity for party activists to meet as a national party, and is therefore a major party-building exercise. Party activists are generally organised around local and state elections. At the convention, they can consider the party as a national institution and focus on electing the candidate to the only nationwide office in the US. The convention is, furthermore, a media event. This is conveyed in a portrait of the 1988 Republican National Convention: 'With a color-coordinated stage; a band playing upbeat, patriotic music; speakers carefully timed, rehearsed, and designed to heighten the campaign themes; balloons set to fall like rain on the nominees and the delegates dressed in all types of garb, the result was pure theater' (Wayne 1992: 161). Although its scope and scale has been progressively reduced, the convention is a major opportunity to attract free national media coverage and win the attention of voters, many of whom are apathetic towards, or alienated from the political process.

If the party is able to promote its candidate and convey a picture of a united party, it may be able to gain a post-convention 'bounce' in the public opinion polls. Between 1964 and 1992, the average 'bounce' for the Republicans and Democrats was eight and five percentage points respectively. The 1992 Democratic National Convention was very effectively orchestrated by Bill Clinton's campaign strategists, and he gained a twelve point 'bounce' (Bennett 1993: 20). In 2000, Al Gore's poll ratings rose from 39 per cent to 47 per cent. Pollsters found that Gore had been able to use the Democratic convention to convey the more positive aspects of his personality and a vision of the future (CNN.com 2000a). The overall size of the 'bounce' does not, however, depends upon the party's media management techniques alone. Stuart Rothenberg argues that it rests upon the public's familiarity with a candidate. The size of Clinton's 1992 'bounce', he asserts, may be attributable to the fact that he had, until then, been a relatively unknown figure. Both Clinton and the Republican challenger, Bob Dole, attracted only small-scale 'bounces' in 1996 because, Rothenberg argues, they were by then familiar to the public (CNN.com 2000b).

At the same time, a divided convention can impede the party's prospects. The 1968 Democratic convention was bitterly divided over the choice of nominee, and there were protests against the Vietnam War. The televised scenes did much to ensure that the Republican contender, Richard Nixon, won the November election. The 1992 Republican convention organisers awarded the abrasively conservative commentator, Patrick J. Buchanan, who had been defeated in the primaries, a prime-time speaking slot. His address to delegates – which called for a cultural 'war' – was widely seen as provocative and divisive. Although there was a 'bounce', it was small-scale. Some observers have attributed the Republican defeat – three months later – to the image of the convention created by Buchanan's speech.

Postnomination (September–November)

From 1845 onwards, presidential elections have been held on the first Tuesday after the first Monday in November. In the past, the nominees began their campaigns after the Labor Day holiday in early September. The beginning of the campaigning process has, however, been edging forwards. Bill Clinton started a nationwide bus tour immediately after the national convention in 1992, thereby giving his campaign a significant boost. In 2000, both Al Gore and George W. Bush concentrated their fire on each other even before the later primaries had concluded.

The candidates, who may have been joined in the contest by independents and minor party nominees, now seek to appeal to the broad interests of the nation. They will almost certainly have to adopt different themes to those that won them the party nomination, if only because the potential electorate is much larger in size. The candidates tour much of the country, speaking to meetings, dinners and breakfasts. However, television opportunities are pivotal, and the campaigns are driven by the need to attract coverage and – although the major party candidates are assigned full funding by the Federal Election Commission – raise the 'soft money' required to purchase paid advertising. Increasingly, although candidate-centred, much of the campaigning is undertaken by interest groups (see Chapter 9).

The televised presidential debates – which are usually held in October – have come to occupy an importance place in the campaign calendar. They were first introduced in 1960, and have been institutionalised from 1976 onwards. They sometimes appear to have played a decisive role. John F. Kennedy's victory in the 1960 presidential election is widely attributed to the perception by television viewers of the debate that his Republican opponent, Richard Nixon, looked evasive. However, although the 1960 debate acquired a legendary status, the claim that the debates play a determining role should be qualified. Firstly, although even small shifts can dramatically change electoral outcomes, only relatively small numbers watch or are influenced by the debates. In 1996, 92 per cent of those asked in a CBS News poll said that the first debate between Bill Clinton and Bob Dole had done nothing to alter their opinion of the candidates (Bennett 1997: 24). Secondly, the debates are outweighed by other political considerations. In 1988, there was a vigorous exchange in the vice-presidential debate between Lloyd Bentsen and Dan Quayle, Democratic and Republican candidates respectively. However, although Bentsen memorably ridiculed his opponent, the Bush–Quayle ticket won the November election. Thirdly, in so far as the debates do play a role, the data suggest that the important factor is not the debate itself but instead the popular expectations of the candidates' performances. In the 2000 presidential election, there were widely shared expectations that the televised debates would offer an opportunity for Al Gore to display his knowledge and experience. There were also predictions that George W. Bush would stumble when confronted by challenging issues, particularly those associated with foreign policy issues. However, Gore failed to match these high expectations. In contrast, Bush exceeded the low level of expectations that had been set for him. As October progressed, Bush established and consolidated his lead.

The Electoral College

The result of the vote is – almost always – known on the day of the election. Indeed, the television networks announce a victor in – or 'call' – states well before the counting of votes has been completed. In the 2000 election, competition between the networks led them to 'call' states, but then retract. The state of Florida was initially 'called' for Gore. It was later called for Bush. It was finally thrown into an undecided category.

However, despite the televised drama of election night, the formal election only takes place – under the terms of the Constitution – at a later stage, through the Electoral College. Each state is allocated a specified number of Electors or Electoral College Votes (ECV) based on its total Congressional representation. Washington DC has a further three Electors. In all, therefore, there are 538 ECV. To compensate for shifts in population, the process of reapportionment that is undertaken every ten years – following the census – leads to changes in state representation in the House of Representatives and therefore the Electoral College. Following the 2000 Census, California has – as the most populous state – fifty-five Electors. Other states with large populations are also well represented. New York and Florida have thirty-one and twenty-seven ECV respectively. The least populous states – Alaska, Vermont and Wyoming – each have three Electors.

In every state – except Maine (since 1972) and Nebraska (since 1996) – the candidate who wins the most votes (a 'plurality') in that state is allocated all its ECV. It is a 'winner-takes-all' system. A few weeks after the November contest, the Electors – who are generally officials and loyalists from the party that has won the presidential vote – meet in their state capitals and the District of Columbia formally to elect the president. These gatherings are – almost invariably – a formality. The Electors simply confirm the judgement of the voters in their state. The results are then dispatched from the state capitals to the vice-president in his role as president of the US Senate. In a joint session of Congress that is customarily a formality, the tellers read the Electoral Votes from each state. There were, however, challenges to the validity of some ECV in both 1969 and 2001.

To win the presidency, a candidate must obtain at least 270 ECV, an absolute majority among the College's 538 Electors. If there is not such a majority, the Constitution specifies that the election is to be conducted by the House of Representatives, although – under the terms of Article II – each state delegation is only assigned one vote.

The Electoral College was established by the Founding Fathers for three principal reasons. Firstly, it offered a degree of reassurance to the states, a number

Table 10.4 *Representation in the Electoral College, 2004 onwards*

State	Electors	% of electors	Population	% of population
Alabama	9	1.67	4,461,130	1.58
Alaska	3	0.56	628,933	0.22
Arizona	10	1.86	5,140,683	1.82
Arkansas	6	1.12	2,679,733	0.95
California	55	10.22	33,930,798	12.03
Colorado	9	1.67	4,311,882	1.53
Connecticut	7	1.30	3,409,535	1.21
Delaware	3	0.56	785,068	0.28
District of Columbia	3	0.56	574,096	0.20
Florida	27	5.02	16,028,890	5.68
Georgia	15	2.79	8,206,975	2.91
Hawaii	4	0.74	1,216,642	0.43
Idaho	4	0.74	1,297,274	0.46
Illinois	21	3.90	12,439,042	4.41
Indiana	11	2.04	6,090,782	2.16
Iowa	7	1.30	2,931,923	1.04
Kansas	6	1.12	2,693,824	0.96
Kentucky	8	1.49	4,049,431	1.44
Louisiana	9	1.67	4,480,271	1.59
Maine	4	0.74	1,277,731	0.45
Maryland	10	1.86	5,307,886	1.88
Massachusetts	12	2.23	6,355,568	2.25
Michigan	17	3.16	9,955,829	3.53
Minnesota	10	1.86	4,925,670	1.75
Mississippi	6	1.12	2,852,927	1.01
Missouri	11	2.04	5,606,260	1.99
Montana	3	0.56	905,316	0.32
Nebraska	5	0.93	1,715,369	0.61
Nevada	5	0.93	2,002,032	0.71
New Hampshire	4	0.74	1,238,415	0.44
New Jersey	15	2.79	8,424,354	2.99
New Mexico	5	0.93	1,823,821	0.65
New York	31	5.76	19,004,973	6.74
North Carolina	15	2.79	8,067,673	2.86
North Dakota	3	0.56	643,756	0.23
Ohio	20	3.72	11,374,540	4.03
Oklahoma	7	1.30	3,458,819	1.23
Oregon	7	1.30	3,428,543	1.22
Pennsylvania	21	3.90	12,300,670	4.36
Rhode Island	4	0.74	1,049,662	0.37
South Carolina	8	1.49	4,025,061	1.43
South Dakota	3	0.56	756,874	0.27
Tennessee	11	2.04	5,700,037	2.02
Texas	34	6.32	20,903,994	7.41
Utah	5	0.93	2,236,714	0.79

Table 10.4 *continued*

State	Electors	% of electors	Population	% of population
Vermont	3	0.56	609,890	0.22
Virginia	13	2.42	7,100,702	2.52
Washington	11	2.04	5,908,684	2.10
West Virginia	5	0.93	1,813,077	0.64
Wisconsin	10	1.86	5,371,210	1.90
Wyoming	3	0.56	495,304	0.18
Totals	538	100.00	281,998,273	100.00

Source: adapted from TheGreenpapers.com (2003), *Electoral College 2004 Allocation,*
www.thegreenpapers.com/G04/ElectorAllocation.phtml?sort=Alph.

of which saw a danger of centralisation in the US Constitution, that they could play an entrenched and institutionalised part in the selection of a president. Secondly, an indirect system allowed the states to maintain their own laws governing the extent of the franchise. Indeed, South Carolina did not choose its Electors by popular vote until after the Civil War. Thirdly, although voting rights were severely restricted in the eighteenth century – and were generally conditional upon property ownership – the Framers feared that the electorate might make an inappropriate choice, and sought safeguards against 'popular passion'. The Electoral College was envisaged as a deliberative institution that could, if necessary, disregard such 'passion' and choose the candidate it considered most qualified.

The College has however been subject to sustained criticism in modern times by those who see it as an undemocratic relic of an earlier age.

1 The mathematics of the Electoral College can allow a candidate with a smaller share of the popular vote than an opponent to win more ECV. This was vividly illustrated in the 2000 presidential election. The result led to bitter criticism of the Electoral College and challenges to the legitimacy of the Bush administration. The phrase 'Hail to the Thief' was heard. The novelist Gore Vidal talked of the 'Bush–Cheney junta'. Michael Moore, the radical television observer and author of *Stupid White Men . . . And Other Sorry Excuses for the State of the Nation* said of the College: 'This is a democracy. One person, one vote. We should have done away with this antique long before now' (Moore 2000). There have, furthermore, been other presidential elections when the winner in terms of the popular vote lost in the Electoral College. In 1876 the Democratic candidate, Samuel J. Tilden, gained 51 per cent of the popular vote, but Rutherford B. Hayes, the Republican had a one vote majority in the Electoral College and thereby gained the presidency. Twelve years later – in 1888 – Grover Cleveland (D) won over ninety thousand more votes than Benjamin Harrison (R). However, Harrison won in the Electoral College by 233 ECV to 168.

Table 10.5 *The 2000 presidential election*

Candidate	Popular votes	ECV
George W. Bush	50,456,002	271
Al Gore	50,999,897	267

Source: adapted from Federal Election Commission (2001), *2000 Presidential Popular Vote Summary for all Candidates Listed on at Least One State Ballot*, www.fec.gov/pubrec/fe2000/prespop.htm.

In the aftermath of the 2000 election, the criticisms of the Electoral College – and the Constitution itself – were compounded by allegations that voting practices in Florida had denied Al Gore a majority of the popular vote in the 'Sunshine State' and thereby given its twenty-five ECV to Bush. In particular, there were assertions that the type of ballot used in some Florida counties had confused a number of voters, and that the rules for the counting of the votes, in a system of voting by punching a hole in the ballot card that sometimes led to rather unclear or uncertain results, had unfairly deprived Gore of votes. The Florida vote was very close indeed, and It was said that if the votes in the state had been counted on the basis of voters' intentions, Gore would have won a majority in the state, been assigned its ECV, and thereby gained the presidency. However, after a prolonged series of recounts which only came to a halt after the US Supreme Court's ruling in *Bush v. Gore*, Bush was finally elected.

2 Even when the Electoral College delivers the 'right' result in terms of the overall victor, it distorts the popular vote. This is because the winner in each state is allocated all that state's ECV regardless of the margin of victory. In 1996, Bill Clinton gained 49 per cent of the vote. This, however, enabled him to win 70 per cent (379) of the ECV. However, although Bob Dole won 41 per cent of the vote, he gained only 30 per cent (159) of the ECV.

3 The Electoral College assures states of at least three ECV. This – in terms of population – is over-representation. Some critics assert that this – like the system of election to the US Senate that assigns two senators to each state regardless of population size – is a denial of the popular will and undemocratic.

4 Although many states have laws prohibiting it, the system allows the occasional 'faithless Elector' to vote for a candidate who did not win the popular vote in a particular state. In all, there have been fourteen instances of this. In 1972, a Nixon delegate from Virginia voted for John Hospers, the Libertarian Party candidate. In 1988, a West Virginia Elector cast her vote for Senator Lloyd Bentsen, the running mate, rather than Michael Dukakis, the Democratic presidential candidate who had won the popular vote in the state. In 2000, one Elector from the District of Columbia abstained in protest against the District's lack of representation in Congress. Although no 'faithless Elector' has changed the outcome of an election, the potential for this in a close race remains.

5 Independent and third-party candidates often fare badly in the Electoral College. In 1992, Ross Perot gained 19 per cent of the popular vote but, because his support was dispersed across the country, received no Electoral College Votes at all. However, having said this, there are exceptions. The popular vote for some minor party candidates has been regionally concentrated. In 1968, George Wallace – who had served as Governor of Alabama and had come to symbolise southern white resistance to desegregation – won in five states, giving him 46 Electoral College Votes. In 1948, both Henry Wallace, a left-leaning progressive, and Strom Thurmond, the segregationist Governor of South Carolina, gained about 2.4 per cent of the national vote. However, because his votes were regionally concentrated, Thurmond won 39 ECV. For his part, Wallace – whose votes were dispersed – gained none.

6 Under the terms of the Constitution, the House of Representatives decides upon the presidency and the Senate the vice-presidency if there is no absolute majority in the College. Each state delegation in the House is assigned one vote. Although this only happened in 1800 and 1824 (while the Senate decided upon the vice-presidency in 1836), a shift of only thirty thousand popular votes would have thrown both the 1860 and 1960 elections to the House (*Congressional Quarterly* 1997: 128). Such procedures can however be seen as a breach of the separation of powers between the legislative and executive branches of government. There is, furthermore, a possibility that the president and vice-president could be drawn from opposing parties.

7 The College distorts the character of the election campaign. In the 2000 election, for example, Al Gore devoted relatively few resources to campaigning in Texas because, despite the size and importance of the state, Bush was – as Governor – a certain victor and would, in a winner-takes-all system, gain all of Texas' ECV.

The reform of the Electoral College has, periodically, been the subject of debate. Many would like to address the problem of the 'faithless Elector' by extending the laws that compel Electors to cast their Vote for the winner of the popular vote in their state. There are, however, also calls for more fundamental forms of change. Some – particularly on the left – hope to see the direct election of the president. This, they argue, would ensure a democratic outcome. However, the role of the states and their Electors is entrenched in the Constitution, and this type of reform would require an amendment. It would almost certainly be impossible to secure the required three-quarters majority among the states, because the less populated states gain in terms of their relative weighting by being assured of at least three ECV. If the election was based on the popular vote alone, campaigns would be concentrated in the metropolitan regions, and the more rural areas would be neglected. Furthermore, those who talk of 'states' rights' also fear that such a step would further denude the states of their semi-sovereign role and correspondingly add to the powers of national government.

There is also a danger that, if the winner simply required a plurality of the votes, a president could be elected with a relatively small proportion of the votes. The presence of third-party candidates increases the likelihood of this. For this reason, proposals for a direct vote are often tied to an insistence that there should be a threshold. The League of Women Voters, for example, backs a 40 per cent threshold. If no candidate gains this, there would be a second, run-off election. Run-off elections are already used for Congressional elections in Louisiana as well as local and statewide races in states such as Texas, Arkansas, and Alabama. These, however, draw out and lengthen the electoral process.

Arthur Schlesinger Jr., the celebrated historian, has put forward another proposal. He argues for the retention of the Electoral College, but suggests that the winner of the popular vote should be awarded bonus ECV. This would almost certainly guarantee that whoever gained a majority of the popular vote would also win in the College. It would, for example, have ensured that Al Gore would have gained the presidency in 2000.

Others call for the proportional allocation of Electoral Votes. In place of the winner-takes-all system, a candidate who wins a particular proportion of the popular vote would be assigned that proportion of the ECV. Although thresholds would have to introduced to prevent the president being elected on a minority vote, this would lead to a fairer, less distorted result, and encourage candidates to campaign across the country. However – in the absence of a Constitutional amendment – it would probably have to be introduced on a state-by-state basis. But the partial adoption of this proposal could give one party an unfair advantage, and, furthermore, it would not address the over-representation of the less populous states.

A more modest proposal would extend the system used in Maine and Nebraska. At present, each state is awarded two Electoral Votes for the state as a whole together with one Electoral Vote for each of its Congressional districts. The Maine and Nebraska system would only give the two statewide votes to the winner in the state as a whole, and would divide the other votes by giving one to the plurality winner in each Congressional district (Center for Voting and Democracy 2003).

Nonetheless, although the 2002 Help America Vote Act provided some funding for the modernisation of voting technology, far-reaching reform is unlikely. There are two reasons for this. Firstly, there is no consensus on the different alternatives. Secondly, many types of reform require a Constitutional amendment requiring the backing of two-thirds of Congress and three-quarters of the states. Thirdly, reform is unlikely to be backed by the Republicans. President George W. Bush owed his victory to the Electoral College system. If Republicans support reform, they are denying the legitimacy of his administration.

Inauguration

An incoming prime minister in Britain takes office the morning after a general election is held. In the US, a new president is sworn in – traditionally by the

Chief Justice – at an inaugural ceremony on 20 January. The two-month transition period allows the president-elect to prepare his administration and appoint senior officials. The Inaugural Address, delivered once the oath of office has been administered, offers signs of the style and direction that will be adopted by the new administration. In 1933, Franklin D. Roosevelt asserted, in a call for government action against economic depression, that 'the only thing we have to fear is fear itself' (Maidment and Dawson 1994: 185). In January 1961, John F. Kennedy spelt out the US's commitment to resisting the expansion of communism: 'Let every nation know, whether it wishes us well or ill, that we shall pay any price, bear any burden, meet any hardship, support any friend, oppose any foe to assure the survival and success of liberty' (quoted in Maidment and Dawson 1994: 190).

Electing Congress

Members of the House are elected every two years. The general election is held using the plurality – or first-past-the-post – system. Districts are roughly equal in population, and are redrawn every ten years on the basis of shifts in population. The process, known as *redistricting*, is carried out by state legislatures, and can be highly partisan. Indeed, some of the 1998 races for state legislatures were fought with a particular intensity, and well funded by the national party committees, because those who were elected would redraw the congressional districts after the 2000 census (*New York Times*, 3 November 1998). Senators represent the entire state, and do not therefore face the traumas of redistricting.

Like the race for the presidency, Congressional elections have a two-stage character and rest on the use of either closed or open primaries. A few states – such as Washington – have held 'blanket primaries'. These allow voters of all persuasions to vote to select the nominees for any of the parties. In 1996, following the passage of Proposition 198, California also adopted the blanket primary. However, it was prohibited by the US Supreme Court in *California Democratic Party* et al. *v. Jones* et al. (June 2000).

Two further characteristics of Congressional elections should be noted. Firstly, the threat of a primary challenge, and the competition for money and workers with campaigns for other elective offices, mean that Congressmen retain their own personal campaign organisation. They are not dependent upon their party apparatus. Secondly, incumbents enjoy a decisive advantage. Once elected, members of Congress are almost certain to be re-elected (see below). Relatively few elections – unless they are held in 'open seats' in which there is no incumbent – have a genuinely competitive character. This, some suggest, contributes to low levels of turnout.

Box 10.4   The role of the mass media

In contrast with Britain, candidates can buy television commercials. These *unmediated* messages have sometimes had a significant impact upon the course of the election campaign.

- In 1964, the 'Daisy Girl' commercial suggested that Barry Goldwater, the Republican candidate, would be too ready to use America's nuclear arsenal. It confirmed him as an irresponsible 'extremist' and, some observers suggest, contributed to Lyndon Johnson's landslide victory.
- In 1984, Ronald Reagan's commercials were structured around the creation of a 'feelgood factor'. The slogan 'it's morning again in America' was used alongside images of secure and stable small town life. These advertisements strengthened the feeling that the US was regaining its strength and rediscovering its national character.
- In 1988, commercials issued by both the Bush–Quayle campaign and Republican-supporting political action committees played a part in establishing an image of Michael Dukakis, the Democratic candidate, as ineffectual in addressing problems such as crime and defence.

During the 1990s, the role of 'spindoctors' attracted particular attention. They are employed by candidates to present, structure or create news stories that will be to their advantage. In 1992, George Stephanopoulos and James Carville are said to have played a pivotal role in 'selling' Bill Clinton. The theme underpinned Barry Levinson's 1997 film, *Wag the Dog*. In the film, an incumbent president is embroiled in a sex scandal just a few days before an election. His spindoctor enlists the assistance of a Hollywood producer to create the appearance of a war with Albania. The war diverts attention from the scandal, and amid a wave of patriotic fervour, the president is re-elected. From this perspective, the media and the American public are the playthings of elite interests who control the information process.

The media has, however, come under fire in other ways. Hillary Clinton spoke – at the time of the impeachment proceedings against her husband – of a vast right-wing conspiracy. Her comments were tied to claims that interlocking conservative media outlets were campaigning – by using both political and personal slurs – against the Clinton presidency and, in the 2000 election, for a Bush victory. Periodicals such as the *American Spectator* and the *Weekly Standard* were cited alongside the Fox News network and talk radio programmes. Each, it was said, played a part in amplifying stories that would otherwise have little credibility.

Financing campaigns

American elections inevitably require large-scale financial resources. Candidates have to fund advertising campaigns, staff salaries, and travel costs. Senate elections in the more populous states involve an electorate of many millions. In 2001, for example, California had an estimated population of 34,501,130. For their part, presidential candidates must reach a voting public in key states during

Others simply point to the negative character of campaign commercials. Many advertisements are simply 'attack-ads' that promote a particular candidate by denigrating his or her opponent. Brit Hume of Fox News suggests that news reporting is also largely negative: 'news is what's exceptional, and bad stuff tends to be exceptional in our world. Reporters have a natural instinct, therefore to look for the negative' (Hume 2003: 4).

However, Hume makes a further point. He suggests – in striking contrast to the claims put forward by figures such as Hillary Clinton – that some reporting is underpinned by liberal thinking. He argues, for example, that many of the networks assumed in the run-up to the 2003 Iraq war that the legitimacy of the action was dependent upon support by the United Nations (Hume 2003: 4).

However, despite this, the overall importance of the mass media should not be exaggerated. Research evidence suggests that the viewer is not a passive consumer of media coverage. Viewers and readers apply 'filters' based on their own experiences and attitudes. Only certain news stories register in the public mind. Furthermore, individuals avoid information that is disturbing or material that conflicts with attitudes that are already held.

The mass media have, then, a limited role. Nonetheless, this should not be disregarded. Firstly, they appear to play a role as a 'gatekeeper' in so far as they determine what is, or is not, 'newsworthy'. Secondly, although they do not change beliefs, they appear to have a *reinforcement* effect. As Leon Sigal has noted: 'newsmen do not write the *score* or play an instrument; they amplify the sounds of the music makers' (quoted in Graber 1997: 263).

References and further reading

Graber, D. A. (1997), *Mass Media and American Politics*, Washington DC, Congressional Quarterly Inc.

Hume, B. (2003), The American Media in Wartime, *Imprimis*, 32:6, June, p. 4.

Websites

Wag the Dog – movieweb.com/movie/wagthedog/.

Fox News – www.foxnews.com.

CNN – www.cnn.com.

New York Times – www.nytimes.com/.

Washington Post – www.washingtonpost.com/.

the primaries and distributed across much of the country in the November contest. Coast-to-coast advertising and campaigning is inevitably costly.

By the early 1970s, there were widespread fears about spending levels in elections. The demands imposed by the need to raise funds prevented some candidates from properly conveying their views to the public. Those without funding were deterred from standing. Candidates, it was argued, were over-reliant on small numbers of wealthy and often anonymous donors. The demands of fundraising prevented some candidates from properly conveying their views to the public. The winner would inevitably be indebted to those who had contributed. Those without funding were deterred from standing. All too often, it was claimed, election victories depended on a candidate's ability to out-spend opponents. Contests had become profoundly unequal.

Congress responded to these arguments by passing the Federal Election Campaign Act (FECA) of 1974. As a consequence of its passage, every presidential election from 1976 onwards has been financed with taxpayer funds. In the primaries, candidates are – subject to stringent conditions – eligible for matching payments. To qualify, candidates should raise over $5,000 in each of twenty states. They must also commit themselves to overall spending limits in each of the states so as to ensure a broadly level playing-field. They must agree, furthermore, not to spend more than $50,000 of their personal funds. The candidates must also allow a full audit of their campaigns. The spending limit is increased every four years so as to keep pace with inflation. In 2000, the candidates who accepted taxpayer funding could not spend more than $40,536,000 on their primary campaign (Federal Election Commission 2000).

In the post-nomination – or general election – phase, the Federal Election Campaign Act envisaged that the candidates nominated by the major parties would receive almost all their funding from the FEC. In 2000, both the Bush and the Gore campaigns were assigned $67,560,000. Patrick Buchanan, the Reform Party candidate, was given $12.6 million because the Party's 1996 candidate, Ross Perot, had won 8 per cent of the vote. The principal parties also receive funding for their national conventions. In 2000, each party received $13,680,292 (Federal Election Commission 2000). Candidates from the minor parties are given some funding, based on a sliding scale, if they attract over 5 per cent of the vote.

There are also constraints on the citizen, although some changes to these were introduced by the 2002 Bipartisan Campaign Reform Act. Individuals may not contribute beyond a maximum of $2,000 to a candidate in the primary or general election campaigns. Organisations wishing to contribute to a campaign must – by law – establish a political action committee (PAC). The first PAC was formed by the Congress of Industrial Organizations – a trade union federation – in 1943 in response to a Congress decision to prohibit direct contributions from the unions to election candidates. PACs have proliferated since 1974. In 1996, 4,079 were registered (*Congressional Quarterly* 1997: 51). In particular, companies established PACs as they sought to influence the decision-making process. Single-issue groups such as organisations campaigning on the abortion issue are also active. Under the provisions of FECA, a PAC can only contribute a maximum of $5,000 to an individual candidate, but there is no total annual ceiling (Grant 1995: 9).

Despite the apparently stringent egalitarianism of FECA, the campaign finance regulations provoked criticism. Some of the limits and restrictions imposed by FECA were bypassed or evaded:

1 Following the 1976 US Supreme Court ruling *Buckley v. Valeo*, those who do not seek matching funds were not bound by the limits imposed under FECA. In 1996, Steve Forbes spent an estimated $38 million of his own money in a bid to win the Republican primaries. Similarly, in 2000, George W. Bush did not seek taxpayer funding at the primary stage. Neither, therefore, had to abide by the Act.

2 Individuals and groups organised well-funded campaigns that may have influenced the election outcome without being restricted by the provisions of FECA. *Buckley v. Valeo* (1976) established that 'independent' campaigns by individuals or PACs either in support of, or in opposition to a particular candidate could not be restricted. Such restrictions would, the Court ruled, be a breach of the First Amendment's guarantee of free speech. Thus, providing there is no formal connection with a candidate's organisation, a campaign could be mounted. Advertisements may expressly advocate the election or defeat of a candidate. In the 1980 presidential election, the National Conservative Political Action Committee (NCPAC) mounted an 'independent' campaign specifically targeted against six Democratic Senators. Four were defeated at the polls. Furthermore, in a 1996 Supreme Court ruling – *Colorado Republican Campaign Committee v. Federal Election Commission* – it was established that political parties could also make unlimited 'independent' expenditures on behalf of candidates.

3 A 'soft money' loophole opened up in the law. Companies, unions, other organisations, and individuals could make donations that were not included in the 'hard money' accounts that had to be submitted to the Federal Election Commission. 'Soft money' was used for state elections and 'party-building' activities such voter education campaigns and voter registration drives, and was not subject to limits. There was, however, a thin line between these forms of spending and the promotion of candidates. At the same time, soft money expenditure freed up 'hard' dollars for candidates' campaign expenditures.

4 The law does not allow organisations to fund candidates directly. However, they could produce 'issue-advocacy ads'. These are forms of political advertising that do not explicitly or expressly call for a vote for or against a candidate. The purpose of the advertisement is instead evident by implication. In 1996, it was reported that the Sierra Club – a longstanding environmentalist organisation – had spent $500,000 on issue ads (FECwatch 2003).

5 FECA had only limited powers if candidates exceeded the spending limits, and the penalties cannot be considered a deterrent. In 1984, Walter Mondale's campaign in the New Hampshire primary spent $2.85 million despite a state ceiling of $404,000. He was later fined $400,000. (*Congressional Quarterly* 1997: 46)

The rise in expenditure as these ways of evading 'hard money' limits grew in scale triggered increasing public unease and disquiet. Against this background, Senators John McCain and Russ Feingold led the calls for campaign finance reform. Their efforts culminated in the Bipartisan Campaign Reform Act (BCRA), which President Bush signed into law in March 2002. As well as increasing the amounts that individuals could contribute to campaigns, parties, and PACs, the Act prohibited 'issue-ads' that refer to a candidate within 60 days of an election and severely curtailed campaign spending by the parties. From November 2002 onwards, they were banned from raising 'soft money'. There have been claims that BCRA's provisions have been watered down by the Federal Election Commission, and some sections of the Act were made subject to a legal challenge in *McConnell v. Federal Election Commission*. BCRA's opponents maintain that limits upon spending represent an infringement of the individual's right to free speech assured under the First Amendment.

Table 10.6 *Spending by winning candidates, 1986–2000 (constant dollars)*

Year	House winners	Senate winners
1986	560,862	4,784,725
1990	544,714	4,257,615
1996	745,040	4,272,182
2000	848,296	7,389,176

Note: the spending levels are shown in 2000 dollars. The figures have been adjusted so as to allow for inflation.

Source: adapted from N. J. Ornstein, T. E. Mann, and M. J. Malbin (2002), *Vital Statistics on Congress 2001–2002*, Washington DC, The AEI Press, p. 86.

Although donations to candidates are regulated by law, there is no system of taxpayer funding in Congressional elections. Campaign spending has risen significantly. Why has this happened? It is partly because the voting age population has grown. At the same time, campaigns have extended in length, are now more professionalised, and depend upon the services of polling organisations. These test public opinion through both conventional sampling techniques and the use of focus groups. These latter are representative gatherings of potential voters who inform pollsters about their responses and feelings towards the candidate, the opponent, and different campaign strategies. At the same time, campaigning is often negative in character, leading to a vicious circle whereby candidates seek to defend themselves against the charges that have been made and make counter-attacks. The 1998 race in New York for the Senate seat between Charles Schumer and Alphonse D'Amato took this form, and cost an estimated $36 million.

However, the overall role of money in politics should not be exaggerated. Firstly, while the sums are large, they should be seen alongside other forms of expenditure. As Stanley C. Brubaker observes, total spending in the 1996 elections was less than half that spent by Americans on cologne and perfume during the same period (1998: 38). Furthermore, although the critics claim that money can 'buy' elections, Congressional votes, and presidential decisions, there is little hard evidence to support this. As Congressional election results show, the outcome depends on other factors apart from finance and the TV advertising that can thereby be purchased. In November 1994, Michael Huffington (R) spent $53 million of his own fortune in an attempt to win a Senate seat in California, and lost. In the 2000 Senate race in New York between Rick Lazio (the Republican candidate) and Hillary Rodham Clinton, they spent $39.6 million and $29.9 million respectively. Although Lazio's campaign broke all expenditure records, Clinton won easily. The role of finance is limited in other ways. Much money is given to candidates who are already in a strong electoral position or have already adopted a favourable policy position from the perspective of the donor, rather than to those who might change their vote. Many PACs give money to competing candidates in the expectation that they will be given a chance to put forward their case before the congressman takes a position, whoever wins. While incumbents are most successful at raising money, there is little evidence that this increases their likelihood of re-election. Instead, the crucial role of money is for challengers, when a well-funded campaign may make a difference.

Evaluating the electoral system

The character of the primaries and the role of money have already been considered. However, other features of the electoral system have also been subject to criticism.

1 The electoral cycle is said to be too long. Campaigning for the House of Representatives is a constant process. The institutionalisation of the 'invisible primary' has extended the presidential contest to almost three years. The primary and caucus season extends over five months. However, although the presidential race could be shortened through the introduction of one national primary, the present system does ensure that candidates are tested in different political environments.
2 Campaigns are conducted on the basis of image rather than policy substance. The mass media, it is said, have trivialised the political process. In particular, critics argue that paid advertisements either present manipulated images or are negative 'attack-ads'. Particular advertisements are said to have swung elections. In 1988, for example, advertisements placed by Republican supporters suggested that the Democratic candidate, the Massachusetts Governor Michael Dukakis, was weak towards criminality. They highlighted the case of Willie Horton, who had attacked a woman while released on weekend leave from a Massachusetts prison. In a brutal phrase employed by the Republican Party Chairman, Horton became Dukakis's 'running mate'.
3 Relatively few Americans vote. The US has one of lowest voting turnouts of all Western democracies. In 1988 barely half the voting-age population (50.1 per cent) cast a vote. The turnout improved slightly in 1992 to 55.1

per cent, but declined again in 1996 to 49 per cent. It then rose to just over 51 per cent in 2000. There is a striking contrast between the US and many other nations. Although turnout fell in the United Kingdom 2001 General Election to 59.4 per cent, it has usually been closer to the 71.5 per cent recorded in the 1997 contest.

Table 10.7 *Turnout in presidential and House elections, 1990–2002 (%)*

Year	Presidential elections	House elections
1990		33.1
1992	55.1	50.8
1994		36.6
1996	49.0	45.8
1998		32.9
2000	51.2	47.3
2002		36.4

Source: adapted from N. J. Ornstein, T. E. Mann, and M. J. Malbin (2002), *Vital Statistics on Congress 2001–2002*, Washington DC, The AEI Press, p. 62.
Nexus (2003), *Voting-Age and Voting-Eligible Population Turnout Rates*, elections.gmu,edu/VAP_VEP.htm.

Table 10.8 *Registration and voting, 2000*

	Registered to vote	Reported voted	Did not vote
All	63.9	54.7	45.3
Men	62.2	53.1	46.9
Women	65.6	56.2	43.8
Whites	70.0	60.4	39.6
Blacks	64.3	54.1	45.9
Hispanics	34.9	27.5	72.5

Source: adapted from US Census Bureau (2002), *Reported Voting and Registration, by Race, Hispanic Origin, Sex, and Age, for the United States: November 2000*, www.census.gov/population/socdemo/voting/p20–542/tab02.xls.

Although there is no conclusive explanation, there have been many attempts to explain the low level of turnout. Firstly, the form of measurement that is used paints an unduly pessimistic picture. Turnout is measured as a proportion of the voting-age population. However, this latter figure includes adults resident in the US, whereas only citizens are eligible to vote. Furthermore, some are barred from voting. Many states have laws limiting the voting rights of those convicted of a felony. These not only apply to prison inmates, but also to those on parole or probation. In some states, the right to vote is permanently forfeited. This has a significant impact on African-American voting patterns in particular. An estimated 15 per cent of black males have either temporarily or permanently lost the right to vote (Flanigan and Zingale 1998: 31).

Eligibility to vote also depends upon registration. Although overall voting rates are low, and while there are significant differences across the racial and ethnic groupings, the proportion of those registered who then vote is relatively high. What are the reasons for this? The registration process is difficult. Although a form is sent to every household in the UK, and officials often follow this up with a personal visit if it is not returned, American voters are responsible for registering themselves. The 1993 National Voter Registration Act (the 'motor-voter law') simplified procedures by allowing citizens to register when applying for a driving licence or other forms of documentation from government agencies. There are also campaigns by voluntary groups.

However, registration barriers provide only a partial explanation of US turnout levels. Estimates suggest that, if they were to be lowered, this would only increase overall turnout by about 8 per cent (Flanigan and Zingale 1998: 45). Other factors should be considered. There is a high level of geographical mobility in the US, particularly among the young. The *Committee for the Study of the American Electorate* suggests that Americans move home at a rate of about 16 per cent a year. Inevitably, if people settle in a different state, they will know less about the process of registration and local candidates and races. Some observers – most notably Robert Putnam – point to a decline in the US civic culture. Individuals are more isolated and detached from the social fabric than in the past (Putnam 2000). Some of the lowest levels of turnout are to be found in low-income communities. Turnout is less than 40 per cent among the poorest fifth of the population (Kuttner 1996: 164). They, in particular, feel little sense of involvement in society and have become increasingly alienated from the political process. Some attribute low turnout to weak party organisation. In the US, the political parties are the main instruments for encouraging the electorate to vote. However, party decline – at least in terms of their place within the neighbourhoods and counties – has reduced the number of activists who are willing to encourage others to register and vote. Others argue that the very large number of elections discourages turnout. Voters, they say, become bored and confused. Although the evidence is unclear, there are suggestions that many contests can be considered 'low-stimulus elections'. This is either because the outcome is regarded as a foregone conclusion or because the candidates are seen as unattractive. The relatively low turnout for the 1988 presidential election – where voters had a choice between George Bush and Michael Dukakis – has been explained in these terms. There are also claims that government plays a much smaller part in everyday lives than in Europe. The contrast in turnout figures between the US and Europe reflects differences in political culture.

Voting behaviour

What determines the way in which Americans vote? Although there is no precise dividing line, a distinction should be drawn between long and short-term factors.

Long-term factors

As Chapter 1 emphasised, American society has a diverse and heterogeneous character. It is fractured by race, ethnicity, region, gender, and religion. These divisions provide a basis for party identification and voting decisions.

In the 1930s – during the New Deal era – the Democrats built up a coalition of support, drawing together blacks, Jews, blue-collar trade unionists, and those employed in the public sector. At the same time, the Democrats retained the loyalty of white southerners who had backed the Party since the Civil War. These groupings formed a *bloc* that constituted the Party's core vote for three decades. However, subsequent strains led to changes in allegiance, and the coalition lost the breadth of support that had formerly characterised it. Blue-collar workers reacted against the Democrats' shift towards social liberalism and their apparent lack of resolve in defence policy. The civil rights revolution of the 1960s swung growing numbers of white southerners towards the Republicans. In the 1950s, as Marjorie Randon Hershey notes: 'The south was the most dependably Democratic region of the country; to be openly Republican was a form of deviance' (1997: 228). Such was the region's loyalty to the Democrats that it had become known as the 'solid south'. In 1952, for example, 85 per cent of southern whites identified with the Democrats. By 1988, however, the proportion had fallen to 46 per cent (Wayne 1992: 73). After the 1994 Congressional elections, the GOP had a majority of House seats in seven of the thirteen southern states. In 1996, the Republicans' overall gains in the House of Representatives were confined to the south (Hershey 1997: 228).

There was another, albeit overlapping, shift in allegiance. During the same period, white evangelical Christians also moved towards the GOP. Supreme Court rulings establishing abortion rights and outlawing school prayer in public schools, and the Democrats' identification with what appeared as an assault against long-established values led to a weakening of traditional political affiliations. Although the evangelicals had initially, in 1976, supported Jimmy Carter's candidature for the presidency, soon the Republicans were 'seen as more attractive, resisting cultural change and an increasingly intrusive government' (Durham 1996: 26). Evangelical Christians gave decisive support to Ronald Reagan in 1980 and to subsequent Republican presidential candidates.

The Republican Party, traditionally the party of business, the farmer and the WASP (White Anglo-Saxon Protestant), gained strength from the Democrats' difficulties. Increasingly, after Reagan had taken office, observers claimed that the Republicans had established a dominant *bloc*. There had been, it was said, a process of *realignment*. As Chapter 9 noted, the concept of realignment rest on the assertion that electoral history is divided into distinct and separate eras. Although there are differences between them, commentators such as V. O. Key, E. E. Schattschneider, and Walter Dean Burnham point to 'critical' or 'realigning' elections, citing 1828, 1860, 1896, and 1932 as examples (Mayhew 2002: 7–12). Each either brought a new party to power or ushered in a period in which one party was predominant. The period from 1932 onwards is seen as an era of Democratic dominance. Although the Republicans won the presidency, as they did during the Eisenhower and Nixon years, and at least one house of Congress, as they did between 1947 and 1949 and again between 1953 and 1955, these were *deviating* elections. They were, in other words, exceptions to the norm. From this perspective, 1968 – or in some accounts 1980 – were however *critical* or *realigning* elections. From then onwards, the US entered an era of Republican dominance. The Senate had a Republican majority from 1981 until 1987, and the GOP won a majority in both houses of Congress from 1994 onwards.

The loss of faith in the Democrats and the process of realignment has been attributed to the shift from an industrial to a post-industrial society. The age of large-scale manufacturing industry demanded the forms of 'big government' with which the Democrats are associated. The modern era is however characterised by the break-up of monopolies and the growth of smaller enterprises. Public opinion is now marked by a 'new mood of doubt' about the role and purpose of government (Ladd 1996: 171). This has led voters towards the GOP.

However, suggestions that realignment has taken place, leading to long-term Republican hegemony, should be qualified. As Richard Wirthlin has observed, realignment has, at most, been partial. The gap between the two parties in terms of identification narrowed, and Republican notions of 'small government' were widely accepted. However, the Republicans have only made limited headway at state and local level (Ladd 1996: 167). The results of the 1998 Congressional elections suggested that Republican hold over the south was rather less secure than it had once seemed. In 2000, Al Gore secured a majority of the popular vote. The US seemed divided between the parties on a fifty-fifty basis. Furthermore, despite the Democrats' long-term difficulties, the Party has won increased support among two groupings:

1 They have made significant gains among minorities. African-Americans have been the Democrats' most loyal constituency since 1964. Other ethnic and racial groupings are firmly within the Democratic fold. In 1992, 61 per cent of Latinos voted for the Party. By 1996, this had risen to 72 per cent; although it fell to 67 per cent in 2000 (Pomper 2001: 138). At the same time, although disproportionately low, minority turnout has risen. There were several reasons for this. The introduction of 'motor-voter' registration increased the numbers in lower-income groups who were able to vote. Furthermore, many long-term Hispanic residents were naturalised between 1992 and 1996, enabling them, for the first time, to cast a vote. More significantly, Republican Party backing for propositions put to the California electorate withdrawing state benefits from illegal immigrants and ending affirmative action programmes created a widely shared feeling that the GOP was hostile to minorities. Even Asian-Americans, whom Republicans had long regarded as the 'model minority', because of their seeming commitment

to conservative values and the entrepreneurial ethos, joined the swing to the Democrats. In 1992, 31 per cent supported Bill Clinton's candidature. By 2000, the figure was 54 per cent (Pomper 2001: 138).

2 There is a *gender gap*. Men – particularly white men – have been drawn disproportionately to the Republicans. In 2000, just 36 per cent of white men backed Gore, compared with 60 per cent who supported Bush (Pomper 2001: 138). In contrast, women were more or less evenly divided. Gerald M. Pomper has emphasised that the gender gap 'remained stable among blacks and whites, among all age groups and in suburbs, and across levels of education and income' (1997: 183–4). There are a number of explanations for the gap:

- There is particular support for the Democrats among women who have a degree of personal independence, either because they are unmarried or because they are in paid employment. They may regard the Republicans – who are associated with a commitment to 'family values' – as a party that believes that women should remain within the domestic sphere.
- Although the ideological differences between the parties should not be exaggerated, the Democrats have often emphasised the protective aspects of government. Like earlier Democratic candidates, Al Gore emphasised the importance of education provision, health care and Medicare. These are issues that have a particular resonance with women. In contrast men think rather more in terms of the economy and taxation rates: 'The social reality of the United States is that women bear a greater responsibility for children's education and for health care of their families and parents, and that women constitute a disproportionate number of the aged' (Pomper 2001: 139).
- Since the 1970s, large numbers of white men have switched to the Republican Party. The shift appears to have been a response to the Democrats' growing association with 'tax and spend' policies, affirmative action programmes, and the expansion of welfare provision. From the perspective of many white men, the Democrats appeared to have abandoned their interests.

However, although there are significant differences in terms of voting behaviour between men and women, the nature of the gap should not be exaggerated. In 2000, more white women voted for Bush than Gore. Furthermore, other gaps are significantly larger than the gender gap. There are bigger gulfs between urban and rural voters, higher and lower income groups, and the different races (Ashford 1996: 66).

Short-term factors

Stephen J. Wayne talks of dealignment. He points to the declining proportion of committed party identifiers, and stresses the weakening of traditional attachments to the parties: 'while class, religion, and geography are still related to party identification and voting behaviour, they are not as strongly related as they were in the past. Voters are less influenced by group cues. They exercise a more independent judgement on election day, a judgement that is less predictable and more subject to be influenced by the campaign itself' (Wayne 1992: 77). As Chapter 9 noted, dealignment – and the associated claim that, as a consequence, short-term variables such as the character of the campaign have become much more important – is open to question. The parties still command strong loyalties. Nonetheless, almost all observers acknowledge that events, issues and personalities play a pivotal role in shaping and structuring electoral contests. Indeed, some portray the electorate as 'consumers' who will 'shop around' for policies that correspond to their interests and switch their vote when they are dissatisfied.

The process is partly retrospective. People make a rational assessment of a party or candidate's record in office. As Morris Fiorina argues, voters keep 'a running tally of retrospective evaluations of party promises and performance' (quoted in Wayne 1992: 67). However, the electorate looks forward as well as backwards. There are widely shared concerns such as the prospects for the economy and the future of education. Particular issues 'pull' voters towards either the Democratic or the Republican candidates. In 2000, about two-thirds of those concerned about health care were drawn to Al Gore. Those who saw world affairs as of importance were, despite Gore's experience in foreign policy making, more likely to be in the Bush camp. The end-result of all this will depend upon the importance – or *salience* – of the issues. The 'percentage mentioning' column offers a rough guide to this. In overall terms, an individual who is primarily concerned with taxation rates will be drawn towards the GOP, while those primarily concerned with the future of education were more likely to be pulled towards Gore.

Table 10.9 *Issues and the presidential vote, 2000*

	% voting for …		
	Gore	Bush	% mentioning
Economy / jobs	59	37	18
Education	52	44	15
Taxes	17	80	14
World affairs	40	54	12
Health care	64	33	8

Source: adapted from G. M. Pomper (2001), 'The presidential election', in G. Pomper *et al.*, *The Election of 2000*, New York, Chatham House Publishers, p. 146.

What other variables affect voting decisions in presidential elections? The state of the economy and public perceptions of it are often felt to play a role. Although the economy was just beginning to falter in 2000, the election followed successive years of growth. The US economy expanded by 4.1 per cent in

1999 and 3.8 per cent per cent in 2000. At the same time, inflation remained at minimal levels (Bureau of Economic Analysis 2003). Unemployment had fallen from 7.5 per cent in 1992 – which had contributed to President George H. W. Bush's election defeat – to 4.0 per cent in 2000 (Bureau of Labor Statistics 2003). Statistics such as these are generally felt to assist incumbent office-holders. There were predictions that Al Gore – who had served as vice-president in the Clinton administration for almost eight years – would benefit from the 'feelgood factor'. However, it was not sufficient to ensure his election.

However, the assessments that voters make may not always be clinically rational appraisals of the economy, overall performance, or policy commitments. The campaign strategy, and the images that candidates construct, also play a role. Bill Clinton's 1992 appearances on MTV and Arsenio Hall's talk-show are said to have helped him build a youthful 'in-touch' image of himself. His strategists were also successful in developing negative images of his opponents. During the 1996 election, the Clinton campaign successfully portrayed Senator Dole as an 'extreme' conservative who would withdraw healthcare provision for the elderly and cut back on funding for education. In their election advertisements, the Democrats tied Bob Dole to Newt Gingrich, the Speaker of the House of Representatives, who was already widely regarded as a far-right figure. At the same time, Clinton adopted a number of 'softer' conservative themes. He called for limited government, signed a bill cutting back on welfare, and spoke in support of tough restrictions on wayward teenagers. Although, for their part, the Republicans promised a 15 per cent tax cut, they were unable to establish either taxation or President Clinton's personal character as campaign issues.

In 2000, representations of the candidates' personalities appear to have been pivotal. An ABC News poll, conducted just over a fortnight before the election, suggested that although Gore was regarded as experienced and – to some degree – empathetic, he was not particularly liked. He was, furthermore, too closely associated with the Clinton administration. Although Clinton's approval ratings had held up during his second term, the Lewinsky scandal had tarnished his period of office and created a mood that favoured change.

Table 10.10 *Perceptions of the presidential candidates, 2000 (%)*

	Gore	Bush
He'd provide a fresh start	32	56
He has an appealing personality	50	60
He's honest and trustworthy	49	53
He knows world affairs	72	55
He has the right experience	72	59
He understands your problems	57	46

Source: adapted from ABCNews.com (2000), *Bush Pulls Ahead*, 16 October, abcnews.go.com/sections/politics/DailyNews/poll001016_election.html.

Voting behaviour in Congressional elections

Congressional elections usually have different dynamics. Firstly, incumbency is crucial. The senator or Congressman who holds the post is almost certain to be re-elected, and will remain in office until she or he chooses to stand down.

Table 10.11 *Number of Congressional incumbents who have been defeated, 1990–2000*

Year	House of Representatives	Senate
1990	15	1
1992	24	4
1994	34	2
1996	21	1
1998	6	3
2000	6	6

Source: adapted from N. J. Ornstein, T. E. Mann, and M. J. Malbin (2002), *Vital Statistics on Congress 2001–2002*, Washington DC, The AEI Press, pp. 67–8.

The importance of incumbency as a determinant of election outcomes is even more graphically illustrated if the figures are considered in percentage terms. Even in 1994, amidst a wave of anger against the Democrats, when the Republicans took control of both houses, 92.3 per cent of the Senators who stood for a further term were re-elected. In the House, the figure was 90.2 per cent (Bureau of the Census 1997: 281).

Although the incumbency figures may be an exaggeration, because weak incumbents might decide not to run, fearing that they will lose the election, incumbency is still an important feature of the American electoral process, and requires explanation. State legislatures are responsible for redistricting every ten years. The boundaries between Congressional districts are, it is said, drawn so as to offer an advantage to many incumbent members of the House. Critics point to the bizarre shape of some House districts, and talk of gerrymandering. At the same time, office-holding, at both state and federal level, provides substantial built-in advantages. These include access to the mass media, name-recognition, the provision of constituency services, and the ability to attract large-scale campaign contributions. Serving legislators and office-holders can also press for, and play a part in allocating, federal government 'pork'. (This refers to the provision of government funding projects for members' own districts or states). There is also a circular process. Potential opponents and the other party will generally believe that an incumbent is electorally safe, and they will not therefore mount a credible challenge nor devote resources to the campaign.

The incumbency factor shapes the outcome of all Congressional elections. Very few seats in which there is an incumbent will be competitive. The overall result of the elections and the composition of Congress therefore depend upon the number of 'open seats' in which there is no incumbent.

Secondly – in Congressional elections – district and state issues have traditionally come to the fore. In the celebrated words of Tip O'Neill, who was Speaker of the House between 1977 and 1986, 'all politics is local'. As Marjorie Randon Hershey notes: 'Typically, an incumbent emphasizes a record of service to the district and individual constituents and at the same time criticizes that distant institution called "Congress" whose members inexplicably waste so much public money' (1997: 206).

However, despite O'Neill's comment, the 'local' character of Congressional elections should not be exaggerated. National factors also play a role.

- In presidential election years, there can be a 'coat-tails' effect. A wave of support for a particular presidential ticket can lead increased numbers to vote for Congressional candidates belonging to the same party. In both 1964, Lyndon Johnson's presidential victory was accompanied by a Congressional swing to the Democrats. In 1980, although the reapportionment and redistricting processes may also have been important, Ronald Reagan's campaign appears to have had a significant 'coat-tails' effect, enabling the Republicans to win control of the Senate. This having been said, few other presidential campaigns have had a 'coat-tails' effect. Between 1968 and 2000, the same party controlled the two houses of Congress and the White House at the same time for only six years.
- Some observers explain the outcome of the mid-term elections that are held between presidential contests in terms of 'surge and decline': 'There is a surge in support for the President's party and in turnout in the presidential election, which is then followed by a decline in the mid-term elections . . . between one fifth and one quarter of those who voted in congressional elections in a presidential year failed to do so two years later' (Owens 1995: 3).

  The November 1994 elections could be seen in this way. The sweeping Republican victories could be understood as a reaction against President Clinton's victory two years previously. However, there is little consistency. Bill Clinton's re-election in 1996 did not lead to a subsequent 'decline' in 1998. Instead, the Democrats gained four seats. Similarly, although George W. Bush held the White House, the Republicans made gains in 2002. This suggests that – in place of cyclical processes – the results of Congressional elections are determined by other, perhaps rather more short-term, variables.
- The national mood and centrally co-ordinated campaigns do appear to play a part in shaping election outcomes. In 1994, the GOP won majorities in both houses of Congress after House candidates adopted the Contract with America – which committed them to conservative policy goals – as a national platform. In 2002, George W. Bush campaigned vigorously and raised about $140 million in funding for Republican candidates. His efforts and his popularity helped the party to make gains in both houses. At the

same time, Democratic candidates suffered because of national feelings and perceptions. They were seen as weak and divided on issues such as the prospect of war with Iraq and tax reductions.

Prospects and trends

What about the future? Arguably, long-term trends are shaping the character of voting behaviour. Some observers point to the cleavages that marked out the 2000 presidential election and suggest that these form a basis for voting patterns over the coming decades. In 2000, the Gore vote was largely concentrated in the metropolitan regions structured around cities such as New York, Chicago, Seattle, and Los Angeles. These have a multi-ethnic character, and within their white populations, a significant proportion are single, highly mobile, and have a college education, and a number work in the high-tech sectors of the economy. Identity politics have a hold, and there are visible gay communities such as the Castro in San Francisco and Greenwich Village in New York. The hinterland – including the 'metros' that have not attracted a significant proportion of immigrants – has a markedly different character. It is overwhelmingly white or – in the south-eastern states – biracial. Indeed, some metropolitan areas, most notably Phoenix and Las Vegas, are attracting growing numbers of white migrants from other parts of the US. Communities in these regions appear to be more conservative, and lean disproportionately towards the Republicans. Those who talk of the divide between the 'metros' and the non-metropolitan regions assert that because the minority population is growing and – at the same time – liberal values have taken hold in these cities, there is a 'coming Democratic majority' (Judis and Teixeira 2002).

However, Republican strategists point to a different scenario. Polling data suggests that those who own stocks and bonds – and thereby have a stake in the successes of the market economy – are sympathetic to calls for lower taxes and deregulation, and minimal government. The 'investor class' – which includes about half of all households who now hold shares either directly or through savings funds and retirement accounts – is, therefore, disproportionately likely to vote Republican (*New York Times*, 7 January 2003). Others are less sanguine. Few, they note, hold significant numbers of stocks and bonds. They point, furthermore, to the long-term fall in share values that marked out the beginning of the new century from 2000 onwards, which may not lead to conservatism, but may instead fuel a sense of disillusionment and anti-corporate populism. Some Republicans have gone further. They have argued that 'swing voters' can be won and that some groupings within the Democratic voting bloc can be levered away. In June 2003, there was talk of an electoral offensive by the Republicans directed at Latinos, married women, white union workers, and Jews (Balz 2003).

Box 10.5   Elections, politics and the internet

The political significance of the internet is growing. Campaign websites and mailing lists have become pivotal. As the *Washington Post* noted: 'Since the late 1990s, the Internet has become the fastest-growing resource in US politics. With more than half the nation online today, campaigns, special interests and political parties are hiring professional webmasters and pouring millions of dollars into websites to reach voters, shape opinion and raise money' (*Washington Post*, 29 June 2003).

However, the use of the internet goes further. During the months preceding the 2004 primaries, some of the Democratic presidential aspirants also used other sites as a means of mobilising and organising their supporters. Howard Dean, a former Governor of Vermont, was particularly effective in using Meetup.com, a website that brings together individuals with similar interests. It played a significant part in collecting campaign contributions, recruiting volunteers, and establishing Dean as a credible national figure. By the beginning of July 2003, 56,563 people had signed up on Meetup.com so as to attend gatherings of Dean supporters, compared with just 4,800 for John Kerry (Meetup 2003).

The importance of the internet is not, however, confined to electoral politics. Since about 2000, 'bloggers' have gained a growing profile. The term refers to those who establish and maintain regular, usually daily, commentaries – or 'web logs' – on the internet. Although many blogs have an amateur character and are, in the words of one observer, simply an outlet for 'ego gratification', there are suggestions that blogs are playing an increasingly important role in setting the political agenda.

There were, in particular, claims that the bloggers played a part in toppling Trent Lott as leader of the Senate Republicans in December 2002. Lott had spoken at a 100th birthday ceremony for Strom Thurmond. Lott said in a light-hearted speech that he wished Thurmond – a former supporter of racial segregation – had been elected when he had contested the presidency in 1948. To many, the comments seemed to constitute an endorsement of institutionalised racism. The story was initially ignored by the established news outlets. It only acquired a momentum – which culminated in Lott's resignation – once it had been fanned by bloggers.

References and further reading

Meetup (2003), *Hot Topics*, www.meetup.com.

Conclusion

The road to both Congress and the White House is long, uncertain and arduous. It has, within recent years, become inextricably tied to large-scale funding, much of which – at the least until the passage of the 2002 Bipartisan Campaign Reform Act – evaded the limits imposed by election law. It compels public officials to devote much of their time to campaigning, and allocate correspondingly less time to the process of governing. Furthermore, as Anthony King notes, this makes 'it harder than it would otherwise be for the American system as a whole to deal with some of America's most pressing problems' (1997: 3–4). Nonetheless, a lack of consensus about alternatives and the constraints imposed by the Constitution make fundamental reform an unlikely prospect.

References and further reading

Ashford, N. (1996), 'Angry white males', *Talking Politics*, 9:1, Autumn, 64–8.

Balz, D. (2003), 'GOP aims for dominance in '04 race – Republicans to seek governing majority by feeding base, courting new voters', *Washington Post*, 22 June, A01.

Bennett, A. J. (1993), *American Government and Politics 1993*, Godalming, the author.

Bennett, A. J. (1997), *American Government and Politics 1997*, Godalming, the author.

Bennett, A. J. (2000), *American Government and Politics 1997*, Godalming, the author.

Boston.com (2000), *South Carolina Gives Bush Major GOP Primary Win*, www.boston .com/news/politics/campaign2000/news/South_Carolina_gives_Bush_major_GOP_primary_win+.shtml.

Brubaker, S. C. (1998), 'The limits of campaign spending limits', *The Public Interest*, 133, Fall, 33–54.

Bureau of Economic Analysis (2003), *Gross Domestic Product – Percentage Change from Preceding Period*, www.bea.doc.gov/bea/dn/gdpchg.xls.

Bureau of Labor Statistics (2003), *Unemployment Rate*, data.bls.gov/servlet/SurveyOutputServlet?data_tool=latest_numbers&series_id=LNU04000000&years_option=all_years&periods_option=specific_periods&periods=Annual+Data.

Bureau of the Census (1997), *Statistical Abstract of the United States*, Washington DC, US Department of Commerce.

Center for Voting and Democracy (2003), *Reform Options for the Electoral College*, www.fairvote.org/e_college/reform.htm#50Runoff.

CNN.com (2000a), *Poll: Convention 'Bounce' Pulls Gore Even with Bush*, 21 August, edition.cnn.com/2000/ALLPOLITICS/stories/08/21/cnn.poll/.

CNN.com (2000b), *Stuart Rothenberg: Understanding the Convention 'Bounce' Not Always Simple*, 3 August, edition.cnn.com/ALLPOLITICS/analysis/rothenberg/2000/08/03/.

Committee for the Study of the American Electorate (1998), *Primary Turnout Reaching Record Lows*, 29 June, http://tap.epn.org/csae/cgans.html.

Congressional Quarterly (1997), *Selecting the President: From 1789 to 1996*, Washington DC, CQ Press.

Durham, M. (1996), 'The fall and rise of the Christian right in America', *Politics Review*, 5:4, April, 26–8.

FECwatch (2003), *Issue Advocacy*, www.fecwatch.org/loopholes/loop3.asp.

Federal Election Commission (2000), *FEC Announces 2000 Presidential Spending Limits*, www.fec.gov/press/preslimits2000.htm.

Flanigan, W. H. and N. H. Zingale (1998), *Political Behavior of the American Electorate*, Washington DC, CQ Press.

Geer, J. G. (1993), 'Assessing the representativeness of electorates in presidential primaries', in E. M. Uslaner (ed.), *American Political Parties: A Reader*, pp. 353–71, Itasca, IL, E. A. Peacock Publishers.

Grant, A. (1995), 'Financing American elections', *Politics Review*, 5:2, November, pp. 9–12.

Hershey, M. R. (1997), 'The Congressional elections', in G. M. Pomper *et al.*, *The Election of 1996: Reports and Interpretations*, pp. 205–39. Chatham, Chatham House.

Judis, J. B. and R. A. Teixeira (2002), *The Emerging Democratic Majority*, New York, Simon and Schuster.

King, A. (1981),'How not to select presidential candidates: a view from Europe', in A. Ranney (ed.), *The American Elections of 1980*, Washington DC, American Enterprise Institute for Public Policy Research, pp. 303–28.

King, A. (1997), *Running Scared: Why Politicians Spend More Time Governing than Campaigning*, New York, Free Press.

Kuttner, R. (1996), 'Why Americans don't vote', in B. Stinebrickner (ed.), *American Government 96/97*, Guilford, CT, Dushkin Publishing Group, pp. 164–6.

Ladd, E. C. (1996), 'The 1994 Congressional elections: the postindustrial realignment continues', in B. Stinebrickner (ed.), *American Government 96/97*, Guilford, CT, Dushkin Publishing Group, pp. 167–80.

Maidment, R. and M. Dawson (1994), *The United States in the Twentieth Century: Key Documents*, London, Hodder and Stoughton in association with the Open University.

Moore, M. (2000), 'Stop Bush's Theft of the People's Will', *disinformation*, www.disinfo.com/pages/article/id515/pg1/.

Norris, P. (1992), 'The 1992 US primaries: if it ain't broke don't fix it', *Parliamentary Affairs*, ksghome.harvard.edu/~.pnorris.shorenstein.ksg/ articles.htm.

Owens, J. (1995), 'The 1994 US mid-term elections', *Politics Review*, 4:4, April, 2–6.

Polsby, N. W. and A. Wildavsky (1996), *Presidential Elections: Strategies and Structures in American Politics*, Chatham, Chatham House.

Pomper, G. M. (1997),'The presidential election', in G. M. Pomper *et al.*, *The Elections of 1996: Reports and Interpretations*, Chatham, Chatham House, pp. 173–204.

Pomper, G. M. (2001), 'The presidential election', in G. Pomper *et al.*, *The Election of 2000*, New York, Chatham House Publishers, pp. 125–54.

Putnam, R. D. (2000), *Bowling Alone: The Collapse and Revival of American Community*, New York, Simon and Schuster.

Salant, J. D. (2000), 'McCain outraised Bush in January', www.boston.com/news/politics/campaign2000/news/McCain_outraised_Bush_in_January.shtm.

Schneider, W. (2002), 'Let the "invisible primary" begin', *The Atlantic Online*, 24 December, www.theatlantic.com/politics/nj/schneider2002-12-24.htm.

Thomsen, S. (2000), 'Gore rolls up delegates in Michigan, Minnesota, Arizona', www.boston.com/news/politics/campaign2000/news/Gore_rolls_up_delegates_in_Michigan_Minnesota_Arizona.shtml.

Wattenberg, M. P. (1991), *The Rise of Candidate-Centered Politics*, Cambridge, MA, Harvard University Press.

Wayne, S. J. (1992), *The Road to the White House 1992: The Politics of Presidential Selection*, New York, St Martin's Press.

11

Interest groups and lobbying

Interest groups are the basis of the 'persuasion industry'. They attempt to persuade – or 'lobby' – decision-makers at federal, state and local level. In contrast to political parties, they do not generally seek to win elected office.

Organised groupings have long been a characteristic feature of American politics. As early as the 1830s, Alexis de Tocqueville was struck by them. 'In no country in the world', he asserted, 'has the principle of association been more successfully used, or applied to a greater multitude of objects, than in America' (1984: 95). Over the past century, interest groups – or political advocacy groups – have developed alongside the religious and civic groupings that Tocqueville described and have, within recent years, proliferated. At the same time, corporations have become much more assertive and astute in terms of lobbying techniques. In 1991, *National Journal* identified 328 groups, ninety-eight think tanks, 288 trade and professional associations, and 682 company headquarters in Washington DC (Judis 1995b: 257). In 1997, an estimated $1.2 billion was spent by those seeking to influence the federal government (Abramson 1998). K Street in Washington DC is now synonymous with the lobbying industry.

Why is there so much group activity in the US?

- The American system of government is particularly open to external influence, and this encourages the creation of organised interests. There are large numbers of openings – or access points – that enable groups to reach decision-makers. These include the three branches of government in Washington DC, as well as the different tiers of state and local government. The courts are open to persuasion in a way that is prohibited in many other countries. At the same time, the use of primaries to determine the parties' candidates and the system of election finance present countless opportunities that enable organisations to advance their arguments and interests.
- Since the turn of the century, commerce and industry have been subject to increasing regulatory control by the federal government. Companies and 'producer groups' have, as a consequence, sought to influence those in

249

Congress and the federal bureaucracy who shape business activity and set a framework for it.

- Some observers describe the US – and other Western nations – as 'post-industrial' societies. Basic, material needs are now more or less guaranteed. This has led people to turn to other issues – such as the state of the environment – with growing vigour.

- During the latter half of the twentieth century, new forms of identity emerged. Increasingly, people defined themselves not only as Americans but also upon the basis of race, ethnicity, gender, and age. There has been a proliferation of sub-cultures. These provided a basis for both new social movements and organised groupings.

- Although American public culture has always incorporated a suspicion of government, there was also a degree of deference towards decision-makers. For example, until the era of Vietnam and Watergate, press coverage of the president was largely respectful, and there was a degree of self-censorship. The breakdown of this, the growth of alternative sources of news and information, and the increasingly ideological and partisan character of US politics, laid a basis for the growth of thinktanks. These are research organisations that publish in-depth reports surveying the rationale behind, and the implications of, particular public policy options. Although the tax-exempt status that many thinktanks have gained prevents them from lobbying or campaigning directly, many are politically aligned, and their work structures the activities of legislators. The Progressive Policy Institute is broadly liberal in its orientation. The Heritage Foundation and the American Enterprise Institute are conservative.

- Growing distrust of government also contributed to the emergence and development of organisations claiming to represent the 'public interest'. Public interest groups address questions traditionally under-represented by interest groups. The most well-known is Common Cause. Founded in August 1970, it was set up to challenge the hold that 'special interests' appeared to maintain over the workings of government. It has, for example, campaigned for the imposition of further spending limits in elections and the introduction of tighter controls on lobbyists. Common Cause has also called for more environmental and urban legislation.

This chapter considers the work of interest groups. It outlines different types of interest group, assesses the methods that they employ, and asks two questions. To what extent do groups influence decision-makers? Do they play a negative or a positive role in the political process?

Types of interest groups

Although the dividing lines are sometimes blurred, interest groups can be classified in terms of *issue* and *protective* groups. Issue groups – which are sometimes also described as *advocacy* or *cause* groups – are organisations that lobby on behalf of others or campaign for a broad political, social or cultural cause. The Children's Defense Fund 'exists to provide a strong and effective voice for all the children of America who cannot vote, lobby, or speak for themselves'. The National Abortion and Reproductive Rights Action League – now renamed NARAL Pro-Choice America – calls for the legal availability of abortion. The Sierra Club campaigns for the preservation of the natural habitat. The Family Research Council promotes a traditionalist approach towards family life.

Protective groupings advance and defend their own interests and those of their membership. They can be divided into a number of categories:

1 There are business groups, including organisations such the National Association of Manufacturers, which claims a membership of about fourteen thousand businesses. Furthermore, companies themselves seek to influence the decision-making process. They might, for example, be seeking federal government contracts. Other companies are affected by regulatory commissions and agencies such as the Interstate Commerce Commission and the Occupational Safety and Health Administration.

2 There are trades – or labour – unions. Sixty-five are brought together by the American Federation of Labor–Congress of Industrial Organizations (AFL–CIO), a voluntary federation created in 1955. By playing this role, the AFL–CIO is – in the language of interest group typologies – a *peak association*. Although the unions do play a role in American industrial life, they are significantly weaker than in Europe. In 2002, only 13.2 per cent of workers were union members. Within the private sector, the figure was – at 8.5 per cent – even lower. The unions were badly hit by the recessions in the early 1980s and 1990s. They were also affected by the long-term process of *deindustrialisation* – the decline of the manufacturing sector, where the unions traditionally had a strong hold. The public sector has, however, held out against the trend. In 2002, those employed by the national, state, or local governments had a union membership rate of 37.5 per cent.

3 There are professional associations, such as the American Medical Association (AMA), representing doctors, and the American Bar Association (ABA), which puts forward the interests of lawyers. Until the Bush administration made a policy switch, the ABA traditionally had an institutionalised role in the selection of federal judges. It awarded 'ratings' to nominees prior to their consideration by the Senate Judiciary Committee.

4 State and local governments also act as pressure groups. As Chapter 8 established, although some of the individual states have offices in Washington DC, they are also represented through organisations such as the National Governors Association and the National Council of State Legislatures.

As well as issue and protective groupings, there are also some *hybrid* organisations that can be placed somewhere between protective and issue groups. They work on behalf of their membership – which has its own distinct, sectional interests – but also campaign for others beyond their own ranks. For example, the National Rifle Association (NRA) protects the rights of gun-owners, but also campaigns, more broadly, to uphold the right to 'bear arms'.

Box 11.1   African-American interest groups

Black politics were dominated for much of the twentieth century by organisations such as the National Association for the Advancement of Colored People (NAACP) and the National Urban League (NUL). The NAACP was formed in 1909. Its strategy rested on lobbying and the bringing of appropriate cases before the courts. It won some important, but inevitably limited, early victories that extended black rights. Founded in 1911, the NUL drew together moderate African-Americans, social workers, and wealthy white philanthropists. It sought to improve living conditions in the cities. While the NAACP and the NUL concentrated on winning modest, incremental reforms, the civil rights protests of the 1950s and 1960s led to the formation of other organisations, most notably the Southern Christian Leadership Conference, which was led by Martin Luther King. They used direct action – such as marches and sit-ins – to protest against segregation.

However, the civil rights organisations have, at times, been challenged by more militant black nationalist groups. In the early 1920s, Marcus Garvey led a 'back to Africa' movement. In the late 1960s, there were calls for 'black power', and groups such as the 'Black Panthers' attracted attention. In recent years, the Nation of Islam (NoI) has been prominent. Under the leadership of Louis Farrakhan, it established the committees that organised the *Million Man March* in October 1995. The NoI calls for separate black territory within the US, and demands reparations for the years of slavery.

Websites

Nation of Islam – www.noi.org/.
National Association for the Advancement of Colored People – www.naacp.org/.
National Urban League – www.nul.org/.

Methods of influence

The methods of influence used by an interest group are tied to the *access points* – openings to the decision-makers – that are available to it. If an organisation resorts to mass action – such as demonstrations or symbolic protests – this can be because access points have been closed off. It could therefore be argued that the October 1995 Million Man March – a mass protest of black men in Washington DC, which mobilised at least 400,000 – reflected the political weakness of black political organisations rather than their strength. More influential and established interest groups seek to influence the political process by working through established channels. They direct their efforts towards all three branches of the federal government, state authorities, and local forms of government.

The legislative branch

The US Congress has long been open to outside influence. This is because party loyalties have traditionally been weak. Voting decisions in Congress are more a matter of individual choice than in the European legislatures, where more rigid forms of party discipline are imposed.

As Chapter 5 noted, a lobbying 'industry' has grown up around Capitol Hill. The Federal Lobby Directory lists 28,005 individual lobbyists, together with 2,771 lobbying firms and organisations, serving 25,714 clients (Political Moneyline 2003). The industry is dominated by corporate interests, and spending levels are vast. In total, during the first six months of 1999, companies and organisations devoted $697 million to lobbying Congress and federal agencies. A watchdog group observed that this represented $116 million a month (CNN.com 2000). The finance, insurance and real estate (FIRE) industry spends the largest amounts on lobbying, although the health sector does not lag not far behind.

Table 11.1 *The top five lobbyists, by spending levels*

	Lobbying expenditure			
	1999	1998	1997	Average growth (%)
1 Chamber of Commerce of the US	18,760,000	17,000,000	14,240,000	14.80%
2 American Medical Association	18,180,000	16,820,000	17,280,000	2.60%
3 Philip Morris	14,820,000	23,148,000	16,248,000	−4.50%
4 American Hospital Association	12,480,000	10,520,000	7,880,000	25.80%
5 Exxon Mobil Corporation	11,695,800	11,960,000	10,454,660	5.80%

Source: adapted from Opensecrets.org (2003), *Who's Giving – Top Spenders*, www.opensecrets.org/pubs/lobby00/topspenders.asp.

What forms does lobbying take? It utilises formal channels, but also employs informal ties and networks. Those engaged in the process will monitor and raise issues that have a direct or indirect impact on their interests or – if they are a lobbying firm – those of their clients. A 1999 study of the 12,113 lobbyists who were active during this period revealed that 2,945 devoted their working time to tax policy. It was the most heavily lobbied issue. More than 2,000 lobbyists worked on budget and appropriations policy, health care, and domestic and international trade. The least important issue – in terms of lobbying time – was unemployment. It was raised by only sixteen lobbyists (Opensecrets.org 2003).

Box 11.2   How lobbyists spend their time

Alerting client about issues	4.3
Developing policy or strategy	4.3
Maintaining relations with government	3.8
Making informal contacts with officials	3.7
Monitoring proposed changes in rules and laws	3.7
Providing information to officials	3.5
Preparing testimony or official comments	3.4
Commentary for press, public speaking	3.2
Mobilising grass roots support	3.0
Monitoring interest groups	2.8
Testifying	2.7
Drafting proposed legislation or regulations	2.7
Making contacts with opposition	2.6
Making contacts with allies	2.5
Resolving internal organisational disputes	2.5
Litigation	2.1
Arranging for political contributions	2.0
Working for *amicus* briefs	1.6

Note: The figures – which were collected during the 1980s – show the frequency of lobbyists' task performance (1 = never; 5 = regularly).

Source: adapted from Fortune.com (2001), www.fortune.com/fortune/power25.

Lobbying efforts can be strengthened and reinforced through advertisements in the papers, and on television and radio. NARAL Pro-Choice America spent $3,407,000 on advertising in 2001. Five of the television advertisements warned against President Bush's position on abortion. NARAL ran three other advertisements, with women using language that stressed personal choice and included 'my right to choose', 'free will', and 'freedom to choose'. For its part, the Club for Growth – a conservative grouping that calls for low taxes and limited government – sponsored a television advertisement in 2001 shown in the Washington DC area. It reproduced the 1950s horror film genre, and said that President Bush's plan for lower taxes would 'stop the Tax Blob' that has 'taken over Washington' and is 'crushing the American economy'. (Annenberg Public Policy Center 2003).

Whereas some, particularly companies, concentrate their resources on lobbying activities, other groups and organisations exploit the opportunities for intervention offered by elections. Some publish 'ratings' of incumbent Congressional candidates based upon their voting record. They seek to highlight his or her attitude towards the issues that they regard as pivotal, and thereby to apply a degree of leverage.

Both Americans for Democratic Action (ADA) and the American Conservative Union issue ratings in the form of percentages. While the ADA is a liberal organisation founded in 1947, the ACU is – in its words – committed to 'capitalism, belief in the doctrine of original intent of the framers of the Constitution, confidence in traditional moral values, and commitment to a strong national defense' (American Conservative Union (2003), *About Us*, www.conservative.org/about/default.asp). A high rating indicates that the senator or Congress generally votes in line with the organisation's thinking. The 2000 ratings confirm that Rick Santorum is unambiguously committed to conservative policies. Nancy Pelosi – who became House Minority Leader at the end of 2002 – is among the more liberal members of the Democratic Party.

Table 11.2 *Interest group ratings, 2000*

	Americans for Democratic Action	American Conservative Union
Senate		
John McCain (R – Arizona)	5	81
Joseph Lieberman (D – Connecticut)	75	20
Edward Kennedy (D – Massachusetts)	90	12
Rick Santorum (R – Pennsylvania)	0	100
House of Representatives		
Nancy Pelosi (D – California 8)	100	8
Barney Frank (D – Massachusetts 4)	95	12
Bob Ney (R – Ohio 18)	20	83
Tom DeLay (R – Texas 22)	0	88

Source: adapted from N. J. Ornstein, T. E. Mann, and M. J. Malbin (2002), *Vital Statistics on Congress 2001–2002*, pp. 194–227. Washington DC, The AEI Press.

The Gun Owners of America also issues ratings on members of Congress and candidates, but these take the form of grades rather than percentages.

Some organisations produce 'voter guides' during pre-election periods. Although they do not explicitly call for a vote for or against a particular candidate, their preferred choice is often readily evident. In the run-up to the November 2000 elections, the Christian Coalition of America distributed 70 million voter guides throughout all 50 states. They list the responses of the different candidates to questions about issues such as part-birth abortion, school prayer, the teaching of Biblical beliefs alongside Darwinist theory, abstinence-based sex education, and educational vouchers that allow a measure of parental choice.

Financial contributions to candidates are also pivotal. They are channelled through 'connected' political action committees (PACs) that may – under campaign finance law – solicit contributions of up to $5,000 from a single individual. PACs may then contribute $5,000 per candidate, per federal election. So long as the PAC acts independently from a particular candidate, and respects limits upon its donations to national political parties during presidential election campaigns, it is not otherwise subject to spending restrictions.

Box 11.3   Gun Owners of America Senate ratings

A+	Pro-Gun Leader: introduces pro-gun legislation.
A	Pro-Gun Voter: philosophically sound.
A– and B	Pro-Gun compromiser: generally leans our way.
C	Leans Our Way: occasionally.
D	Leans Anti-Gun: usually against us.
F	Anti-Gun Voter: a philosophically committed anti-gunner.
F–	Anti-Gun Leader: outspoken anti-gun advocate who carries anti-gun legislation.
NR	Not rated: Refused to answer his or her questionnaire; no track record.

Source: adapted from Gun Owners of America (2003), *GOA Senate Ratings for the 106th Congress*, www.gunowners.org/106srat.htm.

The executive branch

Successive presidents and their aides have been accused of having too close an association with particular interests or organisations. President George W. Bush and Vice-President Dick Cheney are said to have ties with the oil industry. However, in practice, although they are screened by the Office of Management and Budget (OMB), many executive branch decisions – particularly the issuing of regulations – are taken by the departments, agencies, and commissions rather than the administration. Interest groups therefore seek to establish a close relationship with sections of the federal bureaucracy. These ties have been subject to considerable criticism, and a number of observers argue that the personnel working within the government apparatus have, in effect been 'captured' by powerful interest groups. Others go further, and talk of 'iron triangles' (see Chapter 7).

The judicial branch

In contrast with the UK, the courts are open to some forms of lobbying. Interest groups can submit *amicus curiae* – or 'friend of the court' – briefings to the Supreme Court. They can be submitted – in the words of the Chief Justice – by 'someone who is not a party to the litigation, but who believes that the court's decision may affect its interest' (Rehnquist 1987: 89).

Amicus briefs can be put forward at different stages. Some will urge the Court to hear a particular case or, in the language of the Court, grant *certiorari* ('cert'). Some studies suggest that there is a relationship between the number of *amicus* briefs that have been filed and the Court's decision to grant cert. Other briefs urge the Court to rule on a case in a particular way.

The overall number of *amicus* briefs that are being filed to the Supreme Court has grown significantly. Indeed, there has been an 800 per cent increease since the mid-1940s. Controversial cases – such as those concerning affirmative action or abortion – attract significant numbers of briefs. In 1989, seventy-eight were submitted to the Court before it considered *Webster v. Reproductive Health Services*. Of these, forty-seven were put forward by pro-life groups, and thirty-one by pro-choice organisations (McKeever 1997: 109).

If a group is to put forward a brief, it must first seek written consent from all those who are directly involved in the case. If one or the other side has an objection, the group must ask the Court for a 'motion of leave'. However, over 80 per cent of such motions are granted.

To what extent do *amicus* briefs influence Court rulings? Although briefs filed by political advocacy groups such as the NAACP and the ACLU are not accorded the degree of respect that seems to be given to those filed by the Solicitor-General – who acts on behalf of the administration – or those acting for the states, they have an impact. Brendan I. Koerner (2003) argues that, although they rarely decide a case, they can be important in drawing out the long-term consequences of ruling in a particular way. When the cases challenging the constitutionality of affirmative action (*Gratz v. Bollinger* and *Grutter v. Bollinger*) were under consideration in 2003, over a hundred *amicus* briefs were filed. One was on behalf of some former military leaders, including General Norman Schwarzkopf, who led allied forces during the 1991 Gulf War. It argued that a ruling against affirmative action programmes would hold back efforts to build a racially and socially diverse officer corps.

Interest groups can also 'sponsor' a litigant by providing funding and the services of lawyers when cases are brought to the courts. There are some celebrated examples. In 1925, the American Civil Liberties Union (ACLU), and a Tennessee teacher, John Scopes, invited prosecution and a subsequent court battle by teaching Darwin's theory of evolution in defiance of state law. Tennessee legislators still insisted upon the veracity of the account of creation given in the Book of Genesis. Almost thirty years later, in 1954, the National Association for the Advancement of Colored People 'sponsored' a number of school desegegration cases. In the most celebrated of these, *Brown v. Board of Education (Topeka, Kansas)* (1954), the NAACP backed the case of Oliver Brown, who was seeking to ensure that his daughter could attend a nearby school rather than a 'colored school' some distance away.

Groups also play a role in the appointment process. Supreme Court Justices are nominated by the president, but are subject to confirmation by the Senate. Some recent appointments have attracted particular controversy. In 1987, Judge Robert Bork was attacked by critics – who regarded him as an ultra-conservative – both inside and outside the Senate. The ACLU charged that he was 'unfit' to serve. People for the American Way, an organisation established to challenge the claims of the Christian Right, launched a $2 million media campaign opposing the nomination (Hinkson Craig and O'Brien 1993:

180–2). If appointed to the Court, Bork would, it was alleged, oppose rulings such as *Roe v. Wade* (1973), thereby undermining the concept of abortion as a constitutional right.

State government

In a federal system of government, many decisions are made at a state rather than a national level. Interest groups, companies, and the lobbyists who act on their behalf, therefore have a presence in the different state capitals as well as in Washington DC. Indeed, a 2003 study of thirty-nine states suggested that $715 million was spent by lobbyists in the different state capitals during the course of 2002. As the Center for Public Integrity, which conducted the survey, recorded: 'More than 34,000 of those interests – companies, issue organizations, labor unions and others – hired a whopping 42,000 individuals to do just that, averaging almost 6 lobbyists – and almost $130,000 – per legislator' (Center for Public Integrity 2003a).

Table 11.3 *Lobbying in selected states: the biggest spenders*

State	Total 2002 lobby expenditure ($)	Total 2001 lobby expenditure ($)	No. of lobbyists	No. of lobbyist employers
California	197,230,234	188,596,080	1,012	2,359
New York	92,000,000	80,400,000	3,332	1,835
Massachusetts	53,739,651	53,514,941	650	1,000
Minnesota	41,308,993	8,305,408	1,490	1,219
Washington	33,192,837	30,414,601	1,000	1,000
Totals	715,930,207	689,574,646	43,980	35,416

Source: adapted from Center for Public Integrity (2003), *Lobby Spending,* 15 May, www.publicintegrity.org/dtaweb/index.asp?L1=20&L2=10&L3=23&L4=12&L5=0&State= &Display=DRFEC.

The impact of interest groups

What conclusions can be drawn about the overall influence of interest groups in the US political system? Although it does not consider the role of companies, *Fortune* magazine has made a number of studies based upon the perceptions of Washington 'insiders'. Its 2001 Power 25 survey reported that the most effective organisations were – in rank order – the National Rifle Association (NRA), the American Association of Retired Persons (AARP), and the National Federation of Independent Business (Companion). The study compared the ordering of groups with the position that they occupied three years previously, and assessed the different ways in which the groups were perceived by Democratic and Republican supporters. Whereas, for example, the AFL–CIO

Table 11.4 *Washington's 'power 25', 2001*

	Overall rank	Previous rank	Democratic rank	GOP rank
National Rifle Association of America	1	2	2	1
AARP	2	1	1	3
National Federation of Independent Business	3	2	6	2
American Israel Public Affairs Committee	4	4	3	4
Association of Trial Lawyers of America	5	6	5	7
American Federation of Labor-Congress of Industrial Organizations	6	5	4	12
Chamber of Commerce of the United States of America	7	7	9	5
National Beer Wholesalers Association	8	19	28	6
National Association of Realtors	9	15	24	8
National Association of Manufacturers	10	14	26	9
National Association of Home Builders of the United States	11	16	17	15
American Medical Association	12	13	12	18
American Hospital Association	13	31	15	17
National Education Association of the United States	14	9	7	34
American Farm Bureau Federation	15	21	29	11
Motion Picture Association of America	16	17	8	23
National Association of Broadcasters	17	20	13	19
National Right to Life Committee	18	8	31	10
Health Insurance Association of America	19	25	14	22
National Restaurant Association	20	10	34	13
National Governors' Association	21	12	25	20
Recording Industry Association of America	22	40	16	28
American Bankers Association	23	11	23	27
Pharmaceutical Research & Manufacturers of America	24	28	27	29
International Brotherhood of Teamsters	25	23	11	41

Source: adapted from Fortune.com (2001), *The Power 25: Top Lobbying Groups*, 28 May, www.fortune.com/fortune/power25 and J. H. Birnbaum (2001), *Power 25 2001: Whose Party Is It?*, 2 August, www.fortune.com/fortune/washington/0,15704,373095,00.html.

was seen by Democrats as the fourth most influential organisation in Washington DC, Republicans placed them in twelfth position.

Why are some groups – such as the National Rifle Association (NRA) – more influential than others?

- The numerical size of an organisation is important. The NRA claims a membership of three million. The American Association of Retired Persons (AARP) has grown in importance as its membership has expanded. In 1965, it had fewer than a million members. By 1980, it had risen to about twelve million. By the beginning of the new century, it spoke for over 35 million.

- The commitment of the membership to the organisation's goals also plays a role. For many in the NRA's ranks, gun rights define their commitment to liberty and their way of life. For them this is a pivotal issue, and their dedication to gun ownership makes the NRA a formidable opponent. The NRA has a committed group of activists – estimated at about 175,000 – who will turn out with little notice to lobby a member of Congress or canvass for a candidate.
- Size and commitment provide the basis for a third reason why groups such as the NRA exert leverage – they can deliver votes. Although they can only make a difference of a few percentage points, this may be sufficient – in a close race – to ensure victory or defeat.
- An organisation's financial resources can be decisive. A recent estimate suggested that the NRA had an annual budget of $137 million, enabling it to mount campaigns, hire staff, and employ lobbyists.
- The strategic use of campaign finance contributions is also important. The NRA's political action committee – the Political Victory Fund – has about $7 million that is distributed to sympathetic election candidates, who are mostly Republicans.
- The NRA has also been willing to use the courts. It has acted as plaintiff, but has also submitted *amicus curiae* briefs. In 2000, it filed a brief in a case (*US v. Emerson*) heard before the Fifth Circuit Court of Appeals arguing against a federal law prohibiting those with a history of domestic violence – and under a restraining order – from possessing firearms. Citing precedent, the NRA asserted that 'such a sweeping and arbitrary infringement on the right to keep and bear arms violates the Second Amendment' (National Rifle Association – Institute of Legislative Action 2000).
- The political strategy that an organisation adopts also plays a role. One reason for the NRA's successes lies in its resolutely single-minded pursuit of its goals. Others, however, have won influence because they have shown a degree of tactical flexibility. During the early and mid-1990s the Christian Coalition, a conservative grouping committed to 'family values', gained support because it sought to allay the fears of those who saw the organisation's members as religious extremists. Its executive director, Ralph Reed, ensured that it spoke in terms of understanding and tolerance. The abrasively harsh tones that had sometimes been adopted by those associated with the Christian right were eschewed. However, US Term Limits appears to have lost supporters and allies because it was inflexible and refused to compromise. It insisted upon three two-year terms for House members, and two six-year terms for the Senate.
- The influence of an interest group may also rest on the degree to which it can forge a close relationship with key decision-makers in the legislative branch. In her account of the 104th Congress (1995–97), Elizabeth Drew records claims that lobbyists acting on behalf of 'special interests' – most especially

large-scale companies – wrote legislation for Congressmen (1997: 116). It is said that a lobbyist working for the energy and petrochemical industries wrote the first draft of a bill introducing a moratorium – or 'freeze' – on the federal regulations that governed the way in which the industry operated.

- Some observers emphasise the importance of ties between groups – and, to a greater extent, companies – and the federal bureaucracy. They assert that 'subgovernments' or 'iron triangles' have been constructed (see Chapter 7). Some federal government programmes seem to provide particularly fertile ground for their emergence. Theodore Lowi and Benjamin Ginsberg suggest that defence spending is – at least in part – governed by an 'iron triangle'. The Senate Armed Services Committee and the House National Security Committee are bound together with government departments and agencies (such as the Department of Defense or NASA), and large contractors, most notably Boeing, Lockheed Martin, and McDonnell Douglas (1992: 296). They collaborate so as to ensure that defence expenditure is maintained at high levels.

As Paul E. Peterson and Mark Rom note, the development of 'impact aid' was also shaped by an 'iron triangle'. The programme began during the Second World War. It initially offered federal government financial assistance to those school districts that had large concentrations of military personnel living within their areas of jurisdiction. 'Impact aid' was progressively extended so as

---

Box 11.4   Public choice theory and interest groups

Why do some interest groups grow, and why do others fail to attract members? Public choice theory, which employs the language, philosophy and methodology of microeconomics, and assumes that although those involved in politics may talk in terms of ideals and the national interest, they are essentially rational pursuers of their own self-interest, offers one answer.

In his book, *The Logic of Collective Action*, Mancur Olson, a public choice theorist, argues that interest groups seeking potential advantages or benefits that would be distributed among very large numbers of people face particular difficulties. In such circumstances, individuals will generally leave commitment and action to others. They are less likely to join such a campaign, and will instead become 'free riders'. For example, the National Taxpayers Union attracted about a quarter of a million members. However, this only represented about one in 640 taxpayers. In contrast, an interest group seeking tax concessions on behalf of a relatively small group of companies would be much more likely to gain members and establish itself.

Further reading

Ashford, N. and S. Davies (eds) (1991), *A Dictionary of Conservative and Libertarian Thought*, London, Routledge, pp. 214–15.

to provide additional funding for the child of every federal employee – whether military or civilian. The National Association of Impacted Districts used a strategy of 'quiet insider negotiation, partisan neutrality, and the cultivation of key influentials' (Peterson and Rom 1988: 230). Few federal legislators were willing to risk its hostility, and despite their misgivings, successive presidents agreed to the renewal of the programme.

Limits and constraints

Critics of the American political system emphasise what they regard as the disproportionate influence of the most wealthy and powerful pressure groups. They point, in particular, to the role of money and, for example, the implications of 'iron triangles'. However, there are commentators who suggest that these claims are exaggerated. In a study of organisations representing the farming industry, William P. Browne suggests that Congressmen prefer to work with trusted 'confidants' in their home districts or states rather than with Washington-based interest groups (1995: 281). There are a number of reasons why the role of interest groups may, in practice, be limited:

1 The evidence suggesting that candidates can be 'bought' with financial contributions is open to argument. There are, firstly, methodological objections. Timothy Groseclose, Jeffrey Milyo and David Primo argue that: 'The causality can be reversed . . . For example, a member of Congress may represent a district populated by NRA-friendly hunters. The representative may indeed support NRA-backed legislation because he does not wish to alienate voters, not necessarily because the NRA made a contribution' (Groseclose 2001).

   Secondly, even if it is accepted that spending brings influence, other variables may be more significant. In its 1997 Power 25 survey, *Fortune* magazine found that only three among the top ten – the Association of Trial Lawyers of America, the American Israel Public Affairs Committee, and the American Medical Association – owed their influence to substantial campaign contributions. The others, *Fortune* concluded, gained their position by mobilising their grassroots supporters, winning support in a Congressman's district, and building a relationship with a politician's staff members.

2 Many pressure groups face an 'equal and opposite reaction'. This reins in their influence. People for Ethical Treatment of Animals (PETA) was founded in 1980, and by 1994, claimed 370, 000 members. It campaigns for an end to experimentation on animals. PETA's efforts have however been countered by Putting People First (PPF), which insists that human interests should be considered above those of animals. Similarly, the NRA is matched by Handgun Control. Furthermore, although there are large numbers of 'pro-life' groupings – including single-issue organisations such as the National Right to Life Committee – they are opposed by counter-organisations such as NARAL Pro-

Choice America and Planned Parenthood. The trade unions – represented through the American Federation of Labor – Congress of Industrial Organisations (AFL–CIO) – face counter-pressures from business organisations such as the National Association of Manufacturers.

3 The concept of influence should be assessed. A distinction should be drawn between negative influence – through which the proposals put forward by others can be hindered, amended, or halted – and positive influence that enables a group to bring about the forms of change that it seeks.

The influence of US pressure groups is almost always negative in character. The NRA has the ability to prevent further restrictions on 'gun rights' – although it has had to accept the Brady bill, which imposed a five-day waiting period before a handgun could be purchased, and a ban on 19 categories of assault weapons – but, at the same time, it cannot enlarge them. In 1993–94, interest groups could prevent the Clinton health care plan being adopted. The National Federation of Independent Businesses feared the costs that would be imposed by universal coverage. Others were concerned that reform might increase the availability of abortion. The Health Insurance Association of America ran a series of TV advertisements (based around the fictional characters of 'Harry and Louise') asserting that the Clinton plan would deny people the right to choose their own form of health insurance (Cigler and Loomis 1995: 401–3). Interest groups did not, however, have the ability to agree upon and ensure the passage of an alternative plan.

4 Some of the interest groups that became entrenched within the government machine – through the development of 'iron triangles' – lost their grip during the 1980s. The Reagan Administration and Congress worked together in cutting federal government spending. Within this framework, budget proposals put forward by government agencies, which had been regarded as inviolable, became subject to close scrutiny by the Office of Management and Budget (OMB), Congressional committees, and party leaders. Furthermore, in 1986 Congress removed tax concessions from a number of organisations. Peterson and Rom claim that these moves reflect the decline of the 'iron triangle'. Both the President and Congress demonstrated that they had the ability 'to make fairly radical policy changes and are not captive to forces limiting them to minor, incremental adjustments' (Peterson and Rom 1988: 233).

Criticisms of interest group activity

Should interest group activity be seen in negative or positive terms? The 'persuasion industry' has been subject to intense criticism in recent years. Some of these criticisms – such as the hold of 'iron triangles' over the decision-making process – have already been noted. There are, however, further reasons why interest groups and lobbyists are regarded by some observers with a degree of disdain.

Box 11.5   Social movements

A significant number of contemporary pressure groups are tied to social movements. These are broad-based networks of groups and individuals. They seek radical change, and generally have a cultural as well as a political identity. They may, for example, try to develop alternative lifestyles that break with orthodox ways of living. Social movements also often resort to non-institutional methods of campaigning that go beyond formal political channels, including, for example, organised assertions of identity such as street protests. Although some social movements have a long history, most either emerged or were restructured by the events and cultural changes of the 1960s and 1970s.

The women's movement is an example of a social movement. It has had a significant impact on US politics since the 1970s. Feminist texts such as Simone de Beauvoir's *The Second Sex* and Betty Friedan's *The Feminine Mystique* created an atmosphere in which traditional cultural and sexual attitudes were challenged. Groupings such as the National Organisation of Women campaigned, albeit unsuccessfully, for an Equal Rights Amendment (ERA) to the US Constitution. The movement called for the free availability of abortion, equal pay, an opening up of traditionally male occupations, and new attitudes towards domestic labour. Hillary Rodham Clinton's remarks during the 1992 election campaign, stating that she would not be simply standing 'by my man' or staying at home and 'baking cookies', reflect the change in attitudes that the movement engendered.

The gay movement also took shape during this period. In 1969, in a now celebrated incident, the New York police raided the Stonewall bar in Greenwich Village, providing the impetus for the creation of an organised movement. It now has a cultural existence – New York's annual Gay Pride parade is now an important event in the City calendar – and also constitutes a significant lobbying network, particularly within the Democratic Party.

1   The lobbying industry often employs former members of Congress and administration officials. They have valued experience and networks of associates. However, these 'hired guns', the critics charge, exploit their period of public service so as to earn large sums of money. Furthermore, while serving in government, they may be tempted to appease corporate interests so as to ensure that they are offered lucrative posts when the post comes to an end. This, it is said, corrupts the political process. According to Nikos Passas from Temple University: '[These officials] take measures that will benefit companies and interests (while in power) and then they take positions with them ... I call that "deferred bribery"' (The Center for Public Integrity 2003b). A 2003 study by the Center for Public Integrity found that of the hundred most senior officials serving in the Clinton administration in January 2001, 51 are now lobbyists or work for companies that undertake lobbying work (Salant 2003). They were assisted by Clinton's revocation of an earlier exec-

However, the women's and gay movements have not gone unchallenged. Their growing strength contributed to the emergence of *countermovements*. Conservative critics of feminism such as Phyllis Schlafly asserted that the ERA would undermine the traditional role of women and force women into combat units in the armed forces, and that the proposal put forward by the gay movement for same-sex marriage would destroy family life.

Conservative activists were joined by many of the Churches. There are about 336,000 individual churches scattered across the US. Many have an evangelical character. Until the 1970s, they tended to shun the political process, and concentrated instead on spiritual concerns. However, the Supreme Court's 1973 ruling, *Roe v. Wade*, established abortion as a constitutional right. For many Christians, the forcible termination of a pregnancy constituted murder. At about the same time, the Internal Revenue Service revoked the tax-exempt status of Christian schools and colleges, charging that they discriminated against black students. These events, and the apparent threat to family life posed by both feminism and the gay movement, led many evangelical Christians to join forces – in the political arena – with conservatives.

They came together in the New Christian Right. It took a number of organisational forms. In the 1980s, the Reverend Jerry Falwell's Moral Majority sought – with relatively little success – to influence the policies adopted by the Reagan Administration. In the 1990s, the Christian Coalition – led for much of its existence by the Reverend Pat Robertson and Ralph Reed – adopted more developed lobbying techniques. Although its influence has sometimes been exaggerated, it had some success in shaping Republican Party politics.

Further reading

Durham, M. (1996), 'The fall and rise of the Christian Right in America', *Politics Review*, April, 26–8.

utive order that had required officials to wait five years before taking employment as lobbyists. Furthermore, the report asserted, at least 22 per cent of those leaving Congress during the 1990s became lobbyists. Their ranks included some prominent figures, such as the Senate Majority Leaders George Mitchell and Robert Dole (Center for Public Integrity 2003c). At the same time, some lobbyists are the children, wives or siblings of lawmakers. They can use the contacts that they have acquired because of family associations for private gain.

2 Jonathan Rauch (1995) regards the entire lobbying 'industry' as parasitical. The realities of modern politics, he argues, compel companies and organisations to hire an army of public relations specialists, lawyers and persuaders to act on their behalf. This represents a diversion of resources. Rauch refers to 'the whirlpool in Washington, sucking up investment capital, talent, energy'. Inevitably, the American economy pays a price. Furthermore,

Rauch argues, legislators have sought to appease a number of interest groups by offering federal government subsidies. Although less than 2 per cent of the American population live on farms, the farming lobby has been particularly successful in gaining subsidies and 'price supports'. He alleges that the subsidies are enough to buy each full-time farmer a Mercedes-Benz every year. Such policies are justified on the grounds that they protect employment within a threatened industry. However, subsidies require the imposition of taxes on other sectors of the economy.

3 The conservative critique of interest group activity rests on the concept of 'producer capture'. This means that particular groups have used their political influence to secure and maintain a privileged economic position for themselves. This, they assert, happens at a federal, state and local level. For example, in 1937 the New York City taxi drivers persuaded the city authorities to impose a limit on the number of licensed cabs that were allowed to operate. Restrictions such as this prevent would-be competitors entering the market and offering cheaper fares than those charged by the established taxis. Although the taxi driver gains from this, both the passenger and 'outsiders' seeking employment in the New York taxi trade are placed at a disadvantage.

4 Some issue groups have come under fire – particularly from the left – for adopting *covert* tactics. In particular, there have been criticisms of the organisations associated with the Christian Right. They have, it is said, stood candidates to local boards of education as 'concerned parents' or independents. Once elected, they have used their positions to argue for the teaching of 'creationism'. This is the belief that the human race owes its origins to divine creation rather than the process of evolution.

5 Those associated with the left also point to the role of corporate lobbying in obstructing reforms that they regard as essential. They assert, in particular, that health care reform and gun control legislation have been persistently hindered and obstructed.

6 Interest groups are – as a whole – unrepresentative of the public. Companies dominate the lobbying process and other groups are also elite-based. As John B. Judis observes, many do not have an active membership. Their boards of directors are self-appointed. Those groupings that do have an open, democratic structure are dominated by the most affluent sections of American society. Even those groups that champion the interests of the poor are dominated by college students and recent graduates (1995a: 22). As a consequence, it is charged, the mass of the population is marginalised. Kevin Phillips – a political analyst – argues that Washington DC is now a 'capital so privileged and incestuous in its dealings, that ordinary citizens believe it is no longer accessible to the general public' (quoted in Abramson 1998)

7 There have been claims that foreign companies – or their subsidiaries – have used the lobbying process so as to gain a competitive advantage. There have, in particular, been allegations that Japanese businesses have 'bought' influ-

ence on Capitol Hill. In 1993, it was estimated that 125 law and public relations firms were working on behalf of Japanese interests (Hrebenar and Thomas 1995: 359).

8 Political Action Committees (PACs) have been subject to particular criticism. As Chapter 10 outlined, there are – in particular – claims that campaign contributions represent the 'buying' of a candidate. If elected, it is said, they are beholden to the PACs that have financed them. However, the provision of funding not only cuts across and detracts from their responsibilities to those whom they represent, but can also distort the policy-making process. In 1990, there were over eighty PACs supporting the state of Israel. They gave financial support to almost all members of Congress, including $1.2 million to those who served on the Senate Foreign Relations Committee (Uslaner 1995: 386). This, critics allege, tilted US foreign policy in the Middle East.

PACs are said to distort the political process in two other ways. They have also played a role in undermining the political parties. Fund-raising was one of the parties' traditional functions, and part of their *raison d'être*. PACs now represent a primary source of finance for election candidates. They also reinforce *incumbency*. They distribute most of their funds to sitting members. These are the legislators who are already occupying a position, and are seeking re-election. Incumbents already have a built-in advantage – because they attract media attention and are able to deliver 'rewards' and benefits to those they represent – and their chances of winning re-election are therefore disproportionately high. PACs will wish to support likely winners. However, by allocating a very large proportion of their funds to incumbents, they thereby make it even more likely that the incumbent will be re-elected.

9 Many organisations are *single-issue* groups. For example, US Term Limits campaigns to impose restrictions on the length of time that legislators serve in Congress and state and local government. The Federation for American Immigration Reform (FAIR) calls for a dramatic reduction in the numbers entering the US. There is a plethora of 'pro-life' and 'pro-choice' campaigns. However, the activities of these organisations have provoked criticism. Some observers have argued that attempts to focus on one issue alone can distort the political process. Furthermore, a focus on one issue alone tends to lead to inflexibility and an unwillingness to compromise.

Positive features

These criticisms of interest group activity have, however, been countered. Those who are less critical point to the laws regulating lobbying activities. The Ethics in Government Act prohibits senior government officials from lobbying their agency for one year after they leave office; for two years on specific matters over which they exercised supervision while in office; and imposes a lifetime ban on matters for which the official was personally responsible while in office.

Former members of Congress and senior 'staffers' may not lobby Congress for a year after leaving office. Furthermore, both houses of Congress have 'gift rules'. From 1995 onwards, House members could only accept gifts from family and friends. For their part, Senators could not accept gifts of more than $50 and were subject to a $100 annual limit on gifts from any one source.

Interest groups, it is also argued, can strengthen the political process. They can, for instance, provide legislators with specialist information. Although Congressmen have their own 'staffers', groups can offer detailed or technical knowledge that they would otherwise lack. There have however been suggestions that the proliferation of interest groups within recent years has led to a decline in their usefulness as sources of information. William P. Browne has argued that Congressmen are increasingly uncertain about which group has credibility and deserves attention (1995: 284). Groups can also be used as a 'sounding board' by decision-makers at the *policy formulation* stage of the legislative process. President Lyndon Johnson consulted George Meany, head of the trade union confederation, the AFL–CIO, so as to gauge opinion on his proposals for anti-poverty measures. At the same time, organisations offer opportunities for political participation. There is considerable public hostility towards the decision-makers in Washington DC, and group activity can bridge the gap between the electorate and those 'inside the Beltway'.

Conclusion

The US is 'a nation of interest groups' in so far as they play a pivotal role within the political process. They seek to influence all three branches of the federal government as well as the states and the localities. For critics, the process of persuasion is dominated not so much by groups but by lobbyists acting on behalf of companies. However, although spending levels have risen dramatically, there are grounds for believing that group activity has become more open and pluralistic in recent years. As David McKay argues, the decision-making process was – up until the 1970s – 'captured' by a relatively small number of powerful economic groups drawn from business, labour, and agriculture. However, from then onwards a new form of politics emerged. There has been a large-scale growth in issue or promotional groups. No single organisation is predominant. Government has become much more open and receptive to a range of interests (1992: 24–5).

References and further reading

Abramson, J. (1998), 'The business of persuasion thrives in nation's capitol', *The New York Times*, 29 September.

Annenberg Public Policy Center (2003), *IssueAds@APPC*, www.appcpenn.org/issueads/index.html.

Browne, W. P. (1995), 'Organized interests, grassroots confidants, and Congress', in A. J. Cigler and B. A. Loomis (eds) (1995), *Interest Group Politics*, Washington DC, Congressional Quarterly, pp. 281–97.

Center for Public Integrity (2003a), *Lobby Spending*, 15 May, www.publicinteg-rity.org/dtaweb/index.asp?L1=20&L2=10&L3=23&L4=12&L5=0&State=&Display=DRFEC.

Center for Public Integrity (2003b), *Hired Guns*, 15 May, www.publicintegrity.org/dtaweb/index.asp?L1=20&L2=10&L3=23&L4=0&L5=0.

Center for Public Integrity (2003c), *The Clinton Top 100: Where Are They Now?*, www.public-i.org/dtaweb/report.asp?ReportID=516&L1=10&L2=10&L3=0&L4=0&L5=0.

Cigler, A. J. and B. A. Loomis (1995), 'Contemporary interest group politics: more than "more of the same"', in A. J. Cigler and B. A. Loomis (eds), *Interest Group Politics*, Washington DC: Congressional Quarterly, pp. 393–406.

CNN.com (2000), *Interest groups spent nearly $700 million lobbying Washington*, 6 January, edition.cnn.com/2000/ALLPOLITICS/stories/01/06/lobbying.bill/.

Drew, E. (1997), *Showdown: The Struggle Between the Gingrich Congress and the Clinton White House*, New York, Touchstone.

Groseclose, T. (2001), *PAC Contributions: The Mistrust is Misplaced*, Stanford Graduate School of Business, www.gsb.stanford.edu/research/reports/2001/groseclose.html.

Hinkson Craig, B. and D. M. O'Brien (1993), *Abortion and American Politics*, Chatham, Chatham House.

Hrebenar, R. J. and C. S. Thomas (1995), 'The Japanese lobby in Washington. How different is it?', in A. J. Cigler and B. A. Loomis (eds), *Interest Group Politics*, Washington DC: Congressional Quarterly, pp. 349–67.

Judis, J. B. (1995a), 'The contract with K Street', *The New Republic*, 4 December, 18–25.

Judis, J. B. (1995b), 'The pressure elite: inside the narrow world of advocacy group politics', in Walter Dean Burnham (ed.), *The American Prospect: Reader in American Politics*, Chatham: Chatham House, pp. 256–75.

Koerner, B. I. (2003), *Do Judges Read Amicus Curiae Briefs?*, 1 April, slate.msn.com/id/2081006/.

Lowi, T. J. and B. Ginsberg (1992), *American Government: Freedom and Power*, New York: W. W. Norton.

McKay, D. (1992), 'Interest group politics in the United States', *Politics Review*, 24–25 April.

McKeever, R. J. (1997), *The United States Supreme Court: A Political and Legal Analysis*, Manchester, Manchester University Press.

National Rifle Association – Institute of Legislative Action (2000), *NRA's Friend Of The Court Brief In U.S. v. Emerson*, www.nraila.org/FactSheets.asp?FormMode=Detail&ID=114.

Opensecrets.org (2003), *Who's Giving – Top Spenders*, www.opensecrets.org/pubs/lobby00/topspenders.asp.

Peterson, P. E. and M. Rom (1988), 'Lower taxes, more spending, and budget deficits', in C. O. Jones (ed.), *The Reagan Legacy: Promise and Performance*, Chatham, Chatham House, pp. 213–40.

Political Moneyline (2003), *Federal Lobby Directory*, www.fecinfo.com/cgi-win/lb_direc-tory.exe?DoFn=.

Rauch, J. (1995), *Demosclerosis*, New York, Times Books.

Rehnquist, W. H. (1987), *The Supreme Court: How It Was, How It Is*, New York, William Monroe and Company.

Salant, J. D. (2003), 'Half of top Clinton aides now lobbyists', *The State*, 31 March, www.thestate.com/mld/state/5521496.htm.

Tocqueville, A. de (1984), *Democracy in America*, New York, Mentor.

Websites

The Directory of United States Lobbyists (www.csuchico.edu/~kcfount/) offers a guide to cause groups, also known as political advocacy groups: 'this project will provide a starting point to acquaint you with the variety of advocacy groups in the United States'.

12

Ideologies, issues and controversies

There is – as Chapter 2 established – a significant degree of consensus around the basic political principles and the foundations of the political system. Indeed, the pivotal role of these principles has led some commentators to talk of an American 'creed'. The degree to which these values are shared should not, however, be allowed to obscure the cleavages and fault lines that run through public opinion. There are, in particular, significant differences between liberalism and conservatism.

Liberalism

The meaning of the term 'liberalism' has shifted and changed over the past century. Classical liberalism – the liberalism that was associated with the founding of the US and its development during the nineteenth century – rested on principles now more closely associated with conservatism. It emphasised *laissez-faire*, minimal government, and the rights of the individual. However, as the twentieth century progressed, 'liberalism' shifted in terms of meaning. It increasingly referred to the belief that government, particularly the federal government, should pursue social justice by regulating the economy and society.

Liberalism asserts that government can make headway – where private enterprise has failed – in ensuring stable economic growth, generating full employment, and eliminating poverty. Liberal policies are directed towards these goals and include redistributive taxation, the direction of business, and the use of government spending so as to manage overall demand levels. From this perspective, the New Deal of the 1930s holds an important place. It dramatically expanded the federal government's role and authority. Work schemes, most notably the Tennessee Valley Authority (TVA), offered employment and reinvigorated the wider economy. The era established the federal government – and the president in particular – as 'the manager of the economy.' Although the New Deal was not, despite the rhetoric of critics, a form of socialism, or even a 'half-way revolution', it restructured the role of government and the character of the expectations placed upon it.

The 1960s and 1970s built upon 'New Deal liberalism'. In 1965, President Lyndon Johnson called for a 'War on Poverty'. He talked of making the US a 'Great Society'. There was a growing belief that the federal government should commit a much greater level of financial resources to the alleviation of poverty and deprivation. Programmes such as the Job Corps for unemployed young people and Head Start for pre-school children were established. Furthermore, it was increasingly argued that those in poverty should no longer simply be the object of social policy. They should be involved, through political mechanisms, in determining their own fate. These ambitions were not, however, fulfilled. Johnson's 'Great Society' liberalism was discredited by the administration's increasingly evident inability to win the 'War on Poverty' and the spending demanded by US intervention in Vietnam.

However, there was another shift in the character of liberalism. It became increasingly closely tied to the new social movements and notions of identity politics that emerged from the late 1960s onwards. The civil rights movement gave way to calls for 'black power' and organisations such as the Black Panthers. At the same time, the emerging women's movement offered a feminist critique of male dominance – or *patriarchy*. Feminism asserted that women had traditionally been confined to a subordinate status at both work and in the home. It stressed that women had rights, including the ability to control their own fertility and reproduction through the availability of contraception and abortion. For their part, gay and lesbian campaigners demanded an end to discrimination. They were, however, divided between those who wanted to see same-sex marriages and more radical activists who saw 'heterosexism' and family structures as inherently oppressive.

In the foreign and defence policy sphere, liberalism merged with the politics of the anti-war movement. Its opposition to American military intervention in Vietnam and Cambodia led towards a broader opposition to the United States' role in the Cold War. Liberal concerns inspired the 'nuclear freeze' movement of the early 1980s. Its supporters argued that the US should not add to, or modernise, its stock of nuclear weaponry. During the 1990s and at the beginning of the new century, most liberals opposed military intervention against Iraq and instead argued the case for negotiated settlements. There were protests in cities such as New York during the weeks preceding the 2003 war.

However, the overall picture should in some respects be qualified. There have always been limits to the radicalism of the liberal vision. While many liberals point to what they see as the excessive influence of corporate interests and the need to construct countervailing forms of power, American liberalism has remained committed to the private ownership of companies and businesses. It should therefore be distinguished from socialism, which rests upon the collective ownership and control of the 'means of production'. As Michael Foley notes, liberals believe that 'it is possible to achieve substantial change while still conforming to the general ethos of capitalism' (1991: 118). In essence, US liberalism represents an attempt to open up the opportunities promised by the American Dream to all, including those who have been long disadvantaged by prejudice and institutionalised discrimination. In liberal eyes, the contemporary US has failed to live up to the promise offered by Americanism. As Foley puts it, liberals 'seek not the repudiation of American values, so much as their full realisation' (1991: 102).

The decades following the Second World War proved to be liberalism's high tide. By the 1970s – just as it fused with the new cultural and political forces of the period – it was proving increasingly unable to address embedded problems such as economic decline, growing criminality, and welfare dependency. It went into retreat, at least within the economic arena. Although some liberals continued to believe in what their opponents dubbed 'tax and spend' policies, others accepted much of the conservative agenda established during the Reagan years. They accepted that there were limits to the efficacy of government. By the early 1990s, for example, many acknowledged that welfare provision had to be much more limited and selective than in the past. President Bill Clinton was one of those committed to this form of 'neo-liberalism'. Nonetheless, by the end of the 1990s, there were signs of a limited revival. There had been a reaction against the abrasive conservatism pursued by figures such as the House Speaker Newt Gingrich. Against this background, George W. Bush was compelled to structure his presidential election campaign in 2000 around calls for 'compassionate conservatism', which foresaw a much greater role for government than that envisaged during the Reagan years.

However, although economic liberalism has lost ground, cultural liberalism has – at least in a modified form – become entrenched. Pre-marital sexual relationships, cohabitation, some basic notions associated with feminism, 'political correctness', and gay lifestyles have became institutionalised within many of the metropolitan regions.

Conservatism

Conservative thinking is structured around four principal themes. Firstly, although there are small numbers of *palaeoconservatives* who call for protectionist measures so as to limit American industry's exposure to foreign competition, modern conservatism has inherited and integrated classical liberalism's commitment to *laissez-faire* and minimal government. Furthermore, since the late 1970s, the conservative belief in small government has fused with *supply-side economics*. 'Supply-siders' assert that lower marginal rates of taxation and a process of *deregulation* – the phasing out of laws restraining business activities – will generate much higher levels of economic growth. The conservative commitment to 'small government' is thereby justified both as a question of principle and on the more consequentialist grounds that it will generate economic prosperity. There are, however, some tensions between those who believe in market forces and those who think in more traditionalist terms. A commitment to the free movement of both capital and labour and the belief that this creates increased economic growth and prosperity has led some conservatives to back relatively open immigration policies. Others on the right fear that the admission of newcomers on a large scale threatens the living standards of the established population and undermines the cultural integrity of the nation.

Secondly, while there are some who define themselves as economic conservatives – or *libertarians* – and regard cultural and moral questions as matters of personal choice, most conservatives are associated with moral traditionalism. They draw on three principal arguments.

- Some forms of living are natural in character, whereas as others are unnatural. Homosexuality is, it is said, a denial of nature. Similarly, traditionalists often argue that there are important differences in the nature of women and men. Men are instinctively 'providers', whereas women are destined to play a more domestic role as homemakers and 'carers'.
- The US is, traditionalists assert, a Judaeo-Christian nation. The Biblical values upon which it was constructed should be respected. Both the Old and the New Testaments point to the sinfulness of homosexuality and say much about the place of men and women.
- Traditional relationships and family structures offer the most effective basis for the raising of children. Young children, it is said, require both male and female role models. Those from 'broken homes' are less likely to succeed in life and may instead turn to criminality.

The organisations associated with the 'religious right' and committed to moral traditionalism, such as the Christian Coalition, are integral components of the contemporary conservative movement. While they acknowledge that there was a limited process of 'remoralisation' during the 1990s, when for example, divorce rates fell, they fear that traditional institutions such as marriage and the family are in long-term decline. Social or cultural conservatives are committed to the importance of family life and 'Judaeo-Christian values'. Today's public schools, they argue, not only fail to teach basic skills, but do little to instil a respect for morality and tradition. Abortion is regarded as murder. There is deep hostility to the many films and TV programmes that, they assert, depict immoral forms of behaviour – such as homosexuality or promiscuity – in a positive or uncritical way. Again, however, there are some differences among conservatives. Whereas some would use the powers of government at either federal or state level to regulate behaviour – by, for example, seeking to prohibit gay sex – others depend instead upon the force of moral persuasion.

Thirdly, conservatives stress the importance of a stable and assured legal framework. They point to the dangers of lawlessness and criminality, and assert that the security of the citizen requires a firm response by those in authority.

Conservatives stress the need for punishments structured around the principle of deterrence. They see the fall in crime rates during the latter half of the 1990s as a consequence of increased police numbers, the imposition of prison sentences, and a 'zero tolerance' approach, pioneered in cities such as New York, based upon the belief that if anti-social behaviour and small-scale offending is tolerated, it inevitably leads to more serious forms of criminality.

Conservatism is associated, fourthly, with forms of foreign and defence policy that emphasise the national interest and are – in different ways – sceptical of supranational organisations such as the United Nations. From the late 1940s onwards, conservatives accepted that the US had to take the leading role in containing the forces of communism. However, the collapse of the Soviet Union and the end of the Cold War inevitably led to a degree of uncertainty about America's role. While most conservatives backed the Gulf War of 1991, there were tensions between those who backed US participation in peacekeeping missions such as those in the former Yugoslavia and others who feared the lure of 'foreign entanglements'. By the time the Bush administration took office in January 2001, commentators talked of 'neo-isolationism'. Conservative opinion was turning against long-term involvement overseas and, in particular, against attempts at 'nation-building'.

The 11 September attacks led to a significant change of course. With only a few dissenters on the further edges of the right, conservatives backed the 'war on terrorism' and the overthrow of the Taliban regime in Afghanistan. However, the attacks shifted the centre of ideological gravity among conservatives by bringing 'neoconservative' arguments to the fore. For their part, 'neocons' assert that the US should play a role in 'exporting' American values – most notably liberty, representative government, and the free market – to other regions of the world. This, it is said, is not only a legitimate goal in itself but also serves American national security interests. Terrorism, wars and conflicts are, it is said, almost always fostered by repressive, undemocratic regimes. If the Middle East could be 'Americanised', the roots of backward fanaticism would be undermined and eliminated. For many observers, the 2003 Iraq war represented the practical application of neoconservative thought.

Other conservatives are, however, more sanguine. For some, Islamic culture is much more resistant to Western values than the 'neocons' seem to suggest. While national security considerations may justify military interventionism, hopes that the defining ideological character of continents can be transformed are utopian. Echoing the title of Samuel P. Huntington's book, they talk of a 'clash of civilisations' between the east and the west (Huntington 2002). Others fear the construction of an American empire and the abandonment of the traditional nation.

Conservatives regard themselves as the most resolute guardians of American traditions and values. They assert that the US was constructed upon the basis of principles such as liberty, limited government, and self-reliance. However, these values have been – it is said – progressively abandoned.

1 In place of self-reliance, the US has become an *entitlement* society. American people have come to expect secure jobs and rising living standards regardless of individual effort.

> Sixty or seventy years ago, Americans by and large subscribed to the notion of the 'rugged individual' ... Now the spirit has shifted. If something's wrong, it's someone else's fault. Government, business, the schools, or the courts are responsible. Or we are brought down by racism, sexism, ageism or some other 'ism'. What is now called 'victimology' has become widespread and respectable. (Samuelson 1997: 16)

2 Although the US has an ideological commitment to the principle of *laissez-faire*, the federal government has increasingly played an *interventionist* role. The New Deal and the Great Society extended the boundaries of its activities. While the conservative revolution during President Reagan's years in the White House began a process of 'rolling back' government, government spending remained between about 20 and 22 per cent of the country's output – or Gross Domestic Product (GDP) – throughout the 1980s and 1990s.

3 While the American creed rests on the principle of individual liberty and the curtailment of government power, restrictive laws have been introduced. Conservatives point to minimum wage legislation and other forms of economic regulation. They also see gun control legislation as particularly intrusive. They assert that it represents a strengthening of government and is a threat to the fundamental rights of the citizen.

4 Conservatives suggest, furthermore, that the American commitment to equality of opportunity has been undermined by the race- and gender-based programmes introduced over the past thirty years. They oppose 'quotas' and other forms of affirmative action that seek to ensure that minorities and women are more fully represented in higher education and company management structures. Conservatives are similarly critical of 'redistricting', which, until curtailed by the US Supreme Court, redrew the boundaries between electoral areas so as to enlarge the number of black and Hispanic-majority ('minority-majority') districts.

Taxation, the economy and the role of government

Conservatives call for low levels of taxation. In particular, they emphasise the importance of reducing the rate of direct taxation imposed upon individual and corporate income. In part, this is because they want to limit the role of government. They are committed to free market – or *laissez-faire* – economics.

There are, however, some differences within the conservative movement. Those who subscribe to supply-side theories argue that low rates of marginal taxation will encourage entrepreneurship and increase economic growth. This will, in turn, add to the federal government's tax revenues. On the other hand, 'deficit hawks' fear that precipitous reductions in tax rates may create a budget

Table 12.1 *Liberal and conservative attitudes: summary*

Attitudes towards	Liberalism	Conservatism[a]
Government	Should play a pro-active role	Distrust
Industry, business, and commerce	Regulation	*Laissez-faire*
Role of individuals	May require assistance and a degree of collective provision	Self-reliance
'Tax and spend' government policies	High taxes on the wealthy – greater spending on health and education	Low taxes and minimal government
Gun control	For	Against
Crime	Rehabilitation so as to reduce re-offending	Strict penalties to provide a deterrent and serve justice
National security	A 'just' foreign policy	Based upon perceptions of the national interest
Civil liberties	Restrict only in the most exceptional circumstances	Restrict when there is a 'clear and present danger' to national security
Gay rights	For – including same-sex marriage	Against
Abortion	'Pro-choice'	'Pro-life'
Affirmative action	For	Against
Immigration	Relatively open	Restricted
Patriotism and perceptions of the US	Emphasis on the promise of America	Pride in the US as it is

[a] Note that libertarian conservatives are sympathetic to some gay rights (see p. 274). A number have also had reservations about the restrictions on civil liberties that followed the 11 September attacks.

Table 12.2 *Attitudes towards tax cuts, 2003 (%)*

	Mostly help	No effect	Mostly hurt	No opinion
19–21 May 2003	36	23	30	11
5–7 May 2003	47	19	31	3
22–23 April 2003	36	31	26	7

Question text: 'Do you think the tax cuts being proposed by George W. Bush would – [phrases rotated] mostly help the US economy; would have no effect; or would mostly hurt the US economy– over the next year?'
Source: adapted from the Gallup Organization (2003b), *Public Ambivalent About Tax Cuts*, 29 May, www.gallup.com/poll/releases/pr030529.asp.

deficit whereby federal government expenditure exceeds revenue. This would put pressure on interest rates and fuel the long-term national debt.

For the most part, liberals call for increased rates of taxation on higher-income groups. This will, they argue, provide the funding to allow increased government expenditure on education and health care. These policies have been derided as 'tax and spend' by their opponents.

Americans for Tax Reform, www.atr.org/

'ATR opposes all tax increases as a matter of principle. We believe in a system in which taxes are simpler, fairer, flatter, more visible, and lower than they are today. The government's power to control one's life derives from its power to tax. We believe that power should be minimized.'

Gun control

Although not unrestricted, guns are an established feature of the American cultural landscape. The belief that gun-ownership is a defining right of citizenship is tied to conservatism and conservative-leaning pressure groups, most notably the National Rifle Association (NRA). These emphasise that the right to 'bear arms' is protected by the Second Amendment and that it ensures that the government does not become over-powerful. If the people are unarmed, it is said, this opens the way for a government – which would then have a monopoly over the use of armed force – to become tyrannical. Guns therefore represent liberty. Furthermore, guns allow law-abiding citizens – who would otherwise be left defenceless – to protect themselves – and their property – against violent criminals. Violent crime, the advocates of 'gun rights' assert, is not caused or encouraged by the availability of guns. Instead, it has other causes. As the NRA puts it: 'guns don't kill people, people kill people'. From a conservative perspective, these causes include the break-up of the traditional family – which has set individuals morally adrift – and the films and television series that represent criminality in attractive or glamorous terms.

The NRA's arguments are countered by organisations such as the Coalition to Stop Gun Violence and by Michael Moore in his 2002 film, *Bowling for Columbine*. From their perspective, the right to 'bear arms', which is included in the second clause of the Second Amendment, is conditional upon the first clause of the sentence. This talks of a 'well-regulated militia'. The amendment does not, therefore, offer individual gun-ownership, but only a right to 'bear arms' within state-directed organisations and institutions. Furthermore, the availability of guns creates a cycle of escalating violence. As the Consumer Federation of America Foundation observes, more than one million Americans – including many children – have died in firearm homicides, suicides, and unintentional shootings since 1960 (Consumer Federation of America Foundation nd).

Over three-quarters of the American public back a measure of gun control. They want legislation requiring some form of registration before a gun can be purchased. As Table 12.3 suggests, there has been a steady increase in the numbers favouring a permit system and a corresponding fall in the numbers opposing it.

Table 12.3 *Attitudes towards gun control, 1972–2000 (%)*

	1972	1980	1990	1993	1996	1998	2000
Favour	72.4	70.7	80.1	82.5	82	83.6	81.7
Oppose	27.6	29.3	19.9	17.5	18	16.4	18.3

Question text: 'Would you favor or oppose a law which would require a person to obtain a police permit before he or she could buy a gun?'
Source: adapted from General Social Survey (2003c), *GUNLAW*, www.icpsr.umich.edu:8080/ GSS/homepage.htm.

Coalition to Stop Gun Violence, www.gunfree.org

'The goal of CSGV is the orderly elimination of the private sales of handguns and assault weapons in the United States.'

National Rifle Association, www.nra.org

'What members share with every other member is an appreciation of shooting sports, belief in our constitutional right to keep and bear arms and, most of all, a commitment to safety, responsibility and freedom.'

Box 12.1   Guns and gun control: *Bowling for Columbine* (2002)

Director: Michael Moore

Michael Moore's *Bowling for Columbine* is a humorous but also serious film about gun violence in the US. As the film's makers put it: 'It is a film about the fearful heart and soul of the United States, and the 280 million Americans lucky enough to have the right to a constitutionally protected Uzi.'

Bowling for Columbine was the first documentary film accepted into competition at the Cannes Film Festival in 46 years. The Cannes jury unanimously awarded it the 55th Anniversary Prize. It includes coverage of the shootings at Columbine High School and an interview with the National Rifle Association's former president, the film actor Charlton Heston.

Website: www.bowlingforcolumbine.com/

Crime, criminality and punishment

The conservative right has always emphasised the importance of law and order. During the early 1990s, against a background of rising crime levels in many American cities, they talked of 'broken windows' or 'zero tolerance'. They argued that if the authorities tolerated small-scale offending, or allowed an area to become derelict, as had traditionally often happened, more serious forms of criminality would inevitably follow. They called for the adoption of a 'zero tolerance' policy, and many conservatives attribute the fall in crime rates in cities such as New York during the course of the 1990s to this form of measure. They have also backed the use of 'three strikes and you're out' legislation. This has been adopted in states such as California, and provides for a mandatory life sentence if an offender is convicted for a third time.

Table 12.4 *Attitudes towards capital punishment, 1980–2000 (%)*

	1980	1990	1991	1993	1994	1996	1998	2000
Favor	71.6	79.4	76.2	77.4	79.2	76.8	73.3	68.8
Oppose	28.4	20.6	23.8	22.6	20.8	23.2	26.7	31.2

Question text: 'Do you favor or oppose the death penalty for persons convicted of murder?'
Source: adapted from General Social Survey (2003b), *CAPPUN*, www.icpsr.umich.edu:8080/GSS/rnd1998/merged/cdbk/cappun.htm.

Although nearly all Western societies have abolished the death penalty, 38 states and the US federal government allow for capital punishment in their statute books. It attracts particular support from conservatives, although backing for it extends to many self-defined moderates.

For their part, liberals emphasise the broad social causes of crime. They stress the role of urban deprivation, the acquisitive culture that rests upon

---

American Civil Liberties Union (ACLU), www.aclu.org/

'Capital punishment is the ultimate denial of civil liberties. The ACLU opposes capital punishment under all circumstances because it violates the constitutional ban on cruel and unusual punishment, is administered arbitrarily and unfairly, and fails to deter crime or improve public safety.'

Pro-death penalty.com, www.prodeathpenalty.com/

'If we execute murderers and there is in fact no deterrent effect, we have killed a bunch of murderers. If we fail to execute murderers, and doing so would in fact have deterred other murders, we have allowed the killing of a bunch of innocent victims. I would much rather risk the former. This, to me, is not a tough call.'

material gain, and discrimination. There are fears that the police have excessive powers, and the prisons are regarded as brutalising institutions. A number of liberal activists are heavily involved in campaigns against the death penalty.

Backing for the death penalty reached very high levels in the early 1990s, but moderated at the beginning of the new century. Although executions have become routine in states such as Texas and Virginia, some attracted a degree of public disquiet. There were also doubts about the safety of a number of convictions and sentencing procedures. By 2000, there had been a small but marked fall in the numbers backing capital punishment. Against this background, Illinois imposed a moratorium on executions, and Governor George H. Ryan later used his powers to commute all death sentences in the state.

National security

The events of 11 September brought Americans from across the political spectrum together in shared grief. In the immediate aftermath, there was an upsurge of patriotism and widespread support for the US-directed war in Afghanistan.

As was noted above, conservatives – particularly 'neoconservatives' – provided the bedrock of support for the war effort. For their part, although there were celebrated exceptions such as the Washington-based commentator, Christopher Hitchens, many liberals and radicals opposed the Iraq war. There were significant protests in cities such as New York. There was, they argued, no proven link between Saddam Hussein's regime and Al-Qaeda. Furthermore, there was little tangible evidence, despite the Bush administration's claims, that Iraq possessed weapons of mass destruction. Many liberals argued that the roots

---

Box 12.2   Attitudes towards the Iraq war, April 2003 (%)

Support	77
Oppose	16
No opinion	7

Breakdown of support for the war by categories of voters

Conservative Republicans	99
Men	82
Women	72
Liberal Democrats	52
African-Americans	49

Source: adapted from Washington Post (2003), *Washington Post-ABC News Poll: War Support Widespread*, 7 April, www.washingtonpost.com/wp-srv/politics/polls/vault/stories/ data040703.htm.

**The Project for the New American Century,
www.newamericancentury.org/**

'dedicated to a few fundamental propositions: that American leadership is good
both for America and for the world; that such leadership requires military
strength, diplomatic energy and commitment to moral principle; and that too few
political leaders today are making the case for global leadership.'

Antiwar.com, www.antiwar.com/

'This site is devoted to the cause of non-interventionism and is read by libertarians, pacifists, leftists, "greens," and independents alike, as well as many on the
Right who agree with our opposition to imperialism.'

---

of 11 September lay in the nature of US foreign policy. It had often sided with
oppressive regimes and failed to recognise the plight of the Palestinian people.

An opinion poll taken during the war suggested that backing for the war was
overwhelming. There were significant doubts among only two demographic
groupings: liberal Democrats and African-Americans.

Homeland security, civil liberties and terrorism

New 'homeland security' measures were adopted in the wake of the 11
September attacks. These included the holding of detainees and passage of the
Patriot Act, which allows increased surveillance. Although there were some
conservative dissenters, who feared the strengthening of national government
powers, objections came principally from those associated with the radical left
who feared the loss of civil liberties.

Table 12.5 *Attitudes towards terrorism and civil liberties, January–April 2002
(%)*

	Take steps even if civil liberties are violated	Take steps but not violate civil liberties	No opinion
22–23 April 2003	33	64	3
21–23 June 2002	40	56	4
25–27 January 2002	47	49	4

Question text: 'Which comes closer to your view – [phrases rotated] the government should take
all steps necessary to prevent additional acts of terrorism in the US even if it means your basic
civil liberties would be violated, [or] the government should take steps to prevent additional acts
of terrorism but not if those steps would violate your basic civil liberties?'
Source: adapted from the Gallup Organization (2003a), *Civil Liberties*, www.gallup.com/poll/
topics/civil_lib.asp.

While responses differ significantly depending upon the form in which the question is asked, and feelings have to some extent faded since 11 September, public opinion accepts the need for increased FBI powers, but is reluctant to see established liberties abandoned.

American Civil Liberties Union (ACLU), www.aclu.org/

'An immutable characteristic of our nation is freedom. If we allow the interests of "national security" to take away our freedoms, we surrender what it is to be an American.'

'Family values' and gay rights

Although there are some conservatives who favour minimal government but are liberal on cultural issues, many on the right are associated with moral traditionalism. They regard homosexuality as deviant, and do not accept that it has a moral equivalence to heterosexual relationships. Children, it is said, should be brought up in a stable, two-parent home. Many also assert that the entertainment industry has a particular responsibility to convey and maintain 'mainstream' values. They have profound reservations about popular television series – such as *Friends* – that appear to depict sexual relations outside marriage, or single parenthood as a legitimate norm.

Arguments such as these have, however, been vigorously contested. Those associated with contemporary liberalism suggest that the traditional family did not necessarily have a stable or functional character. Instead, the appearance of conventional family life often masked long accumulated tensions and oppressive forms of behaviour. Except for a brief period of relative economic prosperity during the 1950s and 1960s, women not only had to carry a domestic burden but also worked outside the home. In place of an insistence upon traditional family relations, liberal and feminist thinking emphasises the quality of parent–child relationships and maintains that families can take many different

Table 12.6 *Attitudes towards gay and lesbian relationships, 1991–98 (%)*

	1991	1994	1998
Always wrong	75.1	69.7	62.4
Almost always wrong	5	4.3	5.6
Wrong only sometimes	5.6	6.9	7.4
Not wrong at all	14.3	19.1	24.6

Question text: 'And what about sexual relations between two adults of the same sex, is it . . .'
Source: adapted from General Social Survey (2003d), *HOMOSEX1*, www.icpsr.umich.edu:8080/ GSS/rnd1998/merged/cdbk/homosex1.htm.

shapes and forms. They may be based around either heterosexual or homosexual relationships. As Robin Williams observes at the end of the 1993 film, *Mrs Doubtfire*, there are 'all sorts of families'.

Although vocal, conservatism has been in long-term retreat on cultural issues. Although there was a partial and limited swing back towards moral orthodoxy during the latter half of the 1990s, sexual relations and cohabitation prior to marriage are now almost institutionalised. Although something approaching two-thirds of the population still regards homosexuality as 'always wrong', the proportion of the population seeing gay and lesbian relationships in these terms fell during the course of the decade.

Christian Coalition of America, www.cc.org/

'Christian Coalition is leading a growing new alliance of evangelicals, Roman Catholics, Greek Orthodox, Jews, African-Americans and Hispanics who are working hard for common-sense legislation that will strengthen families.'

National Organization for Women, www.now.org

'NOW is dedicated to making legal, political, social, and economic change in our society in order to achieve our goal, which is to eliminate sexism and end all oppression.'

Abortion

The morality of abortion has been a core issue in US politics for at least three decades. In 1973, in *Roe v. Wade*, the Supreme Court asserted that abortion was a constitutional right in at least the first six months of a pregnancy. The ruling was partly based upon a 'right to privacy' that, although not specified in the Constitution, was said by the more liberal justices to be implied in it.

To some extent, abortion cuts across the ideological divide. Nonetheless, although there are many 'pro-choice' conservatives and 'pro-life' liberals, most liberals are 'pro-choice' and most conservatives 'pro-life'. Contemporary liberalism is associated with feminism and calls for women's rights. Liberals therefore emphasise the right of women to control their own fertility and reproduction. Conservatism is more closely associated with religious values and the belief that life begins at conception. Abortion is therefore regarded as a form of killing.

The *Roe* judgement contributed to the political mobilisation of many Christian voters, who were deeply opposed to abortion, and the emergence of the religious right. Nonetheless, despite their commitment, they are in a minority. A narrow majority of the population supports the continued availability of abortion as either a matter of personal liberty or where a clear and serious need can be shown. President Clinton probably caught the popular mood when he said that abortion should be 'safe, legal and rare'.

Table 12.7 *Attitudes towards abortion, 1980–2000 (%)*

	1980	1990	1992	1994	1996	1998	2000
Never permitted	11	12	10	13	13	12	12
In cases of rape, incest, danger	32	33	28	31	30	30	31
Clear need	18	14	14	14	16	16	15
Always as personal choice	35	40	46	40	40	40	39
Don't know, other	4	2	2	2	2	1	2

Source: adapted from National Election Studies (2003), *The NES Guide to Public Opinion and Electoral Behavior – Abortion by Law (2) 1980–2000*, www.umich.edu/~nes/nesguide/toptable/tab4c_2b.htm.

National Abortion and Reproductive Rights Action League (NARAL Pro-Choice America), www.naral.org

'NARAL educates Americans, elects pro-choice candidates and advocates for pro-choice legislation to secure the freedom to choose.'

National Right to Life, www.nrlc.org

'The ultimate goal of the National Right to Life Committee is to restore legal protection to innocent human life. The primary interest of the National Right to Life Committee and its members has been the abortion controversy; however, it is also concerned with related matters of medical ethics which relate to the right to life issues of euthanasia and infanticide. '

Race, gender and affirmative action

The 1964 Civil Rights Act and the 1965 Voting Rights Act brought the era of legalised – or *de jure* – discrimination to a close. Segregation – which had been enforced throughout the southern states – was abolished. However, although there is now a substantial black middle-class, disproportionate numbers of African-Americans remain locked into poverty and the secondary labour market that is characterised by short-term, insecure, and unskilled forms of employment. Despite many individual success stories, blacks have – in overall terms – failed to match white educational achievement.

Why was this? Many liberals and the civil rights organisations argued that these profoundly unequal outcomes were the consequence of 'institutionalised racism'. Companies, universities and other institutions were inherently racist, because blacks under-achieved in them in comparison with whites. This was because, it was argued, a welter of informal – and often hidden – cultural barriers hindered the progress of African-Americans and most other minorities. Women similarly faced a 'glass ceiling' preventing their advancement up the occupational ladder. The answer lay in affirmative action programmes. These seek to ensure that minorities and women are properly represented in senior positions in companies and prestige occupations. Affirmative action can take different forms. 'Soft' forms simply seek to ensure that there are large numbers of applicants for senior posts from groups that have traditionally been under-represented. Job vacancies might, for example, be advertised in newspapers or on television channels likely to be seen by women and minorities. 'Harder' forms of affirmative action rest upon the setting of targets or goals for the recruitment of under-represented groupings. If tests are involved – and they generally provide the basis for admission to many university courses – minority applicants might receive bonus scores so as to improve their chances and thereby meet the overall recruitment target that has been set.

Table 12.8 *Attitudes towards racial preferences, 1994–2000 (%)*

	1994	1996	1998	2000
Strongly support preferences	9.8	10	8.3	11.5
Support preferences	7.3	7	6.9	7.5
Oppose preferences	25.7	26.6	24.9	27.5
Strongly oppose preferences	57.3	56.3	60	53.5

Question text: 'Some people say that because of past discrimination, blacks should be given preference in hiring and promotion. Others say that such preference in hiring and promotion of blacks is wrong because it discriminates against whites. What about your opinion – are you for or against preferential hiring and promotion of blacks?'
Source: adapted from General Social Survey (2003a), *AFFRMACT*, www.icpsr.umich.edu:8080/ GSS/homepage.htm.

American Civil Rights Institute, www.acri.org

'The American Civil Rights Institute is a national civil rights organization created to educate the public about racial and gender preferences.'

Civilrights.org, www.civilrights.org

'civilrights.org is committed to serving as the online nerve center not only for the struggle against discrimination in all its forms, but also to build the public understanding that it is essential for our nation to continue its journey toward social and economic justice.'

These 'hard' forms of affirmative action have provoked bitter controversy. White men, in particular, feel that they are losing out. Opponents argue that affirmative action constitutes discrimination and is unjust. It is also patronising to minority applicants, who will appear to be less qualified than the whites with whom they work or study.

Studies of public attitudes towards affirmative action have shown wide variations depending upon the form in which the question is asked. As Table 12.8 suggests, the use of the term 'preferences' almost always leads to a particularly hostile response.

Two nations?

Although, in overall terms, those defining themselves as conservatives outnumber liberals, US public opinion is divided. As Chapter 10 noted, the divide is to some extent structured around the different regions. Although always outnumbered by the right, disproportionately higher numbers of those living in the bigger cities and the surrounding metropolitan regions (the 'metros') lean towards progressivism and liberalism. There is, for example, greater tolerance of gay lifestyles. The more rural 'heartland' areas are, however, more closely tied to moral traditionalism and conservatism.

Table 12.9 *Political attitudes, 1972–98 (%)*

	Large cities and suburbs	Smaller cities and towns	Smaller areas and open country
Extremely liberal / liberal	48.4	41.3	32.6
Extremely conservative / conservative	51.6	58.7	67.4

Question text: 'We hear a lot of talk these days about liberals and conservatives. I'm going to show you a seven-point scale on which the political views that people might hold are arranged from extremely liberal – point 1 – to extremely conservative – point 7. Where would you place yourself on this scale?'
Source: adapted from General Social Survey (2003e), *POLVIEWS / XNORCSIZ*, www.icpsr.umich. edu:8080/GSS/homepage.htm.

These differences have led some observers to talk in terms of 'two nations' or a '50–50 country'. Although such descriptions edge towards hyperbole, there are significant tensions around core cultural issues. The task for the parties, interest groups, and the political process itself is to respond to this.

References and further reading

Consumer Federation of America Foundation (n.d.), *Which One is More Regulated?*, www.consumerfed.org/gunbro.pdf.

Foley, M. (1991), *American Political Ideas*, Manchester, Manchester University Press.

Huntington, S. P. (2002), *The Clash of Civilizations: And the Remaking of World Order*, New York, Free Press.

Samuelson, R. J. (1997), *The Good Life and its Discontents*, New York, Vintage Books.

Appendix I: a brief chronology of the United States since 1789

1789	George Washington takes office as the first US president.
1791	The first ten amendments – the Bill of Rights – are added to the Constitution.
1803	The acquisition of lands from France – the 'Louisiana Purchase' – doubles the size of US territory.
1812–15	War with Britain.
1820	Missouri Compromise.
1845	Texas is annexed.
1857	*Dred Scott v. Sandford.* The Supreme Court ruled that slaves were mere property, and Congress had no power to forbid slavery in the newly-established western territories.
1860	The US is becoming an industrial nation. 30,000 miles of railway track are in place. Abraham Lincoln (Republican) elected president.
1861–65	Civil War. 618,000 killed by enemy fire, typhoid and dysentery. Following their defeat, the southern states are placed under military occupation.
1868	President Andrew Johnson impeached and acquitted.
1869	Transcontinental railroad completed – linking the east and west coasts.
1896	The Supreme Court rules, in *Plessy v. Ferguson*, that – under the 'separate but equal' doctrine – segregation is constitutional.
1910	National Association for the Advancement of Colored People founded.
1917	The US enters the First World War.
1919–20	The Treaty of Versailles fails to gain a two-thirds majority in the Senate and is therefore defeated.
1919	The eighteenth amendment to the Constitution introduces prohibition.

1921–24	Immigration is severely restricted.
1929	The Wall Street crash ushers in a period of mass unemployment and economic depression.
1933	Franklin D. Roosevelt becomes president. He introduces the Emergency Banking Relief Act and other measures ushering in the New Deal. The federal government becomes much more involved in economic and social affairs.
1937	Roosevelt's 'court-packing' plan.
1941	Following the Japanese attack on the US naval base at Pearl Harbor, the US joins the Second World War.
1945	The Second World War comes to an end with the defeat of Germany (May) and Japan (August). The Japanese surrender follows US atom bomb attacks on the cities of Hiroshima and Nagasaki.
1947	The US commits itself – in the Truman doctrine – to a policy of containment. It will support 'free people' across the world. The countries of Western Europe begin to receive large-scale financial assistance from the US through Marshall Aid.
1948	Alger Hiss, a former State Department official, is accused of spying. Over the next few years, there is a sustained drive against alleged Soviet agents and communist sympathisers known as McCarthyism.
1950	North Korean forces attack the non-communist south. Together with some other United Nations member states, US forces fight a three-year war.
1954	In *Brown v. Board of Education (Topeka, Kansas)*, the Supreme Court rules that segregation in public schools is unconstitutional. It later calls for desegegration 'with all deliberate speed'.
1955	The bus boycott in Montgomery, Alabama, marks the beginning of the civil rights movement's struggle against segregation in the southern states.
1961	President Eisenhower warns, in his valedictory address, about the dangers posed by the 'military-industrial complex'.
1962	The USSR installs nuclear missiles in Cuba. The US 'quarantines' the island. Following a tense stand-off, the USSR removes the missiles.
1963	In an address to civil rights protesters at the Lincoln Memorial in Washington DC, Martin Luther King Jr. proclaims: 'I have a dream my four little children will one day live in a nation where they will not be judged by the color of their skin but by the content of their character.'
	Assassination of President John F. Kennedy.
1964	Following an apparent attack on a US vessel in the Gulf of Tonkin, US intervention in Vietnam escalates. Both air and land forces are committed.

President Lyndon Johnson announces the War on Poverty: 'Our aim is not only to relieve the symptom of poverty, but to cure it and, above all, to prevent it.' The role of the federal government is again expanded.

1965	The Voting Rights Act and the 1964 Civil Rights Act bring segregation and the Jim Crow laws to an end in the southern states.
1969	Woodstock Festival.
1970	Four students at Kent State University are shot dead by the Ohio National Guard. They were protesting against the Vietnam War.
1972	In an abrupt reversal of US foreign policy, President Nixon visits communist China.
1973	In *Roe v. Wade*, the Supreme Court rules that abortion – within the first three months of a pregnancy – is a constitutional right.
1974	President Richard M. Nixon resigns once it becomes clear that he will be impeached for his role in the Watergate cover-up.
1975	The National Liberation Front (Vietcong) and the North Vietnamese defeat the US-backed south. Vietnam is reunited under communist rule.
1979–81	The US Embassy in Tehran is seized by Iranian government-backed militants. The Embassy staff are held as hostages for over a year. In April 1980, a military rescue attempt fails and the Carter presidency loses its credibility.
1983	US invasion of Grenada.
1985	Mikhail Gorbachev becomes Soviet leader. His radical reforms lead to an easing of Cold War tensions.
1986	US bombing raid on Libya. This follows alleged Libyan involvement in a terrorist bomb attack on American servicemen.
	The 'Iran–Contra' affair becomes public, although its overall impact on the Reagan presidency is limited.
1989	The Berlin Wall is opened, signalling the collapse of the communist system. The conflict between the West and the Soviet bloc – the Cold War – comes to an end.
1991	Following the Iraqi invasion of Kuwait in August 1990, the US and other members of the United Nations coalition launch Operation Desert Storm. Iraqi forces are driven out of Kuwait.
1994	The Republican Party wins majorities in both houses of Congress. Most House Republicans are signatories to the Contract with America. Newt Gingrich becomes House Speaker.
1996	Bill Clinton becomes the first Democratic president to win a second term since President Franklin Roosevelt. He just fails to gain 50 per cent of the popular vote.

1998   The Clinton presidency is thrown into crisis by allegations of perjury and obstruction of justice. The President is impeached, but acquitted following a trial by the Senate in early 1999.

2000   Although Al Gore wins a majority of the popular vote, a protracted dispute about the allocation of Florida's Electoral College Vote is only settled after it reaches the US Supreme Court. The Florida Electoral Vote is awarded to George W. Bush, and this gives him the presidency by the narrowest of margins.

2001   The 11 September attacks transforms the Bush presidency. Military intervention in Afghanistan leads to the removal of the Taliban regime that had provided sanctuary for al-Qaeda operatives.

2003   Despite the absence of UN backing for its actions, the US constructs a 'coalition of the willing' and – claiming that Saddan Hussein's regime possesses 'weapons of mass destruction' – invades Iraq. Saddam is removed from power, although US forces later face guerrilla attacks from insurgents.

Appendix II: the US Constitution

We the people of the United States, in order to form a more perfect Union, establish Justice, insure domestic Tranquility, provide for the common defence, promote the general Welfare, and secure the Blessing of Liberty to ourselves and our Posterity, do ordain and establish this CONSTITUTION for the United States of America.

Article I

Section 1.   All legislative Powers herein granted shall be vested in a Congress of the United States, which shall consist of a Senate and House of Representatives.

Section 2.   The House of Representatives shall be composed of Members chosen every second Year by the People of the several States, and the Electors in each State shall have the Qualifications requisite for Electors of the most numerous Branch of the State Legislature.

No Person shall be a Representative who shall not have attained the Age of twenty-five Years, and been seven Years a Citizen of the United States, and who shall not, when elected, be an Inhabitant of that State in which he shall be chosen.

[Representatives and direct Taxes shall be apportioned among the several States which may be included within this Union, according to their respective Numbers, which shall be determined by adding to the whole Number of free Persons, including those bound to Service for a Term of Years, and excluding Indians not taxed, three-fifths of all other persons.][1] The actual Enumeration shall be made within three Years after the first Meeting of the Congress of the United States, and within every subsequent Term of ten Years, in such Manner as they shall be Law direct. The Number of Representatives shall not exceed one for every thirty thousand, but each State shall have at Least one Representative; and until such enumeration shall be made, the State of New Hampshire shall be entitled to chuse three, Massachusetts eight, Rhode Island and Providence Plantations one, Connecticut five, New York six, New Jersey four, Pennsylvania eight, Delaware one, Maryland six, Virginia ten, North Carolina five, South Carolina five, and Georgia three.

---

[1] This provision was modified by the Sixteenth Amendment. The three-fifths reference to slaves was rendered obsolete by the Thirteenth and Fourteenth Amendments.

When vacancies happen in the Representation from any State, the Executive Authority thereof shall issue Writs of Election to fill such Vacancies.

The House of Representatives shall chuse their Speaker and other Officers; and shall have the sole Power of Impeachment.

Section 3.   The Senate of the United States shall be composed of two Senators from each State, chosen by the Legislature thereof,[1] for six Years; and each Senator shall have one Vote.

Immediately after they shall be assembled in Consequence of the first Election, they shall be divided as equally as may be into three Classes. The Seats of the Senators of the first Class shall be vacated at the Expiration of the second Year, of the Second Class at the Expiration of the fourth Year, and the third class at the Expiration of the sixth Year, so that one-third may be chosen every second Year; and if Vacancies happen by Resignation, or otherwise, during the Recess of the Legislature of any State, the Executive thereof may make temporary Appointments until the next Meeting of the Legislature, which shall then fill such Vacancies.

No Person shall be a Senator who shall not have attained to the Age of thirty Years, and been nine Years a Citizen of the United States, and who shall not, when elected, be an Inhabitant of that State for which he shall be chosen.

The Vice President of the United States shall be President of the Senate, but shall have no Vote, unless they be equally divided.

The Senate shall chuse their Officers, and also a President pro tempore, in the absence of the Vice President, or when he shall exercise the Office of President of the United States.

The Senate shall have the sole Power to try all Impeachments. When sitting for that Purpose, they shall be on Oath or Affirmation. When the President of the United States is tried, the Chief Justice shall preside; And no Person shall be convicted without the Concurrence of two-thirds of the Members present.

Judgment in Cases of Impeachment shall not extend further than to removal from Office, and disqualification to hold and enjoy any Office of honor, Trust or Profit under the United States; but the Party convicted shall nevertheless be liable and subject to Indictment, Trial, Judgment and Punishment, according to Law.

Section 4.   The Times, Places and Manner of holding Elections for Senators and Representatives, shall be prescribed in each State by the Legislature thereof; but the Congress may at any time by Law make or alter such Regulations, except as to the Places of chusing Senators.

The Congress shall assemble at least once in every Year, and such Meeting shall be on the first Monday in December, unless they shall by Law appoint a different Day.[2]

Section 5.   Each House shall be the Judge of the Elections, Returns and Qualifications of its own Members, and a Majority of each shall constitute a Quorum to do Business; but a smaller Number may adjourn from day to day, and may be authorized to compel the Attendance of absent Members, in such Manner, and under such Penalties as each House may provide.

Each House may determine the Rules of its Proceedings, punish its Members for disorderly Behavior, and, with the Concurrence of two-thirds, expel a Member.

Each House shall keep a Journal of its Proceedings and from time to time publish the same, excepting such Parts as may in their Judgment require Secrecy; and the Yeas and

---

[1] See the Seventeenth Amendment.
[2] See the Twentieth Amendment.

Nays of the Members of either House on any question shall, at the Desire of one-fifth of those Present, be entered on the Journal.

Neither House, during the Session of Congress, shall without the Consent of the other, adjourn for more than three days, nor to any other Place than that in which the two Houses shall be sitting.

Section 6.   The Senators and Representatives shall receive a Compensation for their Services, to be ascertained by Law, and paid out of the Treasury of the United States. They shall in all Cases, except Treason, Felony, and Breach of the peace, be privileged from Arrest during their Attendance at the Session of their respective Houses, and in going to and returning from the same; and for any Speech or Debate in either House, they shall not be questioned in any other Place.

No Senator or Representative shall, during the Time for which he was elected, be appointed to any civil Office under the Authority of the United States, which shall have been created, or the Emoluments whereof shall have been encreased during such time; and no Person holding any Office under the United States, shall be a Member of either House during his Continuance in Office.

Section 7.   All Bills for raising Revenue shall originate in the House of Representatives; but the Senate may propose or concur with Amendments as on other Bills.

Every Bill which shall have passed the House of Representatives and the Senate, shall, before it become a Law, be presented to the President of the United States; If he approve he shall sign it, but if not he shall return it, with his Objections to that House in which it shall have originated, who shall enter the at large on their Journal, and proceed to reconsider it. If after such Reconsideration two-thirds of that House shall agree to pass the Bill it shall be sent, together with the Objections, to the other House, by which it shall likewise to be reconsidered, and if approved by two-thirds of that House, it shall become a Law. But in all such Cases the Votes of both Houses shall be determined by Yeas and Nays, and the Names of the Persons voting to and against the Bill shall be entered on the Journal of each House respectively. If any Bill shall not be returned by the President within ten Days (Sunday excepted) after it shall have been presented to him, the Same shall be a Law, in like Manner as if he had signed it, unless the Congress by their Adjournment prevent its Return, in which Case it shall not be a Law.

Every Order, Resolution, or Vote to which the Concurrence of the Senate and House of Representatives may be necessary (except on a question of Adjournment) shall be presented to the President of the United States; and before the Same shall take Effect, shall be approved by him, or being disapproved by him, shall be repassed by two-thirds of the Senate and House of Representatives, according to the Rule and Limitations prescribed in the Case of a Bill.

Section 8.   The Congress shall have Power To lay and collect Taxes, Duties, Imposts and Excises, to pay the Debts and provide for the common Defence and general Welfare of the United States; but all Duties, Imposts and Excises shall be uniform throughout the United States;

To borrow money on the Credit of the United States;

To regulate Commerce with foreign Nations, and among the several States, and with the Indian Tribes;

To establish an uniform Rule of Naturalization, and uniform Laws on the subject of Bankruptcies throughout the United States.

To coin Money, regulate the Value thereof, and of foreign Coin, and fix the Standard of Weights and Measures;

To provide for the Punishment of counterfeiting the Securities and current Coin of the United States;

To establish Post Offices and post Roads;

To promote the Progress of Science and useful arts, by securing for limited Times to Authors and Inventors the exclusive Right to their respective Writings and Discoveries;

To constitute Tribunals inferior to the supreme Court;

To define and punish Piracies and Felonies committed on the high Seas, and Offenses against the Law of Nations;

To declare War, grant Letters of Marque and Reprisal, and make Rules concerning Captures on Land and Water;

To raise and support Armies, but no Appropriation of Money to that Use shall be for a longer Term than two Years;

To provide and maintain a Navy;

To make Rules for the Government and Regulation of the land and naval Forces;

To provide for calling forth the Militia to execute the Laws of the Union, suppress Insurrections and repel Invasions;

To provide for organizing, arming, and disciplining the Militia, and for governing such Part of them as may be employed in the Service of the United States, reserving to the States respectively, the Appointment of the Officers, and the Authority of training the Militia according to the discipline prescribed by Congress;

To exercise exclusive Legislation in all Cases whatsoever, over such District (not exceeding ten Miles square) as may, by Cession of particular States, and the acceptance of Congress become the Seat of the Government of the United States, and to exercise like Authority over all Places purchased by the Consent of the Legislature of the State in which the Same shall be, for the Erection of Forts, Magazines, Arsenals, dock-Yards, and other needful Buildings; – And

To make all Laws which shall be necessary and proper for carrying into Execution the foregoing Powers, and all other Powers vested by this Constitution in the Government of the United States, or in any Department or Office thereof.

Section 9.   The Migration or Importation of such Persons as any of the States now existing shall think proper to admit, shall not be prohibited by the Congress prior to the Year one thousand eight hundred and eight, but a tax or duty may be imposed on such importation, not exceeding ten dollars for each Person.

The privilege of the Writ of Habeas Corpus shall not be suspended, unless when in Cases of Rebellion or Invasion the public Safety may require it.

No Bill of Attainder or ex post facto Law shall be passed.

No capitation, or other direct Tax shall be laid, unless in Proportion to the Census or Enumeration herein before directed to be taken.[1]

No Tax or Duty shall be laid on Articles exported from any State.

No Preference shall be given by an Regulation of Commerce or Revenue to the Ports of one State over those of another; nor shall Vessels bound to, or from one State, be obliged to enter, clear, or pay Duties in another.

No Money shall be drawn from the Treasury, but in Consequence of Appropriations made by Law; and a regular Statement and Account of the Receipts and Expenditures of all public Money shall be published from time to time.

No Title of Nobility shall be granted by the United States: And no Person holding any

---

[1] See the Sixteenth Amendment.

Office of Profit or Trust under them, shall, without the Consent of the Congress, accept of any present, Emolument, Office, or Title, of any kind whatever, from any King, Prince, or foreign State.

Section 10.   No State shall enter into any Treaty, Alliance, or Confederation; grant Letters of Marque and Reprisal; coin Money; emit Bills of Credit; make any Thing but gold and silver Coin a Tender in Payment of Debts; pass any Bill of Attainder, ex post facto Law, or Law impairing the Obligation of Contracts, or grant any Title of Nobility.

No State shall, without the Consent of the Congress, lay any Imposts or Duties on Imports or Exports, except what may be absolutely necessary for executing its inspection Laws: and the net Product of all Duties and Imposts, laid by any State on Imports or Exports, shall be for the Use of the Treasury of the United States and all such Laws shall be subject to the Revision and Controul of the Congress.

No State shall, without the Consent of Congress, lay any duty of Tonnage, keep Troops, or Ships of War in time of Peace, enter into any Agreement or Compact with another State, or with a foreign Power, or engage in War, unless actually invaded, or in such imminent Danger as will not admit of delay.

Article II

Section 1.   The executive Power shall be vested in a President of the United States of America. He shall hold his Office during the Term of four Years, and, together with the Vice President, chosen for the same Term, be elected, as follows

Each State shall appoint, in such Manner as the Legislature thereof may direct, a Number of Electors, equal to the whole number of Senators and Representatives to which the State may be entitled in the Congress; but no Senator or Representative or Person holding an Office of Trust or Profit under the United States shall be appointed an Elector.

The Electors shall meet in their respective States, and vote by Ballot for two persons, of whom one at least shall not be an Inhabitant of the same State with themselves. And they shall make a List of all Persons voted for, and of the Number of Votes for each; which List they shall sign and certify, and transmit sealed to the Seat of the Government of the United States, directed to the President of the Senate. The President of the Senate shall, in the Presence of the Senate and House of Representatives, open all the Certificates, and the Votes shall then be counted. The Person having the greatest Number of Votes shall be the President, if such Number be a Majority of the whole Number of Electors appointed; and if there be more than one who have such Majority, and have an Equal Number of Votes, then the House of Representatives shall immediately chuse by Ballot one of them for President; and if no Person have a Majority, then from the five highest on the List the said House shall in like Manner chuse the President, but in chusing the President, the Votes shall be taken by States, the Representation from each State having one Vote; A quorum for this Purpose shall consist of a Member or Members from two-thirds of the States, and a Majority of all the States shall be necessary to a Choice. In every Case, after the Choice of the President, the Person having the greatest Number of Votes of the Electors shall be the Vice-President. But if there should remain two or more who have equal votes, the Senate shall chuse from them by Ballot the Vice President.[1]

---

[1] This paragraph was superseded by the Twelfth Amendment.

The Congress may determine the Time of chusing the Electors, and the Day on which they shall give their Vote; which Day shall be the same throughout the United States.

No person except a natural born Citizen, or a Citizen of the United States, at the time of the Adoption of this Constitution, shall be eligible to the Office of President; neither shall any Person be eligible to that Office who shall not have attained the Age of thirty-five Years, and been fourteen Years a Resident within the United States.

In Case of the Removal of the President from Office, or of his Death, Resignation, or Inability to discharge the Powers and Duties of the said office, the same shall devolve on the Vice President, and the congress may by Law provide for the Case of Removal, Death, Resignation or Inability, both the President and Vice President, declaring what Officer shall then act as President, and such Officer shall act accordingly, until the Disability be removed, or a President shall be elected.

The President shall, at stated Times, receive for his Services, a Compensation, which shall neither be encreased nor diminished during the Period for which he shall have been elected, and he shall not receive within that Period any other Emolument from the United States, or any of them.

Before he enters on the Execution of his Office, he shall take the following Oath or Affirmation: – 'I do solemnly swear (or affirm) that I will faithfully execute the Office of President of the United States, and will to the best of my Ability, preserve, protect and defend the Constitution of the United States.'

Section 2. The President shall be Commander in Chief of the Army and Navy of the United States, and of the Militia of the several States, when called into the actual Service of the United States; he may require the Opinion in writing, of the principal officer in each of the executive Departments, upon any subject relating to the Duties of their respective Offices, and he shall have Power to Grant Reprieves and Pardons for Offenses against the United States, except in Cases of Impeachment.

He shall have Power, by and with the Advice and Consent of the Senate, to make Treaties, provided two-thirds of the Senators present concur; and he shall nominate, and by and with the Advice and Consent of the Senate, shall appoint Ambassadors, other public Ministers and Consuls, Judges of the supreme Court, and all other Officers of the United States, whose Appointments are not herein otherwise provided for, and which shall be established by Law: but the Congress may by Law vest the Appointment of such inferior Offices, as they think proper, in the President alone, in the Courts of Law, or in the Heads of Departments.

The President shall have Power to fill up all Vacancies that may happen during the Recess of the Senate by granting Commissions which shall expire at the End of their next Session.

Section 3. He shall from time to time give to the Congress Information of the State of the Union, and recommend to their Consideration such Measures as he shall judge necessary and expedient; he may, on extraordinary Occasions, convene both Houses, or either of them, and in Cases of Disagreement between them, with Respect to the Time of Adjournment, he may adjourn them to such Time as he shall think proper; he shall receive Ambassadors and other public Ministers; he shall take Care that the Laws be faithfully executed, and shall Commission all of the Officers of the United States.

Section 4. The President, Vice President and all civil Officers of the United States, shall be removed from Office on Impeachment for, and Conviction of, Treason, Bribery, or other high Crimes and Misdemeanors.

Article III

Section 1.   The judicial Power of the United States shall be vested in one supreme Court, and in such inferior Courts as the Congress may from time to time ordain and establish. The judges, both of the supreme and inferior Courts, shall hold their offices during good Behavior, and shall, at stated Times, receive for the Services a Compensation which shall not be diminished during their Continuance in Office.

Section 2.   The judicial Power shall extend to all Cases, in Law and Equity, arising under this Constitution, the Laws of the United States and Treaties made, or which shall be made, under the Authority; – to all Cases affecting Ambassadors, other public Ministers and Consuls; – to all Cases of admiralty and maritime Jurisdiction; – to Controversies to which the United States shall be a Party; – to Controversies between two or more States; – between a State and Citizens of another State;[1] – Between Citizens of different States; – between Citizens of the same State claiming Lands under Grants of different States, and between a State, or the Citizens thereof, and foreign States, Citizens or Subjects.

In all Cases affecting Ambassadors, other public Ministers and Consuls, and those in which a State shall be a Party, the supreme Court shall have original Jurisdiction. In all the other Cases before mentioned, the supreme Court shall have appellate Jurisdiction, both as to Law and Fact, with such Exceptions, and under such Regulations as the Congress shall make.

The trial of all Crimes, except in Cases of Impeachment, shall be by Jury, and such Trial shall be held in the State where the said Crimes shall have been committed; but when not committed within any State, the Trial shall be at such Place or Places as the Congress may by Law have directed.

Section 3.   Treason against the United States, shall consist only in levying War against them, or in adhering to their Enemies, giving them Aid and Comfort. No Person shall be convicted of Treason unless on the Testimony of two Witnesses to the same overt Act, or on Confession in open Court.

The Congress shall have power to declare the Punishment of Treason, but no Attainder of Treason shall work Corruption of Blood, or Forfeiture except during the Life of the Person attainted.

Article IV

Section 1.   Full Faith and Credit shall be given in each State to the public acts, Records, and judicial Proceedings of every other State. And the Congress may by general Laws prescribe the Manner in which such Acts, Records and Proceedings shall be proved, and the Effect thereof.

Section 2.   The Citizens of each State shall be entitled to all Privileges and Immunities of Citizens in the several States.

A Person charged in any State with Treason, Felony, or other Crime, who shall flee from Justice, and be found in another State, shall on demand of the executive Authority of the State from which he fled, be delivered up, to be removed to the State having Jurisdiction of the Crime.

---

[1] See the Eleventh Amendment.

No Person held to Service or Labour in one State, under the Laws thereof, escaping into another, shall in Consequence of any Law or Regulation therein, be discharged from such Service or Labour, but shall be delivered up on Claim of the Party to whom such Service or Labour may be due.[1]

Section 3.   New States may be admitted by the Congress into this Union; but no new States shall be formed or erected within the Jurisdiction of any other State; nor any State be formed by the Junction of two or more States, or parts of States, without the Consent of the Legislatures of the States concerned as well as of the Congress.

The Congress shall have Power to dispose of and make all needful Rules and Regulations respecting the Territory or other Property belonging to the United States; and nothing in this Constitution shall be so constructed as to Prejudice any Claims of the United States, or of any particular State.

Section 4.   The United States shall guarantee to every State in this Union of Republican Form of Government, and shall protect each of them against Invasion; and on Application of the Legislature, or of the Executive (when the Legislature cannot be convened) against domestic Violence.

Article V

The Congress whenever two-thirds of both houses shall deem it necessary, shall propose Amendments to this Constitution, or, on the Application of the Legislatures of two-thirds of the several States, shall call a Convention for proposing Amendments, which, in either Case, shall be valid to all Intents and Purposes, as part of this Constitution, when ratified by the Legislature of three-fourths of the several States, or by Conventions in three-fourths thereof, as the one or the other Mode of Ratification may be proposed by the Congress; Provided that no Amendment which may be made prior to the Year One thousand eight hundred and eight shall in any Manner affect the first and fourth Clauses in the Ninth Section of the first Article; and that no State, without its Consent, shall be deprived of its equal Suffrage in the Senate.

Article VI

All Debts contracted and Engagements entered into, before the Adoption of this Constitution, shall be as valid against the United States under this Constitution, as under the Confederation.

This Constitution, and the Laws of the United States which shall be make in Purusance thereof; and all Treaties made, or which shall be made, under the Authority of the United States, shall be the supreme Law of the Land; and the Judges in every State shall be bound thereby, any Thing in the Constitution of Laws of any State to the Contrary notwithstanding.

The Senators and Representatives before mentioned, and the Members of the several State Legislatures, and all executive and judicial Officers, both of the United States and of the several States, shall be bound by Oath or Affirmation, to support this Constitution;

---

[1] Obsolete. See the Thirteenth Amendment.

but no religious Test shall ever be required as a Qualification to any Office or public Trust under the United States.

Article VII

The Ratification of the Conventions of nine States shall be sufficient for the Establishment of this Constitution between the States so ratifying the Same. Done in Convention by the Unanimous Consent of the States Present the Seventeenth Day of September in the Year of our Lord one thousand seven hundred and Eighty seven and of the Independence of the United States of America the Twelfth. In Witness whereof We have hereunto subscribed our Names.

Go. Washington
Presid't and deputy from Virginia

Delaware
Geo: Read
John Dickinson
Jaco: Broom
Gunning Bedford jun
Richard Bassett

Maryland
James McHenry
Danl Carroll
Dan: of St. Thos Jenifer

South Carolina
J. Rutledge
Charles Pinckney
Charles Cotesworth Pinckney
Pierce Butler

Georgia
William Few
Abr Baldwin

Virginia
John Blair
James Madison, Jr.

North Carolina
Wm Blount
Hu Williamson
Richd Dobbs Spaight

Pennsylvania
B. Franklin

New York
Alexander Hamilton

New Jersey
Wil: Livingston
David Brearley
Wm. Paterson
Jona: Dayton

New Hampshire
John Langdon
Nicholas Gilman

Massachusetts
Nathaniel Gorham
Rufus King

Connecticut
Wm. Saml Johnson
Roger Sherman
Robt. Morris

Thos. Fitzsimmons
James Wilson
Thomas Mifflin
Geo. Clymer
Jared Ingersoll
Gouv Morris

Attest:
William Jackson, Secretary

Amendments[1]

Amendment I

Congress shall make no law respecting an establishment of religion, or prohibiting the free exercise thereof; or abridging the freedom of speech, or of the press; or the right of the people peaceably to assemble, and to petition the Government for a redress of grievances.

Amendment II

A well regulated Militia, being necessary to the security of a free State, the right of the people to keep and bear Arms, shall not be infringed.

Amendment III

No Soldier shall, in time of peace be quartered in any house, without the consent of the Owner, nor in time of war, but in a manner to be prescribed by law.

Amendment IV

The right of the people to be secure in their persons, houses, papers, and effects, against unreasonable searches and seizures, shall not be violated, and no Warrants shall issue, but upon probable cause, supported by Oath or affirmation, and particularly describing the place to be searched, and the persons or things to be seized.

Amendment V

No person shall be held to answer for a capital, or otherwise infamous crime, unless on a presentation or indictment of a Grand Jury, except in cases arising in the land or naval forces, or in the Militia, when in actual service in time of War or public danger; nor shall any person be subject for the same offense to be twice put in jeopardy of life or limb, nor shall be compelled in any criminal case to be a witness against himself, nor be deprived of life, liberty, or property, without due process of law; nor shall private property be taken for public use, without just compensation.

Amendment VI

In all criminal prosecutions, the accused shall enjoy the right to a speedy and public trial, by an impartial jury of the State and district wherein the crime shall have been committed, which district shall have been previously ascertained by law, and to be informed of the nature and the cause of the accusation; to be confronted with the witnesses against him; to have the compulsory process for obtaining witnesses in his favor, and to have the Assistance of Counsel for his defense.

---

[1] The first ten Amendments were adopted in 1791.

Amendment VII

In suits at common law, where the value in controversy shall exceed twenty dollars, the right of trial by jury shall be preserved, and no fact by a jury, shall be otherwise reexamined in any Court of the United States, than according to the rules of the common law.

Amendment VIII

Excessive bail shall not be required, nor excessive fines imposed, nor cruel and unusual punishments inflicted.

Amendment IX

The enumeration in the Constitution, of certain rights shall not be construed to deny or disparge others retained by the people.

Amendment X

The powers not delegated to the United States by the Constitution, nor prohibited by it to the States, are reserved to the States respectively, or to the people.

Amendment XI[1]

The Judicial power of the United States shall not be construed to extend to any suit in law or equity, commenced or prosecuted against one of the United States by Citizens of another State, or by Citizens or Subjects of any Foreign States.

Amendment XII[2]

The Electors shall meet in their respective states and vote by ballot for President and Vice President, one of whom, at least, shall not be inhabitant of the same state with themselves; they shall name in their ballots the person voted for as President and in distinct ballots the person voted for as Vice President, and they shall make distinct lists of all persons voted for as President, and of all persons voted for as Vice President, and of the number of votes for each, which lists they shall sign and certify, and transmit sealed to the seat of the government of the United States, directed to the President of the Senate; – The President of the Senate shall, in the presence of the Senate and House of Representatives, open all the certificates and the votes shall then be counted; – The person having the greatest number of votes for President, shall be the President, if such number be a majority of the whole number of Electors appointed; and if no person have such majority, then from the persons having the highest numbers not exceeding three on the list of those voted for as President, the House of Representatives shall choose immediately, by ballot, the President. But in choosing the President, the votes shall be taken by states, the representation from each state having one vote; a quorum for this purpose shall consist of a member or members from two-thirds of the states, and a

[1] Adopted in 1798.
[2] Adopted in 1804.

majority of all the states shall be necessary to a choice. And if the House of Representatives shall not choose a President whenever the right of choice shall devolve upon them, before the fourth day of March next following, then the Vice President shall act as President, as in the case of the death or other constitutional disability of the President. – The person having the greatest number of votes as Vice President, shall be the Vice President, if such number be a majority of the whole number of Electors appointed, and if no person have a majority, then from the two highest numbers on the list, the Senate shall choose the Vice President; a quorum for the purpose shall consist of two-thirds of the whole number of Senators, and a majority of the whole number shall be necessary to a choice. But no person constitutionally ineligible to the office of President shall be eligible to that of Vice President of the United States.

Amendment XIII[1]

Section 1.   Neither slavery nor involuntary servitude, except as a punishment for crime whereof the party shall have been duly convicted, shall exist within the United States, or any place subject to their jurisdiction.
Section 2.   Congress shall have power to enforce this article by appropriate legislation.

Amendment XIV[2]

Section 1.   All persons born or naturalized in the United States and subject to the jurisdiction thereof, are citizens of the United States and of the State wherein they reside. No State shall make or enforce any law which shall abridge the privileges or immunities of citizens of the United States; nor shall any State deprive any person of life, liberty, or property, without the due process of law; nor deny to any person within its jurisdiction the equal protection of the laws.
Section 2.   Representatives shall be apportioned among the several States according to their respective numbers, counting the whole number of persons in each State, excluding Indians not taxed. But when the right to vote at any election for the choice of electors for President and Vice President of the United States, Representatives in Congress, the Executive and Judicial Officers of a State, or the members of the Legislature thereof, is denied to any of the male inhabitants of such State, being twenty-one years of age, and citizens of the United States, or in any way abridged, except for participation in rebellion, or other crime, the basis of representation therein shall be reduced in the proportion which the number of such male citizens shall bear to the whole number of male citizens twenty-one years of age in such State.
Section 3.   No person shall be Senator or Representative in Congress, or elector of President and Vice President, or hold any office, civil or military, under the United States, or under any State, who, having previously taken an oath, as a member of Congress, or as an officer of the United States, or as a member of any State legislature, or as an executive or judicial officer of any State, to support the Constitution of the United States, shall have engaged in insurrection or rebellion against the same, or given aid or comfort to the enemies thereof. But Congress may by a vote of two-thirds of each House, remove such disability.

[1] Adopted in 1865.
[2] Adopted in 1868.

Section 4.   The validity of the public debt of the United States, authorized by law, including debts incurred for payment of pensions and bounties for services in suppressing insurrection or rebellion, shall not be questioned. But neither the United States nor any State shall assume or pay any debt or obligation incurred in aid or insurrection of rebellion against the United States, or any claim for the loss or emancipation of any slave; but all such debts, obligations and claims shall be held illegal and void.

Section 5.   The Congress shall have power to enforce, by appropriate legislation, the provisions of this article.

Amendment XV[1]

Section 1.   The right of citizens of the United States to vote shall not be denied or abridged by the United States or by any State on account of race, color, or previous condition of servitude.

Section 2.   The Congress shall have power to enforce this article by appropriate legislation.

Amendment XVI[2]

The Congress shall have power to lay and collect taxes on incomes, from whatever source derived, without apportionment among the several States, and without regard to any census or enumeration.

Amendment XVII[3]

The Senate of the United States shall be composed of two Senators from each State, elected by the people thereof, for six years, and each Senator shall have one vote. The electors in each state shall have the qualifications requisite for electors of the most numerous branch of the state legislatures.

When vacancies happen in the representation of any State in the Senate, the executive authority of such State shall issue writs of election to fill such vacancies: Provided, That the legislature of any State may empower the executive thereof to make temporary appointments until the people fill the vacancies by election as the legislature may direct.

This amendment shall not be so construed as to affect the election of term of any Senator chosen before it becomes valid as part of the Constitution.

Amendment XVIII[4]

Section 1.   After one year from the ratification of this article the manufacture, sale, or transportation in intoxicating liquors within, the importation thereof into, or the exportation thereof from the United States and all territory subject to the jurisdiction thereof for beverage purposes is hereby prohibited.

Section 2.   The Congress and the several States shall have concurrent power to enforce this article by appropriate legislation.

[1] Adopted in 1870.
[2] Adopted in 1913.
[3] Adopted in 1913.
[4] Adopted in 1919. Repealed by the Twenty-first Amendment.

Section 3. This article shall be inoperative unless it shall have been ratified as an amendment to the Constitution by the legislatures of the several States, as provided in the Constitution, within seven years from the date of the submission hereof to the States by the Congress.

Amendment XIX[1]

The right of Citizens of the United States to vote shall not be denied or abridged by the United States or by any State on account of sex.

Congress shall have power to enforce this article by appropriate legislation.

Amendment XX[2]

Section 1. The terms of the President and Vice President shall end at noon on the 20th day of January, and the terms of Senators and Representatives at noon on the 3d day of January, of the years in which such terms would have ended if this article had not been ratified; and the terms of their successors shall then begin.

Section 2. The Congress shall assemble at least once in every year, and such meeting shall begin at noon on the 3d day of January, unless they shall by law appoint a different day.

Section 3. If, at the time fixed for the beginning of the term of the President, the President elect shall have died, the Vice President elect shall become President. If a President shall not have been chosen before the time fixed for the beginning of his term, or if the President elect shall have failed to qualify, then the Vice President elect shall act as President until a President shall have qualified; and the Congress may by law provide for the case wherein neither a President elect nor a Vice President elect shall have qualified, declaring who shall then act as President, or the manner in which one who is to act shall be selected, and such person shall act accordingly until President or Vice President shall have qualified.

Section 4. The Congress may by law provide for the case of the death of any of the persons from whom the House of Representatives may choose a President whenever the right of choice shall have devolved upon them, and for the case of the death of any of the persons from whom the Senate may choose a Vice President whenever the right of choice shall have devolved upon them.

Section 5. Sections 1 and 2 shall take effect on the 15th day of October following the ratification of this article.

Section 6. This article shall be inoperative unless it shall have been ratified as an amendment to the Constitution by the legislatures of three-fourths of the several States within seven years from the date of its submission.

Amendment XXI[3]

Section 1. The eighteenth article of amendment to the Constitution of the United States is hereby repealed.

---

[1] Adopted in 1920.
[2] Adopted in 1933.
[3] Adopted in 1933.

Section 2.   The transportation or importation into any State, Territory, or possession of the United States for delivery or use therein of intoxicating liquors, in violation of the laws thereof, is hereby prohibited.

Section 3.   This article shall be inoperative unless it shall have been ratified as an amendment to the Constitution by conventions in the several States, as provided in the Constitution, within seven years from the date of the submission hereof to the States by the Congress.

Amendment XXII[1]

Section 1.   No person shall be elected to the office of the President more than twice, and no person who has held the office of President, or acted as President, for more than two years of a term to which some other person was elected President shall be elected to the office of the President more than once. But this Article shall not apply to any person holding the office of President when this Article was proposed by the Congress, and shall not prevent any person who may be holding the office of President, or acting as President, during the term within which this Article becomes operative from holding the office of President or acting as President during the remainder of such term.

Section 2.   This article shall be inoperative unless it shall have been ratified as an amendment to the Constitution by the Legislatures of three-fourths of the several States within seven years from the date of its submission to the States by the Congress.

Amendment XXIII[2]

Section 1.   The District constituting the seat of Government of the United States shall appoint in such manner as the Congress may direct:

A number of electors of President and Vice President equal to the whole number of Senators and Representatives in Congress to which the District would be entitled if it were a State, but in no event more than the least populous State; they shall be in addition to those appointed by the States; but they shall be considered, for the purposes of the election of President and Vice President, to be electors appointed by a State; and they shall meet in the District and perform such duties as provided by the twelfth article of amendment.

Section 2.   The Congress shall have power to enforce this article by appropriate legislation.

Amendment XXIV[3]

Section 1.   The right of citizens of the United States to vote in any primary or other election for the President or Vice President, for electors for President or Vice President, or for Senator or Representative in Congress, shall not be denied or abridged by the United States or any State by reason of failure to pay any poll tax or other tax.

Section 2.   The Congress shall have power to enforce this article by appropriate legislation.

---

[1] Adopted in 1951.
[2] Adopted in 1961.
[3] Adopted in 1964.

Amendment XXV[1]

Section 1.   In case of the removal of the President from office or his death or resignation, the Vice President shall become President.

Section 2.   Whenever there is a vacancy in the office of the Vice President, the President shall nominate a Vice President who shall take the office upon confirmation by a majority vote of both houses of Congress.

Section 3.   Whenever the President transmits to the President pro tempore of the Senate and the Speaker of the House of Representatives his written declaration that he is unable to discharge the powers and duties of his office, and until he transmits to them a written declaration to the contrary, such powers and duties shall be discharged by the Vice President as Acting President.

Section 4.   Whenever the Vice President and a majority of either the principal officers of the executive departments or of such other body as Congress may by law provide, transmit to the President pro tempore of the Senate and the Speaker of the House of Representatives their written declaration that the President is unable to discharge the powers and duties of his office, the Vice President shall immediately assume the powers and duties of the office as Acting President.

Thereafter, when the President transmits to the President pro tempore of the Senate and the Speaker of the House of Representatives, his written declaration that no inability exists, he shall resume the powers and duties of his office unless the Vice President and a majority of either the principal officers of the executive department or of such other body as Congress may by law provide, transmit within four days to the President pro tempore of the Senate and the Speaker of the House of Representatives their written declaration that the President is unable to discharge the powers and duties of his office. Thereupon Congress shall decide the issue, assembling within 48 hours for that purpose if not in session. If the Congress, within 21 days after receipt of the latter written declaration, or, if Congress is not in session, with 21 days after Congress is required to assemble, determines by two-thirds vote of both houses that the President is unable to discharge the powers and duties of his office, the Vice President shall continue to discharge the same as Acting President; otherwise, the President shall resume the powers and duties of his office.

Amendment XXVI[2]

Section 1.   The Right to Citizens of the United States, who are eighteen years of age or older, to vote shall not be denied or abridged by the United States or by any State on account of age.

Section 2.   The Congress shall have power to enforce this article by appropriate legislation.

Amendment XXVII[3]

No law, varying the compensation for the services of the Senators and Representatives, shall take effect, until an election of Representatives shall have intervened.

[1] Adopted in 1967.
[2] Adopted in 1971.
[3] Adopted in 1992.

Index

U.W.E.L. LEARNING RESOURCES